PRAISE FOR DR FOTUHI

"*The Invincible Brain* is a powerful reminder that we are not prisoners of our genetics. Dr. Fotuhi brilliantly shows how science, lifestyle, and purpose converge to give us the ability to rebuild, rewire, and rejuvenate our brains at any age."
—*David Perlmutter, MD, author, #1* New York Times *bestseller,* Grain Brain *and* Brain Defenders

"Being a six-time USA Memory Champion and having boosted my brain from normalcy to champion status, I can say that Dr. Fotuhi touches on all the important keys to developing a healthy, powerful brain."
—*Nelson Dellis, six-time USA Memory Champion*

"Dr. Fotuhi presents, in a highly readable format, decades of research demonstrating how specific lifestyle interventions can protect the brain from dementia. This book is essential for anyone who wants to stay sharp and reduce their risk of cognitive decline and Alzheimer's disease."
—*George Perry, PhD, professor of Biology and Chemistry at the University of Texas at San Antonio; recognized leader in Alzheimer's disease research; editor in chief of the* Journal of Alzheimer's Disease *for more than twenty-five years*

"Dr. Fotuhi is a consummate educator and writer; in the last three decades, his teaching has made even the most difficult and arcane neurobiology become not only accessible, but also fun and exciting. Amongst the Harvard Medical students (who can be a *very* tough audience, indeed!), he has garnered well over a generation of enthusiastic fans."
—*Richard N. Mitchell, MD, PhD, Lawrence J. Henderson professor of Pathology at Harvard Medical School and former director of the Harvard/MIT Division of Health Sciences and Technology*

"Emerging evidence suggests that specific lifestyle choices and simple interventions can enhance brain health and performance. Dr. Fotuhi translates the latest scientific literature in this field into simple layperson's terms and offers up actionable plans. If you want to think more clearly and effectively, now and as you age, Dr. Fotuhi has the guidance you need."

—*Barbara S. Slusher, PhD, MAS, professor of Neurology, Psychiatry, Pharmacology, Neuroscience, Medicine, and Oncology; director of Johns Hopkins Drug Discovery at the Johns Hopkins School of Medicine*

"Our students at Harvard Medical School consistently praise Dr. Fotuhi for his enthusiastic teaching and his gift for explaining complex neurobiological concepts, making them clear, accessible, and engaging."

—*Stuart A. Forman, MD, PhD, a professor of Anesthesia at Harvard Medical School; director of the Principles of Pharmacology course at the Harvard/MIT Health Sciences and Technology program*

"What Dr. Fotuhi teaches has given me new enthusiasm for life: I now feel confident about my memory and brain performance. Learning how to memorize a list of twenty things, and then forty forward and backward—in just about an hour—made me realize that 'I could do it,'—something I doubted strongly just a few weeks before. I soon applied my newly discovered strategy to remember names at a dinner party and was thrilled to discover that I am now actually good at remembering names, something I always felt was my weakness. Learning about the cutting-edge research on how simple lifestyle changes can increase brain size provided a new incentive to be more conscious about everyday choices. My energy and attitude toward brain aging are supercharged! You're not bound to the brain your birthday says you should have. With Dr. Fotuhi's advice, a bigger, younger brain is yours for the taking. Grab hold. I have, and you can, too!"

—*Michael F. Roizen, MD, former chief wellness officer at Cleveland Clinic, cofounder of RealAge, and author of* YOU: The Owner's Manual *and* RealAge: Are You as Young as You Can Be?

"Want to grow a bigger brain, improve your memory, and save your brain from premature aging? Follow Dr. Fotuhi's advice. I do!"

—*Jean Carper, bestselling author of* Stop Aging Now!, Your Miracle Brain, *and* 100 Simple Things You Can Do to Prevent Alzheimer's and Age-Related Memory Loss

THE INVINCIBLE BRAIN

The Clinically Proven Plan to Age-Proof Your Brain and Stay Sharp for Life

DR MAJID FOTUHI

Neurologist, Adjunct Professor at
Johns Hopkins University

with Eve Adamson

Copyright © Majid Fotuhi 2026

The right of Majid Fotuhi to be identified as the Author of the
Work has been asserted by him in accordance with the Copyright,
Designs and Patents Act 1988.

This book contains advice and information relating to health care. It should be used to
supplement rather than replace the advice of your doctor or another trained health professional.

If you know or suspect you have a health problem, it is recommended that you seek
your physician's advice before embarking on any medical programme or treatment.
All efforts have been made to assure the accuracy of the information contained in
this book as of the date of publication. This publisher and the author disclaim liability for
any medical outcomes that may occur as a result of applying the methods suggested in this book.

Names and identifying details have been changed.

The material on linked sites referenced in this book is the author's own.
The publisher disclaims all liability that may result from the use of the material contained
at those sites. All such material is supplemental and not part of the book.
The author reserves the right to close the website in his sole discretion at any time.

First published in the US in 2026 by Harper Wave
An imprint of HarperCollins Publishers

First published in the UK in 2026 by Headline Home
An imprint of Headline Publishing Group Limited

3

Apart from any use permitted under UK copyright law, this publication may
only be reproduced, stored, or transmitted, in any form, or by any means,
with prior permission in writing of the publishers or, in the case of reprographic production,
in accordance with the terms of licences issued by the Copyright Licensing Agency.

Designed by Bonni Leon-Berman
Illustrations by Tatiana Gandlin

Cataloguing in Publication Data is available from the British Library

Hardback ISBN 978 1 0354 2790 1
ebook ISBN 978 1 0354 2786 4

Offset in 11.55/15.75pt Garamond Premier Pro by Six Red Marbles UK, Thetford, Norfolk

Printed and bound in Great Britain by Clays Ltd, Elcograf S.p.A.

Headline's policy is to use papers that are natural, renewable and recyclable
products and made from wood grown in well-managed forests and other
controlled sources. The logging and manufacturing processes are expected
to conform to the environmental regulations of the country of origin.

Headline Publishing Group Limited
An Hachette UK Company
Carmelite House
50 Victoria Embankment
London EC4Y 0DZ

The authorised representative in the EEA is Hachette Ireland,
8 Castlecourt Centre, Dublin 15, D15 XTP3, Ireland (email: info@hbgi.ie)

www.headline.co.uk
www.hachette.co.uk

To my lovely, brilliant, beautiful, and endlessly energetic wife, Bita

CONTENTS

INTRODUCTION ... ix

PART ONE: A NEW DEFINITION OF INTELLIGENCE ... 1

1: The Unlimited Potential of the Invincible Brain ... 3

2: You Are Smarter Than You Think You Are ... 19

3: The Invincible Brain Mindset ... 29

PART TWO: PLASTICITY, MEMORY, AND OTHER FANTASTIC BRAIN FUNCTIONS ... 43

4: Getting to Know Your Dynamic Brain from the Inside Out ... 45

5: Memory, Plasticity, and Habit Change ... 57

6: How to Improve Your Memory ... 73

PART THREE: UNDERSTANDING AND STRENGTHENING THE AGING BRAIN ... 87

7: Epigenetics Overrides Genetics for Alzheimer's Disease and Beyond ... 89

8: Alzheimer's Disease Is Not What We Thought ... 101

9: A Revolution in the Testing and Treatment of Alzheimer's Disease ... 119

10: The Gracefully Aging Invincible Brain ... 131

PART FOUR: THE INVINCIBLE BRAIN PROGRAM — 145

- 11: The Brain Fitness Program — 147
- 12: Assess Your Brain Function — 169
- 13: Fast-Track Your Fitness — 197
- 14: Fast-Track Your Sleep — 209
- 15: Fast-Track Your Nutrition — 225
- 16: Fast-Track Your Mindset — 243
- 17: Fast-Track Your Brain Training — 261
- 18: Your Invincible Future — 273

APPENDIX: Brain Fitness Calculators and Spidograms for Ongoing Tracking — 285

ACKNOWLEDGMENTS — 289

NOTES — 293

INDEX — 317

ABOUT THE AUTHOR — 331

INTRODUCTION

The human brain is a wondrous organ, complex beyond any computer. During the past thirty-plus years, I have run and published many brain research studies. I've held actual human brains from autopsies in my hands. I've looked at slides with pathological specimens from patients with multiple sclerosis, stroke, Parkinson's, and Alzheimer's. I've taught thousands of students all about the brain at Harvard Medical School and Johns Hopkins University, and I've taken care of thousands of patients with memory loss, ADHD, concussion, mild cognitive impairment, Alzheimer's disease, and other neurological conditions. And now, more than ever before, I am thrilled about the recent revolutionary discoveries in my field that show we can slow and reverse early stages of late-life Alzheimer's disease.

Yet, the brain continues to astound me every day. Three pounds of gelatin-like, slippery, perilously fragile tissue, the brain is stronger and more vulnerable than you might expect. Most wondrous of all, it is ultimately malleable.

The brain is capable of seemingly miraculous feats of growth and rejuvenation. It can reroute and rewire, increase or decrease in size, produce new cells, and fire up new neuronal connections or shut them down. Damage it, and it often finds a way around the damage. Use it, and it gets smarter and better at anything. The brain's capacity to respond to its environment is a testament to why we as a species are so advanced. We can take advantage of that adaptability, flexibility, plasticity, and potential. We can take our brains to the next level, simply by what we do to them, for them, and with them on a daily basis.

How well this happens is based on the genes you inherited from your parents, but even more so on your family environment, education, work, social interactions, hobbies, and dedication to learning and practicing. You may not think about your lifestyle and activities in terms of how they affect your brain, but you're taking care of your brain every day in innumerable ways, through daily habits: You feed your brain nutrients (through food), provide it with blood and oxygen (through exercise), facilitate its natural rinsing and cleaning mechanisms (through sleep), and challenge your brain (by training it).

For decades, scientists and doctors alike believed that we were born with a certain number of brain cells and could never grow new ones, that Alzheimer's disease was mostly genetic and certainly not preventable, and that as the brain aged, there was no turning back the clock. These myths have now been shattered. In fact, at a recent Alzheimer's Association International Conference, the notion that lifestyle impacts brain function was no longer considered radical, debatable, or even surprising. New Alzheimer's drugs are still a matter of debate—do they work, and are they worth the enormous cost? But nobody debates that we can all impact our cognitive function through our daily habits.

This hasn't always been the case. When I wrote my first book, *The Memory Cure*, we decided we could not put "prevent Alzheimer's" on the cover because it was too controversial. Now, most neurologists agree that prevention *is* possible. We understand more than we ever have before about how dementia works and what contributes to it, and that has led to the clear realization that how we use our brains and care for them does influence how well they work—in other words, you have a lot of control over how your brain ages. According to a 2024 report in *The Lancet*, nearly half (45 percent) of dementia cases could be prevented by addressing modifiable risk factors.[1]

Based on my more than thirty years of teaching, clinical practice, and neuroscience research, mainly at Johns Hopkins and Harvard Medical School, I have good news for you: No matter how smart you think you are, or how smart you think you aren't; no matter what kind of cognitive changes you've noticed, or how often you forget what you used to remember; no matter where your brain is sharp, and where you think it might be dull, I am here, as a neurologist and brain researcher specializing in optimizing brain function, to tell you that you could be smarter, sharper, quicker, and clearer tomorrow than you are today. You can protect your brain from decline as you age, in ways that are far simpler than you might expect.

The Genesis of the Invincible Brain

As a clinician-scientist, my mission has always been to make a meaningful impact on the patients I see in my office and the thousands, even millions, of people seeking ways to enhance their cognitive vitality. This passion led me on a journey spanning decades, through rigorous research, clinical practice, and ultimately, creating the twelve-week program shared in this book—a proven plan that has already changed thousands of lives.

My journey to learning how the brain works began during my doctoral research at Johns Hopkins, where I delved into the molecular intricacies of neuronal function. At Harvard Medical School, I continued my research while immersing myself in clinical medicine and researching the hippocampus—the thumb-sized brain area critical for learning and memory—which is highly vulnerable to injuries such as concussions and Alzheimer's disease.

During my neurology residency at Johns Hopkins, I worked part-time as a consultant at the Alzheimer's Disease Research Center, evaluating patients in the Baltimore Longitudinal Study of Aging. As I reviewed cases, I noticed a troubling pattern: Many patients diagnosed with Alzheimer's had underlying, potentially preventable and treatable conditions like strokes, diabetes, or hypertension. Yet, they were given a diagnosis that often felt like a death sentence. They were not receiving information on how they could slow or reverse their cognitive decline by addressing their other, often treatable, medical issues.

Determined to understand this further, I pored over research in the medical literature and uncovered a startling truth: Alzheimer's was being overdiagnosed. Patients were being told they had an incurable disease when, in fact, their memory issues might have been reversible. The weight of this discovery fueled a mission I could not ignore. I was determined to go on rooftops and yell out: "What we call Alzheimer's disease can be prevented!"

To begin spreading this message, I published *The Memory Cure,* in 2003, the same year I started my career as an assistant professor of neurology at Johns Hopkins and as the director of the Center for Memory and Brain Health at Sinai Hospital of Baltimore. I continued to see patients with various degrees of cognitive deficits and participated in several research projects. Over the following decades, I dedicated my career to researching the impact of lifestyle interventions on cognitive decline and Alzheimer's, questioning the prevailing doctrine that genetics determines our destiny by proving how supplements, medications, and physical fitness influence our brain health, and how we have drastically misunderstood these common diseases of aging.

By 2011, evidence suggested that neuroplasticity—the brain's ability to rewire and grow—was more than just a theoretical concept. Inspired by ongoing discoveries in my field, I launched my own neurology practice in Baltimore, designing a multidisciplinary program for patients with mild cognitive impairment (MCI)—a transitional state between normal aging and Alzheimer's disease. In 2015, I moved the clinic to the Washington, DC, area and named it the NeuroGrow Brain Fitness Center. I treated thousands of patients who were worried about their brains for a variety of reasons. Some were recovering from concussions or strokes. Some had migraines, ADHD, or brain fog. Many worried about their memories fading with age or feared impending dementia. I addressed their concerns with my tailored, science-based Brain Fitness Program. This exciting program is the foundation of the book you hold in your hands today.

Even before I began personalizing my program for each patient, I encouraged them to realize how well their brains worked in the many ways they *weren't* worried about. I reminded them that their brains may be the source of their specific struggles, but they are also the source of their particular talents. It's human nature to focus on what's not working rather than on all the amazing things that work perfectly well. After undergoing cognitive testing in my clinic, many of my patients were pleased and excited to realize how well their brains worked in areas they took for granted. I helped them broaden their understanding of intelligence and appreciate just how incredible our brains truly are; many of my patients were thrilled to discover they were already smarter than they thought they were.

I assured them they could get much sharper still. That was when the real work began.

Each patient received a personalized brain rehabilitation program based on an initial neurocognitive and neurobehavioral assessment. The areas where each patient felt they had deficits and the areas where the assessments showed deficits were our focus. The program lasted twelve weeks—

the amount of time I found to be the minimum possible for maximum results. The patients visited NeuroGrow twice weekly over those twelve weeks for brain-coaching sessions. My team and I instructed them on lifestyle changes, helped them to challenge their brains, and trained them on how to practice different forms of biofeedback, including a technique for improving heart rate variability (HRV), a measure of fitness, stress management, and resilience.

Working with our enthusiastic brain coaches, some patients focused on switching to a brain-friendlier diet, others got their sleep in order, some focused on stress reduction, and others dove into intensive brain-training games and other exercises. Most of them focused on several areas simultaneously for maximum effect.

The results were dramatic. Nearly all patients with MCI reported some improvement, and a thorough statistical analysis of data showed 84 percent of my patients gained remarkable improvements in their objective and validated tests, scoring higher on cognitive assessments, and reporting fewer cognitive and emotional symptoms. The MRI results from our patients showed that more than half of them had grown the size of their hippocampi by 3 percent. This meant their brains had become about three years younger in twelve weeks.

The program was so successful that I decided to share the results of our research findings on memory and Alzheimer's disease with the scientific community. I wrote a paper about it, focused specifically on elderly patients with MCI, and it was published in 2016 in *The Journal of Prevention of Alzheimer's Disease*.[2]

Next, I decided to test the effectiveness of this program for patients of all ages who had persistent concussion symptoms for months or even years after brain injuries. Persistent postconcussion syndrome is frustrating for patients, as they suffer from a dozen invisible symptoms including poor attention, difficulty keeping up with their home or work responsibilities, migraine headaches, dizziness, anxiety, insomnia, or depression. Fortunately, the program worked quite well for these patients too. More than 80 percent of them had remarkable improvements in their attention, mood, sleep, and memory, as well as in objective tests of cognitive functions. In 2020, I published these findings.[3]

Encouraged by these much-better-than-expected results, I wondered if our program would be equally effective for children or adults who have been struggling with ADHD symptoms. I enlisted 223 patients with ADHD, postconcussion syndrome, and memory loss, and I evaluated them with tests for verbal memory, complex attention, processing speed, and executive functioning. As with my previous groups of patients, they completed questionnaires about sleep, mood, diet, exercise, anxiety levels, and depression, and underwent objective tests for their cognitive function with standard neurocognitive evaluations at the beginning, after six weeks, and at the end of the program.

The results were just as exciting as those in my previous research.[4] Again, more than 80 percent of patients who completed this program had subjective improvements in their symptoms and objective improvements in their cognitive tests.

This success wasn't limited to adults—to my surprise, children and teens with ADHD improved *as much as my program's adult patients*. Children and teens have their own issues, such as poor diets, irregular sleep patterns, anxiety, and social and academic stress. These results underlined my longtime assertion that what is good for the adult brain is good for the child brain, and even more broadly, what is good for any brain is good for every brain.

With much research under my belt and very little time off, I began to feel like I could do more if I took my message wider. I'd been seeing patients in my clinics for twelve years at this point, but with patients flying in from across the country and our clinic still booked solid seven days a week from 8:00 a.m. to 8:00 p.m., it became clear that this program had the power to help far more people than I could personally see. I realized that anyone could implement these strategies from the comfort of their home with the right tools and guidance. I could stop repeating the same advice day in and day out for patients in my program. I could put it in a book and send that book out into the world.

I made a pivotal career decision in 2023: I retired from my practice to focus on writing this book and developing an app and a course that would empower people everywhere to take charge of their cognitive health and unlock their brain's full potential. I also continue to teach students at Johns Hopkins, George Washington University, and Harvard Medical School to educate the new generation of physicians, showing them a broader view and a more actionable perspective on the brain. I felt this could have a ripple effect through future generations of physicians and anyone who wants an invincible brain.

About This Book

This book will do for you what I did in my clinic for my patients. First, I want you to fully appreciate the intelligence you have right now by understanding how much your brain can do and what it already does for you. I will show you why we've been looking at the brain, intelligence, and cognitive dysfunction in the wrong way. Intelligence comes in many forms, far beyond what a mere IQ test looks at. There are endless ways humans are brilliant. Understanding that can change your mind about what you can accomplish in this life.

I want you to understand in a meaningful way how easy it is to improve your brain function and experience firsthand the remarkable difference that simple changes in your daily routine can make on your cognitive function—differences that will be undeniable. The first step in my program is to complete a series of questionnaires that uncover your strengths and weaknesses, along with a review of specific medical issues you may need to address.

The lifestyle interventions in my program include learning to exercise in a way that works for you and will have maximum impact on your brain health; advice on sleeping better, to maximize your brain's natural cleansing process; a guide to eating for optimal brain function; lessons gleaned from cognitive behavioral therapy for changing mindset to manage stress; an easy way to replicate HRV biofeedback; guidance on brain training and memory tricks; and much more. I want you to feel the positive changes in your mood, memory, energy, concentration, processing speed, and reasoning—within weeks or months, not years.

Furthermore, what we call Alzheimer's disease, I (and many other neurologists and neuroscientists) argue, is the result of a soup of abnormalities rather than a single disease. Dr. Alois Alzheimer, who described the presence of pebble-like "amyloid plaques" in the brains of a few of his middle-aged patients who had confusion and behavioral issues, never claimed he had discovered a disease in older adults with "senile dementia" (a once-common term seldom used today). He knew that aging, vascular issues, and strokes, along with other nonspecific age-related problems, damage and shrink the brain. We have now come to the conclusion that Alzheimer's disease has more complex causes and simpler solutions than we once believed. I'll explain the differences between mild cognitive impairment, dementia, vascular dementia, Parkinson's, Lewy body dementia, actual Alzheimer's disease, and the condition many people call Alzheimer's disease that, in many cases, probably isn't.

You can progress or decline, no matter where you are on that brain spectrum now—your choice. You can get sharper, quicker, and smarter, and improve your executive function and memory. Or you can let your brain go and suffer the consequences of poor circulation, compromised brain waste management, impeded blood flow, dying neurons, and cognitive dysfunction.

In part 1 of this book, we will redefine what intelligence is, assess all the ways you are more intelligent than you may realize, and look at the power of your mindset and how having a sense of purpose in life is a game changer when it comes to brain health and peak cognitive performance.

In part 2, we review the concepts of neurogenesis (the generation of new neurons) at any age and how brain plasticity works. We will take a deep sensory dive into your brain so you can see how powerful, vulnerable, and adaptable your brain is. We will examine the role of dopamine in shaping your habits and how you can learn to develop new productive habits that will shape the future of your invincible brain. We will explore how memory works and teach you fun and easy ways to improve your memory at any age, like how to memorize names, credit card numbers, and a list of twenty items, and how to remember where you parked or where you put your phone.

In part 3, we'll explore the impact of genetics and, more important, discover how to leverage the power of epigenetics to reverse the effects of aging in your brain. We'll explore findings from my research papers about boosting your brain performance by growing the size of your brain, and challenge the assumptions that Alzheimer's is a single pure disease. We will explain in simple terms the nuances of the exciting new discoveries about the prevention, diagnosis, and treatment of Alzheimer's disease in the very recent past. I'll tell you everything you need to know about the latest Alzheimer's biomarkers and whether or not you should take the new medications for Alzheimer's disease, and I'll show you why it's just not true that an aging brain is a less capable brain. I will discuss how the health and vitality of organs below your neck are essential for the optimal functioning of your brain, and teach you how to increase the reserve in your body organs, which can ultimately help to grow and strengthen your brain.

In part 4, you will learn about my Brain Fitness Program—the same one my patients used in my clinic that resulted in such dramatic and impressive cognitive gains. You'll create a Brain Portfolio and get a comprehensive list of tests and questionnaires to complete. You'll assess your brain function to determine where your brain is doing well and where you might want to intervene, with guidance on maximizing your strengths and addressing the areas that could be doing better. You'll learn about the five pillars of brain health and the most critical interventions to fast-track your brain's invincibility. We will consider the real meaning of happiness, quality of life, and sense of purpose. What do you live for?

I'll make the case that intelligence is knowing how to live a happy life and that building an invincible brain is worth every effort. Ultimately, you'll not only learn how to prevent Alzheimer's, you'll learn how to build a brain that can withstand aging with grace and strength. You will learn how to become one notch sharper in a matter of weeks.

There is so much to learn about your brain—but even better, it's never too late to improve your brain functions. Let's figure out what that means for you, what you can do to make it happen, and how to start right now. No matter what you want out of the rest of your life, you'll achieve it more easily with a brain that is bigger, faster, smarter, and practically invincible.

PART ONE

A NEW DEFINITION OF INTELLIGENCE

1

THE UNLIMITED POTENTIAL OF THE INVINCIBLE BRAIN

Do you consider yourself smart—even brilliant? Or do you secretly worry that you're not as smart as others, and possibly losing intelligence over time? Does anxiety about losing your memory loom large in your thoughts? Perhaps you have trouble paying attention or concentrating, and you worry (or know) that you've got ADHD. Maybe you've suffered from a concussion and wonder if your brain will ever fully recover. Have you always wished you were smarter or better at a skill you admire? Maybe you're simply getting older and forgetting names or wondering where you put your keys or why you went downstairs—you're pretty sure you needed to get *something* down there—but what it is completely slipped your mind.

The mind is slippery, and the brain is mysterious. Indeed, there are still parts of the brain we don't fully understand. However, our knowledge about what's happening inside the human skull has improved immensely in the past three to five years, partly thanks to advances in brain imaging. Many of the mysteries about the brain have now become well-established facts, which have helped us recognize that how the brain works is essentially a factor not merely of genetics or fate but of how we live our lives and what we do every day.

The cortex—the outer layer of your brain that, like a blanket, surrounds and communicates with all other brain regions—is where your higher cognitive functions happen. Your brain's cortex has an incredible ability to learn, change, adapt, and grow. The cortex has a thumb-sized extension, called the hippocampus, that is particularly important for learning and memory and is the most malleable part of the brain with the most growth potential.

The brain is not only malleable but exquisitely personalized. Whatever *you* need to do to survive, thrive, and succeed, your cortex will respond,

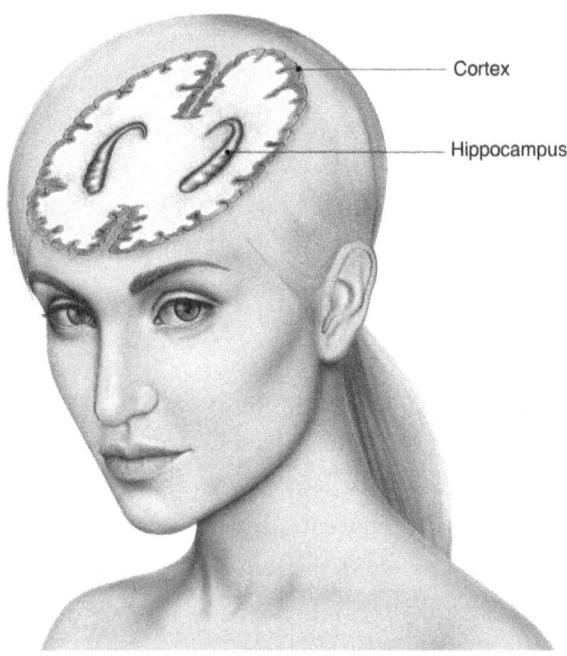

increasing your intelligence in the areas that matter to you and your life and culture. For example, if you were born and grew up in a small village somewhere in the rainforest, your cortical areas for appreciating nature, sensing the environment around you, and hunting would likely develop much better than if you were born in a big city—where you would be more in need of cortical functions for surviving in a crowded urban environment and excelling in your work. Try putting a born-and-bred New Yorker into the middle of the rainforest. That city slicker might not seem intelligent to the locals in that small village. Each type of intelligence, curated by the respective environment, is relevant and beneficial for life in that setting.

This personalization of the brain applies to everyone—will you become street-smart, book-smart, numbers-smart, nature-smart, music-smart, sports-smart, or people-smart? It all depends on how you use your brain, because the brain changes according to how we live and what we do.

Consider, for example, the case of Zohreh Etezad Saltaneh, an Iranian artist born with a congenital disability that stunted the growth of her arms and hands. You may think that because she did not have arms and hands, she would be destined to need constant help. However, she didn't just become capable. She excelled in her tasks. She learned to cook, do chores around the house, play table tennis, and weave carpets. Using her toes to paint, she became an artist; her artwork has been shown in sixty exhibitions worldwide.[1] Her abilities were not located in her arms and hands. They were located in her brain.

Usually, the parts of the cortex devoted to sensation and control of movements in the hands and fingers are much larger than the cortical territory devoted to sensation and movement of the toes, since that is what most humans need. The parts of Zohreh's brain that were initially assigned to control her toes were small. Still, with training, they grew and flourished, and she could achieve fine motor coordination using her toes, far beyond what you or I could ever accomplish, since most of us have never heavily used that part of our brains. Meanwhile, the parts of her brain naturally assigned to operate her arms and hands most likely have shriveled since she never used them. This phenomenon has been demonstrated in animal studies that outline how cortical maps reorganize following the loss of sensory input from a body part.[2]

I recently witnessed this same phenomenon while watching the Paralympics. One of the athletes was an archer, Matt Stutzman, born without arms. Growing up on a farm in Iowa, he learned how to use a bow and arrow with his feet and toes. He won the gold medal for archery in the 2024 Paralympics at forty-one. Like Zohreh, the parts of his brain that control the feet and toes have expanded, giving him abilities most of us couldn't even imagine.

I was also astounded by Ezra Frech, who has only one leg and won Paralympic gold in both the high jump and the 100-meter sprint, and Hailey Danz, who also has only one leg and learned how to ski and then to do triathlons—swimming, biking, and running her way to a gold medal in 2024. The Turkish swimmer Scvilay Öztürk has no arms, and she competed in the Paralympics in swimming. She won a bronze medal in the backstroke and competed in the butterfly and freestyle.

The brains of these and other Olympic athletes have rewired and grown throughout their adult lives to such an extent that they can perform at these impressive levels. They were not born with these talents. These are all examples of neuroplasticity, the technical term for the brain's ability to grow, rewire, and change in response to trauma, the environment, or a person's aspirations in life.

Your brain is no different from those of people who compete in the Olympics and persist at what they love to do. What you use grows; what you don't use shrinks. Remember this! You can increase your brain's size and computing power at any age and stage of life. You can form new neurons, and you can create new connections. You can build a bigger, more intelligent brain and become more adept at anything simply by training and being determined to reach your goals. If you want to be smarter at anything, practice, practice, and practice. Learning by practicing something over and over again grows your brain.[3]

What Is Cognition?

> I often talk about cognitive skills or cognition, but what does that mean, exactly? Cognition consists of mental processes that help you acquire knowledge and make sense of the world through your experiences and senses. These higher brain functions include the ability to pay attention to certain things and not others (selective attention); exercise impulse control; switch back and forth between different thoughts or tasks (flexibility); form categories and recognize patterns; understand complex concepts such as philosophy; solve problems; engage in specific tasks like cooking, playing sports, and having conversations; and carry out such functions as processing speed, working memory, imagination, manual dexterity, and the performance of dozens of different tasks in day-to-day life. These cognitive functions arise mostly from the cortex and hippocampus, and the more you use them, the more they grow.

Take, for example, a well-known and often-cited study on London taxi drivers.[4] The study examined MRIs of taxi drivers' brains alongside a control group of individuals who did not drive taxis. The researchers found that the taxi drivers had larger hippocampal regions, and the longer they had been working in their jobs—some for twenty to thirty years—the greater their hippocampal volume, particularly in the posterior region of the hippocampus, which is important for spatial representation of the environment and learning navigational skills.

But could it be that people with larger hippocampal regions in spatial representation and navigation gravitated to becoming cabdrivers? To find out, the researchers studied a group of people who wanted to become taxi drivers. In London, to qualify to become a taxi driver, candidates must pass a difficult qualification exam that requires a four-year study of the complex layout of London's 25,000 streets and 60,000 points of interest. The candidates must learn every street and the direction of every one-way street. It's a tough test, and only about half the people who take it can become taxi drivers.

The researchers performed initial MRIs on the people in this group before they started their four-year course. After completing the program, the researchers conducted follow-up MRIs. In the beginning, the hippocampal volume of all the candidates was approximately the same. At the end of the four years, the people who passed the test had significant growth in the posterior part of the hippocampus. Those who studied hard grew their brains and could pass the test, while those who failed the exam had brains that revealed they probably hadn't studied very hard. You study, and your brain grows. You don't study, and your brain stays the same—or, depending on how you live, it might even shrink.

Researchers from Sweden studied fourteen young adults in the Swedish Armed Forces who were in a three-month program of daily intensive training in the Arabic or Russian language, so that they could serve as interpreters.[5] This program resulted in language fluency in just three months. They compared this group of students to regular college students of the same age. Before-and-after MRIs showed more brain connections and significant increases in the hippocampus volume and cortical thickness of the students in the intensive language training, and no change in the regular college students.

Even something as seemingly simple as learning to juggle can grow the cortex. Researchers demonstrated this concept by taking twenty-one college students who didn't know how to juggle and doing MRIs to look at their brains.[6] After the baseline MRI, they taught the students how to juggle and had them practice for three months. When researchers did MRIs of the students after the three months had passed, they found a measurable increase in brain volume in the areas of the cortex for hand-eye coordination. When the students stopped practicing juggling, they did another MRI three months later, and their brain volume had decreased again, although not back to what it was before they learned to juggle.

Another study showed that medical students had larger hippocampal volumes after three months of intensive studying for their national board exams.[7] In their case, the extra brain volume did not decrease after the board exam, likely because these medical students had to keep learning and remembering information.

Three months may sound like a short time to grow a brain enough to be measured with a brain MRI, but another study of fifteen college students showed increases in cortical volume of the motor cortex, sensory cortex, and hippocampus after just five days of learning a visual-motor task. And, on the first day of training, several hours after the first learning session, MRIs already showed increased brain volume—even one learning session caused microstructural changes in the brain. Again, brain volume decreased after students stopped doing the task, but not back to what it had been before learning the task.[8] This kind of growth isn't limited to young people. A similar study in older people showed similar brain volume increases in the areas most important for learning and memory.[9]

This concept of neuroplasticity can apply to other forms of learning as well. Researchers took twenty-eight subjects[10] in their twenties and taught them how to balance on a platform. They trained for six days and practiced for forty-five minutes daily, learning to balance themselves. MRIs at baseline and then on training days one, three, five, and seven showed significant increases in brain volume in three cortical areas related to balance. The first hints of anatomical change were evident after only two forty-five-minute training sessions, and those who had practiced more intensely and improved more had gained more brain volume during these six days.

A similar study of fifteen college students in Japan[11] who practiced the visual-motor task of mirroring image movements of the hands for five days showed increases in the cortical volume in the motor cortex, sensory cortex, and hippocampus. MRIs on the very first day, several hours after the first learning session, showed increases in brain volume. A month later, while they lost some of this extra brain volume, their brains didn't return to baseline.

Memory is yet another cognitive skill you can improve upon at any age. Consider my friend Nelson Dellis, the six-time US Memory Champion. When his grandmother died of Alzheimer's disease, he started to worry that he might develop it too, so he decided to do intensive memory exercises.

Eventually, he practiced four to five hours daily and became highly skilled at remembering things. He won some local competitions in the Miami area, and just one year later, he won the US Memory Championship. He memorized the order of a deck of cards in forty-five seconds—I saw it with my own eyes because I was invited to be the keynote speaker at that event.

Nelson Dellis was not a "natural" Memory Champion. He was never particularly into reading literature or language. He was a computer guy. If his grandmother had died of some other disease, he might never have cultivated the memory areas of his brain to such a degree that he would become known around the world for his formidable memory.

He has continued to compete, and his world ranking has fluctuated. Yet, in 2024, he won the USA Memory Championship again at forty. This is phenomenal, as he beat many much younger competitors who had also trained intensely. If he had done a brain MRI when he began his memory training fifteen years ago and repeated one now, we would have seen a significant boost in the size of his hippocampus.

Even after reading this chapter and learning new concepts, your brain will be slightly different structurally than before you picked up this book. The more you learn, the bigger your brain will get. If you practice remembering things, you could become a memory champion too.

Practice Makes Cortex and Hippocampus

One of the things I love the most about our brains is how easily they can change with practice, in ways you can actually see. Shown as darker shadings in these illustrations, different combinations of cortex and hippocampus grow and become stronger and more resilient with different types of learning and challenges. With continous practice, the fiber bundles that link these brain areas also thicken and become larger, as shown in the following diagram.

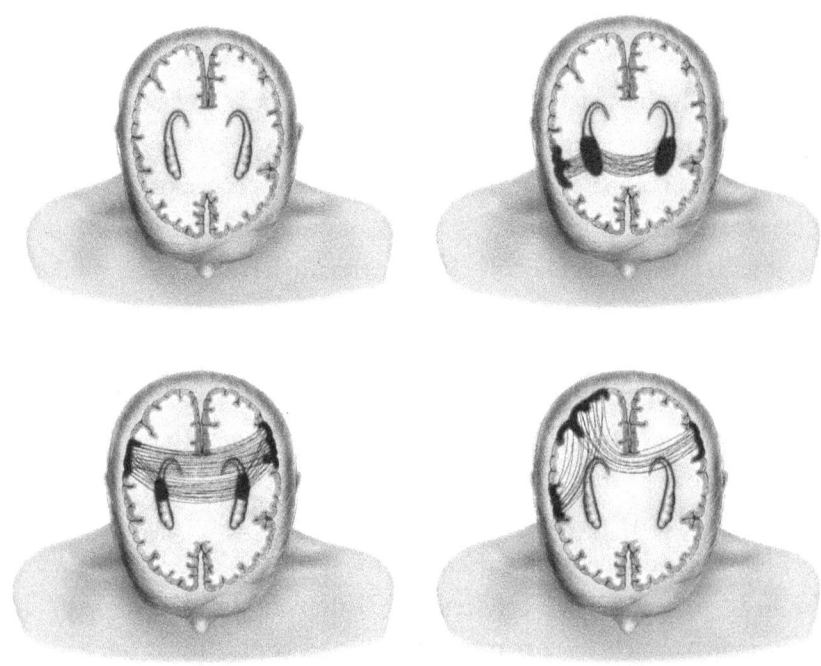

What Is Intelligence?

What if I told you that intelligence isn't what you think it is? That you are smarter than you think you are? That you probably aren't headed toward an Alzheimer's diagnosis, or don't have to be, even if you sometimes forget names or can't remember why you walked into the kitchen?

What if I told you that an IQ test isn't the absolute measure of intelligence we once thought it was? That memory, problem-solving, reasoning, logic, creativity, abilities, and even happiness are ever-changing brain functions over which you have significant control?

Neurologists and brain researchers have known for some time now that each person's brain is unique, that people learn in different ways, and that intelligence comes in a multiplicity of forms and expressions. There are culturally accepted markers of intelligence, like professional success, advanced degrees, or a high income, but these are not, as some believe, the only signs that someone is intelligent. So you're not good at math, logic problems stump you, you can't do a crossword puzzle to save your life, or you never know the answers on *Jeopardy!*? Those are just a few forms of intelligence. Maybe you have an intuitive sense about people, know how to make people laugh, can find your way around a strange city, or can put together a fantastic meal without a recipe. Or maybe you've figured out how to build a life full of love and contentment, and it makes you happy. I would argue this is one of the most important kinds of intelligence! Who wants to be a physics genius who feels miserable all the time?

You must admire the intelligence potential in humans. I certainly do. Every day, I am in awe as I watch people around me—colleagues and patients, friends and family members—displaying their brilliance in interesting ways. I'm often amazed by people on TV or in the movies who take on different roles and can embody a variety of personalities. Comedians who perform in front of large audiences have an admirable talent for understanding the nuances of humor. Gymnastic or ice-skating athletes can maintain their balance and posture as they perform the most amazing maneuvers with their bodies. I am also impressed when I see someone who is blind use the tips of their fingers to read Braille or when someone who is deaf communicates through sign language.

Everyone has areas in which they are brilliant, as well as areas in which they struggle—everyone is good at something, and nobody is good at everything. Albert Einstein was brilliant but reportedly struggled with personal and professional relationships. A master chef can be brilliant, even if they can't understand $E=mc^2$. Someone may not know how to make boeuf bourguignon or fix a dripping faucet, but can easily detect when someone else is sad or depressed and understand how to help them reframe. Someone else may have trouble reading emotions in other people, but can figure out the most complex tax problems or have an innate sense of navigating in the wilderness. These are all forms of intelligence.

One of my pet peeves is that some people think that other folks are less intelligent than they are: "Why would anyone make such a stupid decision?" or "Why can't these people do their job right?" or "Why can't they see the obvious?" One person may be good at writing, another at fixing things. Someone who can handle finances may not be good at performing high-dexterity tasks, while someone who can memorize many facts may not have good people skills. We each have our unique package of cortical functions, with some things above average, thanks to our genes, parents, schooling, financial situation, and environment. We all have different childhood experiences and life exposures, so our brains develop differently because our brains are malleable. I believe intelligence is about 30 percent genetic and at least 70 percent environmental.

If only we could all learn to appreciate that we are each intelligent in our own way and be humbled by that understanding, we might all be a little more tolerant and get less frustrated when we see other people struggling with things that come easily to us. This could reduce our stress level as we interact with others, whether at work, the post office, in traffic, or even at home, dealing with family members.

Let's broaden our definition of intelligence to empower people, especially children, to gain confidence about their unique talents and set out to challenge themselves to achieve a higher level of success in their lives. Even if you value certain types of intelligence over others (we all have intelligence bias), I hope you can see the importance of expanding the idea of intelligence to include all the many exceptional skills humans have and celebrating those.

Before you embark on this journey to strengthen your brain and fight or reverse age-related decline, it's important to pause and assess your current baseline, not just to track progress, but also to appreciate the strengths you may not realize you have. Research shows that you are more likely to take on new challenges and succeed if you feel confident about your abilities, intelligence, and potential to learn and grow (which psychologists call self-efficacy). This is an excellent place to begin your journey. Believe in your ability to grow your brain and increase your intelligence. Celebrate your skills and those of others—even those you may not have appreciated before now.

Amazon founder Jeff Bezos said, in a 2010 speech at Princeton University,[12] "When you are 80 years old, and in a quiet moment of reflection narrating for only yourself the most personal version of your life story, the telling that will be most compact and meaningful will be the series of choices you have made.... In the end, we are our choices. Build yourself a great story." He is right that success in life doesn't depend on just talents, but also on your choices and decisions. In the following pages, you will learn just how your choices can impact your intelligence and brain health in a variety of ways.

What About IQ and Other Cognitive Tests?

There is no single accurate definition for "intelligence." Psychologists often call intelligence the ability to think logically, plan, and solve problems. In our society, we generally consider intelligent people to be those who are highly educated, have professional careers, or are financially or intellectually successful. If someone gets good grades or has a job as a professor or a scientist, they must be intelligent, right? We talk about IQ, or intelligence quotient, as the proof of intelligence.

Not so fast! The reason IQ tests are popular is that they are quantified. They are about measurable aspects of brain function but are not exhaustive. These intelligence tests focus only on intellectual abilities like problem-solving, logical thinking, and math. They come up with a single number to describe a person's intelligence. That seems pretty reductive to me.

The original IQ test was never meant to identify the most intelligent people. The IQ test was invented in 1905 by Alfred Binet to identify children in the French public school system with cognitive challenges.[13] The test measured certain aspects of cognitive functioning in children—judgment, comprehension, and reasoning—but the point was to identify children who needed help, not to champion the ones who were "the smartest." You could say we've been misusing IQ tests all along.

Offshoot tests have been refined and improved over the years. Nearly a decade after the invention of the IQ test, psychologist Lewis Terman at Stanford University created the Stanford-Binet IQ test,[14] which continues to be revised and updated. Many other tests have emerged to measure various aspects of intelligence. However, Binet believed his test was insufficient to determine overall intelligence. Even today most, if not all, tests developed to measure intelligence and cognition have serious limitations.

Consider why. For one thing, to create a test, you must decide what you will measure. Most cognitive and intelligence tests measure only a select number of cognitive functions. You can't measure every possible brain function. For example, the fifth (most recent) edition of the Stanford-Binet IQ test includes just five different aspects of cognitive function: fluid reasoning, quantitative reasoning, visual-spatial reasoning, working memory, and knowledge. That may sound comprehensive, but the test doesn't consider many other skills and talents. A variety of alternative standardized IQ tests have been developed in recent years. However, none of them can capture and measure the many different forms and combinations of intelligence any one person can possess. Because of this limitation and the broad nature of intelligence, every person could get very different scores on different IQ tests.

Another limitation is cultural bias. Tests are based on "population norms," so people from different cultures would likely score lower, even if they are equally as or more intelligent than someone within the culture of the test. It's virtually impossible to eliminate cultural bias from an IQ test. In our increasingly global world, this is undoubtedly problematic. Someone who is not a native English speaker or comes from a very different culture or environment may not do well on an American IQ test, even though they may be highly intelligent.

Is the answer to include more types of intelligence on these tests? Today's popular intelligence test, called the Wechsler Intelligence Scale, is widely used to assess intelligence in children. It tests verbal comprehension, perceptual reasoning, working memory, and processing speed. But is that enough? Howard Gardner, a Harvard Graduate School of Education professor, has proposed that intelligence is more complex. He named eight types of intelligence: body-kinesthetic, linguistic, logical/math, spatial/navigational, naturalistic, musical, interpersonal, and intrapersonal. But again, are these the only categories of intelligence? I can think of a dozen more off the top of my head, from cooking intelligence to street-smart intelligence to mechanical intelligence.

For instance, many years ago, my family and I visited Costa Rica and traveled to the rainforest. Our tour guide pointed out different trees and animals. Suddenly, he stopped. "Listen carefully," he said. "I hear a mother bird, distressed because an animal has taken her chicks." We all listened but couldn't hear anything beyond a general humming of nature sounds and the breeze through the trees. Our tour guide, however, seemed utterly changed, overcome with sadness. As we continued our walk, it took him a while to recover from the tragedy he felt he had just experienced. He had a special kind of intelligence—nature or sensory intelligence. He was able to do something none of the rest of us could do.

Intelligence should not be reserved for qualities that can be measured by paper-and-pencil or computer-based testing. My younger brother, Leo, teaches psychology at the University of Pittsburgh and is an expert in learning innovations (he's also a TEDx speaker and an Ironman athlete). He once told me, during one of our lengthy conversations about the brain, "I think the current view of intelligence is highly dictated by the mentality of 'what is measured matters,' which is to say that people have taken a lazy approach to understanding intelligence based largely on the things they can measure . . . and since most of that measuring happens in school, it also restricts the domains of what people come to think about as examples of intelligence. It's also a fascinating argument about the spectrum on which skills and abilities versus intelligence and talent lie. We've been taking a dichotomous approach to skills versus intelligence."

As Leo observes, people have been using "intelligence" to refer to just a few ways the brain is capable. The dogma is that intelligence means being good at math, writing, and reading, which is quite limiting. There is no reason verbal fluency should be a sign of intelligence, but the ability to play the piano well should not be. The skill of woodworking, the talent for dancing, the ability to problem-solve in the moment, the ability to see how complex things work, the ability to grow a beautiful garden or navigate over a mountain are all just as valid as the ability to do math, read Shakespeare, or write a novel (or even an excellent email).

We may not assume a quarterback is as intelligent as someone with a PhD in chemistry or medieval literature, but let's see those professors figure out how to throw a ball precisely sixty yards away to one person in a group of four or five people, with exactly the right amount of force and direction. There are three moving objects—the quarterback, the ball, and the receiver, not to mention a group of aggressive men charging at the quarterback like angry bulls. That's an incredible skill and an impressive example of body movement intelligence. (The athlete probably makes more money than the professor too.)

Additionally, intelligence is not static—even an IQ score can change. We used to believe IQ stayed the same throughout your life, but we now know this is untrue. According to one study, learning relational skills (improving the ability to perceive connections between disparate things and find common elements) significantly raises IQ scores.[15] You can improve your cognitive function in the tested areas by practicing.

I agree with my brother that there are many things you can't measure. Emotional intelligence, social skills, a sense of humor, natural or acquired talents, and, perhaps most important, the ability to build, enjoy, and take pride in a meaningful life are each different types of intelligence.

The Value and Limits of Cognitive Tests

What about cognitive tests? These are different from intelligence tests. In neurology and neuropsychology, we often order cognitive tests to measure attention, concentration, processing speed, problem-solving, and executive function. These tests have been used for decades to assess patients with ADHD, concussion, learning disabilities, memory loss, mild cognitive impairment, or Alzheimer's disease. A typical report provides a series of numbers, in the form of percentages, based on how a person's cognitive functions compare to others in their age group with an equivalent education level.

Like the original IQ test, these tests were designed to detect deficits, not talents. In my neurology practice, I used these tests as a baseline to get a general idea of where my patients stood so we could see how their cognition improved after completing our brain rehabilitation program (which I will outline for you in chapter 11). I was always careful to explain to my patients that the results of their cognitive tests reflected only a minor portion of their full cognitive capacity and that we used them only to monitor their progress. Still, patients sometimes became discouraged when their brain scores were below average.

I vividly remember one of my patients, a middle-aged woman named Sue, who came to see me as her last resort. Sue had postconcussion syndrome, a constellation of symptoms that can persist long after a concussion. She was devastated by cognitive test scores from shortly after her brain injury four years earlier.

Sue had been a successful chemist at a pharmaceutical company in Maryland, but after her concussion, she had frequent migraine headaches, sensitivity to light, poor sleep, and general malaise. Her cognitive test showed many of her brain functions were below the 30th percentile for her age. She was especially alarmed when she saw that her executive function score (reflecting her ability to plan, decide, and get things done) was ranked at the bottom 1 percent for her age. Because of these scores, Sue lost all confidence in her ability to handle complex problems and had given up on pursuing her career goals.

After I talked with her about the concept of neuroplasticity and how I was certain she could improve, Sue agreed to start our program and indeed gained remarkable improvements in her cognitive performance. Within twelve weeks, she felt much better, and her cognitive scores rose—to 70 percent for her executive function, and 99 percent for her processing speed! She regained her confidence.

She had spent four years worrying about something she could repair and improve in twelve weeks. She believed that she was doomed to have poor brain function for the rest of her life. She was wrong. She had tears in her eyes when she returned to her job and discovered she could perform her tasks just as well as she had done before her postconcussion syndrome. She was just as intelligent as she had been before.

I cannot overemphasize the adverse psychological effect that can result when a doctor tells a patient, without context or nuance, that their cognitive test scores are poor. They may give up, get depressed, and stop trying to improve their brain function or even enjoy life. When you cease using your brain, it degenerates just like a muscle would, so giving up can reduce your function even more. Instead, you can regain that function and beyond with confidence and a plan. The gains I've seen in people who were told they had permanent brain deficits are incredible. Your brain has a built-in healing kit, and your mindset and lifestyle can support or thwart your ability to recover and improve.

People who aren't happy with their brain performance need to know that how your brain works today does not indicate how it will work next month, next year, or in five years or ten. You can get faster, smarter, and better at whatever it is you want to do, starting right now.

And even though you can continually improve at anything you decide to work at, there are also many ways in which you are already quite intelligent. Read on to discover exactly what those ways are.

2

YOU ARE SMARTER THAN YOU THINK YOU ARE

I bet you're good at something. I bet you're good at a *lot* of things. Nobody is good at everything, but everybody is good at something. Where you excel is where your unique intelligence lies, and it is highly individual.

Forget your grades or what anyone else has told you about your intelligence, and ask yourself what you excel at. No matter what an IQ test might indicate, what score you received on your SATs, or how smart you felt in school or at a job you didn't enjoy, I want you to begin appreciating your unique areas of intelligence. I invite you to look at a list of various types of intelligence I have outlined below. Reflect on each one and rate yourself from 1 to 10 for each type, with 1 being "I'm not good at this at all," 5 being "I'm probably average at this," and 10 being "Hey, I'm brilliant at this!"

This may feel challenging. Many of my patients struggle to see where they are skilled or where they are intelligent. Try to be honest with yourself here. This is not the time to be self-deprecating or humble. It's the time to recognize and consciously admit to your talents! If you feel you can't do this, go through this list with a friend or family member to get their opinion on where you rank on each item, then return the favor and help them assess their different types of intelligence too.

This exercise aims to show you where you are naturally intelligent so you can refine and sharpen those areas, and/or to show you where you might want to work to bring up your score. You may not care that you aren't naturally musical, but you might like to get better at doing math in your head. What areas make you think, "I want to be better at this"? Because you can be. No matter how smart you are in any number of areas now, with the program in this book, you will be more intelligent in other areas too, in three months, after which you can go through this list again.

Thirty Types of Intelligence

This list isn't comprehensive, and there is overlap between some of the types of intelligence listed here; just as every part of the brain is connected, different types of intelligence are connected and can't be completely isolated. You can probably think of other types of intelligence you could add to this list—go ahead and make this list longer if you are so inspired. This is just a start to help you appreciate the complexity and range of your own talents. Let's assess where you, from your admittedly subjective perspective, stand right now. Read the following list and track your score on the form at the end of this chapter.

SCORE FROM 1 TO 10

Emotional intelligence: Are you good at assessing your emotions and behaviors? Are you able to express your feelings appropriately and helpfully? Do you use your emotions to get along better with others, or do your emotions use you? People with emotional intelligence can perceive emotions in themselves and others, interpret emotions, and use emotions to communicate better.

Social intelligence: Can you adapt easily to a new social environment? Do you get along with most people? Can you have an interesting conversation with just about everyone? Related to emotional intelligence, social intelligence is the ability to understand and get along with all kinds of people, with an awareness of the emotions and intentions of others.

Intrapersonal intelligence: Do you examine your role or reactions when something terrible happens? When you detect problems in your reactions or behavior, do you seek to improve yourself rather than blame others? As opposed to interpersonal or social intelligence, intrapersonal intelligence is the ability to have insight about your own feelings, thoughts, biases, and skills.

Logical/analytical intelligence: Are you good at problem-solving? Do you love to test a reasonable hypothesis? Can you reason out problems with logic and set aside emotions? Are you fascinated by science? This is the ability to identify the components of a complex issue, see how the parts fit together, and think of practical solutions.

Street-smart intelligence: Do you adapt easily to novel environments? Do you see the big picture in a way that makes solutions evident to you? Do you sense when a situation is safe or dangerous? Are you coolheaded in an emergency? This is the ability to solve problems and reason out conflicts. It's a valuable survival instinct to figure out how to get out of difficult situations and even profit from them.

Body movement intelligence: Are you a natural at sports, or at one particular sport? Are you good at dancing, yoga, gymnastics, or racket sports? Do you dream of doing one of those obstacle course or elaborate dance competitions on television? This is the ability to move your body in space in an extraordinary fashion, in significant ways, and with fine motor coordination or dexterity.

Book-smart intelligence: Do you always have the right words and an extensive vocabulary? Do people say things to you like, "Well said!" or "I couldn't have said it better!"? Is it easy for you to express yourself? This is the ability to understand and express complex thoughts in written or spoken words.

Numerical intelligence: Is math easy and fun for you? Can you do math problems in your head? Do you remember numbers with little effort? This is the ability to understand and manipulate numbers easily. Some people have an affinity for numbers, percentages, probabilities, savings, and interest rates, or like to memorize number sequences.

Foreign-language intelligence: Do you quickly understand how to use a language with some basic learning before you travel somewhere? Can you speak more than one language fluently? Do you find it fun to try to learn new languages or read in other languages? Some people learn different languages with little effort, while it can feel virtually impossible for others, especially as adults.

Persuasive intelligence: Were you good at debate in school? Do people often come around to your point of view after you talk to them about it? Does your mind easily come up with methods of persuasion? Do people tell you that you should be a lawyer? Persuasive intelligence is the ability to convince others of your point of view or to argue effectively for any opinion, whether or not you agree.

Memory intelligence: Do you easily remember what happened in the past, people's names, phone numbers, details of books you read, names of actors in movies, models and makes of cars, or anything else, general or specific? Some people with memory intelligence have photographic memories or can remember details of events and conversations from long ago, but some people can't remember what they did yesterday. However, it is important to remember that memory intelligence, like any other form of intelligence, can be significantly improved with practice and training (see chapter 6).

Sensory/intuitive intelligence: Do you get a feeling about people? Do you notice every little change to an environment? Do you often detect odors, sounds, or minute details others miss? Can you pick up on the mood of a group? Do you often guess accurately about what is going to happen? This is the ability to sense subtle cues in your environment or people and to have an inner knowing about what is happening.

Nature intelligence: Are you an "animal whisperer"? Do you feel your best outside, around trees or water? Are you good at orienteering? Do you get a sense about changing weather, hear sounds, and notice impressions from nature more acutely than when you are inside or with people? Nature intelligence is something most people probably had when humans primarily lived outdoors and nature intelligence was a matter of survival. Many have lost this intelligence, but some, especially those who spend a lot of time in nature, still have it or have relearned it.

Cooking intelligence: Do you have a knack for putting together dinner without a recipe? Do you know what will taste good, or have a sensitive palate so you can season as you cook and know what goes together? Are you a foodie? The search for food is tied to survival, so I believe the ability to appreciate different food ingredients' flavors, tastes, and aromas and prepare delicious meals is an important type of intelligence.

Musical intelligence: Did you begin playing a musical instrument or begin singing at an early age? Do you write music or teach music to others? Do you feel compelled to listen to music whenever you can? Do you get how music works? Master musicians and composers have musical intelligence, but many others have an affinity and understanding of music, even if music is not a profession for them. Most people enjoy music, but some have a special knack for it.

Imitation intelligence: Are you good at doing impressions or imitating the voices, expressions, or movements of other people, celebrities, or people you know personally? This is the ability to capture someone else's body movements, voice, expressions, or speech. This type of intelligence may be a product of advanced mirror neuron activity. Mirror neurons are activated when we do things while we watch other people do them.[1] They likely play a role in learning from observing, but they may also play a part in the advanced ability some people have to imitate.

Humor intelligence: Were you the class clown? Are you good at making people laugh? Do people say you are "so funny"? This is the ability to make people laugh. I'm always amazed at how some people, like stand-up comics, can make people laugh for an hour with seemingly little effort. Humor is a great gift because it makes people happy.

Creative intelligence: Are you drawn to art, literature, or music? Do you love creating, designing, or making things more beautiful? Do you have a gift for translating inspiring concepts into words? Creative intelligence is the ability to conceive and create art, whether painting, sculpture, poetry, music, performance art, or fiction. Many people have undeveloped creative intelligence.

Tactile intelligence: Do you have to touch things to understand them? Are you a hands-on person? Are you obsessed with textures? Are you choosy about the clothes you wear or the food you eat because of their texture or feel? Some people are particularly tuned in to how things feel. My wife is like this—she loves to touch carpets and figure out how well they have been made and which country produced them. People with good dexterity often have tactile intelligence, such as surgeons or people who work with small electronic parts or make jewelry. Tactile intelligence can be learned. For example, someone who goes blind later in life can learn to read Braille, which seems incomprehensible to sighted people.

Spiritual intelligence: Are you naturally attracted to philosophy or religion, or do you feel a connection with something beyond yourself? People with spiritual intelligence have a deep sense of God or spiritual energy and put their faith in things they can't know. This isn't about religion. It's a natural interest in and affinity for pursuing spiritual growth.

Empathic intelligence: If you are with someone in a sad mood, do you feel sad? If someone is joyful, do you feel the joy inside you? If someone is physically hurt, do you hurt? Do you consider yourself to be an empath?

Related to emotional intelligence, this is the ability to feel the thoughts of others and understand their emotions, wishes, and desires. Some people may possess high social intelligence and understand and appreciate the emotional experiences of others intellectually. Still, they may not necessarily feel the feelings of others or relate to them. This is the difference between social intelligence and empathic intelligence.

Organizational/procedural intelligence: Do you love to straighten up your desk, sort through files and organize them on your computer, put items into categories, or redo a workspace for maximum efficiency? Do you think organizing is fun? Do you love a numbered list, working through the steps, and checking off the boxes? Some people are naturally good at organization and enjoy it. They are good at following step-by-step procedures and creating systems. Thank goodness for the people who love to come in and make things work more efficiently through their organizational intelligence!

Visualization intelligence: Can you envision complex systems and see all the parts in your mind? Do you daydream in detailed pictures? If someone tells you a story, do you "see" it? Are you a visual learner? This is the ability to see vivid images in your mind and manipulate them, whether visualizing a creation, a model, a physical technique like a dance move, or a story. People with visualization intelligence may also be good at solving a Rubik's Cube, recognizing and remembering faces, or mentally rotating and flipping 3D images.

Lifestyle intelligence: Do you eat a healthy diet, exercise regularly, get enough sleep, manage your stress, and generally live in a way that prioritizes your health? This is a simple habit for some, but for others it takes a great deal of effort. People with lifestyle intelligence enjoy their daily habits that make them feel fit and strong. They easily choose what is good for them and avoid what is unhealthy. Like all forms of intelligence, you can get smarter at this very important intelligence, which is essential for living a long and healthy life.

Navigational/spatial intelligence: Do you have a good sense of direction? Do you know how to get places? Is your GPS only a backup? Do you naturally know which way is north, even without environmental cues? This is the ability to sense where you are in the world, physically, and how to get somewhere else, when driving, walking, hiking, or sailing.

Inspirational/motivational intelligence: Do you have a gift for getting people fired up? Are you the team leader, a coach who inspires team spirit, or a teacher who makes students passionate about history or politics? This is the ability to motivate people and crowds. You can stand up in front of people without feeling nervous and give a speech, do a presentation, perform, or teach a class in an absorbing manner that motivates people to change, act, or learn.

Cognitive flexibility intelligence: Can you switch from doing one task to doing something totally different quickly and easily? Can you reinvent yourself or change your life without fear or resentment, when necessary (or just because)? This is the ability to be flexible when dealing with the challenges and obstacles of daily or professional life. You can adapt easily to any situation, even in a crisis.

Quick learning intelligence: Do you often feel like people can't keep up with your train of thought? Do you listen to podcasts at a faster speed? Do you read a book in a day or two? Have you already solved a problem before people fully realize they have a problem? This is the ability to absorb or manipulate information quickly, whether fixing a friend's dilemma, learning a new skill, or calculating a tip. Quick learners are always three steps ahead of everyone else. Often, they have to slow down just to let others catch up.

Digital/machine intelligence: Does technology come easily to you? Do you love machines and have a sense of how they work? Would you much rather enter a note in your phone than write it down on a sticky note? Does it feel easy to learn a new video game or software? You could argue this is a new kind of intelligence—the ability to use technology efficiently and intuitively. Many young people have this, but even some older folks have adjusted quickly to a digital world. Using smartphones and computers has taught our brains to orient to the digital world, and the older generation can get better if they keep doing it.

Happiness intelligence: Do you tend to be a cheerful optimist? Do you default to seeing the good in people and situations? Do you feel content with your life? For some people, this comes easily (just like it's easier for some to learn to play an instrument). For others, it's more difficult, just like all the types of intelligence on this list. However, also like other types of intelligence, happiness intelligence can be improved. According to experts in the field of positive psychology, you can learn to become happier.[2] This is one of the most important kinds of intelligence for quality of life and is worth the effort it takes to become good at it.

Note: Some people may have a genetic predisposition to suffer from major depression or chronic anxiety, which can make this kind of intelligence more challenging for them. Individuals with severe forms of such mental health conditions may need consultation with a psychiatrist, cognitive behavioral therapy, and/or medications. But they too will benefit from changes in their mindset, which can make them feel more content and happier (as we will discuss in more detail in chapter 3). The key is to believe you can change and then set reasonable goals to achieve in the short term. Anyone can achieve better happiness intelligence—anyone.

How did you do? Chart your findings here, then think about how many of these areas of intelligence you have within you and which ones you wish to improve.

	1	2	3	4	5	6	7	8	9	10
Emotional intelligence										
Social intelligence										
Intrapersonal intelligence										
Logical/analytical intelligence										
Street-smart intelligence										
Body movement intelligence										
Book-smart intelligence										
Numerical intelligence										
Foreign-language intelligence										
Persuasive intelligence										

	1	2	3	4	5	6	7	8	9	10
Memory intelligence										
Sensory/intuitive intelligence										
Nature intelligence										
Cooking intelligence										
Musical intelligence										
Imitation intelligence										
Humor intelligence										
Creative intelligence										
Tactile intelligence										
Spiritual intelligence										
Empathic intelligence										
Organizational/procedural intelligence										
Visualization intelligence										
Lifestyle intelligence										
Navigational/spatial intelligence										
Inspirational/motivational intelligence										
Cognitive flexibility intelligence										
Quick learning intelligence										
Digital/machine intelligence										
Happiness intelligence										

Take a moment to feel proud of how brilliant you are in the areas where you have high scores. Even one high score is proof of your intelligence in that area. Before going through this list, did you realize how intelligent you truly are?

Never let a number, score, test result, or someone else's careless comment convince you that you aren't smart or that there is no hope. Instead, celebrate where you excel, then consider which areas you want to improve. Would you like to increase your emotional, lifestyle, or digital intelligence? Whatever you want to get better at, you can! Whatever you don't care about, don't worry about.

Work on the parts of your brain that matter most to you, and believe you can do it! It's just like going to the gym. Do you want a strong core? Work your core. Do you want strong arms? Do biceps curls and overhead presses. Do you want to be good at math, or socializing, or music, or humor, or happiness? Practice those things. Your brain is like a muscle. The more you use it and challenge it, the stronger it gets. Learning to do things you're not naturally good at is a kind of cross-training for your brain. Engaging your brain not only makes you smarter but also makes you more resilient against brain degeneration as you get older. That's how you make your brain invincible.

The most important thing I would like you to take away from this chapter is that how you think about yourself significantly affects your happiness, life satisfaction, and performance in anything you choose to do. When it comes to the brain, to a large extent, it is mind over matter. That brings us to the next chapter, which is all about how your mindset is a significant factor not just in your growth and success but also in the size and health of your brain.

3

THE INVINCIBLE BRAIN MINDSET

You've now determined—maybe even happily discovered—that you're smarter than you may have thought. You are certainly smarter than some test scores might suggest. You're above average at some things, and that's great. Now, how do you get even better at your innate talents? And how do you improve in the areas where you aren't necessarily naturally talented?

There are mindset changes, and there are lifestyle changes. Mindset changes come first. Developing an invincible brain mindset comes down to three things: know why you are doing it, believe you can do it, and find the motivation to practice it repeatedly. The lifestyle part—keeping your brain as healthy as possible—is something we will talk about in detail in part 4. Lifestyle changes can profoundly impact your brain health and function, and they will become much easier to maintain if you've got the right mindset.

To achieve that mindset, I suggest you begin by asking yourself: "Why?"

Finding Purpose

Why do you want an invincible brain? This is a serious question. You may think at first, "Who *wouldn't* want an invincible brain?" Of course, getting smarter and aging better sounds great to everyone, but that's not what I'm asking. Why do *you personally* want an invincible brain?

Finding purpose is about knowing why you want to change, or what you want to change into. It's about what makes life exciting and meaningful *for you*. When you have purpose, you will want to keep pursuing that purpose and those passions for as long as possible, with a strong brain that is clear and sharp enough to keep on going for as long as you need it.

I ask this of all my patients: "What are you trying to achieve by boosting your brain power? If you are working to get from point A to point B, what is your point B?" Many of them are concerned about success in their career, recovering from a setback (such as a concussion), earning a higher income, or preventing Alzheimer's disease. What are *you* getting or staying healthy for? Think of the positives you want, not the negatives you want to avoid.

Do you want to be able to play chess with your grandchildren, even in your nineties? Perform better at your job? Learn something entirely new in midlife, starting a fresh career, or picking up a passion you left behind when you were younger? Get really good at your favorite hobby? Learn to paint flowers with watercolors or self-publish a slim volume of your finest poetry?

Do you want to travel the world and see all the places you've dreamed about? Get your groove back and start dating again? Achieve higher scores in school, or finally get an advanced degree? Learn how to be a great cook, play an instrument, or finally learn French? Develop and grow in your spiritual quest?

Whatever it is, I want you to start thinking about the reasons that are unique to you and inspire you to work to grow your brain, get smarter, and resist degeneration. I want you to know how to answer the question: "Why are you doing this?"

A sense of purpose is the belief that there is meaning in what you do. For instance, I love taking care of patients and teaching. I become excited when I see my patients who had suffered for years improve in a matter of weeks with our program. I love seeing how they become more confident, happier versions of themselves.

I also feel passionate about increasing public knowledge about the brain. I enjoy it. I get excited waking up in the morning on the days I'm going to teach a class. That gives me a sense of purpose, especially when I see my students begin to change their lifestyle choices and their mindset to become sharper and healthier. And, above all, my family gives me purpose—along with my lovely wife, whom I admire, I look forward to helping our two daughters build happy and successful lives by themselves. All of these things give me a sense of purpose.

A sense of purpose provides a compass. It tells you where you are going, so your day-to-day actions have an orientation. It fills you with excitement and motivation, so you want to do the work to get where you are going.

Without a sense of purpose, life can feel less meaningful, directed, and enjoyable. A sense of purpose gives you a reason to live, which can motivate lifestyle change, but even without lifestyle change, research has shown that a sense of purpose by itself contributes to better health and a longer life.[1]

The Brain Benefits of Purpose

Having a purpose may seem like a quality-of-life issue, but it is also a quality-of-brain issue. There are psychological and measurable physical brain benefits to having a sense of purpose. One researcher is determined to quantify purpose and its brain benefits, and her research is revealing. Dr. Carol Diane Ryff is a psychologist at the University of Wisconsin–Madison and the director of the MIDUS (Midlife in the United States) national study of Americans' health and well-being. A pioneer in this field, she studies how purpose benefits people.

Dr. Ryff has developed a six-factor model of psychological well-being, including purpose in life, autonomy, environmental mastery, personal growth, and positive relations with others. She also created the Ryff Scale of Measurement,[2] a seven-item inventory that assesses psychological well-being based on these elements, to determine the level of a sense of purpose in her research subjects.

Along with her colleagues, Dr. Ryff published a study in 2024[3] about how purpose in life builds brain resilience. Using the data from her MIDUS study, researchers took brain MRIs of 132 people with an average age of sixty-five. They found that those people with a sense of purpose in life had positive changes in the brain's microstructure consistent with better brain health, including in the right hippocampus, which had a higher density of dendrites and axons (we call this neurite density). Typically, neurite density declines with each decade of life, but those with a sense of purpose seemed to have a buffering effect, with neurite density suggestive of a younger brain. (I'll introduce you to white matter, dendrites, axons, and the hippocampus in chapter 4.)

Another study, a meta-analysis of eight previously published papers in the literature,[4] included data from 62,250 adults and found that having a sense of purpose in life was associated with a 19 percent reduction in cognitive impairment and dementia. The study compared a sense of purpose to optimism and a positive mood, which did not contribute to a reduced risk of dementia like a sense of purpose did.

A sense of purpose might even thwart Alzheimer's symptoms, even in people whose brains show signs of Alzheimer's disease. In a study[5] of 246 older adults who agreed to donate their brains to research after death, researchers found that those who were in the 90th percentile for having a sense of purpose in life demonstrated better cognitive function, even if they had visible Alzheimer's plaques and tangles in their brains. They also had a slower rate of cognitive decline in their last decade of life.

A sense of purpose can also boost lifestyle habits. It's been associated[6] with more physical activity, a better diet, better sleep, less depression, less incidence of diabetes, and lower blood pressure. Even after diagnosis with Alzheimer's, those with a sense of purpose still feel happier. They have fewer behavioral and psychological symptoms and better experiences with their caregivers.

In another study,[7] 443 participants were monitored for twenty years and agreed to donate their brains for research after passing. The participants with a higher sense of purpose had 50 percent fewer strokes, even when the researchers adjusted for other risk factors like smoking, diabetes, high blood pressure, obesity, and a sedentary lifestyle. Imagine that. Having a sense of meaning in your life and pursuing your dreams and passions can cut your risk of strokes by half.

Similarly, a study of 137,000 participants[8] from ten studies analyzed by researchers at Mount Sinai Hospital found that those reporting a sense of purpose had 19 percent fewer heart attacks and needed heart bypass surgery or cardiac stenting procedures less often. They also had a 23 percent lower risk of death from all causes. Another study monitoring 13,770 adults in the United States over eight years with three waves of testing and data analysis[9] showed that those in the top 25 percent for having a sense of purpose were 33 percent less likely to have sleep problems, 22 percent less likely to be overweight, and 24 percent less likely to have a sedentary lifestyle.

A similar study[10] of 12,998 adults over age fifty who were monitored for four years showed that people with the highest sense of purpose had a 43 percent lower risk of depression, were more likely to be optimistic, and were less likely to be lonely. Not having a sense of purpose in life and not seeking activities that bring meaning and value to life could, in itself, be a sign of depression or anxiety.

It also turns out that people with a sense of purpose have just as many stressful events in their life as anyone else—they get stuck in traffic, they get fined for something, they need a new roof or have a leak in the basement—but their response to these everyday stressors tends to be less negative. They have fewer physical symptoms on stressful days, such as gastric reflux, stomachaches, or high blood pressure. This was according to a study[11] of 1,949 adults with an average age of fifty-six. A Swiss study[12] of 2,312 people with an average age of fifty-two showed that those with a high sense of purpose were less likely to be lonely and more likely to report positive social interactions.

Now, an important question: Do people with a sense of purpose have better sex? A study[13] of 677 women between the ages of forty and sixty-five showed that while they don't have sex any more often, they enjoy sexual activity at a level three times higher than those who had a low sense of purpose, and also reported feeling a better sense of emotional well-being.

People with a sense of purpose live longer too—a study[14] of 6,985 people with an average age of sixty-eight showed that a strong sense of purpose correlated with less heart disease and a longer lifespan. In contrast, people with a low sense of purpose were twice as likely to die during the study.

The benefits of having a sense of purpose go on and on. This is all very exciting to a neurologist, and I hope it is to you too. While you can certainly influence brain health with lifestyle changes such as dietary alterations or cognitive training (as you'll see later in this book), having a sense of purpose improves brain health without doing anything other than adjusting your mindset. It seems a sense of purpose—a "mere" belief, in essence—is quite a powerful prophylactic against brain diseases such as Alzheimer's disease and stroke, and leads to better physical and mental health.

The psychological benefits are also significant. According to Dr. Ryff, people with a high sense of purpose feel their life has meaning and a sense of fulfillment, value, and satisfaction. They enjoy their daily routine. They look forward to the future. Conversely, she sees in her work that people without a sense of purpose tend to do what they need to do each day without thinking much beyond that. They get by.

I'm sure you can think of people who live their lives uninspired. Imagine a woman with a husband and children who goes to work in an office every day. She doesn't like her job, but she needs the paycheck. She has just enough time to get the kids to school, go to work, come home, get dinner ready, put the kids to bed, and maybe take a family vacation once a year. When asked why she does the job she does, she may say, "I have to pay the mortgage." If she once had hopes, dreams, and expectations for her future, she no longer thinks about those because she is too busy getting by.

Now imagine if she had found her passion and changed careers to do something that utilized her natural intelligence, that was personally meaningful to her, that filled her with purpose and joy. Would she still say she *just* has to pay the mortgage? Or would her hopes, dreams, and expectations still be intact, and even fulfilled?

Ask yourself why you do what you do. Do you work at your job only to pay your mortgage and your bills? Are you in a relationship because it is what is expected of you? Do you put off doing what you love because you don't have time? Do you think beyond today, or next week? Are you working toward something, or just working? Do you get excited about aspects of your life? This is something to consider seriously because if you don't have one right now, you can develop a sense of purpose by changing your mindset.

The way to tell if your work is also your passion is to ask yourself if you would do it, even if you weren't paid for it. However, a sense of purpose doesn't have to come from your job. Some people work to make money but pursue their passions outside of their jobs, like sailing on the weekends, taking classes in the evenings to earn an advanced degree, or simply carving out time in their schedules for dedicated family activities or travel. Even if you can't make a career of it, make room for it in your life and let yourself indulge in your true talents and passions.

Find *Your* Sense of Purpose

So, what if you don't have a sense of purpose? Are you doomed? No! There is a way to find your sense of purpose. We all have something deep in our hearts that we believe in and find exciting. We may have forgotten it, or feel we've lost it.

Maybe you haven't thought much about your purpose, but it's never too late. Even if you have thought about this, consider the following seven questions to see whether it might be time for a purpose update.

1. What activities have you enjoyed the most in the past? Why do you think you enjoyed those activities so much? Go further than "I used to love playing soccer." Ask yourself why.
2. What do you love to do the most these days? Why do you think you love to do that thing so much?
3. What things do you enjoy reading the most? What about those things interests you?
4. How would you spend your days if nobody were watching and you had no responsibilities? Why would you spend your time this way?
5. Who is your role model? Who do you admire? Why do you think you admire that person or those people?
6. What do you really care about? Why do you care about those things?
7. What do you want people to say about you when you aren't around? Why is that how you want people to think of or remember you?

I suggest you take the time to write answers to these questions, emphasizing the "why" part. There are no wrong answers. As you ponder these questions, a picture will emerge. You will begin to see what gets you excited and passionate about life, how you want to spend your time, and what kind of person you want to be. These are the seeds for developing and growing your sense of purpose.

After contemplating the above questions, please write down a few things that give meaning to your life and fill you with excitement for the future.

Adopting a Growth Mindset

After knowing your why, the next step is to believe in your capacity for growth. "Growth mindset" is a psychological term indicating the belief that you can get better at things. When something is difficult, do you give up? Or do you persevere because you know you can do it?

My father used to tell me that Thomas Edison, John F. Kennedy, Mahatma Mohandas Gandhi, and Sir Isaac Newton were all once regular kids. They were not born famous geniuses. They were people who worked hard and kept pursuing their dreams. He insisted that I had all it takes to become a famous scientist, author, and physician one day. He often inspired me to have a growth mindset—to think to myself, "I can do this."

People with a fixed mindset tend to avoid challenges because they assume the things they are already good at are the only things they will ever be good at. They may dislike feedback or advice because they can't imagine it will help them.

Someone with a growth mindset believes intelligence can be developed, and they can get good at anything. They think, *If other people can do it, I can too. I may not be as good as the best person in that field, but I can still do it. I can learn to play football. I can learn to play Ping-Pong. I can do math. I can learn to make art. I can learn to play the piano. I can make a friend. I can learn a new language. I can get that promotion or job. I can do whatever I want because my brain has the capacity to do it. And if I don't succeed at first, I'll keep trying.* They see the value and opportunities in feedback and advice, and see others who excel as inspirational. They know it will take effort to get there, but they aren't afraid of the effort because they know it will lead to growth.

Here's a personal example. I'm not a handyman. I'm an academic guy. I take care of patients. I read, I write, I teach. I do research. This is my element. So, when my wife asked me to figure out why the heater wasn't working, I used to tell her, "Honey, I can give a lecture to an audience of three thousand people and motivate them to change their lives. I can't be both a handyman and a great speaker. Why don't you appreciate *that*?"

This response did not amuse her, nor did it get the heater working, so I finally decided to take my own advice and stop making excuses. I developed a growth mindset—I thought, "Hey, I'm a smart guy, I can learn how to fix things around the house. If others can do it, I can do it too."

Now I always do things around the house, and my wife loves it. Things break down, and I fiddle with them, watch a couple of YouTube videos, and figure it out (most of the time). And if I don't, I'm not defeated by calling in a professional. Nobody can do it all, but, the more I learn about how things work around the house, the better I get at repairing them—at least the simple things, which most things around the house are. The more I do it, the easier it gets, because my growth mindset has resulted in those parts of my brain growing. I'll never be a master electrician, plumber, or even a professional handyman, but I have improved at something I didn't think I could do.

My wife has had a similar experience. When she was a child in elementary school, she saw someone drown in the ocean. She became fearful of water. A couple of years into our marriage, we attended a pool party, and somebody pushed her into the deep end of the pool, not knowing she didn't know how to swim. She almost drowned. My brother Leo saw her going down and dove in to save her. After that, she became even more afraid of water. For years, she refused to swim. She didn't think she could do it. She had a fixed mindset.

Recently, I said, "Honey, I believe you can learn to swim! After all, I'm writing a book about how anyone can learn to do anything they wish!" Eight lessons later, she was swimming. She decided she could learn it—she developed a growth mindset—and she was right. Now she's not just safer. She's more confident and "smarter" at swimming.

I've heard many people, including my patients, say things like "I'm too old to learn that," or "I'm not smart enough to go to graduate school," or "I'm just bad at math." People tend to focus on their own brain's apparent shortcomings, assuming they are set in stone. Humans are hardwired with a negativity bias, meaning we tend to notice what's wrong more than right.[15] People often default to a fixed mindset, but you can switch to a growth mindset whenever you decide. You'll see many examples of this throughout the book, when I tell you about some of the patients who came to me believing they were not smart or capable, and who were able to embrace a growth mindset after going through my program at NeuroGrow.

Not only are fixed-mindset beliefs untrue (except to the extent that a person makes them true because of their mindset), but they keep people from growing their brains in ways that can improve their lives. If you go skiing for the first time, you'll fall a lot on the first day. You are failing at skiing. But as my brother Leo said in one of our recent lively brain-related conversations "Look forward to failing. It means you're trying. You're moving out of your comfort zone. It's not really failing. It's learning. The learning process is one of trial and error, so if you're making mistakes, give yourself a pat on the back and say, 'Good job!'" If someone gives you advice about how to ski better, listen and benefit from the feedback instead of getting angry, so you can enjoy getting better. When you see other people who are good at skiing, get inspired to become good at skiing like they are. That's a growth mindset.

If you recognize your tendency to have a fixed mindset but choose to work on developing a growth mindset, you can get good at what you thought you couldn't do, and you can also get better at what you are already good at doing. Take some pride in and appreciate your many spectacular natural talents, and use a growth mindset to take your skills and talents to the next level.

How to Cultivate a Growth Mindset

Researchers have proven the brain benefits of a growth mindset. One study showed that when students adopted a growth mindset, this change in their beliefs about themselves resulted in significant anatomical growth in their brains. They selected seventy-nine children, ages seven to ten, who lived in California.[16] They gave fifty-two children four weeks of training for a growth mindset and math tutoring, for sixty minutes three times per week. The twenty-seven students in the control group received their usual schooling, without training in developing a growth mindset or improving their math skills.

Not only did the children who developed a strong growth mindset do better in cognitive tests and math, but MRIs showed they increased neuronal connections and activity in specific parts of their brain while solving math problems compared to the control group, which showed no gains in growth mindset or brain growth. The more students adopted growth mindset principles, the more robust was the strength of the new connections in their brains.

What I have found to be true in my decades of practice and research, and what I want to impress on you now, is that mindset alone can grow your brain, and your opinion of your brain's abilities plays a significant role in your quality of life, happiness, and success. Hush that voice in your head telling you that you can't do something because you're not smart enough. Yes, you can. I've seen remarkable brain changes in thousands of patients, and this is proof. Here are some things you can do to flip your script and change your inner voice:

Instead of saying . . .	Tell yourself . . .
"This is too difficult for me."	"Let me give it a try."
"I don't like learning or practicing new things."	"It will be fun to improve and impress myself."
"I just can't do this."	"I can do anything I want to do."
"I'm not as smart as my friend."	"I'm smart in my own ways."
"I've never been good at this."	"I bet I could get better at this."
"I always fail at new things."	"Mistakes teach me how to do things better."
"I hate people criticizing me."	"Feedback helps me improve for next time."
"I can't produce outstanding results."	"With focus and practice, my results can improve."
"I hate it when my colleagues rise in the ranks and I don't."	"I'm happy for their success. They worked hard."

The final part of the invincible brain mindset, after knowing why you want it and believing you can do it, is to use your sense of purpose and your growth mindset to inspire you to practice—to *do it*, and do it again, and again, and again, whatever it is, whether that is to get better at a skill or adopt healthier lifestyle habits that you know will help to make your brain more invincible. This is how you can start accelerating your brain growth in ways you will learn about in the following few chapters.

Practice Makes Cortex

You may have heard that with ten thousand hours of practice, you can master any skill. The author Malcolm Gladwell wrote about this in his book *Outliers: The Story of Success*. While many believe this is an oversimplification and that the quality of practice matters more than the quantity, I think it's generally true that if you want to learn something, you can learn it with a lot of dedicated practice. Practice grows the brain and increases the thickness of the cortex, which is why I (and others[17]) often say, "Practice makes cortex."

I talked about this in chapter 1, when I gave examples of people who were missing arms and could compensate by using their feet to paint, do archery, or compete in other sports. I talked about how the challenges of your environment can shape which parts of your brain you use, according to what you need to do to survive (as in the example of surviving in a rainforest versus a big city). This is also true on a more modest scale. Similar to how someone's brain can reroute around a missing limb or grow according to survival needs, your brain can get bigger and better at something just by repeating it, whether it comes naturally to you or not.

Did you know that the brilliant basketball player Michael Jordan was once mediocre at sports? Did you think he was born a basketball genius? Actually, Michael Jordan was not selected for the varsity team when he was a sophomore. He worked hard, he practiced constantly, and little by little he got better. Sure, he has natural talent, but he still had to do a lot of work to achieve the level he ultimately achieved. As a junior, he improved and made the team. As a senior, he got even better. Eventually, he became known as one of the greatest athletes in the world. If he had never practiced, we might never have heard his name.

Michael Jordan once said, "I've missed more than 9,000 shots in my career. I've lost almost 300 games. 26 times I've been trusted to take the game-winning shot and missed. I've failed over and over again in my life.

And that is why I succeed."[18] How's that for inspiring? He also said, "I can accept failure. Everyone fails at something. But I can't accept not trying."[19] Wise words, Michael!

Practice can be fun and affirming. I love ballroom dancing, and I want to become a better dancer, so I enjoy the process of honing this skill. I may never be the Michael Jordan of dancing, but I can certainly get to a level that feels good to me and, I hope, to my wife, my lovely dance partner. (We ranked second in a "Dancing with the Stars" competition as part of an Alzheimer's fundraising gala in Baltimore!)

Practice can also help you to improve at things that don't come naturally to you. There is a difference between innate talents and acquired talents. Innate talent could include the natural ability to communicate, connect with others, handle numbers, code computer programs, learn new languages, or analyze details. Acquired talent comes from improving the networks of connections in your brain, even if you are not born with the deluxe version. You can make it deluxe through practice, practice, and practice. *Practice makes cortex!* Remember that.

But what about memory—something many people worry about? Can you practice your way into a better memory? Can you rewire your brain so that you have a much sharper memory? Absolutely. Your brain is designed to do precisely that. In the next section, you're going to learn a lot more about the fascinating interplay of neurons and their supporting cells that make neuroplasticity possible and allow you to rewire your brain to achieve any goal you set for yourself, including achieving a super memory.

PART TWO

PLASTICITY, MEMORY, AND OTHER FANTASTIC BRAIN FUNCTIONS

4

GETTING TO KNOW YOUR DYNAMIC BRAIN FROM THE INSIDE OUT

When something happens to your skin, hair, teeth, even your bones and joints, you can often see it. You can scratch the itchy rash, see the hair coming out in your brush, feel the cavity in your molar, or ice the swollen knee. But your brain may seem more mysterious. You can't see, touch, or feel it inside your head. Even an MRI of your brain is just a black-and-white representation of light and shadow, a mere impression that doesn't begin to show all a brain really is.

Imagine seeing Manhattan (or any large city) from a plane. Your view wouldn't reveal all the exciting activities going on down there. The city is alive with tourists coming and going, subways running underground, skyscrapers brimming with people working, shops filled with customers, and galleries and studios sheltering creative geniuses. No matter the time of day or night, something is always happening.

That's a lot like your brain.

Yet, for all that mystery—how little you might see from above or even on an MRI—your brain essentially makes you who you are. It is both enigmatically unfamiliar and intimately familiar. Your thoughts, emotions, plans, and dreams all originate in your brain, in the form of cells—just regular cells made from biological materials, which, like other cells in your body, require oxygen and nutrients. It's pretty incredible, if you ask me, that these basic components—proteins, minerals, salts, sugar, and water molecules—are responsible for everything the brain does: manufacture and deliver signals to do things like walk and talk, laugh and cry, work and eat and sleep; pondering the most profound philosophies, the most complex scientific theories, and the most ambitious of plans; and fostering the awareness, when we look in the mirror, that we are a "self" and different from any other person who has ever lived.

You know how your brain makes you feel. You know that you are reading these words and thinking about these ideas because of your brain. You know the incredible things your brain can help you do. But how does it look in there? How does it work? What happens inside your skull as you live your life and make it through your day? And what happens to your neurons and supporting cells when certain lifestyle choices limit the rinsing mechanisms and blood flow to your brain? Let's find out!

Different Parts, Connected by Networks

For centuries, clinicians and scientists who studied the brains of patients who had strokes concluded that each part of the brain, and especially the cortex, was associated with specific functions. For example, Dr. Paul Broca, a French physician in the nineteenth century, discovered that patients who had lost a patch of their cortex in the left frontal lobe lost their ability to speak. He theorized that this part of the cortex, known as "Broca's area," was the brain station for generating speech. Dr. Carl Wernicke, a German neuropathologist around the turn of the twentieth century, found a patch of cortex in the temporal lobe important for understanding speech. Later, this patch of cortex, labeled "Wernicke's area," became known for its role in language comprehension. Based on studies of stroke victims, we have come to think of the hippocampus as the center for learning and memory, the motor cortex as the center for moving our body, and the visual cortex as the center of sight.

All these notions are true, to an extent. However, advanced imaging techniques in the past twenty to thirty years have provided compelling evidence that individual brain functions result from activity in an elaborate network of brain connections. While there are nodes of activity that are primarily involved in certain functions, the reality is that the brain is more about networking than islands of tissue that function independently. Like so much else in the body, it's all connected.

You can think of the different areas of your brain as neighborhoods in a bustling city like New York or Shanghai. Each neighborhood has its own character. Some are filled with towering skyscrapers, others with leafy parks or busy marketplaces. The basic ingredients of a neighborhood are always there—roads, buildings, gathering places—but the mix looks different in each one. Importantly, these neighborhoods don't operate in isolation. They are woven into the larger city, linked together by an intricate Metro system.

The brain's networks operate in much the same way: they are like green, yellow, red, and purple subway lines that connect a specific set of neighborhoods across the city. Just like a real Metro system, some stations are shared, allowing passengers—and in this case, brain signals—to transfer from one line to another. At any given moment, every line is buzzing with activity, carrying the constant flow of information that keeps the whole "city" of your brain alive and thriving.

In our brain, we have five major networks that mediate our main cognitive functions:

1. **The language network**, which includes Broca's and Wernicke's areas (its main station hubs) and ten other brain regions, handles understanding language and generating speech.
2. **The salient attention network** helps us focus on important details, guiding our attention to significant stimuli like a loud sound or a familiar face in a crowd.
3. **The visual network** helps us understand what we see in the world around us.
4. **The limbic network** manages our emotions, adding depth to our experiences, from joy and excitement to sadness and nostalgia.
5. **The executive function network** takes charge of planning and decision-making, helping us set goals and follow through with them, whether a simple task like setting the dinner table or a major life plan to obtain a university degree and launch a career.
6. **The motor network**, with its central hub in the motor cortex, controls and regulates the movements of our body parts and facial muscles.

What's really interesting is that how you use your brain can strengthen connections within and between networks. For example, if you dedicate yourself to daily violin practice, you first engage, enlarge, and strengthen key cortical regions in the attention network, visual network, executive function network, and motor network. Over time, as you refine the rapid and intricate movements of your arms and hands, these networks become more synchronized, processing information with greater speed, ease, and precision. Becoming a master musician, like any other form of intelligence, emerges from persistent growth and more intricate connectivity within and between brain networks.

Even the simplest activities and cues use many distinct parts of the brain. Please look at the illustration below, and let's take a quick look at what happens in your brain when someone asks you a simple question.

When someone asks, "How are you?" the sound of those words activates the nerves that extend from your ear to several nuclei in your brain, until they reach the Wernicke's area in your cortex. Here, random sounds are transformed to meaningful words.

Next, your prefrontal cortex is activated; the parts of the lateral prefrontal cortex for attention and motivation help you pay attention to the question and decide how to answer, considering options ("I am fine," "I'm sad," "I'm completely miserable!" or "I'm thrilled because . . . ," etc.) and choosing one.

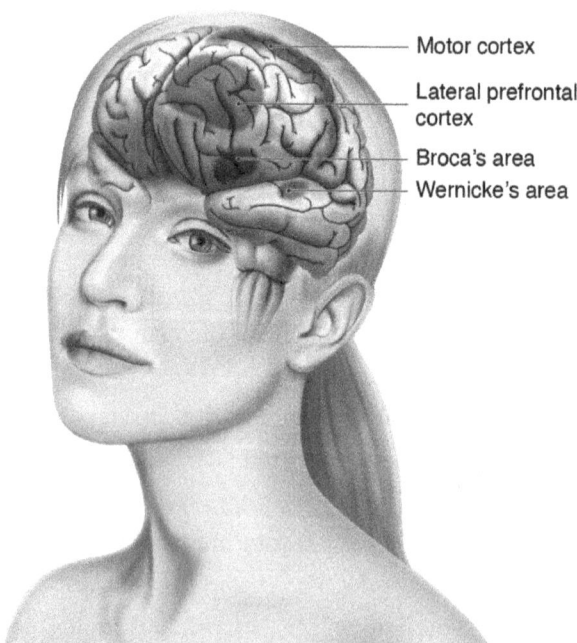

Once your prefrontal cortex decides what your answer will be, the information travels to your Broca's area, where the grammar and details of your response will be determined and processed.

Next, the information goes from Broca's area to parts of the motor cortex in charge of the control of your mouth and face muscles so that you can articulate your response: "Just fine, thanks for asking. How are you?"

Now you understand how many different parts of your brain jump into action to respond to a straightforward question. Just imagine what goes on if you are taking a high-stakes test, learning a complicated skill, or debating an important subject with someone. Every part of your brain is essential and requires care and training for optimal functioning. The healthier your brain cells are, the better they function and the better your brain performance will be.

A Deep Tour of Your Brain in Broca's Area

Earlier, I explained the brain networks as a series of neighborhoods that are interconnected by specific metro lines. Now that you have become even more knowledgeable about the brain, let me take you for a deep dive into the brain and show you what it is like to be inside one of these neighborhoods, Broca's area.

Imagine you have shrunk to the size of a pebble and are standing inside Broca's area, in the human brain. Look around and you will see that millions of brain cells called neurons surround you. Each neuron has tens of thousands of dendrites extending from its bowl-like center, like the branches of a tree. As you run your fingers along these branches, you feel the velvety texture and countless little bumps, called dendritic spines. Each bump holds a synapse—a small junction where neurons pass signals to one another. Neurons communicate by releasing chemical messengers across these synapses, which either excite or inhibit the receiving cell.

Walking around Broca's area, you notice millions of synapses arriving from the Wernicke's area (part of the language network important for understanding language) and from patches of the prefrontal cortex (parts of the attention network and executive function network).

Millions of axons that travel from Wernicke's area and the prefrontal cortex to Broca's area weave together to form ropelike nerve cables called fiber bundles that provide highways for information to flow smoothly, with clear starting points and destinations. This intricate network of fiber bundles enables communication across the entire brain.

As you explore Broca's area more closely, you realize neurons work well thanks to three types of dedicated supporting cells. You first notice star-shaped astrocytes—cells with extended "arms" like an octopus—that pamper the neurons. Astrocytes are like attentive and energetic caretakers. They reach out and set a foot on a neuron and a foot on a blood vessel, forming a bridge between them. They transport nutrients—glucose, proteins, oxygen, minerals, and vitamins—from the blood to the neurons, ensuring that these busy cells have the fuel they need to keep firing every millisecond, twenty-four hours a day.

Strolling past the neurons and astrocytes in Broca's area, you come across a second type of supporting cell: the microglia. These small but mighty cells function as the brain's immune defense. Like microscopic security guards, microglia are always on patrol, monitoring the brain for any signs of trouble, like viruses or bacteria. When they detect an issue, they spring into action, releasing toxic levels of inflammatory free radical molecules (such as hydrogen peroxide) that destroy harmful elements to ensure your brain remains sterile and healthy.

The final group of supporting cells you meet in Broca's area are oligodendrocytes (not shown in the illustration below). You can think of them as the brain's electricians, wrapping axons in a protective coating called myelin. This insulation is what allows signals to race through your brain at lightning speed—up to 250 miles per hour! Unfortunately, conditions such as vitamin B_{12} deficiency can wither the myelin sheaths and cause

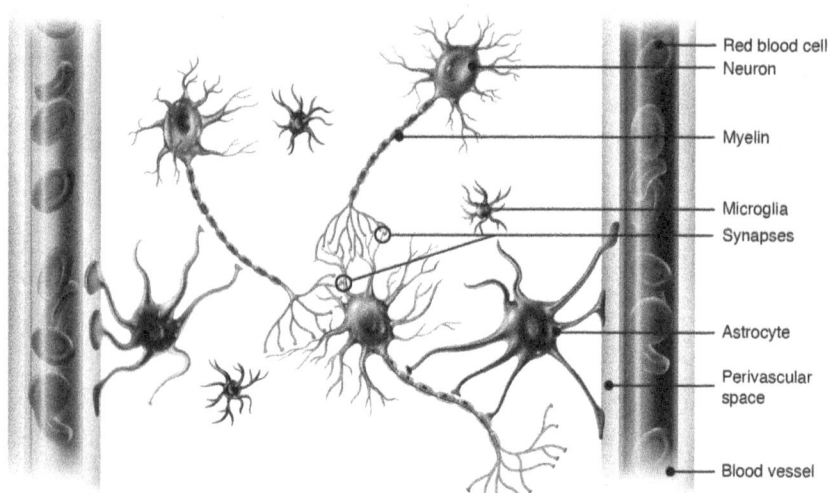

what we call "white matter abnormalities," a key feature of accelerated aging in the brain.

What's the Matter?

You've probably heard of gray and white matter when hearing or reading about the brain. These are distinct brain structures with quite different functions.

- **Gray matter** refers to the cerebral cortex, hippocampus, and other brain structures that contain a high density of neuronal cell bodies, dendrites, and synapses, as well as astrocytes, microglia, and oligodendrocytes. The brain integrates and processes information and generates signals in the gray matter areas.

- **White matter** consists of fiber bundles, or bundles of myelinated axons, which connect various parts of the brain and spinal cord. Myelin is lighter in color compared to the cell-rich gray matter. This gives the "white matter" its lighter hue on an MRI. When there is damage to fiber bundles, such as with poor blood supply or with high levels of inflammation, your brain operations slow down and complex thought becomes difficult because it requires simultaneous communication among different networks.

Both areas can shrink with lifestyle factors like daily stress, an inflammatory junk food diet, or insomnia. Likewise, lifestyle factors like exercise, learning, and practicing complex activities can grow and strengthen both areas. In most cases, what shrinks gray matter also shrinks white matter, and what grows gray matter also grows white matter, but in some cases, actions or conditions will affect only one or the other.

On your tour of Broca's area, the last thing you notice is a whooshing pulse. Come to think of it, you realize the whole brain is pulsing around you, in a steady thrum, sixty to seventy times a minute. Curious about where this pulsation is coming from, you venture toward the blood vessels surrounding the brain's cells. You notice that the sound and movement around you—the watery, steady beat of the brain, ba-BUM ba-BUM, ba-BUM—is coming from those blood vessels.

The heart transmits its pulsation, via the blood vessels in your neck, all the way to the tiny blood vessels inside your brain. With each heartbeat and the vibration it causes in these vessels, a clear fluid in the brain, called cerebrospinal fluid (CSF), rinses the space around neurons and clears all the debris that has accumulated from the billions of chemical processes that happen in the neurons every second. This elaborate waste management operation in the brain is called the glymphatic system, and it is most active during deep sleep at night—one of the most important things that happens during sleep.

As you end your tour of Broca's area, you realize that you now understand how neurons, astrocytes, microglia, and oligodendrocytes always work harmoniously. They have a standard mode of communication with one another and the blood vessels surrounding them. This is not unique to this one part of the brain we have toured. Every other part of the brain has the same components: neurons, astrocytes, microglia, oligodendrocytes, blood vessels, and the glymphatic system. They all work together in the same basic way, and they are all affected by your healthy or not-so-healthy lifestyle choices.

While each area belongs to a handful of nodes in different networks, the fundamental operations of the brain are remarkably consistent everywhere you go. At any given millisecond, all the cells in your brain are busily involved in their routines to ensure you can read, type, walk, talk, eat, use the bathroom, sleep, laugh, be romantic, make love, be active, remember things, or just sit and think about your life's purpose.

Chaos in the Brain?

Under normal circumstances, your neurons and their support team work together like a well-run city. Oxygen and nutrients arrive through blood vessels, astrocytes feed neurons, waste is cleared away, microglia security guards keep intruders out, and oligodendrocytes make sure electrical signals race across networks with perfect timing. Everyone does their job, and you feel sharp, focused, and ready to tackle work, school, or home life with ease.

And When It Doesn't

But what happens when a city's essential services start to falter? Imagine garbage collectors stop working, electricians cut productivity in half, and trains on the metro run only irregularly. Sides of the roads become filled with garbage bags, deliveries slow, and communication between neighborhoods breaks down. Before long, the city becomes clogged, chaotic, and unpleasant to live in. This is exactly what happens in your brain when the operation among neurons and their support systems are disrupted.

What Throws the System Off

Challenges like high blood pressure, obesity, or uncontrolled diabetes damage blood vessels, limiting oxygen and nutrient delivery. Poor sleep interferes with the brain's nightly cleaning cycle, and excessive stress or alcohol disrupts the brain's normal firing patterns, resulting in faulty operation of the brain's networks. For a while, astrocytes, microglia, and oligodendrocytes can keep things stable, but if problems persist, even they get overwhelmed and add to the inflammation that can damage your neurons. The result is a brain that feels foggy and sluggish.

Built-In Repair Systems

The good news is that your brain is resilient. With rest, exercise, and healthy habits, neurons can sprout new connections, astrocytes and microglia can restore balance and reduce inflammation, and protective molecules like BDNF (brain-derived neurotrophic factor) help repair damage. Like any great city, your brain has crews prepared for damage control, to help you recover—up to a point. It is up to you whether you live a life that promotes your brain's innate healing mechanisms or choose lifestyle habits that harm it.

Your Brain Chemistry, Thoughts, and Emotions

Thoughts and emotions reflect the biology of your brain and what happens in the symphony of interactions among neurons, astrocytes, microglia, and oligodendrocytes. When you eat something you enjoy, the pleasure network in your brain produces the chemical dopamine, which helps to reinforce behaviors and experiences you enjoy.

When you are worried about something bad happening, changes in the levels of another neurotransmitter called serotonin activates the parts of your brain that regulate fear (such as the amygdala, which is a part of your brain's emotional network). When your amygdala activates, it sends chemical messages to the hypothalamus to regulate hormones that increase the adrenaline levels in your blood, making your heart beat faster.

When you fall in love, the chemical changes in your brain (not your heart) give you that magical feeling, a result of other parts of your emotional network signaling the hypothalamus to release hormones and make your heart race faster when you see the person you love. When you start a romantic conversation and flirt with someone, your thoughts alone can activate your hypothalamus to release hormones that prepare your body for sex (e.g., lubrication). Sex hormones like testosterone and estrogen in the body can affect your brain, just as romantic thoughts in the brain affect your body. (By the way, sexually active people usually stay fit and have fewer cognitive deficits in old age, so love and intimacy can have significant long-term brain benefits.)

Meanwhile, negative and stressful thoughts not only activate the amygdala, but when high stress levels become chronic, new chemical changes happen in the brain that lead to inflammation, impaired blood flow, and excess cortisol secretion. Similarly, chronic medical conditions like uncontrolled hypertension and sleep apnea that impair blood flow in the brain can impact the chemistry of your brain in ways that can lead to negative thoughts, apathy, and depressed mood. Whether it's physical or mental (and as you can see, they aren't so separate after all), all negative thoughts and untreated medical conditions can hurt your brain.

Bottom line: Taking care of your brain and body can make you happier, and taking steps to increase your happiness can improve your brain vitality and overall health.

The Brain's Endless Possibilities

I hope you have enjoyed your tour of the brain. Now that you've experienced the sparkling, pulsating, awe-inspiring harmony that happens within the brain every second, and understand how every part of the brain works in concert, isn't it humbling to realize that everything we think of as intelligence, talent, or skill arises from this intricate dance of neurons, astrocytes, microglia, and fiber bundles in different brain networks?

It's a profound thought: Intelligence in all its forms is not a mysterious gift but the product of countless tiny interactions within your brain's networks. Each neuron firing, each astrocyte balancing ions, each glymphatic pulse cleansing the brain, each signal passed down the spinal cord to send messages to the rest of the body—they all contribute to your capacity to think, learn, create, and grow your intelligence.

One of the most amazing discoveries of modern neuroscience is that your brain is not fixed like concrete—it is plastic, meaning it can rewire and reshape itself throughout your life. Every time you learn a new skill, practice a habit, or even recall a memory, networks of neurons strengthen and expand their connections. This is why musicians can refine their craft with practice, why stroke patients can relearn to speak, and why your own brain can stay sharp well into old age if you challenge it. The intricate anatomy we've explored—neurons, astrocytes, microglia, oligodendrocytes, and fiber bundles—is not static architecture but a living, breathing system that constantly remodels itself in response to how you use it and how much you challenge it. This is what we call neuroplasticity.

All higher brain functions depend on the optimal functioning of these essential cells and structures. Our every thought and every movement from crown to toe, from the conscious to the automatic, all begin in the brain. The cortex and hippocampus, the most critical components of all brain networks, are central to these processes, serving as the foundational platforms from which intelligence and higher cognitive functions emerge.

Now, what can you do with all this fantastic material inside your skull? You can grow it and change it, and you can use it to improve your memory beyond what you ever thought possible, especially if you believe you are "memory challenged."

In the next chapter, you will learn how the memory parts of your brain work and how the memories you make today can physically modify your brain to shape your future habits (for better or worse). You will also learn about how neuroplasticity can contribute to addiction.

5

MEMORY, PLASTICITY, AND HABIT CHANGE

It seems like everywhere I go, people tell me they are worried about their memories. Often, they are concerned that having memory problems is a sure sign of Alzheimer's disease. I assure them, and I want to assure you, that most of the time this is not the case. Memory problems in midlife are common and happen for many reasons. And, they can almost always be fixed if you work at it. But first, let's get a better understanding of what memory is.

Memory seems like an elusive thing. You remember some things and not others. You remember some things at first, but not later, or you remember things later that you didn't think you noticed at first. Memories come and go in ways we seem to have little control over. And yet, memories are not out there in the air. Memory is physical. It is one of the forms of intelligence we discussed in chapter 2, and like other forms of intelligence, it relies heavily on the malleability of the cortex and hippocampus.

Optimal memory requires optimal functioning of all your brain cells and blood vessels. When you learn something, your neurons develop more connections. When you acquire new knowledge or practice something, you make more synapses (contact points between neurons). The more you practice and practice, the more you develop new synapses and fiber bundles that connect different brain areas.

This phenomenon explains why people who learn a new language, practice a new challenging brain game, or learn a complex skill like juggling grow the corresponding parts of their brains. The brain literally becomes larger. We can observe the growth on brain MRI—sometimes, even one session of intensive brain training can result in noticeable changes. For example, a study of forty-three young adults who practiced learning new vocabulary words for one forty-minute session showed small but visible microstructural changes in their brains on MRIs.[1] Imagine that—only a single period of learning vocabulary can create millions of new synapses and make measurable changes in the anatomy of your brain!

When you learn with a growth mindset—you believe you can learn, grow, and improve at things when you work at them—you prime and boost the neuronal connections involved in learning, and as a result, you can memorize things more easily. On the other hand, the synapses and connections regress when you stop learning and stimulating your brain. "Use it or lose it" applies to your brain just as much as to your muscles, and it also specifically applies to your memory.

Memory Is Now

People often think of memory as recalling things from the past. "I remember my childhood. I remember names. I remember faces. I remember that family trip. I don't remember if my older sister was with us." We think of memory like a scrapbook of the past, and we worry about the missing pages—will we retain the memories of our childhood, the names of our loved ones, all the things we have learned in our lives? Or we worry about the recent past—where we put our keys, where we parked the car, how we completely forgot about that dentist appointment.

The past could be an hour ago, yesterday, last month, or decades ago when you were a child. But the truth is that the more interesting parts of memory, and the more frequently used parts, are about the present, not the past. Remembering the past is only a fraction of our memory. Memory is constantly being interpreted through our present understanding of the world, and we act and think according to those interpretations.

You think thoughts based on memories—not just facts you have learned, but how people have treated you, how you have handled struggles and triumphs, what you have experienced, how you responded, and even your mindset. Those memories have changed your brain and activated your neuroplasticity so that everything you have experienced, learned, and remembered has influenced you in large or small ways, making you who you are today. Memory influences what you do and how you respond to what happens to you now. It informs your decisions, habits, preferences, attitudes, and opinions.

Let's say you go to a nearby town and visit an ice cream parlor, and you really enjoy that ice cream. The next time you're in that town, you remember how much you liked the ice cream, so you decide to go back and get ice cream again. Without that memory, you might not have considered getting ice cream a second (or third, fourth, or fifth) time. This is a very simple example of how the memory of what you did influences what you do.

Memory can also keep you from doing something. Let's say a colleague at work was rude to you. You remember those rude words the next day, so you act differently around that person or avoid them altogether. Your behavior changes based on what happened yesterday because you remember it. The more you avoid them, the more your future actions around that person will be shaped because each new memory reinforces (or contradicts) the older memories.

You may also remember something differently than you initially experienced it. Let's say you went to Europe as a college student, got lost, and wandered alone for hours before you found your way back to your hotel. It was scary and you were afraid, but you also saw many interesting things and met some helpful, kind people. Even though you were fearful when it happened, you look back later and remember that day as an adventure. You were stressed beyond belief, but when you describe it to a friend, you describe that trip as a lot of fun. It was an experience you will never forget. Furthermore, now you have opinions about travel, Europe, tourists, and people from the country you visited that will continue to influence your opinions and actions, all because of your memories.

Sometimes, those stored memories don't turn out okay, or we later interpret them as being traumatic. If someone you love dies, depending on the circumstances (losing a grandfather versus losing a child), you may store that memory as trauma that you can't get over. You remember that experience with deep sadness. You may recover somewhat a year later and decide that life moves on. Or you may need some help recovering from the trauma caused by that memory. Either way, you are changed in some ways. You see things differently and feel differently about death, illness, or tragedy. You have emotions permanently connected with that memory, which influence how you act and respond to things now, for better or worse.

You weren't born with the complete set of beliefs and behaviors you have now. There are basic human impulses that we have built in to help us survive, but everything else is behavior, and our behavior is influenced by our memory: things that have happened to us in the past that we remember and act upon accordingly. So, memory, as you can see, is essential to nearly everything you do. Therefore, the hippocampus—the part of your brain essential for consolidating memories—is essential to nearly everything you do. That is how important it is, and why it is the most changeable part of your brain. It must constantly remodel to accommodate your active and engaged memory system.

The Anatomy of Memory

Neuroscientists have long been fascinated by how memory works, and research has distilled these key steps in the process of creating and retaining memories:

Acquisition. Memory formation begins with acquisition. This is when your brain takes in the sights, sounds, and sensations of the world around you, like a camera snapping pictures. Often, memory problems begin here when individuals skip this step—you can't remember something later if you never recorded the memory in the first place. This step relies on your sensory systems and attention. What you focus on becomes the foundation of your memory. This part of your brain helps you stay motivated, attentive, and engaged during your learning process, and it relies on the part of your cortex called the prefrontal cortex. It is responsible for registering something new and holding all that information in one place—your "memory bank"—ready to be processed further.

Consolidation. This next step is the behind-the-scenes process where the brain organizes and stabilizes the information it has just gathered. Think of it as sorting snapshots into an album, ensuring they don't fade or get misplaced. The hippocampus helps determine which information is worth remembering in the future, like when your library book is due or the time of next week's doctor's appointment. It also helps delete memories, like you would toss an irrelevant advertising flyer into the trash. Trashing useless memories is important because your "hard drive," while massive, can't store every memory. We don't remember every meal we had, every shower we took, every conversation we participated in, or every commute to and from work. The hippocampus registers the things you do remember. It says, "Okay, this memory looks like a keeper."

Storage. Once memories are organized and encoded, each memory component is stored in the corresponding parts of the cortex, which acts like a file cabinet. If you see somebody you met two months ago and recognize their face, you pull that memory from the visual cortex. If you hear a song and you remember hearing it before, or you can recall the sound of your teacher's voice or your mother singing a lullaby, you are pulling that memory from the auditory cortex.

Retrieval. Finally, retrieval brings those memories back to life, allowing you to recall a vivid scene, a long-forgotten song, or the steps to riding a bike. During memory retrieval, an event's components come together in a process that involves many parts of your cortex. Think about a wedding you've attended. There are a lot of things to remember about a wedding: the way the bride and groom looked, the music they played, the taste of the wedding cake, the feel of your dance partner's hand, the smell just before it started to rain, and the excitement when everybody ran under the tent. Yet somehow, all those pieces of memory come together in your brain to form one coherent story, along with all the sensory and emotional impressions you have added to the memories. We don't know exactly how it happens: You see one piece of the jigsaw puzzle, and suddenly the whole puzzle—the whole memory—comes together.

These four steps work together seamlessly, turning experiences (both meaningful and fleeting) into lasting memories.

Now that you know about the overall mechanisms of how memory gets acquired, consolidated, stored, and retrieved, let's discuss different, specific forms of memory and the brain areas involved for each of them.

Types of Memory

Memory involves a network of brain areas called the memory network. Memory is like a grand symphony, with different brain areas playing their unique parts—the prefrontal cortex, amygdala, hippocampus, basal ganglia, and cerebellum are the players. These are all different nodes in the memory network:

Short-term memory. This is the memory of the recent past that you hold in your prefrontal cortex while you learn something, like the cache in your computer. Short-term memory typically lasts for about fifteen to thirty seconds. If someone you just met tells you their name, you will remember it only briefly unless you need to repeat it to someone else or try to remember it for later (I'll show you how to do that in the next chapter).

Working memory. This type of memory kicks in when you need to use the information in short-term memory to do something. It can last thirty seconds to a few minutes while you play and manipulate the information. Let's say you try to enter a website, and they send you a code to type in for security. You remember that code briefly—that is short-term memory—but you must also type it into your phone to open the website. That is working memory.

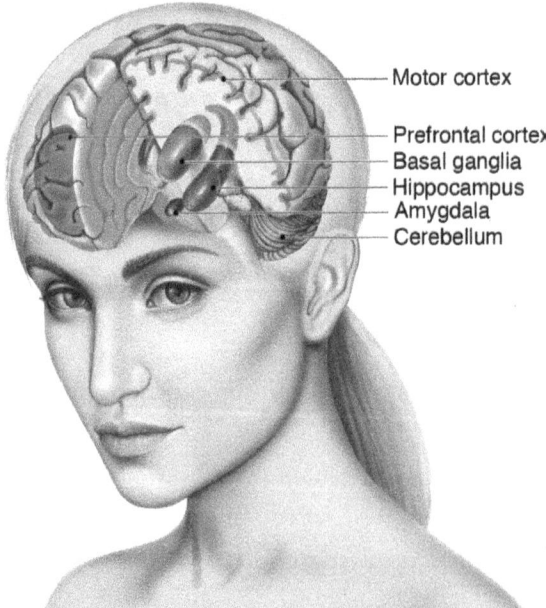

Long-term memory. If the information in your short-term or working memory is meaningful—you want to remember that person's name because you would like to get to know them better—your brain will convert that memory into long-term memory. Your hippocampus is the star of your orchestra for long-term memory. It oversees what events, facts, or experiences are worth remembering for the future and what needs to be discarded. If you hear information that piques your interest during a conversation with friends, such as a hot new bargain on Amazon or the new stock that is skyrocketing, then your hippocampus hits the "save" button. Only that portion of the conversation remains active in your brain for the next day or week.

I still vividly remember one day when I was about six or seven years old. I was gardening with my father in our backyard. It was a beautiful, sunny morning in spring, and I was enjoying the feeling of wet soil in my hands as I was planting some flowers. We discussed my plans for the future, and then my father said, "Majid, remember, everyone is the architect of his own life." I never forgot that moment and those words, even though I have had millions of conversations with him over the last six decades. I remember pausing for a moment and thinking about the meaning of what he was telling me, picturing myself building my future and wondering what it would look like.

Procedural memory brings in a few additional parts of the brain. This type of memory involves how to ride a bicycle, play golf, do a line dance, or hit a tennis ball with power and precision. The hippocampus is always involved, but two other brain structures, the cerebellum and the basal ganglia, are the primary players for procedural memory.

When I practice new dance steps with my wife, I can't help but marvel at how my cerebellum springs into action during our lessons. It helps coordinate the precise timing when I take two steps to the right, then one back, and turn around with my arm raised so my wife can spin gracefully. After repeating these steps a few times, something magical happens: The dance begins to feel effortless. This is thanks to the basal ganglia, which steps in after practice to automate my dance movements. The basal ganglia ensures I can glide through the dance without consciously thinking about each move, freeing up my prefrontal cortex and hippocampus for other tasks.

Have you noticed that when you first practice something, like juggling or Ping-Pong, you need to pay attention and cannot have a conversation? Your brain is occupied following the steps and repeating them. But after practicing the same movements dozens of times, you can talk and dance, juggle, or hit the Ping-Pong ball and think about other things simultaneously. When you learn the steps to doing something new, many new synapses and connections form in different parts of your brain. Once they are established, all you need to do is to access them. You practice, but once it's in your brain, you'll remember it for years to come. Riding a bike is a good example, which is why people say, when talking about something you learn and never forget, "It's just like riding a bike."

The more you learn each day, no matter what you are doing, the more your hippocampus and cortex grow, so you can learn from your experience and remember what you learned. This is one of the most essential survival mechanisms in our brains.

Memory Is Emotional

Of all the types of memory, emotional memory probably impacts our lives the most. Almost all the memories from our distant past involve a strong emotional component. It may surprise you that emotion is one of the primary criteria for remembering something, but the more emotional an event is, the more the hippocampus will be engaged to consolidate it for long-term storage.

Imagine the difference between being introduced to someone you don't know and probably won't see again or interact with much in the future (let's call him Bob, from human resources), and being introduced to someone a friend wants to set you up with because they know you are hoping to find a love match (let's call her Sally, your buddy's wife's friend). An hour after meeting Bob and Sally, you might wonder, "What was that human resources guy's name again? I can't think of it. Bill? Ben?" You might also think, "Wow, I really connected with Sally. I think I'll ask her if she would like to go out for coffee with me sometime." You have more of an emotional connection with Sally, so you remember her name but can't recall poor Bob's name at all.

Anatomically, the prefrontal cortex governs working memory and attention, where we attend to the world with different levels of heightened awareness. You can sit there during that safety lecture you've heard on the plane a thousand times. Still, you couldn't recite it. Or you can get really into that same safety lecture because you're in the exit aisle, and you may be just a little emotionally stressed—you want to be sure you know what to do if you're going to be responsible for the safety of others.

The amygdala, an almond-shaped structure sitting right in front of the hippocampus on either side of your brain, is the star player in your emotional memory—especially those memories involving fear and danger. A neighbor to the hippocampus, the amygdala acts like a trigger, urging the hippocampus to store emotionally important memories with extra vividness. If you burn your hand while cooking with a new pot, you will remember that sensation for a long time and be extra cautious when using the same pot again. If a movie really scared you as a kid, you will probably remember vivid scenes from that movie decades later.

Do you remember your first kiss or the first time you held your newborn baby? That unforgettable, heart-racing feeling is courtesy of a part of the prefrontal cortex in your brain that has a strong link to the dopamine reward pathway. This area is called the orbitofrontal cortex. This part of the cortex, sitting right above and behind your eyes, can also rev up the firing in the hippocampus. The more emotional such rewarding experiences are, the more your orbitofrontal cortex is activated and the more you will remember every detail about them: the look, the sounds, the smells, the touch—everything is firmly etched in your mind about those highly emotional moments.

Beyond their role as prominent members of the memory network in the brain, the hippocampus, orbitofrontal cortex, and amygdala are also key components of the limbic, or emotional, network in the brain. As a part of their membership in this brain network, these structures have tight links with the dopamine, or reward, pathways in the brain. Our brain's wiring is such that the orbitofrontal part of the prefrontal cortex, the central hub in our brain's reward pathways, is also critical for emotional memory.

This overlap of the memory and emotional networks makes sense from an evolutionary perspective—remembering dangers (like predators or reactions to poisonous plants) and rewards (like the location of a grove of fruit trees or a good hunting ground) helps increase your chances of survival.

Menopause and Memory

One common complaint of women going through menopause is memory problems, and many women worry that this signifies the onset of Alzheimer's. Don't worry! The hormonal changes women go through during this time of life often cause memory problems, brain fog, and other cognitive issues as your brain adjusts to shifting hormones. Menopause-associated memory problems are *temporary*. Your memory will return once your body has adjusted to the new hormone balance. You are not on a downward cognitive slide. You are experiencing a transition. This is, however, a good time of life to refresh your lifestyle and start practicing brain-boosting habits (like those in part 4 of this book) —to guard against future cognitive issues that could potentially be more permanent.

Why We Forget Things

You can't remember everything that you experience every day—and sometimes it's distressing if you try to remember something and simply can't. What's really going on when that happens, whether it's where you put your car keys or the name of your new coworker?

Sometimes, forgetting is related to a medical problem, but more often, people forget things because they never transferred a memory to long-term storage. As I've already explained, if you are uninterested in something, you will be less likely to remember it, especially if you have no emotional attachment to the thing you want to remember. This is why students do better in classes that interest them. If the information is irrelevant to you, you're even less likely to remember it. If a friend tells you a long story about someone you don't know doing something you don't care about, chances are you won't take up brain real estate remembering all the details.

It's natural to forget something if you don't have to remember it.

For example, if you don't fully and intentionally memorize the name of a person you met for the first time an hour ago—maybe while you were being introduced, you were thinking about something else, or distracted because you notice that they strongly resemble your Aunt Susan—chances are you will not remember their name if you see them again tomorrow. (You might even mistakenly call them "Susan.") You heard the information but didn't consolidate it into long-term memory. Technically, it's not that you forgot it. It's that you never memorized it in the first place.

Ten Reasons Middle-Aged People Forget Things

"Can't do it" mentality: When you (falsely) believe you can't remember anything, you don't try hard and so you forget things easily, which "proves" to you that you have a poor memory.

Poor sleep quality: Sleep is essential for memory consolidation, especially deep (slow-wave) sleep.

Distraction and multitasking: Divided attention reduces the brain's ability to encode new information.

Sedentary lifestyle: Lack of physical activity reduces blood flow and BDNF, a key brain growth factor.

Poor diet: Diets high in sugar and processed foods can cause inflammation and insulin resistance in the brain.

Depression, anxiety, and chronic stress: These conditions reduce focus, shrink the hippocampus, and impair the memory network in the brain.

Hormonal changes: Thyroid, estrogen, or testosterone abnormalities can affect learning and memory.

Sleep apnea: Repeated nighttime oxygen deprivation damages memory-related brain areas.

Alcohol and substance use: These can shrink the hippocampus and damage synaptic connections.

Medication side effects: Common drugs for anxiety, sleep, blood pressure, and allergies can interfere with memory.

Aging can also be the reason for forgetting—some information, especially if you don't use it, might decay over time. For example, you may forget the names of elementary school friends because you haven't thought about them in decades. Some cues can dredge memories from long ago—things you thought you forgot but that you actually stashed away. Smells can be a potent reminder of past memories. Maybe you smell chocolate chip cookies, and that activates a memory of your grandmother who used to love baking cookies, and then you may find you are remembering other things about your grandmother that you haven't thought about for years.

Recently, I was driving in a Baltimore neighborhood and passed by a house I used to live in almost forty years earlier, when I was a graduate student at Johns Hopkins University. I remembered the very nice owner of that house, Barbara, who had rented one of her rooms to me. I could vividly remember (and see) her soft voice and kind face. Then suddenly, the phone number of that home just popped into my head. To confirm I had the correct number, I called. To my surprise, Barbara answered. We arranged to meet a week later and chatted about my years in her house. A flood of memories from those days filled me with joy.

Without a cue, you may never actively recall a stored memory, even at the back of a "file cabinet" buried deep inside your brain's archives. If I hadn't driven that way that day, I might never have known I still kept that phone number somewhere in my brain. You never know what will trigger a stored memory.

Memory Is the Key to Habit Change

You probably don't think of neuroplasticity as having much to do with your daily decisions, especially when it comes to health. And yet, habits are essentially the formation of new wiring in the brain via neuroplasticity. Whether they are bad or good habits, what we do on repeat, especially when it taps into our brain's reward centers, changes the brain. Understanding this is key to changing your habits because pleasure often overrides logic.

Let's take the example of a fifteen-year-old kid named Fred. One day after school, Fred goes over to his group of friends, and they're all vaping.

Memory, Plasticity, and Habit Change

Fred has never vaped before, and he heard it was a bad idea, but his friends all said it was great and there was nothing wrong with it. Normally, Fred wouldn't do such a thing, but he wants to fit in, and his best friend, Harry, convinces him to try it, just this once. After some back-and-forth, Fred agrees... just this once, because it's Friday and he's had a long week of tests and homework.

So Fred tries vaping, and it tastes great. He gets a burst of energy. He admits he enjoys it, and he also enjoys the approval of his vaping peers. Even so, he knows he would get in big trouble if his parents found out, so he says firmly, to his friend and himself: "I'm never doing that again."

The problem is that Fred's brain created an enjoyable memory of that experience. The rush of nicotine and the social approval were emotionally charged, so his brain remembered that good feeling. The next time Fred sees his friends in the parking lot vaping, the rewarding memory rises to the surface. He wants to have that good feeling again, so he agrees to vape "just one more time."

The problem with "just one more time" is that when Fred does this activity again, his brain reinforces those pathways that made him want to vape. The next time Fred sees his friend, who offers him his very own vaping device, he accepts. He wants to vape again, even more than he did last time. Every time he reinforces that pathway, it gets stronger. He may still say, "I'm not addicted. I do it for the fun of it. I do it with this one group of friends. I only do it on Fridays after school. I can stop whenever I want." But this is precisely how addiction happens.

Every time you repeat a behavior, you reinforce and strengthen those pathways even more, whether it's a good habit or a bad habit. Meanwhile, nicotine—an addictive substance—can create neuronal pathways in the brain by releasing dopamine, especially in the orbitofrontal cortex, which cues you to remember things with emotional connections. Every time Fred craves that good feeling and vapes again, he further reinforces and strengthens those pathways in the brain.

Think of it like walking on grass in a field. You walk on it once, and it makes a dent in the grass. You can detect a slight path if you walk on it a few times. You walk on it thousands of times, and the grass is completely worn away, creating a clear path. This is what happens when these brain pathways are formed and strengthened. But stop walking on the path, and although the path persists for a while, the grass will grow back and the path will fade away. Breaking a habit takes time, but with time and a growth mindset, you can be successful.

So what about Fred? Pretty soon, he has trod a clear path through that metaphorical grass. He is thinking about vaping even when he doesn't see his friends. He's vaping in his room with the door locked. He doesn't need the cue anymore because he's developed a habit. Now he's doing it on weekdays. Then his parents catch him and take away his vape, and he is grounded for months! Poor Fred . . . he didn't realize how easy it would be to rewire his brain into addiction. This is an example of negative neuroplasticity—that is, the formation of neuronal pathways that are harmful to us in the long run.

This process can happen with anything that accesses your reward system: shopping, alcohol, chocolate, social media, or a person you're madly in love with. Whatever it is, the more you expose yourself to the dopamine, the more you will shop, drink, scroll, eat candy, or spend time with that person you can't get enough of, and the more those pathways are reinforced, for better or for worse.

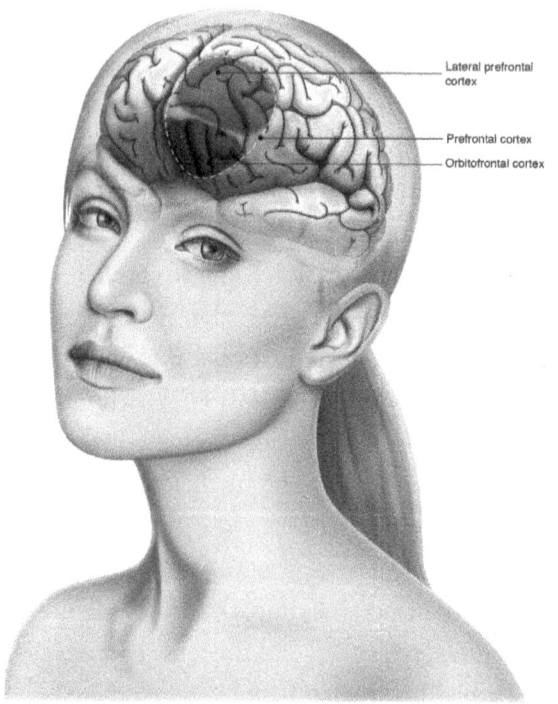

Fortunately, we have a brain area that can help regulate our natural quest for dopamine. A large part of the prefrontal cortex located above and behind the orbitofrontal cortex, called the lateral prefrontal cortex, is responsible for analyzing behavior and its consequences. This part helps us make decisions based on common sense. When we engage in activities that demand logical thought or self-discipline, such as exercising daily or working toward long-term goals, this part of the brain becomes more active. It suppresses the impulsive tendencies of the orbitofrontal cortex and supports decisions that align with our broader aspirations and values. It considers future consequences and actions or thoughts with clear-cut logical consequences—for example, studying hard to do well and get admitted to medical school or not eating too much pizza to avoid heartburn.

The dynamic interplay between these two brain regions—the pleasure-seeking orbitofrontal cortex and the logical, goal-oriented lateral prefrontal cortex—determines our behavior at any given moment. Striking the right balance between these areas is crucial for making decisions that feel good now and benefit us in the future.

The brain does not change effortlessly. The trick in building these pathways is to remind yourself of the pain you will avoid and the joy you will have if you persist. This is also where people with a sense of purpose in life have an advantage; they have a clear vision of where they want to be in their lives, so envisioning things that will get them there makes sticking with new habits easier.

Even better is to have a motivator that has a strong emotional component. When I was a kid, maybe ten or twelve years old, I had a best friend whose mother was a smoker. He was like my brother, and she was like my second mom. I used to say, "Why do you smoke? It's bad for you." She would say, "Honey, I've smoked a pack or two a day for thirty years. I can't quit now. I just can't."

I visited them every year or two after we grew up and his family moved to Florida. She was constantly coughing, and then one day she was diagnosed with lung cancer. From that moment on, she never smoked again. The strong logical assessment—realizing she had cancer and wanting to beat it—was charged with enough emotion (probably fear) to let her lateral prefrontal cortex override the programmed reward-driven habit enforced by her orbitofrontal cortex, and she was finally able to quit. Unfortunately, this happened too late. Sadly, she died one year later.

The formation of habits is about a constant battle between logic and emotion. Knowing this means you can use emotion to help you stick with behaviors that you know are logical. You can boost the activity in both your lateral prefrontal cortex and your orbitofrontal cortex by believing strongly (and emotionally) in the logic of your choices. Imagine as vividly as you can the joy you'll experience when you have achieved your goal (e.g., losing five or ten pounds, or running your first 5k); feel the excitement you will have in that moment, and then let that dopamine rush drive you to stick to your new habits. In this process, you will rewire your brain for success. Habit change is all about neuroplasticity.

Memory is a curious thing—mysterious even to those who study it. Yet understanding how it works can help you learn to use it to your advantage. In the next chapter, we're going to have some fun. I will show you some tricks for improving your memory in ways you never thought possible!

6

HOW TO IMPROVE YOUR MEMORY

If you think your memory is horrible, you are not alone. Throughout my career, giving lectures to thousands of people in academic or large organizations in about twenty-five countries, I have always been amazed at how many people believe their memory is not as good as the memory of others. Whenever I ask my audience members to raise their hands if they feel their memory is poor for remembering names, more than 90 percent respond!

Obviously, it's not the case that more than 90 percent of all the people in the world have early brain decay.

In my experience of treating thousands of patients who came to see me about their fading memory, especially those in their midlife, a diagnosis of Alzheimer's disease has always been a rare possibility. As you'll see in chapter 8, rates of Alzheimer's are actually dropping.[1] It's strange to me that most people never intentionally try to improve their memories. People often think memory should just be there, working perfectly all the time, without any effort—that information should go into their brains and stay there. When it doesn't, they think they have a "bad memory" or "memory problems." But did they try to attain and keep that memory? Usually not.

You wouldn't expect to be able to run a marathon with no training—having a stellar memory is no different. It's not your fault if you didn't know this or don't do this. Our brains are wired with a system for deciding what information is vital for our survival. If you go to a party and hear the names of fifty people, your brain knows there is no survival benefit to memorizing these names, so it doesn't remember most of them. But that doesn't mean you *can't* remember fifty names.

We often want to remember things that are not critical for survival, and we can. We just have to put in the effort. When you do that, you can memorize whatever you want. It's true! Learn to quiet that inner voice that says, "My memory is fading!" I want you to decide today to be different from those who have negative beliefs about their ability to remember things. You can boost your memory by 5 to 10 percent with minimal effort, and even more with greater effort, but the first thing you need to do is stop the repetitive negative thoughts (RNTs). I suggest you start practicing repetitive positive thoughts (RPTs) by repeating a mantra that appeals to you.

My favorite mantra is "If I really want something, I always get it eventually." Here are some other positive affirmations you might like to adopt:

Where there's a will, there's a way, or The will makes the way.
Dream it, do it.
Desire fuels action.
Commit, conquer.
I can do anything I choose to do.
I can remember!

Or make up your own. Repeat your mantra when you wake up in the morning, or when you are taking a shower, driving, or taking a break from work. When an RNT comes to mind, replace it with your chosen RPT. These words and your attitude toward improving memory help you develop a growth mindset. They excite your prefrontal cortex, the engine that revs up the rest of your brain.

I am confident you can boost your memory with my instructions and impress yourself and people around you in a matter of days to weeks. Anyone can learn to play tennis or cook a meal if someone shows them how. Memory is no different. I can teach you to become a star memorizer.

Memory Tricks from a Memory Champion

Many years ago, I worked with my friend and colleague Nelson Dellis, the six-time US Memory Champion. We organized a one-day memory-boosting event in Baltimore. We divided the concepts that can help people improve their learning and memory into two categories:

1. Things that improve the biology of your brain and make it a more efficient engine

2. Tricks and skills that can help people improve memory performance in a matter of hours and days

In our presentations, he and I took turns discussing these essential concepts. I talked about the science of the brain and how we can make our brain healthier through diet, exercise, sleep, stress management, socialization, and brain games. He talked about his favorite tricks.

In this book, you will learn a great deal about how to make your brain work better through lifestyle changes. But first, I'll share some memory tricks I learned from Nelson Dellis, which will help you overcome day-to-day memory issues, including memorizing names and where you parked your car.

Memory tricks can be fun, especially as you observe your memory steadily improving. They are also great exercises for your brain. These tricks work. I've seen it many times in all kinds of people, from college students to seniors in assisted living facilities.

Recently, I got into a minor bicycle accident and broke my kneecap. I was off my feet, in a straight leg brace, for many weeks. Usually, I'm a pretty active guy, so I was unhappy that I couldn't exercise, walk, or drive. In general, I have a motto that when something bad happens, I should try to make something good come out of it. So instead of feeling sorry for myself, I decided this would be a perfect opportunity to do memory exercises for two to three hours daily, so I could boost memory further.

Even I could not believe how quickly and easily I became better at memorizing things. For two to three weeks, every day, I memorized multiple credit card numbers, multiple phone numbers, two decks of cards, and refreshed my ability to read and speak Spanish. Now I'm hungry for it—whenever I hear a useful number or bit of information, I jump to memorize it! And guess what? It's fun! It's entertaining. It keeps getting easier. And I have come to really enjoy it. You can too. These memory tricks may feel challenging at first, but after you do a few of them, you will begin to enjoy the process.

And just in case you still think you can't do it, here's a true story: I once lectured a group of about one hundred senior citizens in a retirement community. The average age was about eighty, with most residents between seventy-five and eighty-five. Some were in wheelchairs, others used walkers, and while this particular group did not have dementia, they were all at an age where many people think their memories are certainly impaired.

I picked a list of twenty random words. Using the tricks I will teach you in this chapter, within forty minutes the entire group of seniors had memorized all twenty words and could repeat them to me in unison, forward and backward. I made a video of this and put it on my Facebook page. I recently had the video appear as one of my Facebook "memories," but I'll never forget that day.

So don't think you are too old or forgetful to learn these memory tricks. You are going to amaze yourself!

Improve Your Memory for Names

With consistent practice, you can begin to memorize the name of every person you meet. I have been practicing name memorization for years, and now I have become quite good at it. I once memorized the names of seventy people during one of my lectures for the Inova Health System in Northern Virginia. I always memorize all my students' names (usually about fifty of them) within the first two classes in a semester.

Before meeting someone new, one easy, quick trick is to use your imagination. Tell yourself that you will get $10,000 if you memorize their name and its correct spelling. The more excited you are, the more your prefrontal cortex will get revved up. Remember, this part of your brain is the engine that energizes all other parts of your brain to be primed and function at their best, including your hippocampus.

Once you've got yourself motivated, try this four-step process for remembering names, using the acronym N.A.M.E.:

Notice: When you first meet a new person and want to remember their name, begin by *noticing* their face in detail. Look at their eyes, eyebrows, nose, and mouth. Listen to their tone of voice, observe how they speak, and guess their approximate age. Pick one feature of their face that stands out the most; do they have thick eyebrows, a small nose, or a charming smile? This allows your mind to focus on them and block out distractions. You want them to be at the center of your attention and be ready to discover their name. Get excited to earn that $10,000!

Ask: The next step is to *ask* their name. When you hear the name of the person you just met, repeat their name loud and clear. People tend to give their name quickly, but you want to ensure you hear it fully. Be ready to tell them: "Nice meeting you, Fredricka." This is an important moment in the learning process. You need to grab their name with complete confidence, and say it out loud. People often feel shy to repeat the name of the person they just met, as they worry they may not be pronouncing it correctly. This is the moment to be bold. Ask them to repeat their name if you are not 100 percent sure how it is pronounced or spelled. You need to grasp the details of their name, especially if it is unfamiliar to you.

Memorize: Memorize their name by repeating it two to three times during your conversation. There is a good chance that despite your best effort to grab and register this person's name, their name vanished in your mind. There is nothing to worry about. They don't know your name either. I often make a joke and ask people if they remember my name (which they rarely do). Then, while smiling, I give them my name and ask them to repeat their name (and how to spell it, if necessary). You are on a mission to register this person's name into your hippocampus. Repeat their name as you talk with them: "Fredricka, tell me, how do you know our host?" Listen with heightened attention. The more you connect with and learn about them (what they do, where they live, etc.), the more likely you'll remember their name.

Ensure: *Ensure* you have their name fully memorized. As your conversation ends, be 1,000 percent confident you know how to pronounce and spell their name. Confirm that you know this person's name without a doubt. Picture in your mind that you are about to receive your $10,000 reward, and pat yourself on the back for your victory, having accomplished memorizing their name. Remember, the more emotions are involved in an event, the more likely you will remember it later, so remain upbeat and enthusiastic.

Like any other learning process, you will get better at memorizing names with practice. The most critical factor about this process is your attitude about your brain's capabilities. I love the quote from Henry Ford: "Whether you think you can or you think you can't, you are right." Tell yourself you are good at remembering names, and you will be.

"Where did I put that...?"

It's such a common scenario—you can't find where you put your wallet, glasses, or car keys. The trick to avoiding this is always putting that thing in the same place every time. Your keys always go in a dish by the front door, your wallet goes in the nightstand drawer, and your glasses belong on the bookshelf—*every time*. However, we all know this doesn't always happen. Maybe you aren't in your usual environment. You put your glasses down in a hotel or your hat down somewhere at work. The trick is, whenever you put something down, to say in an exaggerated British accent or some other accent you know (French, Indian, or Italian, for example):

"I am putting my wallet here, darling."
"My reading glasses belong on the bookshelf, old chap!"
"Why, I say, I'll set my keys right here on this desk!"

The idea is to make it sound funny so it's memorable. Remember that when you attach an emotion to an event, you are more likely to remember it. Humor counts. Whatever it is, amuse yourself and you will remember.

Another way to attach emotion to something is to always be nice to the future you. Consider when you need to remember this information—in an hour, tomorrow, or in a week—and make it obvious so you can find something easily again and not put yourself in distress. For example, you bought tickets to a concert you can't wait to see. You will need them in a week. Think to yourself, "I wouldn't want my future self to run around in a panic looking for these tickets on the day of the concert! I'll put them right here in the drawer by the front door, and I'll remember this so future me can find them!" Or maybe you know you will be leaving the country next month. Think to yourself, "My future self would be so upset if he couldn't find his passport on the day of the trip. I'll put it right here in my suitcase's front pocket, and I'll remember this so future me doesn't think it's lost."

Either way, attaching humor or empathy to the information will help it solidify as a memory.

"Why did I come into this room?"

Many people complain that they come into a room and forget why. They worry that this is a sign of a degraded memory. Researchers have studied this phenomenon[2] and have determined that the best way to remember why you came into a room is to go back to where you were before you came into the room and start there. This will often trigger the reason, whether you see something that reminds you or you remember what you were thinking about.

Let's say you go from the kitchen into the garage, and now you can't remember why you went into the garage. Go back into the kitchen and look around. You may see a note on the calendar that reminds you there's something in the car you wanted to retrieve. Or you remember noticing a stain on the counter, and you went into the garage to get the heavy-duty stain remover.

"Where did I park the car?"

We've all been there—you park the car to go to an event (or a shopping mall), and when you return, you can't remember where you parked. If you are in one of those big parking garages, you might panic that you will never find your car again! Here's a trick to avoid that.

When you first park your car and then go to the elevator, stairwell, or exit, there may be a sign with a picture of an animal or a color to help people remember their level. People often ignore this helpful cue. Notice and visualize it. You can usually find some indication of the location—maybe it is parking garage B, level 4 north, or something like that. Whatever it is, always notice it before you get on the elevator. You could write it down or photograph it with your phone, but that's cheating. Why not use a memory trick and grow your brain a little?

If you are in parking garage B, level 4 north, you might imagine four giant bears (*B* is for "bear," *4* is the level) looking up at the north star. Or maybe you imagine the parking garage is a giant letter *B*, and your car sits on top of the *B* with a number *4* rocking back and forth. Whatever the picture, think about it the whole time you are making your way out of the parking garage. The funnier it is, the better.

How to Memorize Your Credit Card Number

This is a lot easier than you think. You can do this through a process called the memory palace. In ancient Greece, messengers had to carry news across the vast landscape of the Greek city-states. To ensure they remembered every detail accurately, they used a memory technique that transformed their minds into intricate maps of imaginary palaces. Each room in these mental palaces was associated with specific information, such as a leader's decree, a treaty term, or a battle strategy. As they visualized walking through these palaces, they could "retrieve" the information from the rooms, step-by-step, as if reading from a scroll.

This method was beneficial in an era when written records were rare and unreliable during long journeys. The technique allowed messengers to travel for days or weeks, relaying complex messages with perfect accuracy. Memory champions still use this technique. Here's how to use a memory palace technique to memorize your credit card numbers:

1. Get your credit card and look at or write down the number, expiration date, and code. Let's say it is 5500 6602 8653 3362, Expiration: 04/48, Code: 629. We will place each of these groups of numbers on a familiar path you take every day, from when you wake up to when you leave the house.
2. Imagine a path you take every morning (for example) from your bedroom to your bathroom, kitchen, door, and garage.
3. Use your imagination and picture each of these groups of numbers in each of the locations. See them large and clear, as big blocks in vibrant and vivid colors.

For example, in your mind, place an image of 5500 on your nightstand. Close your eyes, and see these numbers as white blocks next to your lamp or your alarm clock. Picture these thick white blocks in your head and ask yourself a few times what the numbers are. Make sure you have 5500 firmly in your memory. This should take no more than three to five minutes when you try it for the first time. Once you are sure you have memorized this number, we can now move to the bathroom.

4. Picture 6602 written in large bold red letters below your shower (perhaps with dripping blood, if you want to make it extra dramatic). Seeing such a random number in your shower is ridiculous, but that's the idea. The sillier, scarier, or funnier, the better you will remember it. Repeat this number and memorize it for three to five minutes.

5. Go back and picture seeing 5500 on your nightstand, then walking to the bathroom and seeing 6602 in your shower. This reinforces the memories and the order.

6. Picture walking into the kitchen and seeing 8653 in large black block numbers next to your coffeemaker (perhaps with some coffee spilled over the blocks). Close your eyes and repeat 8653 as you envision your kitchen counter with these numbers. Repeat for three to five minutes.

7. Repeat all the numbers, going back to the beginning of your route: 5500 on the nightstand, 6602 in the shower, and 8653 by the coffeemaker. Smile and have fun with this process. You are doing it for the fun of it, in addition to the convenience of knowing your credit card number wherever you are.

8. Repeat the same process for memorizing 3362—picture it in large brown blocks standing in your front doorway (with letters almost as tall as you are), blocking your way out of your home. Again, go back through the journey, starting at your nightstand, visualizing and repeating the numbers at each location.

9. Now you have stepped into the garage and see 04/48 written on your windshield. That's weird; who did that? Imagine getting upset because you must clean 04/48 from your windshield glass. Repeat 04/48 as you are cleaning the glass. Now repeat the entire number: 5500 6602 8653 3362, Expiration: 04/48.

10. Picture opening your car door and seeing 629 etched on your seat with a knife. Vividly see how your seat is damaged with these letters. The more

clearly you visualize it, the better you will remember it. What terrible vandalism! You can even get slightly upset about it—you will remember it more easily that way.

11. Finally, repeat the whole thing from the beginning to the end: 5500 6602 8653 3362, Expiration: 04/48, Code: 629.

And *voila!* You have memorized your credit card number and can confidently rehearse it (and impress your family and friends!). For the fun it, try to rehearse all of these numbers backward.

When you do this memorization drill for the first time, it may take thirty minutes, but as you get better at it, you can memorize a credit card in five to ten minutes. The point is that this is ultimately doable and requires no exceptional talent or skills.

Train Your Prefrontal Cortex Like You Train Your Muscles

As you know by now, your prefrontal cortex is the king of the learning process because that is where the first step—acquisition—happens. The more you use and challenge this part of your brain, the stronger it will become. Here is a hands-on game to work out your prefrontal cortex: You will play rock-paper-scissors with yourself!

First, decide that you will let your left hand win three times, then let your right hand win three times. This isn't as easy as it sounds, because usually people play rock-paper-scissors without planning what they will do. It requires some attention. Play the game using both hands and let the designated hand win. You can mix up what you decide. Maybe you will let the right hand and left hand win in an alternating pattern.

Memorize Twenty Things

This next trick uses the brain's natural tendency to remember stories, combined with elements of the memory palace you learned when memorizing your credit card number. I often use this exercise to show people they can memorize a random list of twenty things—this is the trick I taught the senior citizens I told you about at the beginning of this chapter. But why not make it more useful? You will be so impressed with how you can do this!

When I tell people I can show them how to memorize twenty items in twenty minutes, they often decline. They feel intimidated. They worry they will be the one person who will fail. I try to convince them that they are not special in this negative way—anyone can do it. I say, "Come on, guys, let's do this!" They often continue to refuse, and I think it is because they are embarrassed, just in case they really can't do it. But I am telling you right now that you *can* do it. If those retirement home residents in their seventies and eighties can do it, so can you. So let's give it a try, shall we?

Begin by making your list of twenty words. Maybe it's your grocery list—you can learn to memorize that list and never forget anything at the store again! Let's imagine, for illustration, that your list looks like this:

Salad mix
Tomatoes
Mushrooms
Carrots
Apples
Sourdough bread
Bagels
Baked beans
Canned corn
Flour
Spaghetti
Ground beef
Chicken breasts
Sliced turkey
Swiss cheese
Milk
Vanilla yogurt
Sour cream
Frozen broccoli
Frozen blueberries

That may sound like a lot for anyone to remember, but just wait! We're going to make up a few silly stories and place them around the grocery store you go to frequently. Your story will occur in groups of four items, so you will have five short stories of four items to memorize twenty things. The goal of this practice is to turn trivial daily items into large, exaggerated, and funny things that are ridiculous and memorable. The storyline helps you keep the order of the items in your mind so that you can rehearse them later. I usually have a lot of fun when I do this and laugh along the way. Here is just an example of how to do this:

We will begin with the first four items: salad mix, tomatoes, mushrooms, and carrots. Imagine a story like this:

"I arrive at the grocery store, and as I enter the usual way, I realize my path is blocked by a giant pile of salad mix, just as I try to walk in the door. Who piled salad mix ten feet high in front of the door? I look up to the top of the salad mix mountain and see a ring of bright red tomatoes, like a crown on top of the mountain of salad mix. As I get around the salad mix with its tomato crown, I see that the biggest mushroom I've ever seen is in the center of the produce aisle, like a giant twelve-foot umbrella. Hanging from the underside of the mushroom cap are hundreds of carrots, pointing down like icicles, as if they were hooked onto the gills of the mushroom cap."

Take your time to visualize all these four items in your head as vividly as you can. Repeat them forward and backward a few times.

Now let's memorize our next four items: apples, sourdough bread, bagels, and baked beans. This should be fun!

"As I walk through the store, I see a line of round red apples, like basketballs, which ends in a giant slice of sourdough bread, blocking my way. Or is it a giant door made from a slice of bread? I notice that right where a doorknob would be is a hot bagel. I reach out and turn the bagel, and the sourdough bread door opens right onto a river of baked beans. Yes, a whole lot of baked beans flowing like a river!"

Vividly picture each of these four items, and repeat this short list forward and backward. Then repeat the eight items from the beginning to the end, and then backward. Practice this list a few more times until you know them perfectly well.

Our next four items are: canned corn, flour, spaghetti, and ground beef.

"In the next aisle, I see a giant ear of corn sticking out of a large aluminum can and decide to take a bite. It tastes delicious! Soon after I see that snow is falling on me, and as I brush it off, I realize it isn't snow but flour falling like snow. In the center of the aisle I encounter a giant white plate filled with ten pounds of hot spaghetti and topped with red ground beef. I can vividly see the mix of spaghetti and red meat!"

Think about this segment of the story and remember your items. Now go back through the store and recall all the items, story by story. Repeat them a few times, forward and backward.

We're over halfway there! Next up: chicken breasts, sliced turkey, Swiss cheese, and milk.

"As I continue my fascinating journey in this weird supermarket, I encounter an interesting scene: a chicken and a turkey, facing off, glaring at each other, and circling and flapping their wings like they are getting ready for a fight. Behind them, a towering block of Swiss cheese stands like a scoreboard, showing their scores. Just as the turkey lunges toward the chicken, a waterfall of milk pours down from above and drenches the birds. They run away in opposite directions."

Recall all the items in order by remembering each story. Repeat them a few times, forward and backward. Now we have just one more story to go, using vanilla yogurt, sour cream, frozen broccoli, and frozen blueberries.

"As I wade through the flood of milk on the floor, with every step the milk parts. Half of it flows to the left, where it solidifies and turns into vanilla yogurt. On the right, it also begins to solidify, but on this side it turns into sour cream. As I make my way toward the exit, I see a colorful arch made with frozen broccoli over the exit. It's very pretty. I step through the arch and almost slip on an icy path of frosted, deep blue blueberries. I decide to pick and taste a few of them as I walk to the parking lot to my car."

Do you remember the last four items? Can you go through all twenty grocery items featured in this epic tale, forward and backward? Repeat the story in your mind, as vividly as possible, for fifteen to twenty minutes, and you are ready to head to the actual grocery store, without your list!

You did it! Now you get the process. Of course, you can make the story anything you like—the weirder, funnier, or more dramatic, the better. And the more you do this, the less time it will take you. With practice, you can memorize your grocery list in minutes. You can use this technique to memorize any list of 10, 20, 30, 50, or even 100 items. Even most of our patients with cognitive decline, concussion, or ADHD who completed our twelve-week program learned how to memorize a list of one hundred items (twenty words a week) and/or a deck of cards. Use this technique often and you will be exercising your prefrontal cortex and your hippocampus, gaining memory confidence, impressing your friends, and never doubting your memory abilities again.

If you want to try a more condensed method to memorize twenty items, imagine a very familiar room in your home and place groups of items around the room, such as in your kitchen, with little stories to go with each, arranged clockwise. For example, you make a story with four items by the coffee machine, four next to the dishwasher, four next to the sink, four in the fridge, and four next to the door. When you need to know your twenty words, all you have to do is imagine that one room and look around it in your mind.

If you enjoyed memorizing your list of twenty items and feel ready to take memory tricks even further, check my website, drfotuhi.com, where I will teach you how to memorize the order of an entire deck of cards. This one takes a little more time at first, but it's a lot of fun once you get into it. It can take your memory skills to the next level.

Every one of these memory tricks can help you gain confidence and expand your growth mindset about your ability to improve your memory further. Keep in mind that your ability to memorize things depends on the harmony of actions between your brain cells, your brain blood vessels, and the CSF fluid that rinses your brain with each heartbeat. They all come together to create the magical and vibrant brain environment that allows you to keep boosting your cognitive functions every day.

Now let's get to the reason why, I suspect, many of you came to this book. What happens to your brain's anatomy and environment as you age, and what can you do to optimize aging and avoid cognitive decline? Can you slow down or reverse the effects of Alzheimer's related genes in your brain? These are the focus of the next part of the book.

PART THREE

UNDERSTANDING AND STRENGTHENING THE AGING BRAIN

7

EPIGENETICS OVERRIDES GENETICS FOR ALZHEIMER'S DISEASE AND BEYOND

With advancing age, your brain changes every day. That doesn't mean it declines. Your brain is constantly readjusting and adapting in response to your environment. You've already seen examples of how this happens. While the primary structures remain the same, you can grow and shrink your cortex and hippocampus according to what you do.

However, there is one thing my patients often ask about: genetics. What if they are predisposed to Alzheimer's disease, or some other condition that can compromise brain health? They think they are surely doomed and may as well get their affairs in order because you can't change your genes, right? Your DNA is your DNA, so to what extent is your brain a victim of its genetic destiny? Is your brain a time bomb ticking away as the years go by?

I'm happy to tell you that in most cases, the answer is no. It's understandable that people worry about genetics, especially now that almost anyone can do a cheek swab or spit in a tube to get a genetic portrait. Knowing what genetic variations you have and what disease risks correlate with them can be interesting, but it can also be frightening and defeating because it seems so set in stone. People often say, "Heart disease runs in my family," or "Obesity is in my genes," or "My grandmother had Alzheimer's, so I'll probably get it too."

Take heart! While it is true that many genes and their variants can increase susceptibility to certain conditions, it's simply not true that your genetics equal your health destiny. Genes play only a small to moderate role (depending on the condition) in most common health conditions, including the most common type of dementia, late-onset Alzheimer's disease. Understanding how this works, and how much influence you actually have over your so-called genetic destiny, can help to ease your worry and motivate you to make the necessary adjustments.

Genetics vs. Epigenetics

Let's begin with some simple information. You probably know that you inherit your DNA from your parents. DNA contains genetic sequences that provide instructions for building and maintaining living organisms. Genes code for proteins that determine an organism's traits and characteristics, like eye color or height. Different versions of a gene, called alleles, can result in variations in these traits.

The gene variants code for the manufacture of proteins that may vary from person to person. A gene influencing eye color may have one allele for blue eyes and another for brown eyes. In some cases, they may increase or decrease the risk of certain diseases.

The problem is that people often think genetics is all there is to it. If they have a gene that codes for a process that increases risk, they believe they will be doomed to get that disease. In reality, it's not so simple. There are typically many gene variants that can increase or decrease the risks associated with most chronic diseases, and they may cancel each other out or build on each other. Even more important, though, is that how you live your life and the choices you make can determine whether these genes get activated or not—whether they get "turned on" (expressed) or "turned off" (suppressed).

Epigenetics is the interaction between genetics, environment, and lifestyle.

Methylation: A Key to the Epigenetic Effect

Methylation is a biochemical process that influences whether genes are expressed or suppressed, which can affect the synthesis of proteins involved in essential cellular functions such as generating ATP (adenisone triphosphate, energy for cell operations), BDNF (brain-derived neurotrophic factor), reducing inflammation, building structures, and regulating growth and development.

BDNF: A Tonic for the Brain

Brain-derived neurotrophic factor (BDNF) is one of the most important protective proteins produced mainly in the brain, especially in the hippocampus and cortex (some are also made in other organs like the heart, muscle, and kidneys). BDNF helps to support the survival of existing neurons, promotes the growth of new neurons and synapses, and is involved in neuroplasticity. It is vital for learning, memory, overall cognitive function, and the prevention of Alzheimer's disease. Lifestyle factors such as poor sleep and prolonged stress can add methyl groups to the DNA gene that codes for this critical protein, reducing BDNF production. Fortunately, positive lifestyle choices such as exercise, eating a heart-healthy diet rich in omega-3 fatty acids, and challenging your brain mitigate this effect and increase levels of BDNF in the brain.

Your genes get turned on and off all the time, according to your body's needs. Usually, this is a tightly regulated process. Your body plays your genes like a piano, and everything works in concert. Sometimes, however, we get in the way of this natural process by living a lifestyle that interferes with a balanced and healthy methylation level. Poor lifestyle choices and environmental factors, from pollution to a high-sugar diet to too much stress, can trigger hypermethylation via inflammation in ways that increase the risk of health problems such as cancer or late-life Alzheimer's disease.

Methylation is also closely correlated to aging, so closely associated that some researchers use methylation patterns to estimate biological, or "epigenetic," age. They can make a pretty good guess of how old you are based only on your methylation patterns.[1] Higher levels of methylation are generally associated with faster aging and also with an increased likelihood of mental health conditions like depression[2] and addiction.[3]

Although you can't affect how old you are, you can do something about methylation, so you might be able to outsmart the epigenetic clock.

Positive lifestyle choices can make favorable methylation changes in your DNA. You might be fifty-five, but your epigenetic clock might say you have an epigenetic age of forty-five, implying that you are likely to live longer than usual. Or consider the opposite—your epigenetic clock could say you are sixty-five, meaning you have less time left if you keep living the way you are.

In many ways, your epigenetic age is up to you. For example, one study found that even six weeks of physical exercise resulted in positive epigenetic changes in skeletal muscle cells.[4] Another study published in *Epigenetics* investigated the effects of long-term endurance training on DNA methylation in human skeletal muscle.[5] Researchers analyzed muscle biopsies from individuals before and after a six-month endurance training program. The findings revealed significant changes in DNA methylation at specific gene sites associated with muscle function and energy metabolism. Notably, genes involved in energy production in the cell exhibited decreased methylation, correlating with increased gene expression and enhanced muscle capacity.

Recent research has shown that DNA methylation age can influence the brain's structure, even in healthy young adults.[6] By studying saliva samples and brain MRIs in seventy-nine healthy volunteers, scientists found that higher DNA methylation age correlated with smaller surface area and volume in many cortical regions associated with memory, decision-making, emotional regulation, and mood. Understanding how our cells age at an epigenetic level could provide important clues about changes in our brain structure and help identify ways we can remain sharp later in life.

Another study published in *JAMA Network Open* investigated the relationship between DNA methylation-based biological age and cortical thickness.[7] Individuals who aged faster than their biological age, as noted by higher DNA methylation levels, had smaller brains. This cortical atrophy was most pronounced in the hippocampus and its adjacent areas, which are critical for learning and memory. This study further supports that faster epigenetic aging affects cortical structural changes. In other words, too much methylation can shrink your brain, and lifestyle and environment influence the level of DNA methylation.

Methylation is complex and isn't the only epigenetic influence. Rather than go into any great detail about how methylation works, the main thing I would like you to take away from this section is that methylation is an action going on all the time. Genes are not static, and you can definitely influence this process through your lifestyle choices.

What About the "Alzheimer's Gene"?

This may be one of the most common concerns patients have expressed to me: "But I have the Alzheimer's gene!" Whether you know that you have this gene variant (which is not really an "Alzheimer's gene"), you may be wondering at this point whether you can influence its effects on the brain. Yes, most definitely.

Here is what we are talking about: We all have two copies of the ApoE gene (apolipoprotein E). We inherit one from each parent. There are three ApoE variants. ApoE3 is the most common version and does not affect Alzheimer's risk. However, you might have inherited one or two copies of ApoE2 or ApoE4 alleles.

The ApoE2 allele correlates with a lower-than-average risk of developing Alzheimer's disease and/or developing it at an older age (perhaps not until the nineties). In contrast, the ApoE4 allele correlates with a higher-than-average risk of developing Alzheimer's disease and/or developing it at a younger age (perhaps in the sixties or seventies).

But here's the good news: Having one or two copies of the ApoE4 variant does not mean you will definitely get Alzheimer's disease. In fact, while it increases your *risk*, numerous other variables can add to that risk or subtract from it, including lifestyle influences and other genes that are susceptible to methylation or can be protective. We don't know all the gene variants that influence Alzheimer's risk, but we know there are many, not just ApoE4.

As for lifestyle, here's an exciting fact: There is an easy way to substantially eliminate the added risk. It's exercise.

Exercise is a powerful risk leveler when it comes to ApoE4. One way this happens is through exercise's influence on amyloid, one well-known marker of late-onset Alzheimer's disease. An observational study conducted at St. Louis University by my colleague, the renowned Alzheimer's neuroscientist Dr. John Morris, examined the levels of amyloid accumulation in sedentary people versus those who were highly active, both in those with and without the ApoE4 risk variation.[8] Brain imaging showed that ApoE4-positive people with high levels of physical activity had the same low level of amyloid as those who were ApoE4-negative (i.e., for those with ApoE3 and/or ApoE2 genes). Exercise alone basically completely negated the elevated risk, at least in terms of amyloid accumulation in the brain.[9] It did not technically suppress the ApoE4 gene, but its actions elsewhere canceled out the influence of the gene, as you can see in this bar graph:

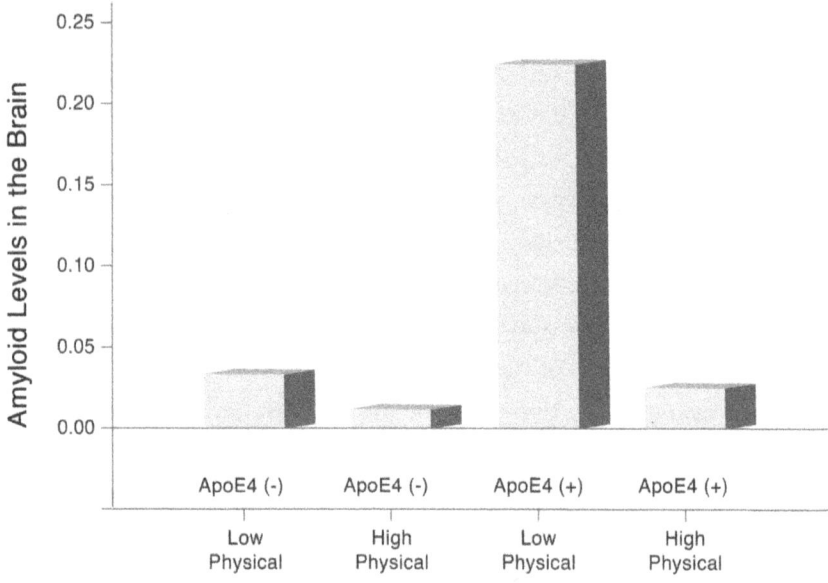

Another recent study of 204 older adults with an average age of seventy-four showed a similar effect.[10] One quarter of these individuals had ApoE4 variants while others had either ApoE3 and/or ApoE2 variants. Researchers found that ApoE4 carriers who engaged in high levels of leisure activities and sports had the same low level of amyloid in their brains as those who did not have this variant. You can see the effects on the graph on the following page.

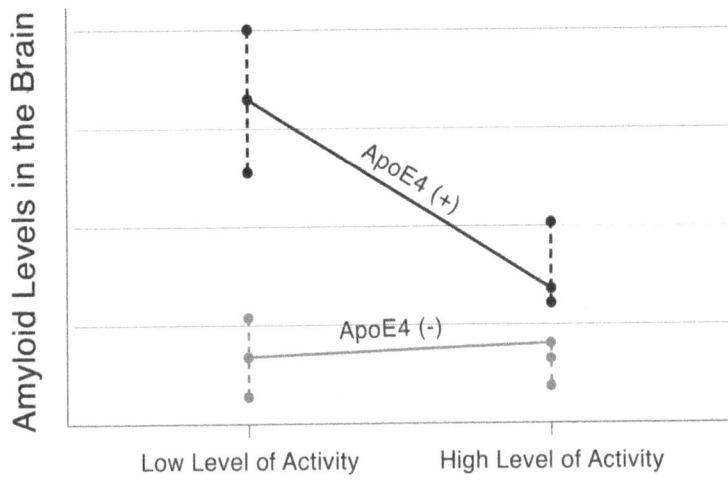

Other research has demonstrated similar effects. A review found that many studies support the role of exercise in mitigating the effects of ApoE4.[11] The review concludes that people with ApoE4 who engage in physical exercise have lower amyloid levels, higher blood flow to their brain, less inflammation, more neuroprotective proteins (such as BDNF), and better cognitive performance. All these factors influence Alzheimer's risk—exercise reduces risk in many different ways. If you have one or two copies of the ApoE4 gene, the best thing you can do is exercise most days.

Also, those with ApoE2 should not be misled—just as ApoE4 does not automatically mean you will get Alzheimer's, ApoE2 does not automatically mean you won't. If you pile on the risk factors by sleeping poorly, having high blood pressure or diabetes, never exercising, eating junk food, and being chronically stressed, you will negate the favorable genetic benefits of ApoE2.

Isn't it exciting that you can virtually eliminate an elevated disease risk just by doing something as rewarding and fun as exercise? Even if you don't love exercise (yet), this information might be just the motivation you need to feel empowered and in charge of your health and aging.

Before we leave the subject of ApoE4, I want to say something about genetic testing—something that has become increasingly popular and which can, on some tests, uncover the presence of ApoE4. Having seen thousands of patients with cognitive decline and Alzheimer's disease over the years, I've seen how knowing you have one or two copies of the ApoE4 gene can do real damage to your morale and even your growth mindset. For many, knowing they have the ApoE4 variation can make them unnecessarily preoccupied and sometimes obsessed with getting Alzheimer's. They worry about it every day for decades, fearing the worst.

Yet, they may not appreciate that obesity, diabetes, insomnia, sleep apnea, and many other issues all increase the risk of developing Alzheimer's disease as much if not more than having a copy of ApoE4—and having all these risk factors together can increase the risk of Alzheimer's disease sixteenfold,[12] which is a much higher contribution than having that one gene variation in ApoE.

Years ago, the prolific bestselling health writer and medical journalist Jean Carper was interested in Alzheimer's, so she did genetic testing and found that she tested positive for ApoE4. She saw a doctor who told her (irresponsibly) that yes, she would likely get Alzheimer's disease eventually, so she should get ready. But she had seen some of my published research papers and flew to Baltimore to see me. I did some testing, and although she was already eighty, she was as sharp as a healthy fifty-year-old, if not someone even younger.

I said to her, "Jean, you do not have Alzheimer's disease. You may have that one bad gene, but you may have ten good genes that lower your risk, and how you live your life has kept you healthy." She was immensely relieved, and most important, she stopped worrying so much about getting Alzheimer's disease. Worry alone can cause stress that increases your risk of brain problems, so just knowing your risk could increase your risk!

My conversations with Jean Carper, which she included in her 2016 documentary about Alzheimer's disease (titled *Monster in the Mind*), helped ease her concerns. Instead of giving up on her life, Jean wrote more books about the effects of nutrition on the brain. She came out with another book, *101 Ways to Avoid Alzheimer's & Dementia*, in 2022. As I write this, Jean is ninety-three years old and is still as sharp as ever and energetic with a cheerful nature that is quite contagious. She is a perfect example of how a "bad" gene does not control your future. You do.

I also once had a patient who was a successful attorney in her fifties and had found out she was positive for ApoE4. She was anxious and scared when she came to visit me. After I explained that ApoE4 was not a definitive indicator for getting Alzheimer's, she calmed down a little bit. After completing my twelve-week program, her scores for memory improved measurably (from the 40th percentile to the 55th percentile), and she was thrilled. As a part of our program, she had learned to organize her busy family and work life better, be less stressed, and make more time for exercise and brain training. She also learned skills and tricks for improving her memory. She memorized a list of one hundred words. Excited by doing something she thought she could never accomplish, she was energized and determined to keep improving her memory—and beat her genes! With her new attitude and lifestyle habits, one year later, her memory score had increased to the 70th percentile when she repeated her testing with us.

I wish more physicians would educate their patients on how their weight, fitness, sleep pattern, and stress levels have a more profound effect on their risk of developing Alzheimer's disease in the future than merely having the ApoE4 gene, especially since these are factors over which we have control. In my opinion, we need a total paradigm shift in the way we think about cognitive decline with aging and the importance of how our day-to-day habits have a profound impact on the health and vitality of our brain—more so than having ApoE4.[13]

There are countless people who have one or both copies of ApoE4 who never develop Alzheimer's disease, even in their nineties (like Jean). There are also many people with other risk factors who do not have ApoE4, but who develop Alzheimer's disease. Until we have the complete picture for all the genes related to optimal brain function or Alzheimer's disease and how much they influence risk for an individual, getting this test doesn't help and can very well hurt.

The bottom line is that genetics is about susceptibilities, not destiny. Being susceptible or predisposed to something does not mean it will happen, but every day, with everything you do and every choice you make, you could be influencing your susceptibility, via the expression or suppression of specific genes that can affect your brain, as well as having direct effects on your health and disease risk. Temporary changes, like occasional dietary indulgence or short periods of high stress, probably don't make much difference in how your genes are methylated and expressed, but persistant good or bad lifestyle habits over the course of decades can profoundly affect your gene expression and your brain vitality.

Lifestyle Can Increase Hypermethylation and Shrink Your Brain

I've been waiting to give a list of the things to avoid and watch out for regarding your risk for Alzheimer's disease—because who wants to start with what *not* to do? But here's a fact you now understand: There are multiple proven habits and conditions that we know can trigger negative epigenetic changes, increasing methylation and shrinking your brain.

An underlying mechanism to all these negative changes is inflammation, so your cheat sheet could be: "If it causes inflammation, it's bad for my brain." We'll talk in more detail about all the factors that increase inflammation and cause brain atrophy and what factors can grow your brain and make it healthier in part 4. As you will soon see, the things that increase hypermethylation are exactly the same things that decrease brain health (and heart health and total health): poor diet quality, exposure to pollution and toxins, stress, physical inactivity, smoking, sleep deprivation, obesity, and social isolation. The more you learn about the many different factors influencing brain health, the more these lifestyle issues will come up. Conversely, many of the things that regulate and contribute to a healthy low level of methylation are the same things that contribute to a healthy brain, a healthy heart, and health in general. Just remember that as you begin the program in part 4, methylation is just one of the many things that will begin working in your favor.

What I hope you will take from this chapter is that fundamental changes, from gene expression to brain size, happen in response to how you live. Epigenetics is something you can manipulate, which undermines the notion of genetic destiny. Isn't that great news?

So, if you are ever on the fence about eating the donut, skipping the gym, or staying up late to binge-watch a show, remember epigenetics and the fact that your choice could result in excessive methylation of your DNA, which in the long run could make you ill, shrink your brain, and even shorten your life.

Next, we will turn to Alzheimer's disease ... or should we call it that? In my view, and the view of a rapidly expanding set of forward-thinking neurologists, Alzheimer's isn't so much a pure disease as it is a multifactorial cognitive decline—or, as I like to call it, a soup of problems.

8

ALZHEIMER'S DISEASE IS NOT WHAT WE THOUGHT

Many people are terrified that they are already on the road to decline—even those in the best of health. I know firsthand how concerned people are about losing their precious memories and brain functions. I see the fear that strikes when people hear the dreaded words "Alzheimer's disease."

A lot of that fear is based on misunderstanding and a lack of knowledge about what Alzheimer's disease is. People think that they "just get" Alzheimer's disease, like they "just get" cancer. It just happens, luck of the draw. But what we have learned quite recently is that you have more control than you think.

It's hard to fully express how surprising and meaningful this realization has been in the world of neurology. In fact, it is still hard for some practitioners to accept—they tell you that if you're going to get it, you're going to get it. But I'm telling you no! That is simply not true for most people, and we now have the research support to say this with confidence. Even if you have a family member who has had dementia (and I know how troubling and traumatic that can be), believe me when I tell you that you are not doomed to follow. Alzheimer's is *not* what we once thought it was.

Based on my four decades of research, clinical, and teaching experience, I am now more certain than ever that we can slow or even reverse the mixture of abnormalities that come together to damage the brain and lead to what we call late-life Alzheimer's disease. This is an exciting time in my field, and I am thrilled to share with you the secrets of how you can keep your brain young and remain sharp way into your eighties and nineties.

Now pay very close attention, as I am going to explain to you in this chapter exactly how we have come to understand the underlying causes of late-life dementia and how we have, for the first time, established solid evidence that shows we can indeed mitigate or even reverse mild cognitive impairment (MCI) and the early stages of Alzheimer's disease.

Alzheimer's Rates Are Declining

Let's start with some good news. Despite what you might have heard, Alzheimer's rates are going down—progressively, over decades—in some affluent countries (such as those in Western Europe) and some parts of the United States. The incidence of dementia in France, the Netherlands, Sweden, the UK, and Iceland shows a decline over the past twenty-five years of about 13 percent lower incidence per year.[1] In the U.S., the Framingham Heart Study tracked the cognitive status of more than five thousand volunteers aged sixty and over since the 1970s in Framingham, Massachusetts, and found a progressive decline in dementia of about 20 percent per decade.

Not only are rates going down, but the age of dementia onset is later, from an average age of eighty in the 1970s to age eighty-five in the 2000s.[2] Researchers also found brain volume increasing, specifically in the hippocampus. According to MRI data, participants born in the 1970s had a 6.6 percent larger brain volume on average compared to those born in the 1930s.[3]

Remember how older adults used to look in their fifties, sixties, and seventies? It's much more common now to see people in these age groups looking energetic and vibrant. They are more often mobile and cognitively sharp. People are more health-savvy than ever, and the new generation of seniors, especially those who spend a lot of time in gyms and engage in community activities, has caught on. How they live influences how they age, and this is becoming increasingly apparent at an epidemiological level. This is excellent news! This can be you.

However, this decline is not happening everywhere or for everyone, so let's not get ahead of ourselves. People with metabolic issues like uncontrolled diabetes and obesity do not have declining rates of Alzheimer's.[4] Nor do people with little to no higher education, or people with heart disease.[5] This demonstrates that environmental and lifestyle choices do indeed affect Alzheimer's risk.

The Evolving Understanding of Alzheimer's Disease

To understand what people think about Alzheimer's now, it helps to see how our thinking about aging has evolved—and continues to evolve. One of the earliest references to age-related cognitive decline is attributed to Pythagoras, a Greek philosopher who lived from 570 to 495 BCE, and who reportedly wrote that after the age of eighty, people return to the "imbecility of infancy."[6] Both Plato and Aristotle linked cognitive decline to old age. In 44 BCE, Cicero presciently argued that aging did not have to be related to mental changes and that an "active mental life could prevent cognitive decline in old age."[7]

Before the Renaissance, many believed dementia was God's punishment for sinners. However, during the Renaissance, doctors realized there were physical causes for dementia, such as syphilis, alcoholism, and depression. On autopsy, doctors could see that the brains of the cognitively impaired had more strokes and were smaller in size.

In Germany in the 1890s, Dr. Alois Alzheimer started his work as a young clinician-scientist, when microscopes and brain staining for neurons had recently been invented.[8] Dr. Alzheimer used these inventions to discover plaques and tangles in the brains of a handful of his middle-aged patients who had experienced confusion and behavior changes before they died. He noted these but did not believe they were the cause of dementia in late life, which he attributed to strokes and hardening of the arteries. He called his common finding of strokes in people with dementia the "gradual strangulation of the blood supply to the brain."[9]

At the time, the chairperson of Dr. Alzheimer's department, Dr. Emil Kraepelin, was updating his book *Textbook of Psychiatry*. He included

Dr. Alzheimer's case studies, coining the term "Alzheimer's disease," even though Dr. Alzheimer himself never claimed to have discovered a disease. (I think if Dr. Alzheimer were to return to life today, he would be shocked at how his name has become so well known worldwide for something he never claimed to have done!)

Throughout the 1950s, hardening of the arteries was considered the primary driver of dementia, so people took blood thinners and vasodilators to prevent what was called "senile dementia" at the time. In the 1960s and 1970s, a debate began about who did and did not have Alzheimer's disease, based on a renewed interest in plaques and tangles. The term "senile dementia of Alzheimer's Type (SDAT)" was coined.

In the 1980s, scientists discovered that the plaques Dr. Alzheimer had described in his papers were made of a small protein (a peptide) called amyloid, and that the tangles in the brain consisted of a protein in the axons of neurons called tau. Tau clumps together, forming tangles that block the flow of nutrients and chemical messengers from the neuron's center to the end of the axons.

Researchers John Hardy and Gerald Higgins in England proposed the Amyloid Cascade Hypothesis in 1992.[10] They suggested that the formation of amyloid in the brain leads to the formation of tau tangles, which then cause atrophy in the cortex and hippocampus. The new consensus became that plaques and tangles were the primary cause of Alzheimer's disease in older adults. There was great excitement in the field because researchers believed they had discovered a path to a cure for Alzheimer's: blocking amyloid.

Throughout the early 2000s, pharmaceutical companies poured their efforts and billions of dollars into finding a drug that could block amyloid (blocking tau proved more difficult). After more than thirty clinical trials to see what happens when amyloid is removed from the brains of older adults with Alzheimer's, there were few and only minor successes. Some patients died from the drugs due to brain swelling and bleeding. These disappointing results led researchers to focus on the influence of other factors beyond amyloid. For example, they found that people with obesity had significant hippocampal shrinkage,[11] vascular damage throughout the brain, and amyloid plaques.[12] Stress correlated with shrinkage in the hippocampus; the greater the stress, the more shrinkage.[13] More concussions seemed to result in more shrinkage in the hippocampus,[14] as well as the development of severe memory loss.[15]

What nobody saw until very recently is that they were *all* right (well, except for the ones who implicated black bile or divine retribution—I haven't seen any research support for those!). Yet, they all missed the big picture, until now.

The reality is that a soup of a dozen+ different factors causes brain shrinkage and cognitive decline, and the more you clear the soup through how you live, the lower your risk.

The Most Common Types of Cognitive Impairment (Dementia)

Many people use the term "Alzheimer's disease" to refer to all forms of cognitive impairment, but it's just one type of what doctors call dementia, a blanket term for any cognitive impairment caused by brain degeneration that impairs a person's ability to function independently. Here are the most common forms:

Late-onset Alzheimer's disease: The most commonly diagnosed form of cognitive impairment, late-onset Alzheimer's disease, is caused by a soup of abnormalities that leads to the gradual degeneration of brain cells, beginning in the hippocampus and leading to memory loss and confusion.

Early-onset Alzheimer's disease: Also called familial Alzheimer's disease, this afflicts people in their thirties to sixties. It is rare and characterized by the rapid accumulation of plaques and tangles that destroy the brain.

Vascular dementia: Vascular dementia is caused by reduced blood flow to the brain, leading to multiple small or large strokes.

Frontotemporal dementia (FTD): FTD is caused by the progressive aggregation and clumping of several proteins, including a form of tau that is different from the one that forms tangles in Alzheimer's disease. FTD causes damage to the frontal and temporal lobes, leading to problems with behavior and language.

Lewy body dementia (LBD): LBD is a close relative of Parkinson's disease, a degenerative brain condition caused by the clumping of a protein called alpha-synuclein. Symptoms include hallucinations, confusion, and difficulty walking.

Limbic-predominant age-related TDP-43 encephalopathy (LATE): A major contributor to cognitive decline in aging individuals, LATE is characterized by the abnormal accumulation of TDP-43 protein in the brain, particularly in parts of the brain for memory and regulation of emotions.

Normal pressure hydrocephalus (NPH): This form of dementia is caused by a slow buildup of fluid in the brain, causing pressure on the surrounding brain tissue and suppressing its functions.

The Revelation of the Dynamic Polygon Theory, aka the Soup of Problems

I like to think I have contributed to the recent recognition that Alzheimer's is not a pure disease but instead has multiple contributing factors that can be treated to prevent or even regress symptoms in the early stages. It all began, as I recounted in the introduction, when I was doing my neurology residency at Johns Hopkins and was working as a consultant at the Alzheimer's Disease Research Center, evaluating patients in the Baltimore Longitudinal Study of Aging (BLSA).

As I looked over the patient files, I noticed something striking—nearly all those in the study who were diagnosed with Alzheimer's disease had a pattern of other underlying conditions, like strokes, diabetes, or hypertension. What if treating the underlying conditions could head off their Alzheimer's? I couldn't stop thinking about it. I spent a lot of time going through the medical literature and concluded that what we call Alzheimer's disease was being tragically overdiagnosed. This was the beginning of the mission I've been on ever since.

Over the next few decades, as I began my career as assistant professor of neurology at Johns Hopkins and as the director of the Center for Memory and Brain Health at Sinai Hospital, I encountered many more patients with the same pattern of underlying treatable conditions that damage, shrink, and inflame the brain.

Then I began to notice other neurologists talking about the same idea. In 2009, I contacted Dr. Vladimir Hachinski, author of more than one thousand articles in neurology, who discovered that vascular risk factors can increase levels of amyloid plaques in the brain. He argued that there were connections between cognitive impairment caused by vascular issues, strokes, and Alzheimer's disease.[16] Dr. Hachinski and I, along with another well-known neuroscientist, Dr. Peter Whitehouse, wrote a review paper[17] in which we encouraged a paradigm shift about how we should view, diagnose, and treat elderly people with cognitive impairment. In it, we proposed what we called the Dynamic Polygon Hypothesis.

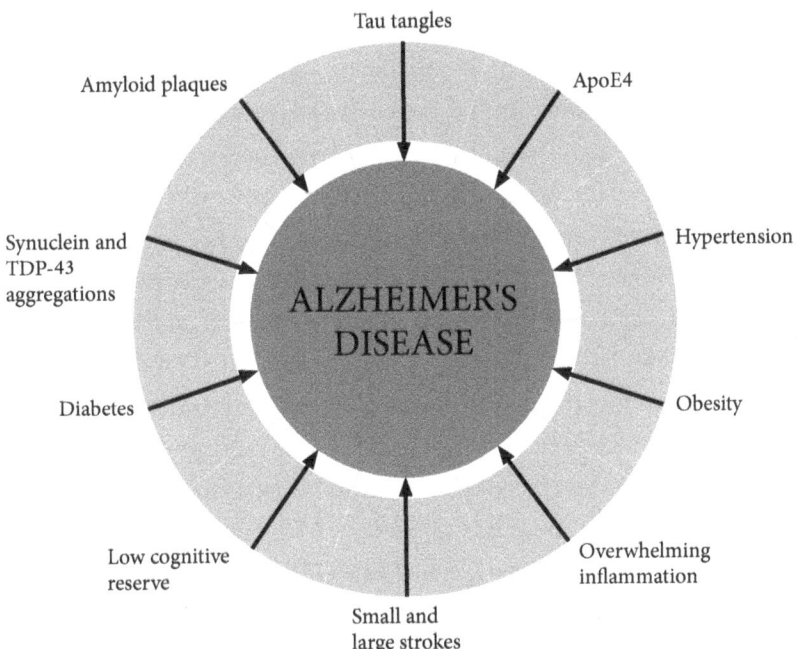

The Dynamic Polygon Hypothesis suggests that late-onset Alzheimer's disease is the result of a much different process than early-onset Alzheimer's, which is a pure disease of rapidly accumulating amyloid plaques and tau tangles. In late-onset Alzheimer's, we argue, the factors that cause shrinkage in the hippocampus and cortex are many—the disease is multifactorial, as you can see from the previous image. It is not just a simple downstream effect of an abnormal accumulation of plaques and tangles.

This theory is in opposition to the popular Amyloid Cascade Hypothesis, which suggests that Alzheimer's results in a very particular process: Amyloid plaques form for some reason (likely genetic), leading to tau tangles, leading to synaptic loss and dementia. Diagnosis: late-onset Alzheimer's disease. If this is true, you probably could not do much about developing Alzheimer's disease.

Our theory counters that late-life dementia is more complex. There is a set of pathological processes that shrink the cortex and hippocampus: amyloid aggregation and tau formation, yes, but also inflammation, strokes, synucleinopathy (the abnormal accumulation of another protein called alpha-synuclein, which we often see in Parkinson's disease and Lewy body dementia), as well as the contributing effects of concurrent health issues, including hypertension, obesity, diabetes, and environmental exposures and lifestyle issues from diet and exercise to education and stress.

Our paper on the Dynamic Polygon Hypothesis was not the only one coming out at the time, arguing that late-onset Alzheimer's disease was multifactorial and not just a result of amyloid and tau. For instance, my dear friend and colleague Dr. Miia Kivipelto, professor of geriatrics at the Karolinska Institute in Sweden, published a study in which she and her team monitored more than 1,400 individuals at midlife and over the following twenty years. She discovered that having multiple vascular risk factors can increase a person's risk for a diagnosis of Alzheimer's disease sixteenfold.[18]

In response to this emerging realization, many people began to develop lifestyle intervention programs to prevent Alzheimer's disease. Dr. Kivipelto started an extensive study called FINGER[19] (Finnish Geriatric Intervention Study to Prevent Cognitive Impairment and Disability). Over two years, 1,260 participants followed a program combining nutrition, exercise, cognitive training, social engagement, and vascular risk management, leading to a 25 percent improvement in cognitive performance.[20] This study was replicated in several other countries around the world.

Around this time, another flood of new studies showed that many lifestyle factors, such as exercise, meditation, brain training, and treatment of sleep apnea can actually grow the size of the hippocampus within a matter of weeks to months, to such a high degree that it can be detected on a brain MRI. Since a shrinking hippocampus is one of the hallmarks of Alzheimer's disease, I was excited by these discoveries. I did more research and published a paper about this with another prominent neurologist from the Mayo Clinic, Dr. Clifford Jack.[21]

By 2014, I felt compelled to put together a clinical program myself, for older adults with MCI. I wanted to prove that lifestyle modification can indeed help memory. It worked. I was among the first in the field to offer a twelve-week program tailored to a patient's specific issues and needs, which resulted in the reversal of cognitive decline and the regrowth of the hippocampus in a significant percentage of my patients. (You'll find the details of this program in part 4 of this book—my results were also published in 2016 in *The Journal of Prevention of Alzheimer's Disease*.[22])

Maybe you have never heard of any of these studies, but you might have heard about the most famous research supporting the multifactorial nature of late-onset Alzheimer's disease: the Nun Study, helmed by Dr. David Snowdon.[23] This study followed Catholic nuns ranging in age from their seventies to their hundreds, living in a small community together in the United States. The results revealed that many of the nuns had significant amyloid plaques and even tau tangles in their brains, but surprisingly, had *no significant cognitive deficits*. How could they have the pathology of Alzheimer's in their brains but with no signs of Alzheimer's in their memory or behavior?

The surprising result of this study was that the nuns who had multiple small bean-sized strokes in their brains did develop substantial cognitive decline, even with only a small amount of plaques and tangles in their brains. Meanwhile, those who did not have such strokes remained cognitively sharp, despite having a significant load of plaques and tangles. It was the strokes, not the plaques and tangles, that seemed to make the difference. According to this study, the odds of developing dementia were 20.7 times higher in participants with multiple strokes than in those with plaques and tangles but no strokes!

Why such unusual outcomes? There are some exciting theories. These nuns were models of a healthy lifestyle—most had higher education levels and a lifetime of mental stimulation, which allowed their brains to work better despite degeneration in some parts. (As you already know, the brain is good at working around areas that don't function.) They had a sense of purpose and a spiritual life. They exercised regularly, even lifting weights. They ate a healthy diet and kept their minds active. They were socially connected and supported, both by each other and by their community, where they often volunteered. They were not lonely or bored, sedentary, or addicted to junk food. They were less likely than the general population to have other conditions often associated with Alzheimer's disease, like cardiovascular disease and depression.

We can learn a lot from the Nun Study about how to live for a healthy brain. In my opinion, the way these nuns lived built up their brain reserve. They were cognitively resilient so even with plaques and tangles, they maintained their memories and executive function, unless they had the added burden of strokes. (You'll learn more about brain reserve and resilience in chapter 10.) If there was ever an argument for a multifactorial lifestyle intervention to address the multifactorial nature of Alzheimer's disease itself, those nuns are it.

Optimal Rinsing and Blood Flow: Keys to Building a Fresh and Vibrant Brain

So what does lifestyle actually do to mitigate risk? Mounting evidence has clarified that glymphatic drainage in the brain may affect how much waste products and toxins (like amyloid, tau, and other misfolded proteins) can accumulate over time. As I mentioned in chapter 4, your brain gets rinsed with CSF with each heartbeat, especially during deep sleep. The CSF in the sleevelike area around the arteries (called the perivascular space) gets pushed out into the brain with each heartbeat, rinses the brain, and then gets collected in the perivascular space in the veins. This waste management system clears the brain of most chemical byproducts that may accumulate during the day. Some of the debris that gets rinsed away includes amyloid and tau molecules. In a healthy brain, the rinsed CSF that washes away the debris in the brain milieu drains out of the brain through the lym-

Alzheimer's Disease Is Not What We Thought

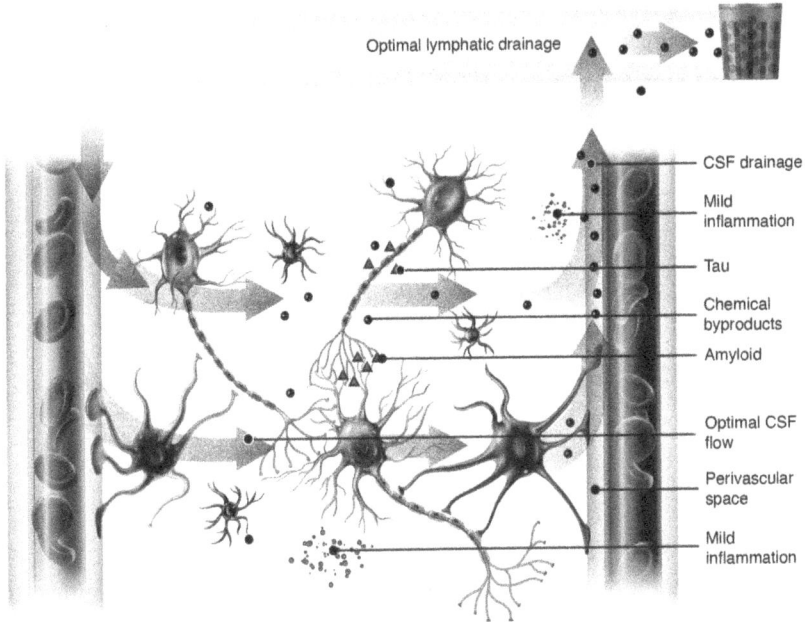

phatic system. As you can see in this illustration, a thoroughly rinsed brain appears nice, clean, and fresh.

However, a lack of sleep that impedes the glymphatic system operation leads to accumulation of an overwhelming amount of debris. The glymphatic system can't pump it out, so little is collected in the lymphatic drainage system. The gunk remains stuck in the brain milieu, choking neurons, astrocytes,

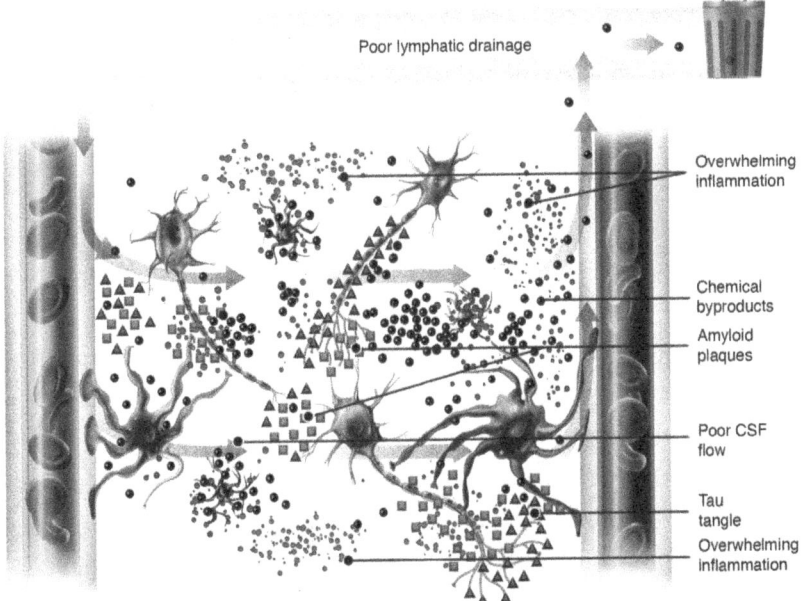

and glia, depriving them of the nutrients and oxygen needed to function. In response to these problems in the brain, astrocytes and microglia produce more inflammatory free radical molecules to clear the debris. However, this overwhelming inflammation ends up killing more neurons.

You can optimize the action of the glymphatic system with lifestyle interventions such as optimizing your sleep and fitness. We will review these factors in part 4.

Now let's consider the significant impact of blood flow issues. Neuropathological studies have shown that 90 percent of older adults with a diagnosis of Alzheimer's disease have vascular abnormalities in their brains.[24] Individuals with vascular risk factors such as untreated high cholesterol, sleep apnea, hypertension, sedentary lifestyle, poor diet, and obesity often harbor tiny "silent strokes" (the size of a grain of rice) they never knew they had, or small strokes (the size of a bean) like the ones found in some of the nuns in the Nun Study, or large strokes (the size of a Ping-Pong ball or an apple).

These conditions also make the arteries become stiff and damage the blood-brain barrier, the protective layer in and around the blood vessels in the brain that protects from the seepage of blood content into its internal environment. When this barrier erodes, blood contents like red blood cells, the components of the blood clotting system, and many inflammatory proteins leak into the brain. Called "leaky brain," this causes the brain to begin falling apart.

Yet another soup ingredient, caused by lifestyle and medical conditions that impair blood flow to the brain, is damage to white matter fiber bundles. The thinner they get, the slower the communication between different corners of the brain will be, and the more a person would have difficulty with executive function, such as problem-solving and remembering.

An older person's brain may already be suffering from a great many abnormalities at a microscopic level that impair their ability to remember and function, even before the brain MRI shows significant atrophy.

These microscopic changes that deprive neurons and their supporting cells of oxygen and nutrients accumulate over decades until a person begins to show serious memory loss, like forgetting the names of their children or getting lost in their own neighborhood. As you will see in part 4 of this book, you have many options to make sure your brain's waste management system and blood flow system are in tip-top shape before you get to your eighties.

Successful Aging

One of the most vivid memories I have from my medical school years was during my rotation in neuropathology at Massachusetts General Hospital. I remember how some brains from older people looked quite fresh and young. Other brains looked shriveled and wasted, with blood vessels that felt like stiff straws. When I held those vessels in my hand during autopsies, I could pinch them and feel them cracking. I used to think to myself, "I never want to have a brain like this!"

In postmortem brain autopsy, you can see this soup of different problems. If you look at a cross section of the brain of a twenty-year-old person (who, for example, might have died in a motorcycle accident), you will see a beautiful ribbon of cortex around the periphery and a pair of vibrant, thumb-sized hippocampi deep in either side of the brain. In such a person, who has not had significant obesity, diabetes, hypertension, chronic stress, or concussion, there would not be a measurable degree of inflammation, leaky brain, blocked arteries, silent strokes, or plaques and tangles. Cognitive functions, perhaps other than poor judgment in risky motorcycle riding, would be intact.

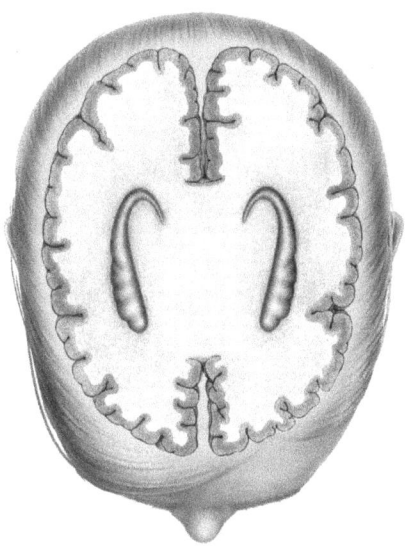

20-years old brain

The brain of a healthy eighty-year-old would harbor some of these abnormalities. By the time most people reach their late seventies and early eighties, they have some vascular damage. This will be worse in smokers and heavy consumers of alcohol. A low level of these conditions affects the brain's size and vitality to a mild degree, with no significant cognitive decline beyond occasionally forgetting names, appointments, or details of some conversations, movies, or events.

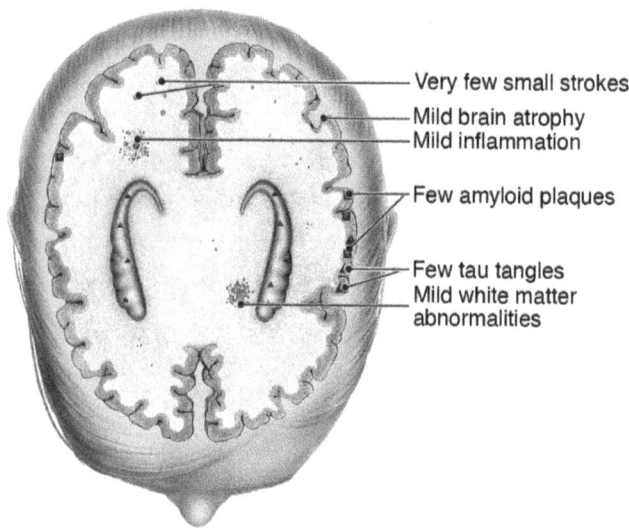

80-year-old healthy brain

However, an eighty-year-old with Alzheimer's disease would have an overwhelming degree of leaky brain, inflammation, small or large strokes, white matter abnormalities, plaques, tangles, and possibly some other pathologies such as synuclein, TDP-43, and FTD-tau aggregates. According to a neuropathological study, 100 percent of patients with late-onset Alzheimer's disease have at least one additional non-Alzheimer's pathology in their brains.[25] The more of these brain abnormalities they have, the worse their cognitive decline and the severity of their Alzheimer's disease.

This difference between these two eighty-year-old brains is largely a difference in health, which is largely a matter of lifestyle and successful management of medical issues.

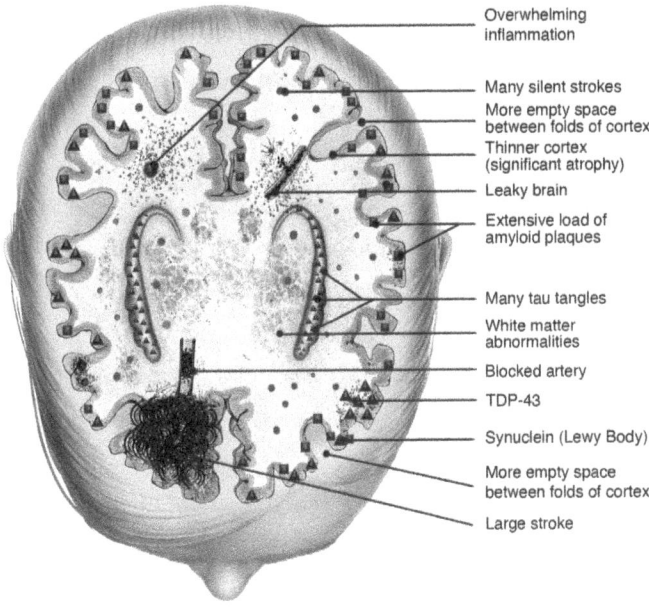

80-years old with Alzheimer's disease

Didn't Your Cardiologist Tell You This Already?

Antonio, one of my patients, who was a successful businessman in his seventies, came to see me because his wife had noticed his memory was fading. He was making millions of dollars every year buying and selling stocks. He loved his job, which was mostly sitting in front of his computer and tracking the stock market. He was happy, but tended to repeat himself often. For example, he would ask his wife, "What are we having for dinner?" ten times during the day, and each time, he would not remember that she had answered his question already. They were told he had mild cognitive impairment, and he was referred to me for further evaluation and treatment.

As I reviewed his case in more detail, I noticed he had high cholesterol, hypertension, obesity, sleep apnea, poorly controlled diabetes, and a sedentary lifestyle. I talked to him for about twenty minutes about the importance of exercise, a healthy diet, treating his sleep apnea, and lowering his cholesterol to improve his memory. After our long conversation, he said: "You are telling me the same things my cardiologist has been telling me for twenty years. What do these things have to do with Alzheimer's disease?"

I get excited when I get to explain to my patients (or large audiences) the link between vascular risk factors and Alzheimer's diagnosis, as I know once they truly understand the physiology of what is going on in their brains, they are far more likely to change their behaviors and take on healthy lifestyle habits. So, with much enthusiasm, I told him all about the discoveries in my field: The very same vascular risk factors that contribute to a higher risk of heart attacks and strokes also contribute to brain inflammation, atrophy, cognitive decline, and a diagnosis of Alzheimer's disease.

After our long conversation, he had an "aha!" moment. Suddenly, he could not wait to start our twelve-week program and receive training for improving his memory, getting in shape, addressing his sleep apnea, and reducing his risk for strokes and progressing to develop Alzheimer's disease. By the time he completed our program, his memory had improved greatly—from the 15th percentile for his age to the 45th percentile for his age. With the help of our cheerful brain coaches, he learned to memorize a list of one hundred random things. He had gotten into regular walking daily and lost ten pounds. His wife was thrilled to have a husband who had upgraded his brain (and was now even more handsome!).

Recent discoveries in the field of Alzheimer's have also shown that the factors that cause heart attacks aren't just the things that are bad for your brain in general—many of those same things actually lead to the accumulation of amyloid, too.[26]

I hope you come out of this chapter convinced that amyloid is just one of many abnormalities in the brain of a person who experiences cognitive decline and develops dementia in old age. Dr. Alzheimer said this beautifully more than one hundred years ago (without the benefit of CT scans, MRIs, genetic testing, biomarkers, or advanced imaging) when he wrote, "The plaques are not the cause of senile dementia, but only an accompanying feature of senile involution of the central nervous system."[27] We now know that many treatable factors can shrink the brain, especially the cortex and hippocampus, and thus we need to focus our attention on these factors daily. The same interventions that reduce the risk of heart attacks also prevent amyloid accumulation, inflammation in the brain, strokes, and mitigate risk of MCI and Alzheimer's disease.

Here's another parallel between the heart and the brain: Just as cholesterol is only one factor among many that contribute to heart disease, amyloid is only one factor among many that contribute to Alzheimer's disease. And just as taking statins to lower cholesterol only modestly reduces the risk of heart attacks, even powerful new drugs that remove almost all the amyloid from the brain have only modest effects on memory and thinking. To really reduce the risk of heart disease, doctors recommend a combination of medications and lifestyle changes—like exercising more, eating better, sleeping well, managing stress, and quitting smoking. The same is true for preventing and treating Alzheimer's disease.

How Not to Get Alzheimer's

So what's the big secret for how to avoid Alzheimer's disease? The power is in multimodal lifestyle intervention programs like mine, which focus on personalizing a set of specific lifestyle interventions that can improve blood flow to your brain, reduce the level of amyloid in your brain, slow inflammation in your brain, and boost levels of protective proteins like BDNF. You'll learn much more about how to keep your brain young and strong as you work through my Brain Fitness Program in part 4 of this book.

But as a sneak preview, you may be interested in an influential and widely cited study published in *The Lancet* in 2024[28] that highlighted the importance of prevention to reduce the risk of dementia. This paper was written by twenty-seven leading experts in the field and is one of the most commonly cited papers in the field of Alzheimer's disease. The international group of authors in this study concluded that 45 percent of dementia cases in the world could be prevented by addressing these fourteen lifestyle factors:

1. Low education level
2. Hearing impairment
3. Traumatic brain injury/concussion

4. Hypertension
5. Excessive alcohol consumption
6. Obesity
7. Smoking
8. Depression
9. Physical inactivity
10. Diabetes
11. Social isolation
12. Air pollution
13. Vision impairment
14. High levels of LDL cholesterol

So far, we have reviewed all the factors that contribute to cognitive aging and lead to what we call late-life Alzheimer's disease—and we've taken just a peek at what we can do to prevent this dreaded disease. In the next chapter, you'll learn about some of the most exciting recent developments in my field with regards to blood-based tests for diagnosing Alzheimer's disease, the new medications for treating MCI or early-stage Alzheimer's disease, and the most important strategy to reverse cognitive decline with aging.

9

A REVOLUTION IN THE TESTING AND TREATMENT OF ALZHEIMER'S DISEASE

I have been attending the Alzheimer's Association and American Academy of Neurology meetings regularly for the past twenty-five years and have *never* felt anything close to the level of excitement in the conference halls as I felt this year. The years 2024 and 2025 have marked one of the most exciting eras in the history of brain aging and Alzheimer's research. After decades of effort and frustration, we are finally gaining a clearer, more measurable view of what happens in the aging brain. The result has been a simultaneous leap ahead in two important areas: Alzheimer's testing and Alzheimer's treatment.

A Sea Change in Alzheimer's Tests

Scientists have long searched for a simple blood test that could offer the same kind of insight that brain scans provide—something as routine and affordable as a cholesterol panel, but for the brain. That goal, once considered out of reach, is finally within sight.

The discovery of blood tests that show the presence of plaques and tangles in the brain and the FDA approval of new drugs that target amyloid in the brain have created a fresh sense of hope and positive outlook for the future. Many neurologists and Alzheimer's researchers alike believe we are at the beginning of a new era where Alzheimer's is like diabetes—a condition with a straightforward diagnostic procedure and treatment protocols.

I am optimistic too. I believe we will soon have complementary blood tests that can also give us a glimpse into the severity of vascular abnormalities in the brain so that we can have a complete picture of *all* the issues that impact cognitive function with aging. Multimodal lifestyle interventions such as my Brain Fitness Program are increasingly recognized as the most powerful tools to treat patients with MCI or early-stage AD (not just to prevent these conditions). As you will soon see, we are on the cusp of finding medications that can supplement such programs, just as people with diabetes may work on their lifestyle issues and take medications like Metformin or GLP-1 agonists.

So what about these new tests? Should you take them?

Traditionally, the diagnosis of Alzheimer's disease has been based on the observation of cognitive decline over time, confirmed through memory testing and clinical evaluation. Imaging or cerebrospinal fluid (CSF) testing would then be used to support the diagnosis. For many years, CSF testing and advanced brain imaging, both of which required specialized equipment and trained personnel, were primary diagnostic tools. While accurate, obtaining CSF through a lumbar puncture (which requires inserting a long needle in the lower part of your spine) is invasive, and people usually don't want to do it.

Another commonly used approach has been brain PET imaging. Amyloid PET scans can detect the buildup of amyloid plaques in the brain, and tau PET scans can show where tau tangles are forming and spreading. These imaging methods have been valuable in research settings and sometimes in clinical care, but they are expensive and not widely accessible, especially outside of major academic centers.

Brain MRIs have been helpful to show the presence of strokes, white matter abnormalities, and level of shrinkage in the cortex and hippocampus.

Now, however, a simple blood test can detect certain Alzheimer's biomarkers. Researchers worldwide have spent more than twenty years trying to identify proteins in the blood that could act as windows into the brain. Now, those efforts are producing real results. This has transformed our ability to detect Alzheimer's earlier, track its progression, and monitor treatment effects. These new tests are helping to shift the focus from late-stage diagnosis to early detection and prevention, opening the door to a more proactive approach to brain health.

A series of extensive studies presented at major conferences and published in top-tier journals have shown that specific blood-based biomarkers can mirror the findings we see on PET scans and MRIs. These blood tests can detect changes years before symptoms appear.[1] But the excitement isn't just in the research community. These tests are already being used in clinical trials and are starting to appear in specialty clinics.[2] They are transforming how we screen for Alzheimer's risk, monitor brain health over time, and track the effects of lifestyle or medical interventions. In short, we are moving from a world where brain aging was invisible and mysterious to one where it is increasingly visible and measurable.

That said, these tests are still in the early stages of use and have not become fully standardized worldwide. Several companies have developed their own versions, each with different methods and cutoff values. Some focus on the ratio between various markers, while others recommend ordering the full panel. Like a lipid panel, each part of the test has its own meaning. And just like with a cholesterol panel, interpreting the results correctly requires experience. You wouldn't take medications for cholesterol based only on abnormal LDL test results you obtained online. Your doctor would order a panel of tests relevant to you, then look at the full picture and recommend the appropriate treatment (which may or may not involve taking medications). The same is true with these new tests.

As you know, Alzheimer's and other brain diseases are complex. The biomarkers these tests measure mostly reflect changes in amyloid and tau proteins, inflammation, and injury to brain cells. Many different issues can affect brain function that these tests do not measure. For example, they don't tell whether your brain's blood vessels are healthy. In the last chapter, I described how vascular issues are a significant factor in the development of Alzheimer's. People in midlife and beyond often develop blockages in the small or large arteries that supply the brain. These blockages may result from high blood pressure, diabetes, smoking, or high cholesterol, and can lead to memory problems on their own, even in the absence of Alzheimer's pathology. These vascular issues are usually detected through brain imaging, not blood tests.

These tests also don't indicate whether your blood-brain barrier is functioning correctly. As I've already described, this is the brain's natural protective system that keeps harmful substances in the blood out of the brain. It can become "leaky" with age, stress, trauma, or chronic illness.

A leaky blood-brain barrier has been linked to cognitive decline, but there is no simple blood test to measure its integrity right now. (A new brain MRI, called Dynamic Contrast Enhancement,[3] can show the severity of brain leakage in a person with cognitive issues, but this has not yet become commercially available. Initial results are promising, and I can't wait to see when this critical test can be ordered.)

Importantly, these biomarkers are primarily focused on amyloid plaques and tau tangles. They don't yet detect other causes of dementia that involve different brain proteins. Conditions like frontotemporal dementia (FTD) or Lewy body dementia (LBD) involve the accumulation of a different protein than is found in Alzheimer's disease. LATE (limbic-predominant age-related TDP-43 encephalopathy) is also caused by the accumulation and aggregation of TDP-43 protein. Some cases of memory loss may stem from fluid buildup in the brain, as in normal pressure hydrocephalus (NPH), which requires a brain MRI for initial evaluation. The new biomarker tests can detect none of these conditions. These blood tests are blind to blockage in brain arteries or the presence of small or large strokes, and also cannot provide any data about the severity of conditions such as poor sleep, anxiety, or depression, which could be the real cause of your memory loss.

Just like a cardiologist would obtain a complete history, perform an exam, and order relevant tests, a neurologist needs to listen to the story of your symptoms—when they started, what made them worse, and how you have managed them so far—then obtain a neurological exam, and, finally, order a series of tests that may include a brain MRI, a cognitive evaluation, a sleep study, and a comprehensive set of blood tests. They may also provide questionnaires that check for your level of anxiety, depression, stress, sleep apnea, and insomnia. A practical and targeted treatment requires a complete understanding of all the medical or neurological issues affecting your brain. Alzheimer's blood biomarker tests cannot accomplish this.

So, as exciting as they are (and they are exciting!), they should always be interpreted by a trained expert. When used correctly, they are up-and-coming tools that bring us closer to the day when we can detect and treat brain changes early, perhaps even preemptively. I predict there will be many additional elements that these tests will be able to detect in the near future.

The New Alzheimer's Drugs

Along with the excitement about these new blood tests, there is a similar or even greater excitement about a new class of Alzheimer's drugs that has recently been approved. These drugs aim to slow the progression of the disease by targeting amyloid plaques in the brain. Called anti-amyloid monoclonal antibodies, these drugs, including lecanemab and donanemab, are designed to help the immune system clear out amyloid plaques from your brain.

These drugs can indeed clear almost all the amyloid plaques in the brain. PET images of patients who received drugs showed more than 80 percent of the amyloid had cleared during the eighteen months of the trial. Both drugs also improved the blood biomarkers. Both showed favorable improvements in Alzheimer's biomarkers for amyloid and tau. While this may sound like a breakthrough, the hype is overstated, at least for now. The clinical benefits of these drugs are minor or imperceptible to actual patients and their caregivers.

A common test assessing cognitive function is the Alzheimer's Disease Assessment Scale—Cognitive Subscale, or ADAS-Cog for short. This tool evaluates memory, language skills, attention, problem-solving abilities, and orientation to time and place, with tasks like word recall, naming objects, and following instructions. Test scores range from 0 to up to 90, with higher scores indicating more impairment, so lower scores are better. These tests have been an important way to compare the effectiveness of drugs for patients with Alzheimer's disease.

On ADAS-Cog, the difference between those who received these new drugs and those who received a placebo for eighteen months of treatment was minuscule; it was 1.4 points for lecanemab[4] and 1.52 points for donanemab.[5] This is a modest difference on a 0–90 scale. The change is too small for most people to notice in everyday life.

There is more to consider. These drugs come with serious safety concerns and require a high level of medical oversight. Before starting treatment, individuals must undergo genetic testing to determine if they carry the ApoE4 gene, which not only increases the risk of developing Alzheimer's but also raises the risk of dangerous side effects from these medications. Those who are ApoE4 positive are more likely to have a brain bleed if they receive anti-amyloid medications. Clinicians now routinely order this test when evaluating a patient for these drugs.

Moreover, before treatment can begin, patients need to have a brain MRI to check for existing microbleeds, strokes, or other abnormalities. If any are found, they may not be eligible for treatment. Once treatment starts, the person must return for IV infusions every two to four weeks. They must also undergo frequent brain MRIs, particularly in the first year, to monitor for a potentially life-threatening complication known as ARIA, short for amyloid-related imaging abnormalities. ARIA indicates swelling (ARIA-E) or bleeding (ARIA-H) in the brain. These changes may be detected on an MRI before symptoms appear, so regular scanning is required to preempt complications. When symptoms do occur, they can include confusion, headache, dizziness, nausea, vision changes, or weakness. The FDA has issued a black box warning for the risk of ARIA with these drugs. In some cases, ARIA can be fatal, particularly in older adults or those with underlying vascular disease.[6]

What makes this even more complicated is that the symptoms of ARIA—fatigue, fever, feeling "off"—can resemble a mild flu, a urinary tract infection, or a viral illness. If someone on these drugs develops these symptoms, doctors are advised to obtain a brain MRI to rule out ARIA. This is not a routine precaution. It is a potentially life-saving step. If left untreated, ARIA can lead to seizures, severe brain injury, or death. That means whenever the patient feels sick, they had better get an MRI or suffer potentially lethal consequences. It's probably nothing, but if it's *something*, the patient could die, so the expensive MRI is a necessity.

There is also a necessary consequence that many patients and families are not aware of: People taking these drugs are no longer eligible for some specific emergency treatments. If someone on lecanemab or donanemab has a stroke, they generally cannot receive clot-busting medications like tPA or TNK. These drugs are the standard of care for an ischemic stroke and are lifesaving. However, for people on anti-amyloid drugs, the risk of bleeding into the brain is considered too high. This means that a person on these medications might be excluded from the most effective emergency stroke treatment available.

As you can see, these treatments are not simple prescriptions—they require significant testing and monitoring (not to mention access to a major medical center), and come with significant compromises and risks.

Then there is the cost of these drugs: around $30,000 per year, but that doesn't include all the PET scans, MRIs, frequent blood tests, and physician appointments required for safety. Altogether, the expense can add up to $50,000 to $80,000 per year. For now, they may be covered, at least partially, by insurance in the United States. Still, if only 5 percent of eligible Medicare patients take one of these drugs, the total financial burden on Medicare would be $5.1 billion a year.[7]

All that being said, some people still choose to take these drugs. For them, any improvement is worth the cost, even if the improvements are only the reduction of amyloid levels in the brain, without any noticeable improvements in everyday life. I personally prefer to wait until these drugs have evolved to have fewer risks, pose less responsibility on caregivers and doctors, are not prohibitively expensive, and involve only a weekly shot, a nasal spray, or a daily pill. I would happily take such a drug, to prevent one of the contributors to Alzheimer's soup of abnormalities in my brain. Others may feel differently, which is of course their choice.

In any case, I believe we are headed in the right direction. I am hopeful that the next generation of safer and more effective drugs will become available in the next five to ten years. As tests and treatments evolve, late-onset Alzheimer's, like diabetes, may someday be fully preventable and treatable with a combination of lifestyle and pharmaceutical interventions. In the meantime, I'm putting my money on lifestyle, which we know, thanks to the new blood tests, can improve both biomarker levels and clinical symptoms.

The Proven Power of Lifestyle over Drugs

When I say I'm still putting my money on lifestyle over drugs, I do not say so lightly. In fact, the evidence comparing lifestyle interventions with the new AD drugs is pretty dramatically in favor of (surprise) lifestyle interventions. Five multimodal lifestyle interventions studies, which used the same standard ADAS-Cog used in Alzheimer's clinical trials, have shown that they are more effective than anti-amyloid drugs.

1. One randomized controlled trial in South Korea showed that patients with MCI not only improved their ADAS-Cog scores by 1.3 points more than the placebo group, but also reported having better quality of life when they received exercise, brain training, group interactions, and music therapy.[8]
2. Another multimodal randomized controlled trial in South Korea showed twenty-four weeks of exercise and cognitive training improved cognitive functions in patients with MCI. Their cognitive tests showed the intervention group also had better working memory, executive function, and lower depression symptoms.[9]
3. Another multimodal study in France showed a combination of exercise, cognitive training, and social interactions for seven months resulted in significant improvement in ADAS-Cog test scores by 2.17 points, compared to the placebo group. Patient MRIs showed better blood perfusion in the brains and better efficiency of neuronal communications. At follow-up evaluations seven months later, patients had maintained the improvements they had gained during the study period.[10]
4. Another study in Canada showed similar results. A combination of exercise and cognitive training in patients with MCI resulted in a 2.64-point difference in ADAS-Cog scores as compared to the placebo group. Again, during the follow-up evaluation six months later, participants who were in the lifestyle intervention group maintained their initial gains in better cognitive performance.[11]
5. Finally, the lifestyle intervention study by Dr. Dean Ornish and his colleagues in California came up with the same results. In this study, fifty-one individuals were assigned to either lifestyle modifications or control (usual care without lifestyle changes). They were encouraged to eat a plant-based healthy diet, exercise at least thirty minutes daily, practice yoga, meditate or do breathing exercises daily, and participate in a support group three times a week for twenty weeks. They all had biomarker and cognitive testing at the program's beginning and end. Results showed an actual improvement of 1.92 points in ADAS-Cog (not just less decline), as compared with the control group. These lifestyle interventions reduced levels of amyloid in the brain. LDL-cholesterol,

A Revolution in the Testing and Treatment of Alzheimer's Disease

ketone bodies, insulin levels, and microbiome health all improved as well.[12]

Encouraged by the research, I recently decided to compare the results of the clinical trials for anti-amyloid medications and multimodal lifestyle interventions side by side, with specific attention to the ADAS-Cog tests (the same tests used in all these trials). My findings, which I presented at the Alzheimer's Association International Conference in Toronto in July 2025, showed lifestyle interventions are *far* more effective.

I evaluated three clinical trials for the three new monoclonal antibody drugs for Alzheimer's disease versus five randomized clinical trials for multimodal lifestyle interventions. In the lifestyle trials, the control group usually declined. As you can see in the figure below, the treatment group in all these trials showed significant improvements in cognitive scores. By contrast, significant improvements were not shown in any of the trials for the new Alzheimer's drugs.

The figure on the next page shows the percent difference in changes in the standard cognitive test (ADAS-Cog) that was used for both multimodal

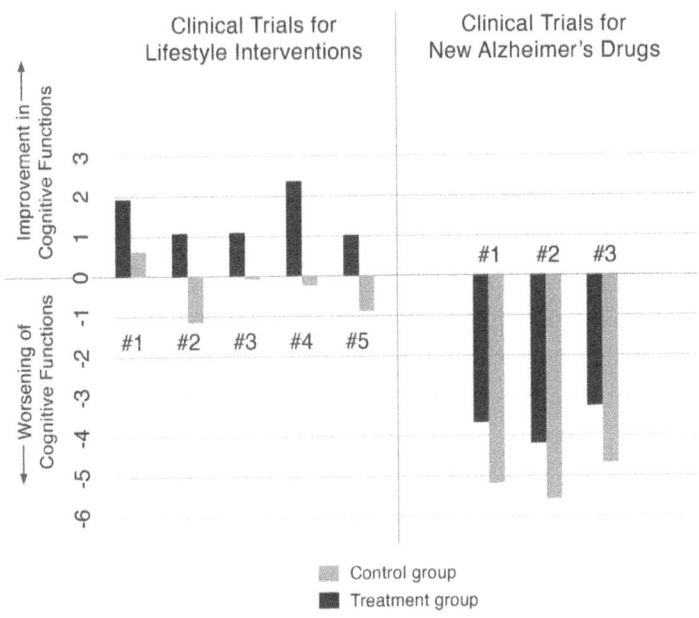

lifestyle interventions (left) and for the new Alzheimer's drugs (right). As it can be appreciated easily in this figure, programs that combine healthy lifestyles are orders of magnitude more effective than the new Alzheimer's drugs.

These clinical trials showed that patients who had received the anti-amyloid drugs declined during the 18 months of the study, but by just about 27 to 32.4 percent less than the control group. Patients in these trials did not gain better memory and continued on their downhill course. In contrast, patients in clinical trials for lifestyle interventions actually improved their cognitive functions by as much as 204.7 percent to 1147.8 percent.

The chart on the next page summarizes the short-term and potential long-term risks and benefits for the anti-amyloid drugs versus a combination of lifestyle interventions:

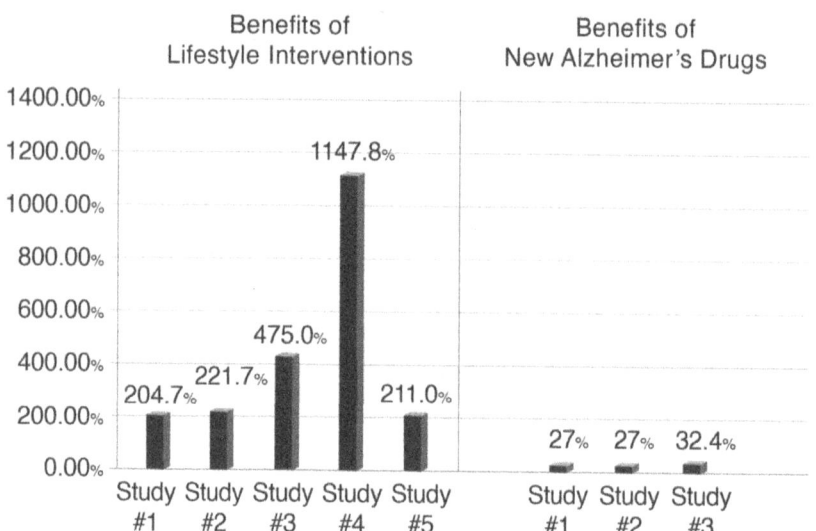

	Anti-amyloid drugs	Multimodal lifestyle interventions
Amyloid levels in the brain	Decrease	Decrease
Risk of heart attacks and strokes	No change	Usually lower
Sleep quality	No change	Usually improved
Life expectancy	No change	Usually improved
Brain shrinkage	Worse (a known side effect of these drugs is brain atrophy)	No brain atrophy. The hippocampus and cortex may grow larger in some people.
Benefits for the heart, skin, or other body organs	None	Overall health of all body organs usually improves
Risk of swelling and bleeding in the brain	High	None
Eligible to receive lifesaving anti-stroke medications	Not eligible	Yes. Eligible for all medications needed for stroke treatment.
Fear that the side effects may be due to a potential life-threatening ARIA	Yes	No
Need for frequent MRIs to check for brain swelling and bleeding	Yes	No
Cost	$50,000 to $80,000/year	$2,000 to $4,000/year

Please make what you will of this information—my point is not to keep you from trying these new drugs, but to make clear the risks, and to show you the potent positive effects of lifestyle, whether you choose to take the drugs or not. In the meantime, let's all hope for more effective, safer drugs in the near future!

It is indeed an exciting time. I can vividly imagine a day when a combination of safe and affordable medications paired with lifestyle interventions turns a devastating, incurable Alzheimer's disease into a condition that we can successfully prevent, manage, and treat. But we already know one thing for sure: Creating a robust brain will make it more resilient to any damage that can happen with aging. Now, let's learn how to make your brain more invincible by building more reserves in all your organs.

10

THE GRACEFULLY AGING INVINCIBLE BRAIN

Early in my career, I covered the hospital's inpatient unit for one week a month. As a consultant, I would provide recommendations for patients in the oncology, ICU, pediatric, obstetric, and dialysis units who had developed neurological symptoms such as weakness, headaches, confusion, or coma.

One of the patients I remember quite well was a seventy-two-year-old man who had become confused, lethargic, and weak. John was admitted to the general medicine unit for further evaluation and treatment. He had a prior history of uncontrolled diabetes, hypertension, high cholesterol levels, alcohol abuse, and smoking. My assessment revealed that John had developed kidney failure and that his dangerously low serum sodium levels were the main culprit for his neurological symptoms. I urged his medical team to correct his sodium levels promptly because he would otherwise be at a high risk for developing a seizure in the hospital.

But I remember his brother, Brian, even more vividly than John. He was eighty-two years old and had been taking care of John for the previous eight years (since John had lost his wife to cancer). Brian was quite fit, healthy, and sharp. Unlike his younger brother, Brian was active daily, participated in community activities for his church, and his only medication was a statin for his high cholesterol.

I remember contemplating how two brothers living in the same general environment, with the same socioeconomic status, had experienced aging on such different trajectories. John had not taken care of himself and his medical issues. Brian had. The brother, who was ten years older, took care of the younger sibling while remaining quite functional in his eighties.

The sad truth was that unless John drastically changed his lifestyle and took charge of reviving his health, he was more likely to develop strokes and dementia and die before Brian.

Young Brain, Old Brain, Alzheimer's Brain

As you now know, the brain of a 20-year-old does not look the same as the brain of an 80-year-old. If you put them next to each other, you will notice that the 20-year-old brain is bigger, fuller, and more vibrant in color. However, while brains do shrink with aging, a healthy 80-year-old brain looks only slightly smaller than a 20-year-old brain. The brain of an 80-year-old with advanced Alzheimer's disease, on the other hand, looks totally different. It is significantly more shrunken, grayish, dull, dry, and has more space between the folds.

The brain area most sensitive to shrinkage with aging and Alzheimer's disease is the hippocampus. A recent meta-analysis determined that, on average, the hippocampus shrinks at a rate of about 1.18 percent per year after age fifty.[1] With advanced Alzheimer's, that rate increases to about 4.7 percent per year. The average size of a hippocampus in the brain of a healthy eighty-year-old is about 3.5 to 4.0 cm^3. In someone with Alzheimer's, it is just 2.0 to 2.5 cm^3. Although your hippocampus is probably a little smaller than your thumb, for the sake of size comparison, look at your thumb and your pinky, and you can visualize roughly the difference between a hippocampus that has aged typically and one that has atrophied from Alzheimer's disease.

Functionally, a healthy older brain will likely have a slightly slower processing speed than a younger brain, but it is wiser. It functions better at problem-solving and understanding the nuances of information. We all know that speed isn't everything. For example, when it comes to an international conflict, you'd much rather have seasoned politicians with a deep knowledge of history and a calm demeanor at the negotiation table than a recent college graduate who is new to politics but can type twice as fast as his older colleagues.

But we cannot deny that learning new things becomes more difficult with aging, especially when we reach our eighties and nineties. Older individuals require more time to figure out the automated check-in machines at the airport, use new apps on their mobile phones, or complete their tax returns. Some of this age-related slowing in figuring things out is related to

The Gracefully Aging Invincible Brain   133

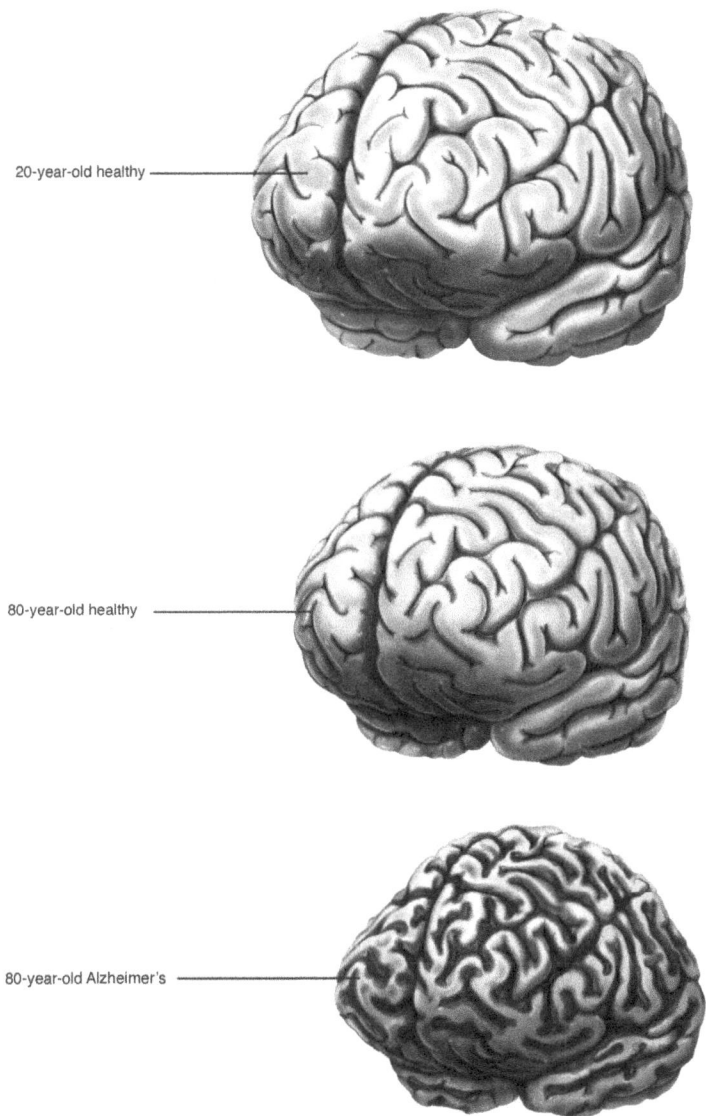

20-year-old healthy

80-year-old healthy

80-year-old Alzheimer's

mild atrophy in the cortex and hippocampus in late life. However, given that the brain atrophy with normal aging is mild, older individuals should be able to thrive, take on new hobbies, travel, manage their finances, go on dates, and live a full life without restricting their physical or mental activities.

The following chart shows the acceptable level of cognitive slowing with aging, marked as lines 1 and 2. However, in some older adults, memory fades faster, and they may have more challenges completing their daily tasks. They still get everything done, but they are at the border of having significant cognitive decline, more than would be acceptable with aging (the third line). These individuals are preclinical and may easily decline to Mild Cognitive Impairment, MCI (the fourth line). In the MCI stage, they may repeat themselves often, but can still live independently. Once their cognitive decline progresses beyond MCI, they lose their ability to function by themselves and are diagnosed with Alzheimer's disease.

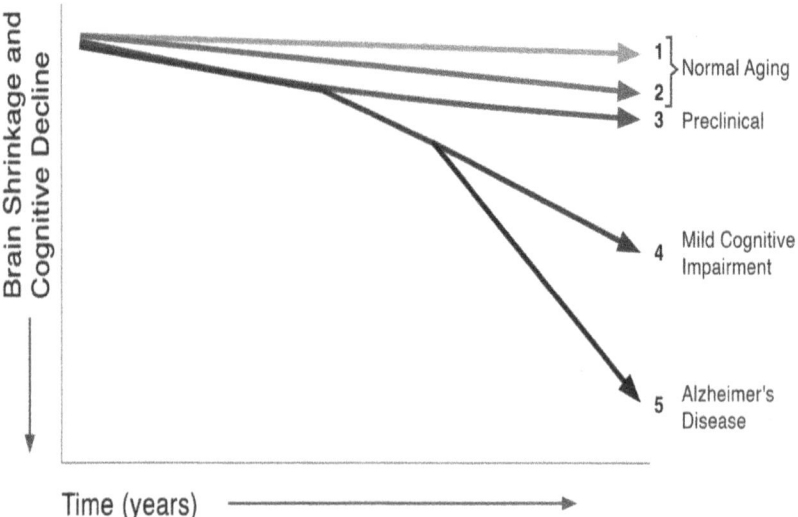

Fortunately, your brain possesses a remarkable degree of neuroplasticity and has the potential to switch from a preclinical or MCI trajectory back to normal aging. If you feel you are somewhere on trajectories 3 and 4, please know that you can improve your brain functions and become one or two levels sharper. I have researched and witnessed this firsthand. I've seen hundreds of patients with MCI, or even early-stage Alzheimer's disease, significantly improve their cognitive functions in my clinic time and time again.

While it is true that some people with MCI do go on to develop Alzheimer's disease or other forms of dementia, others may remain stable or even improve. For example, one study in Japan[2] monitored 396 older adults with a diagnosis of MCI for four years and found one-third of them reverted to normal when they started to take care of themselves better and engaged in more activities. Individuals who transitioned back to normal had begun to read books, take cultural classes, participate in community meetings, take up new hobbies, exercise, and spend more time gardening.

Attitude has a powerful effect as well. Recent research by scientists at Yale University has shown that people who have a positive attitude and positive beliefs about aging are less likely to convert from MCI to Alzheimer's disease.[3] In the study, individuals with an optimistic attitude toward aging had a 30.2 percent greater likelihood of recovering from MCI to normal than those with negative beliefs about aging. Additionally, those with more positive beliefs recovered more quickly.

Even when some people with MCI make only minor or seemingly insignificant changes in their life circumstances, their cognitive problems may disappear. For example, an older person living alone may develop depression, which can cause memory loss and apathy, and then feel sharper and happier when moving to live closer to their grandchildren. MCI due to depression can resolve with a change in life circumstances. Sometimes we don't know the reason. According to a meta-analysis of many studies, 18 percent of patients with MCI seem to revert to normal cognitive function spontaneously.[4]

If you want to age gracefully, not just avoid Alzheimer's disease but remain sharp, mobile, energetic, and able to pursue your passions and purpose, there is a straightforward formula: Keep growing your brain. The more neurons, synapses, and fiber bundles you have, the greater your brain reserve will be. That translates into more efficient and harmonious connections between your brain networks, and your brain will be better able to resist aging effects. Even better, build reserve into all your organ systems because the health of your organs—heart, lungs, liver, kidneys, pancreas, bones, muscles—supports the health of your brain.

You can begin doing this at any age. Whether you are eighteen or eighty-one, it is never too late to build more reserves and slow the aging process. I find it remarkable that after I teach a class to college students who are barely into their twenties, the most common response I get when I ask them to evaluate the class is that they have made lifestyle changes that will protect and grow their brains so that they will never experience brain decay and precipitous decline. How amazing is that? Young people are notorious for not thinking much about their future health. Yet, understanding the concept of brain reserve motivates even these college students to start making meaningful changes in their lifestyle habits.

The Secret to Graceful Aging Is Organ Reserve

Reserve is the extra resource your organs need to withstand challenges. You can think of reserve like a bank account. If you live paycheck to paycheck, you are always at the end of your reserve, so if there were an emergency—car repairs, a new roof, a big hospital bill—you would not have the resources to pay for it. But if you accumulate money in an emergency savings account, you would be able to handle the occasional unexpected expense.

Your organs are the same. You don't usually need to tax your organs to their maximum, but in the case of a health emergency, you might. Imagine someone who runs fifteen miles every week versus someone who smokes cigarettes, has emphysema, and doesn't exercise. If both these people contracted pneumonia, the runner would have much more lung reserve and, therefore, milder symptoms and a better chance at a quick recovery than the smoker.

The same goes for your heart, liver, kidneys, bones, and brain. A healthy brain reserve can mean better cognitive function as the brain ages. We should all have the organ reserves to last us 110 years or more, to protect us against the inevitable challenges of life and the increasing likelihood of decline with aging in all our organ systems. This is how you age more gracefully.

Accumulate Brain Reserve

Having brain reserve means having more synapses, neurons, fiber bundles, efficient neuronal networks, and resilience than you need to overcome challenges that can affect your brain. More brain reserve is a reflection of more neuroplasticity and a higher ability to rewire and expand your brain. If you are limping along with untreated depression or anxiety, unresolved concussions, persistent insomnia, untreated sleep apnea, poor diet causing inflammation in your brain, or a long-standing sedentary lifestyle, you are less likely to recover well from a big event like a concussion, stroke, or long period of extreme stress. Someone with plenty of brain reserve will recover faster with fewer residual cognitive symptoms. Brain reserve is the likely answer to why some people with plaques and tangles in their brains show no signs of cognitive decline (like the nuns in the Nun Study I told you about in chapter 8).

Resistance + Resilience = Reserve

You can increase brain reserve in two ways: *resistance* to atrophy and decline, by avoiding things that cause problems in your brain, and *resilience* in the face of challenges, by doing things that are good for the brain. For example, you can build resistance by avoiding smoking, drinking too much alcohol, and eating junk food. You can build resilience by exercising regularly, eating nutrient-dense foods, and challenging your brain to learn new things daily. Together, this two-sided strategy increases brain reserve and grows the brain.

Every day, you make hundreds of decisions. If building brain reserve is a part of the criteria for your decisions, you can add a little bit of brain reserve every day by choosing what to eat, whether to go on a walk, or how to manage your stress. Lifestyle changes have a cumulative effect, so you will feel the impact of your years less as you age. The more reserve you have to spare, the longer it will take for your brain and body to notice that you are getting older, and the later you will reach the threshold of becoming frail—hopefully beyond the age of one hundred.

Whole-Body Organ Reserve

Aging gracefully is about increasing brain reserve, but it is also about increasing reserve (through resistance and resilience) in all body organs. The brain talks to the body all the time, and the body also talks to the brain. Each of your organs gets information from your brain and sends information to your brain. How well these organs work and how much reserve they have affect your brain, growing or shrinking it.

HERE ARE SOME WAYS THAT THE BRAIN AND OTHER ORGANS DEPEND UPON ONE ANOTHER:

Liver-Brain Connection

Liver problems cause brain problems. Unfortunately, fatty liver disease (triggered by obesity, poor diet, uncontrolled diabetes, sleep apnea, and/or excessive alcohol consumption) is quite common, accounting for two million deaths worldwide every year. In 2023, one out of twenty-five deaths was due to liver disease![5] When the liver begins to fail, a buildup of toxic chemicals (such as ammonia) in the blood erodes the protective linings of the blood vessels in the brain, inflames fiber bundles, and dirties the pristine environment between neurons, astrocytes, and microglia. Brain cells cannot tolerate the presence of foreign chemicals and waste. Brain MRIs of patients with liver disease often show white matter abnormalities.[6]

Advanced liver disease can result in profound memory loss, brain atrophy, and a higher risk of Alzheimer's disease, as the brain experiences reduced cerebral blood flow, vascular injury, and brain inflammation. A recent analysis of more than 1,500 older adults with various degrees of memory loss showed that individuals who have signs of liver abnormalities are more likely to develop Alzheimer's disease and have more plaques and tangles in their brains.[7]

Kidney-Brain Connection

When kidney function declines, waste products accumulate quickly in the blood, and high blood urea nitrogen can damage multiple organs, including the brain, causing confusion. Low vitamin D levels, which can also result from reduced kidney function, can cause memory loss, slow thinking, and brain fog. High blood pressure caused by kidney damage can reduce blood flow to all organs, including the brain. Built-up potassium levels can cause muscle weakness and fatigue (this is why people with kidney disease must limit their potassium-rich foods).

As with liver disease, patients with kidney disease show more white matter irregularities on brain MRIs, as well as significant brain atrophy.[8] One study showed that poor kidney function, even without kidney failure, was associated with a smaller brain volume and more damage to the fiber bundles. When kidney failure was severe, it was associated with more strokes and small brain bleeds.[9] Disturbingly, chronic kidney disease is surprisingly common, affecting one in seven adults in the United States, many of whom are unaware they have it. Over time, chronic kidney failure can lead to a higher risk of Alzheimer's disease and significant brain atrophy.[10]

Bone-Brain Connection

Your bones affect your brain? Yes. As you age, bones can become more porous and brittle, sometimes leading to a condition called osteoporosis, which is caused by low estrogen in women, excessive smoking and alcohol consumption, and a poor diet with not enough protein, calcium, or vitamin D. Osteoporosis is associated with a higher risk of cognitive impairment and Alzheimer's disease—we aren't entirely sure why, but it could be related to lower levels of osteocalcin or other bone-related neuroprotective hormones.[11]

On the flip side, Alzheimer's disease can also increase the risk of osteoporosis and fractures,[12] possibly due to shared risk factors like low estrogen, inflammation, low vitamin D, a sedentary lifestyle, and other brain changes. The same factors that are culprits for poor bone density also seem to be culprits for brain atrophy with aging. Fractures and the immobility they cause are another major cause of rapid cognitive decline in older people.

Muscle-Brain Connection

When you use your muscles, they release myokines (such as BDNF and irisin) in the blood, impacting the brain by improving neuroplasticity, memory, and accelerated learning. People with low muscle mass associated with obesity, aging, or being sedentary have low brain-boosting myokines.

Muscle mass appears to be related to brain volume. A study published in *BMC Geriatrics* examined the relationship between sarcopenia, i.e., low muscle mass, and brain volume atrophy. Researchers assessed 1,284 participants for muscle mass and handgrip strength over four years. Those with sarcopenia showed significantly more gray matter volume loss on MRIs compared to the control group.[13] Another MRI study of 284 people[14] with an average age of eighty-three found a correlation between faster walking and higher gray matter brain density. Yet another study with forty thousand participants showed a correlation between greater handgrip strength, larger brain volume, and better cognitive function. Those with stronger handshakes often have stronger brains.[15]

Lung-Brain Connection

Lung diseases such as chronic obstructive pulmonary disease (COPD) reduce lung elasticity and capacity. Airways narrow, the chest wall stiffens, inflammation increases, and the number of alveoli—tiny air sacs in the lungs that exchange oxygen and carbon dioxide as you breathe in and out—decreases. Inflammatory components from the lungs can leak into the bloodstream, disrupt the blood-brain barrier, cause leakage of blood content inside the brain, and lead to significant neuroinflammation and cell death.

In a study of 115 people with COPD and thirty-five healthy adults as a control group, researchers compared the severity of COPD and the changes in gray matter density and white matter integrity in the brain.[16] They found that patients with more severe COPD had significantly lower gray matter density and white matter integrity and a smaller brain overall.

Heart-Brain Connection

The heart spontaneously generates a pulse that affects the blood vessels in the entire body, including the glymphatic system that cleanses the brain of waste. That pulsation, conveyed to the brain's blood vessels, is what pushed the CSF fluid that rinses out the waste. But the conversation between the brain and the heart is more than just a pulse. The brain suffers as the heart ages or becomes weaker, with slower electrical activity, stiffening heart muscles, blockage of coronary arteries with cholesterol plaques, and a less vigorous pulse. Heart failure is linked with significant brain atrophy, and the hippocampus is particularly vulnerable to the effects of poor blood supply to the brain. It shrinks the most when the heart is inefficient.

You can see on an MRI how a patient with congestive heart failure has a much smaller hippocampus than someone with a healthy heart and a normal brain. In a study of 148 patients with heart failure in their sixties in Germany, researchers examined the link between measures of heart failure and brain deficits. They found that more than 40 percent of the heart failure patients had memory loss or were slow to process information, and the worse the heart failure, the smaller the brain.[17]

As you can see, your whole-body health really does drastically influence your brain. So what can you do to improve function in all your organ systems?

Resist organ decline by avoiding too much alcohol, smoking, vaping, chemical fumes, caffeine, drugs, and unnecessary medications. Avoid junk food and eating too much sodium, red meat, or sugar. Don't sit too much.

Avoid developing obesity, diabetes, high cholesterol, and high blood pressure. Manage chronic stress. Treat sleep issues.

Build organ resilience by eating a low-fat Mediterranean-style diet rich in leafy green vegetables, fiber, and protein. Take omega-3 fatty acid supplements. Exercise regularly. Walk a lot. Lift weights a few days a week. Drink water throughout the day. Get seven to eight hours of sleep on most nights. Practice deep breathing exercises.

When you think about building reserve, remember how connected everything is. The more reserves you have in all the organs, the more protected your brain will be, and the less it will decline. Build and maintain your reserves as you age, and you can recover from challenges like a young person would. You'll also enjoy less obvious and less symptomatic aging.

The program in part 4 will help you assess your specific issues and learn how to incorporate the necessary healthy lifestyle habits into your life in a way that is easy and fun, and at a pace you can handle. You can do this! Your brain and all your other organs will thank you for it. The higher your organ reserves, the longer you will live, the sharper you will be as you reach your eighties and nineties, and the happier you will be in these golden decades of your life.

Telomeres: Markers of Longevity and Brain Health

Telomeres are a chain of DNA molecules (called nucleotides) that cap the ends of your chromosomes and appear to be directly correlated to cellular aging and longevity. At birth, a telomere has approximately 10,000 to 15,000 nucleotides. By midlife, depending on your lifestyle choices and health conditions, your telomeres may shorten to 5,000 to 7,000 nucleotides, and by the time you are in your eighties, your telomeres may be as short as 2,000 to 4,000 nucleotides.

The longer your telomeres, the longer you are likely to live. Every time a cell divides, the telomere length shortens, so telomeres gradually become shorter over time and with age. However, lifestyle and environment can also prematurely shorten telomeres, just as healthy behaviors and a healthy environment can keep telomeres longer. The inflammation (and other factors) leading to too much DNA methylation also appears to shorten telomeres prematurely. In two people of the same age, the one with a healthier lifestyle, that is, the one with longer telomeres, will live longer.[18]

A meta-analysis of many studies reviewed evidence that exercise and nutrition influence telomere length.[19] The researchers concluded that physical activity and a diet high in fiber and unsaturated fat are associated with longer telomeres. In a study of sixty-eight people who were caregivers for dementia patients, researchers assigned half of the participants to an exercise intervention of approximately forty minutes of aerobic activity three to five times per week. Throughout the twenty-four-week study, the exercising group not only increased telomere length compared to the decrease in the control group but also experienced a significant loss of body fat, reduced feelings of stress, and better cardiorespiratory fitness.[20]

Meditation helps too. A German study monitored three hundred participants, assigning some to a meditation program. The researchers compared telomere length and cortex volume every three months. The meditators increased their telomere length and cortical thickness, while those who did not meditate had slight decreases, or no change at all.[21]

A clinical trial that involved a combination of lifestyle changes, stress management, and socialization showed a remarkable 10 percent increase in the length of telomeres in the intervention group. In comparison, the control group experienced a 3 percent reduction in the lengths of their telomeres.[22] Those who had adhered to the program more intensely on average during the five-year study period saw a more significant lengthening of their telomeres.

Shorter telomeres correlate with Alzheimer's pathology, and longer telomeres are associated with a thicker cortex, including a larger hippocampus and a lower risk of dementia.[23] Fortunately, to increase your telomere length and lifespan, you don't have to do anything other than what you are already doing to grow your brain, but it's nice to know you are getting that extra longevity boost!

So, Grow Your Brain!

Aging gracefully ultimately means resisting brain shrinkage and increasing brain resilience by growing your cortex and hippocampus. Most of the interventions that lead to brain growth, which we will review in part 4 of this book, depend on the health and vitality of all other organs below your neck.

As you grow and build your brain reserve, your brain will expand to a full, vibrant, healthy size, and then it will continue to grow not so much in size but in function, complexity, flexibility, and reserve. It will develop more sophisticated neuronal networks that work harmoniously and lead to higher intelligence. And you will experience graceful aging for yourself.

Now that you have a big-picture view of what to do to age as gracefully as possible by building reserve in your brain and other organs, let's get you started on the Brain Fitness Program, so you can start increasing your resistance and resilience to build your brain reserve, for a more invincible brain both now and far, far into your future.

PART FOUR

THE INVINCIBLE BRAIN PROGRAM

11

THE BRAIN FITNESS PROGRAM

Carol was one of my unforgettable patients. She was in her early seventies when her sister brought her to my clinic. Her sister told me, "Carol doesn't do anything. The TV is on, but I think the TV watches her because she just sits there staring. She sits there all day." The sister wanted me to confirm that Carol had Alzheimer's disease so she could obtain power of attorney, sell Carol's house, and use the money to place Carol in a nursing home.

I thought, "Wait a minute. This lady is relatively young. I need to figure out what's going on here." She had retired eight years earlier from a job as a manager in the Social Security Administration. As I spoke with her sister more, I learned that Carol had severe sleep apnea and back pain and was on six different pain medications that made her very sleepy. No wonder she wasn't moving much! She also had depression, high blood pressure, and type 2 diabetes. Given her complex medical issues, she was a mess.

I suspected that could change if Carol started my Brain Fitness Program.

The first thing I did when I began working with Carol was to taper her medications one by one, as much as possible. I treated her sleep apnea by placing her on a CPAP machine. Initially, she couldn't walk very well and used a wheelchair, but as her medications were reduced, she was able to stand and then take a few steps. Our program was structured to meet twice weekly, and at each meeting, Carol worked for ninety minutes with our brain coaches. The more medications Carol stopped taking and the more she worked on the program, the more she could do things for herself.

About six weeks later, I remember sitting at my desk, and as I looked out my office window, I saw a woman walking by. I thought, "Wait a minute, is that Carol?" I couldn't believe she was the same barely responsive lady who had come to see me in a wheelchair just six short weeks earlier.

During the program's second part, Carol memorized words, started a hobby, and resumed attending church. By the end of the program, she was back to being the Carol she used to be. She was happy, cheerful, and engaging. It was like meeting a new person. On her before and after MRIs, I could see that the size of her hippocampus had increased. Her baseline brain MRI showed a few small strokes and significant atrophy in her hippocampus and cortex. When Carol started the program, the total volume of her left and right hippocampus measured 7.29 cm^3; afterward, it was 7.92 cm^3. This represented a growth of about 8.6 percent in size in just twelve weeks; in other words, her brain MRI was similar to someone eight years younger. Carol's progress was one of the best cases we had seen in our program. Her brain was growing!

I saw Carol every three months after her initial twelve weeks. At the first visit, she was doing well. On the second visit, six months later, she came in looking sad. I asked what had happened, and she said her husband had died. I remembered him because he had come with Carol on her first visit, along with her sister. He had severe emphysema and used an oxygen tank.

On her third visit, she was cheerful and happy again. I said, "Carol, what's going on?"

She replied, "Dr. Fotuhi, I'm in love again! When I was in high school, I had a crush on a guy in my class, but I never told him, and then I got married right out of high school and never saw him again. He went to California, but since my husband passed away, I tried to find him. I found him in California! It turned out his wife had died too—and now we are together!" She spoke like a giddy teenager.

On her fourth visit, one year after she participated in the program, she asked for a repeat brain MRI. She wanted to see if her progress had continued or if her brain had reverted. Rather than regressing in size, her hippocampus had grown another 1 percent. She had adopted more new habits and hobbies—walking, memorizing things, and so forth—so her brain continued to grow, even as she aged. And let's not forget the power of social connection or, in her case, love!

All these positive activities and attitudes must have improved blood flow to her brain, reduced inflammation, mitigated amyloid levels, enhanced the glymphatic rinsing processes, and diminished any leaky brain she might have had in her hippocampus. Despite this being a charming story, think about what could have happened to Carol and how her life would have been if she had never changed her routine and reemerged from her shell of sitting at home in a wheelchair, drained of energy and life. She would probably be in a nursing home today. Instead, she's happy, in love, and full of vitality.

This is the power of the Brain Fitness Program.

I continued to provide this program for other patients with MCI and, time and time again, saw remarkable stories of these older adults coming back to life. Many of them were in their seventies and eighties, and they had felt that their destiny was to develop Alzheimer's and die in misery. However, after they had completed the program, they felt as if they had regained many of their cognitive abilities. They felt revived and looked forward to enjoying more years with their grandchildren and pursuing their passions.

When I reviewed the results of objective cognitive tests in 129 patients who had completed my program, I saw that 84 percent of them had gained significant improvements. When I analyzed the before and after MRIs of these patients, I saw that more than half of them had grown the size of their hippocampus by an average of 3 percent. I felt these findings were incredible and published them in *The Journal of Prevention of Alzheimer's Disease* in 2016.[1]

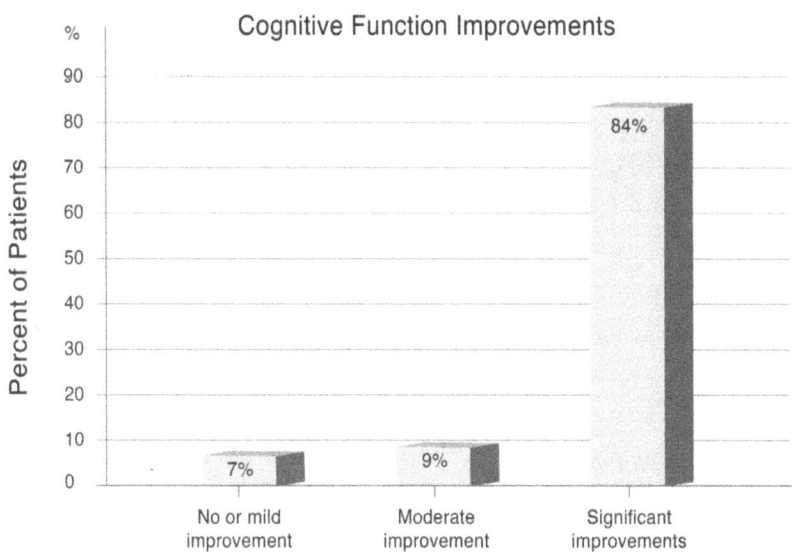

I also provided this program for my patients who had postconcussion syndrome. In this condition, patients continue to have persistent dizziness, headaches, memory loss, poor executive function, irritability, or depression for months or years after their initial traumatic brain injury. When I reviewed the results from the questionnaires and cognitive tests in several hundred of my patients with these conditions, I saw that more than 80 percent had improved their symptoms and had better scores. I published those findings in 2020.[2]

Excited by these results, I provided my program for patients with ADHD. Again, I saw that more than 80 percent of my patients reported significant improvements in their daily lives and had objective improvements in their cognitive evaluations. I published my findings about similar results of the program for patients with ADHD, concussion, and MCI in 2023.[3]

Now it's your turn to be an amazing story.

The Brain Fitness Program Adapted for You

Of course, I can't welcome you into my clinic, but I can welcome you to a new incarnation of my Brain Fitness Program: the program you can do for yourself, with the help of this book. It won't be the same as what I did at NeuroGrow, but it can have the same effect because every intervention we did there, you can do too—or you can do something similar that will work in the same way.

In the first step of this process, you'll take the same brain fitness calculator assessment and fill out the same questionnaires I used with my NeuroGrow patients to get clear on where you are now and what your most troubling symptoms and deficits are today. We'll narrow down what you want to work on and in what order.

Once you've assessed where you are and feel mentally prepared to tackle your concerns and grow your brain, we will begin the program. The great thing about this program is its simplicity. There are five pillars of brain health. Not a thousand, not a hundred, not even twenty-five. Just five pillars to focus on:

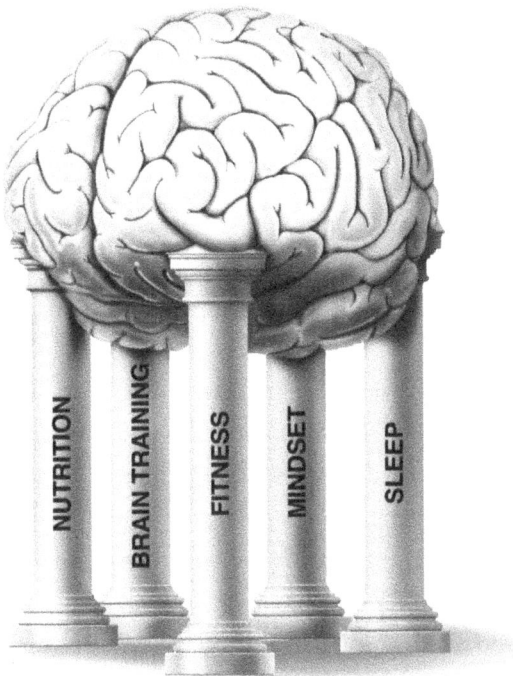

1. Fitness, for more oxygenation and BDNF
2. Sleep, especially deep sleep for its glymphatic system effects
3. Nutrition, especially food items that reduce inflammation and improve blood flow in the brain
4. Mindset, for stress reduction as well as the power of belief and confidence in your abilities
5. Brain training, to strengthen and increase neurogenesis and synaptic connections

You've heard of these things before and may have had vague ideas about how to work on them, but we will be systematic in this program. You probably won't tackle all five pillars at once—where you concentrate your efforts will depend on where you most want and need to improve. I'll help you identify those areas over twelve weeks by taking small steps. We'll cover each area in a series of five "Fast Track" chapters:

Fitness Fast Track: Depending on your fitness level, you'll begin increasing the amount of exercise you get and monitoring your fitness through your VO_2 max (which I will explain in detail in chapter 13). You'll get a list of interventions. Pick which ones to do each week, according to your current fitness level and subsequent progress throughout the twelve weeks.

Sleep Fast Track: Sleep problems can be the primary cause of your cognitive symptoms. You will learn how to identify and address all your sleep issues, with different prescriptions according to whether you have sleep apnea or insomnia, or need better sleep hygiene. You'll get a list of interventions you can choose each week to address your personal sleep issues, which can change as your sleep improves.

Nutrition Fast Track: You will learn about the brain-friendliest diet—what to eat, when to eat, and how to get more comfortable with whole foods as you transition off ultra-processed foods. I'll help you take meaningful steps toward integrating nutrient-dense, fiber-rich, whole-food, moderately portioned meals into your life. I'll give you a list of interventions, a brain-friendly food list, and a few key supplements to focus on as you incrementally improve your diet.

Mindset Fast Track: You will assess your current stress level, mindset, life enjoyment, purpose, and contentment. By learning how to track your heart rate variability (HRV), you can determine how much you are stressed so you can intervene with items on the list of peace-inducing activities that will increase your quality of life and lower your cortisol. I'll also show you how to improve your HRV and state of mind through DIY biofeedback.

Brain Training Fast Track: There are many ways to train your brain to boost your memory and other areas of your cognitive capacity (i.e., intelligence). Depending on your schedule and preferences, I'll give you many options, resources, and a prescription for how much and how often to train your brain. Choices range from old-fashioned games and puzzles to high-tech brain-training programs. More important, I will show you how to focus better, become more creative, and get more done every day.

Each week, you'll rate how you did on different aspects of following through with the program with a simple tracker at the end of each Fast Track chapter, or track your progress in your own way or on my app. You may also consider using some of the tools I have provided on my website, drfotuhi.com, and on the app.

After six weeks, you'll do another full brain-fitness calculator and assessments. As you gradually build up your brain and body reserves and increase the invincibility of your brain, you'll begin to feel better, have more energy, and notice that your brain is working better and better. After twelve weeks, you'll do another assessment, at which point the differences will be obvious. The more strictly you follow the program and apply yourself to changing your habits and revamping your health practices with a growth mindset, the more you will see jaw-dropping results.

Then, to keep you moving forward and motivated, you will repeat your assessment questionnaires at three months, six months, and one year. I also encourage you to repeat basic blood tests at your yearly physical to monitor your health progress. This is where you will truly appreciate how far you have come, just by making a few simple changes here and a few more alterations there, resulting in a brain-friendlier lifestyle. The longer you stick with the new habits you develop during the program (I hope it will be for life), the more progress you will enjoy, and you'll see those results every time you retake the assessments.

No drug can completely fix your cognitive decline. Not yet, at least. There is no one practice, food, exercise, sleep trick, memory hack, brain game, no one *anything* that can significantly grow your brain and build your reserve and resilience. You know that brain health is not about doing just one thing, but that's great news because it means you can do all kinds of things to achieve better brain fitness.

After completing the program, most of my patients comment on how easy it was for them to improve their symptoms and their scores on our tests. They seemed in awe that they had memorized a list of one hundred words or the sequence of cards in a deck with relatively minor effort. But this was never a surprise to me. I know well how strong the brain is and how little of our brains we use daily. We each have a powerful machine in our heads, but may neglect to make the effort to use it even at half capacity. I believe boosting your cognitive performance is easier than the efforts you need to build muscles in your arms. You must believe in your brain's extraordinary prowess and take the first steps to harvest its incredible powers.

A Real Patient Reversing Her Cognitive Decline

What's it like to go through my Brain Fitness Program step-by-step and experience brain transformation? Let's follow another one of my patients, a fifty-five-year-old schoolteacher named Lisa.

Lisa came to my clinic fearing the worst: Alzheimer's disease. She had trouble remembering her students' names and keeping up with her responsibilities at work. She was often tired, woke up frequently in the middle of the night, and had almost daily headaches. The noise in the classroom, like desks moving and students talking, had become extremely irritating to her. She had gained twenty pounds in one year, which wasn't typical for her, and she was plagued with knee pain. She was also in the middle of getting a divorce. Lisa was anxious, depressed, and overwhelmed.

After I spent a long time talking to Lisa during our first visit and getting to know her, I had her do the same three assessments you will do in the next chapter. The first evaluation was the Brain Fitness Calculator. According to her answers, Lisa was low on energy, stressed, disorganized, had a negative attitude and a poor memory, and was having trouble sleeping. She no longer felt like being social and felt sad much of the time. She had a poor diet (although she did take omega-3 fatty acid supplements). She received a low brain fitness score of just 44 out of 75. On the next page, you can see what her Brain Fitness score looked like, according to the calculator.

The second assessment was for neurocognitive symptoms. For these assessments, Lisa filled out a spidogram (my term for the spiderweb-shaped diagrams I used in my clinic), ranking herself from 1 to 10 in different categories, depicted as dots on the web. These dots indicated the intensity of her symptoms. What I call the red zone (8, 9, or 10 out of 10), depicted by the outer ring, meant she was having a lot of difficulty with those symptoms. The yellow zone (5, 6, or 7 out of 10), or middle ring, meant she was having moderate difficulty. The inner ring (1, 2, 3, or 4 out of 10), or green zone, meant little to no difficulty. The further out she marked a symptom, the more intense it was; the further in she marked a symptom, the less intense it was.

BRAIN FITNESS CALCULATOR

	Your score
Energy level throughout the day (low: very tired to high: very energetic)	1 2 ③ 4 5
Fitness (low: totally out of shape to high: in great shape)	1 ② 3 4 5
Peaceful state of mind (low: stressed out and nervous to high: calm and in control)	1 ② 3 4 5
Organized (low: chaos at home and work to high: well-organized most of the time)	1 ② 3 4 5
Positive attitude (low: life is tough; everything will fail to high: life is beautiful; everything will work out just fine)	1 2 ③ 4 5
Satisfactory sleep (low: trouble falling sleep or up all night to high: sleep well, about 8 hours a night)	1 2 ③ 4 5
Memory for names (low: can't remember "anybody's" name to high: remember "everybody's" name)	① 2 3 4 5
Taking Omega-3 fatty acid supplements (low: never or one day a week to high: 5 or more days a week)	1 2 3 4 ⑤
Social engagement (low: prefer to stay alone by myself to high: busy with lots of social activities every week)	1 ② 3 4 5
Sense of curiosity (low: not too much into figuring things out to high: love to discover new things and solve puzzles)	1 2 3 4 ⑤
Love your daily routine (low: dread my day-to-day routine to high: enjoy and love my daily routine)	1 2 ③ 4 5
Heart-healthy diet choices (low: fast food, donuts, French fries to high: lots of fruits and vegetables)	1 2 ③ 4 5
Mindful of portion size (low: eat large portions and second servings to high: prefer small and reasonable portions)	1 2 ③ 4 5
Extracurricular activities / hobbies (low: do not enjoy participating in activities to high: enjoy trying new hobbies, participating in community activities, volunteering, or helping others in my community)	1 2 3 4 ⑤
Usual mood (low: down and depressed to high: happy and cheerful)	1 2 ③ 4 5
Add up your score:	41

Green (Good job, keep it up): 60-75   Yellow (Need some work): 45-59   Red (Need lots of work): 15-44

The categories were: paying attention, calculating, concentrating, making decisions, multitasking, navigation, processing information quickly, understanding instructions, finding words during conversation, expressing yourself, short-term memory, remembering names, forgetting what you read, difficulty planning, and organization.

Here is how Lisa ranked her difficulty in each of these categories:

Neurocognitive Symptoms

● Pre-program

- Difficulty paying attention
- Difficulty with calculating
- Difficulty with concentrating
- Difficulty with making decisions
- Difficulty with multitasking
- Difficulty with navigation
- Difficulty with processing information quickly
- Difficulty with understanding instructions
- Difficulty with finding words during conversations
- Difficulty with expressing yourself
- Difficulty with short-term memory
- Difficulty with remembering names
- Difficulty with forgetting what you read
- Difficulty with planning ahead
- Difficulty with organization

Total 126

As you can see, she had quite a few dots in the outer (red) zone. She had three dots in the middle (yellow) zone, and only one symptom—difficulty calculating—was in the inner (green) zone.

Next, we gave Lisa a neurobehavioral symptoms assessment, also depicted on a spidogram. This assessment tracked difficulty with fatigue, falling asleep, staying asleep through the night, pain, hypersensitivity to light and sound, headaches, mood swings, obsessive thoughts, compulsive behaviors and/or thoughts, depression, difficulty socializing, general anxiety, hyperactivity, agitation, impulsive behaviors, low motivation and apathy, frustration, anger, and irritability. Lisa did a little better on this one. She had seven dots in the inner (green) zone, but she still had many moderate to severe issues in other areas:

Lisa also had extensive blood tests, a sleep study, and formal cognitive evaluations (you'll learn how to do those in the next chapter). After I reviewed all her test results with her, I sat down and talked with her for about an hour. I explained the three elements needed for her successful recovery: believing she can improve, working hard to improve, and making her body more fit and healthy. She was a great candidate for our program, and I told her I expected great results. She agreed to start the program with some hesitation, but with a positive attitude.

I tailored Lisa's program for her, addressing the areas where she needed the most help. She was particularly concerned about her ability to manage all her personal and professional responsibilities (handling appointments with her divorce lawyer, taking care of her knee pain, keeping up with her teaching responsibilities, and dealing with students) and her memory (forgetting names of her students and worrying about developing the early stages of Alzheimer's disease).

At a biological level, my goal was to increase the blood flow in her brain, reduce inflammation, and help her grow and expand parts of her brain for memory and executive function—critical for planning and managing her many life challenges simultaneously. These were the areas she wanted to work on, so we set out to tackle improving these areas of her brain first: namely the hippocampus and the prefrontal cortex.

Lisa came to our brain center twice a week and worked closely with our brain coaches and biofeedback team for ninety minutes each time. She enjoyed the specific brain games we picked to challenge her brain. For

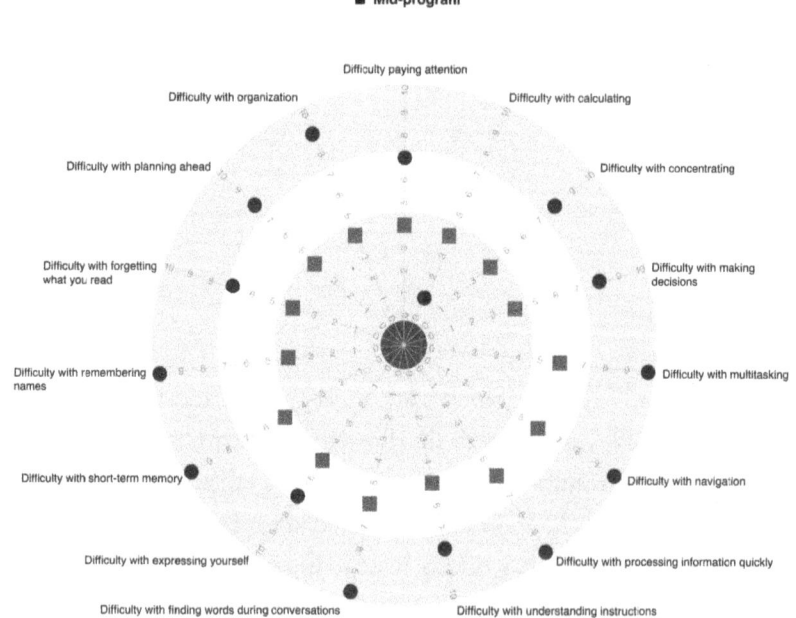

example, she learned how to memorize a list of twenty words each week, and could not believe it when she had memorized one hundred words, forward and backward. She also enjoyed eating a Mediterranean diet, walking thirty minutes daily, and practicing meditation daily for ten minutes. She talked with our social worker about her stressful life issues, and together they came up with solutions on how to manage her stress. After just six weeks, Lisa started feeling better, calmer, more energetic, and hopeful.

As we do with all our patients, we reassessed Lisa's neurocognitive (see the image on the previous page) and neurobehavioral (see the image below) symptoms halfway through this program. She had improved noticeably, as you can see by the location of the squares in her spidograms, which were her measurements at six weeks. All the measurements in the red zone had moved into the yellow or green zones.

Neurobehavioral Symptoms

Encouraged by these results, Lisa began the second half of our program with more enthusiasm. At the end of the twelve weeks, we assessed her again. Her improvements were dramatic, not just on her spidograms but in her self-reported mood, manner, and appearance. She took more pride in her appearance, and her students noticed she looked younger and healthier. She had fewer headaches, was no longer sensitive to light and sound, and was enjoying her work again. She was managing the stress of her divorce with a smile—instead of dwelling on the loss. She focused on being happy that she was getting out of a negative relationship—and she loved her new, more fit, and stronger body, which could do more for her without pain or fatigue. She was back—sharper, more confident, and feeling much better than when she came in for her initial assessment.

You can see how much she improved by comparing the dots, squares, and the final score triangles in her twelve-week spidograms. Her responses indicated that all her triangles were in the green zone, which was our goal.

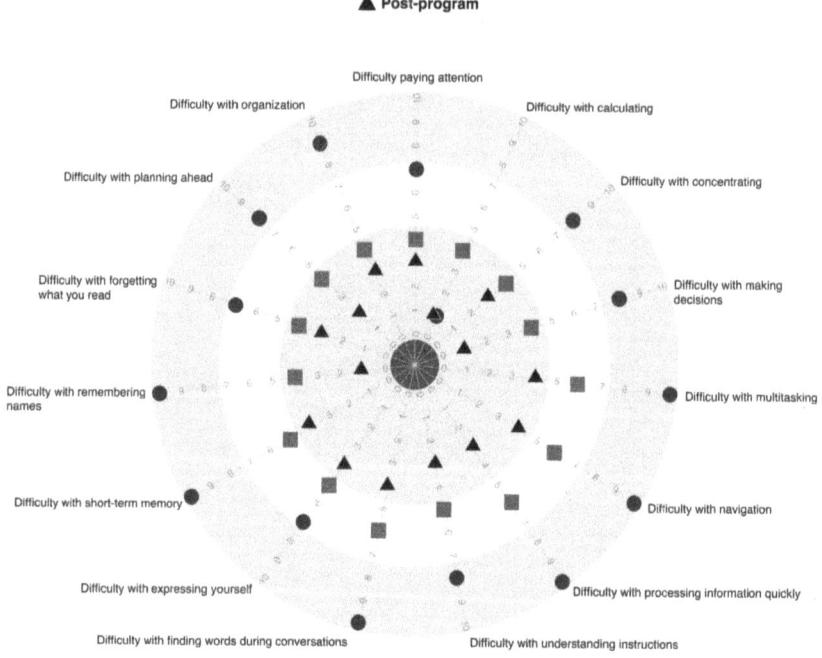

For more perspective on the difference the program has made for Lisa and others, we measured the change in total symptom load by adding the numbers patients had assigned to each of the items in the neurocognitive and neurobehavioral spidograms at baseline, six weeks, and twelve weeks. Below are the results for Lisa, showing that her neurocognitive symptoms declined from 126 to 43 (66 percent less), and her neurobehavioral symptoms declined from 111 to 53 (52 percent less).

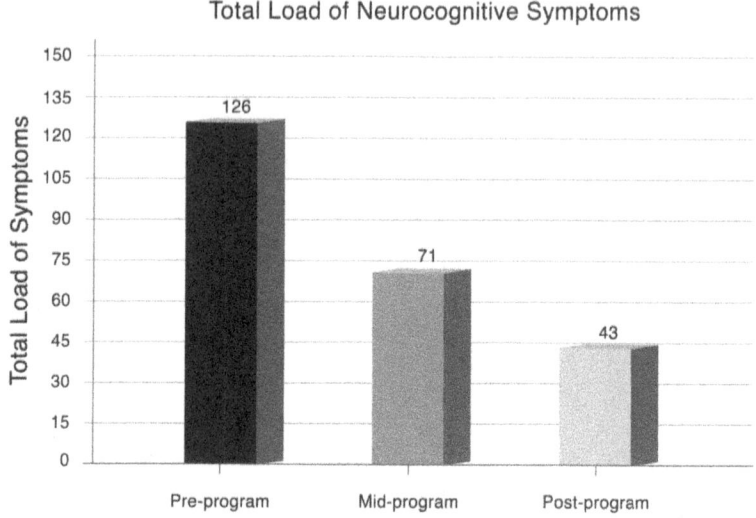

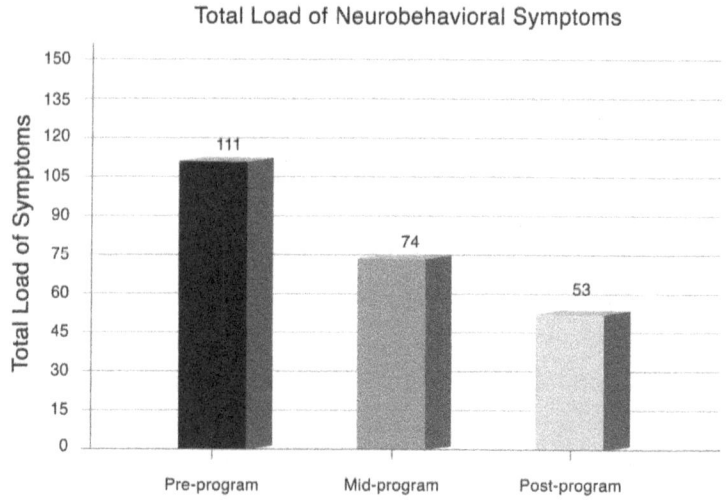

While her spidogram assessments were subjective (based on her reports), Lisa also showed dramatic improvement on her objective tests of cognitive performance as shown in the following graph. This computer-based cognitive testing measures the levels of verbal memory, attention, processing speed, and executive function with specific tests that often look like brain games.

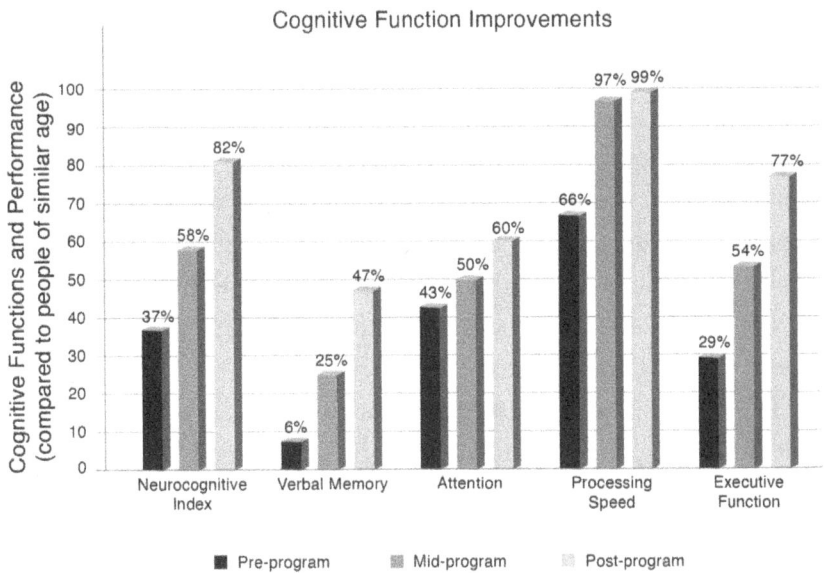

At baseline, her neurocognitive index, which summarizes all her cognitive functions, was at the 37th percentile for her age group. This measure of her overall cognitive capacity increased to above the 50th percentile for her age by the time she had completed the first half of her program. Then it reached the 82nd percentile for her age by the time she finished the twelve-week program. Her scores for each individual cognitive domain had improved greatly as well.

Lisa wasn't just a fluke. No way! Her results were *typical* for people going through my program. Most of the patients who completed my program achieved the goal of getting their final spidogram scores into the green zone.

Here are two other typical examples.

Hannah was a forty-four-year-old accountant who came to see me for her long-standing challenges with ADHD. She was diagnosed with this condition in high school and struggled to do well in college. She had tried taking Adderall but did not like how this medication made her feel jittery, so she stopped taking it. She often misplaced her belongings, jumped from one task to another, and was irritable. For example, she frequently argued with her family members or her boss. She was particularly frustrated with her low motivation to get things done, procrastination, poor attention, horrible memory, fatigue, and mood swings. She had brought her teenage son with ADHD to our brain center and was impressed by his remarkable improvements in just three months (he took no medications). So she decided to do our program herself.

Her initial assessment showed that in addition to ADHD, she also suffered from low levels of B_{12} and vitamin D. Her spidograms revealed that most of her neurocognitive symptoms fell in the red (outer) zone. Her responses regarding irritability, frustration, low motivation/apathy, anxiety, and mood swings were also in the red zone. Her formal cognitive tests showed her attention score was at the 26th percentile for her age, and her memory was at the 30th percentile for her age.

Like Lisa, Hannah received a personalized set of treatments within our multimodal protocol focused on her specific reported symptoms and objective findings. Her vitamin B_{12} was so low that I had to put her on biweekly B_{12} injections for three months. She collaborated with our social worker to change her mindset about dealing with people in her family and work environment, to respect them more and expect less from them.

She also received specific brain games that challenged her attention and memory. For example, she learned how to pay attention and memorize the sequence of playing cards in a deck.

Once her attention improved, her memory scores spiked to the 90th percentile. This confirmed that her memory problems were due to challenges with the attention part of her brain, not the memory part of her brain. As you can see in her spidograms on the following page, she gained remarkable improvements in all of her symptoms. She, too, was a brand-new woman!

Finally, let's look at the case of Carlos, a thirty-eight-year-old mechanic who had had a severe concussion when a heavy box on the top shelf of his garage fell on his head. He passed out for a couple of minutes and woke up feeling confused. He did not remember anything hitting his head. He also had nausea, a headache, and felt weak overall.

In the emergency room, his head CT showed he did not have a bleed in his brain. As he was feeling better gradually, he was sent home with the plan to see his primary care doctor about treating his concussion symptoms. Carlos did not improve as expected; he found that he had become

The Brain Fitness Program

Neurocognitive Symptoms

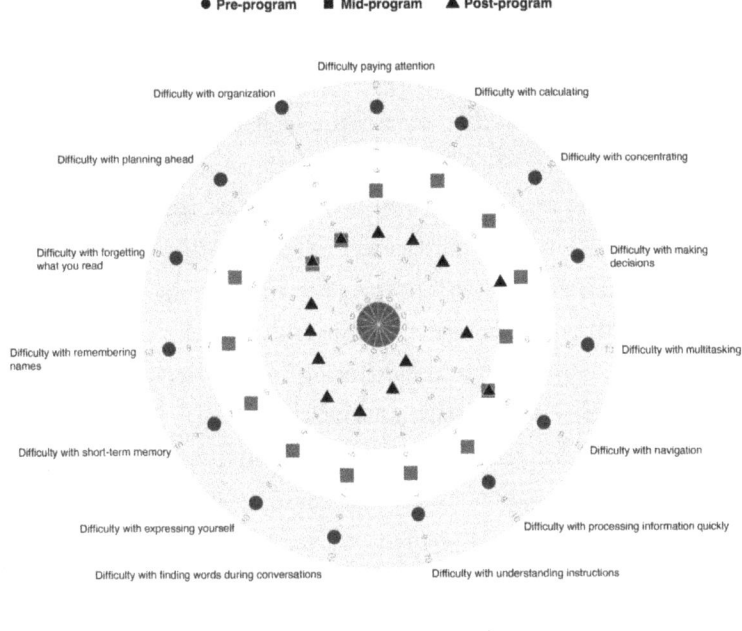

Total ● 132   Total ■ 81   Total ▲ 43

Neurobehavioral Symptoms

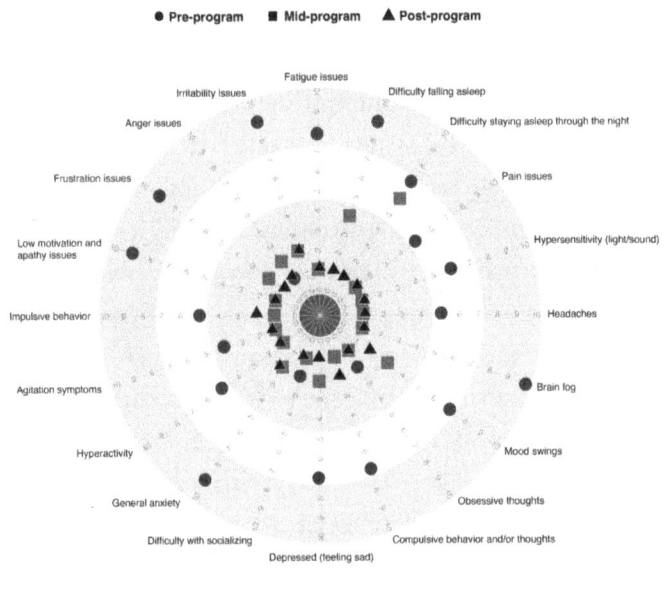

Total ● 126   Total ■ 35   Total ▲ 25

much slower than he used to be. Everything, from brushing his teeth to eating his breakfast to fixing an engine, took twice as long as it used to. He felt he had to think extra hard to drive, calculate his balance sheets, and conduct conversations. Not able to sleep well most nights, he also had developed frequent headaches, something he had never dealt with before. His income dropped by more than 50 percent.

Carlos visited a neurologist who recommended some medications for his headaches and insomnia, and suggested that he reduce his workload for a few weeks. His frustrating symptoms persisted. He saw a psychiatrist; she suggested his difficulty with getting things done at his usual speed could be related to his depression and frustration in dealing with the trauma of having had a significant concussion and the changes in his relationship with his wife. He decided not to take the antidepressant medication she had prescribed for him. He saw another neurologist. This doctor spent fifteen minutes with him and seemed annoyed at how Carlos was perhaps exaggerating his symptoms (and looking for an excuse to collect disability insurance). After all, Carlos could talk, walk, drive, and work.

Nobody recommended a cognitive evaluation to assess how his brain was functioning. Six months later, he was still struggling with all his concussion symptoms. He seemed desperate when he came to see me, having been referred by one of our other patients and reading positive reviews about our center online. He said I was his last stop. He was giving up on the chance that he would ever improve and return to his baseline.

As you can see from his spidograms on the following page, all his responses shifted to the inner green zone after completing my program. His headaches, slow thinking, and frustration issues all resolved in just three months. His cognitive test results were also remarkable. His processing speed increased from the 42nd percentile to the 94th percentile.

I learned a lot while putting my patients through the Brain Fitness Program. I got to know those patients so well that they felt like family. I watched not just their objective scores change but their subjective feelings about their intelligence change too. Many of the patients who came to visit me at my NeuroGrow Brain Fitness Center believed themselves to be less intelligent than they used to be, or thought they were on the brink of diagnosable cognitive impairment. They were wrong.

The Brain Fitness Program 167

Neurocognitive Symptoms

Total ● 109   Total ■ 49   Total ▲ 32

Neurobehavioral Symptoms

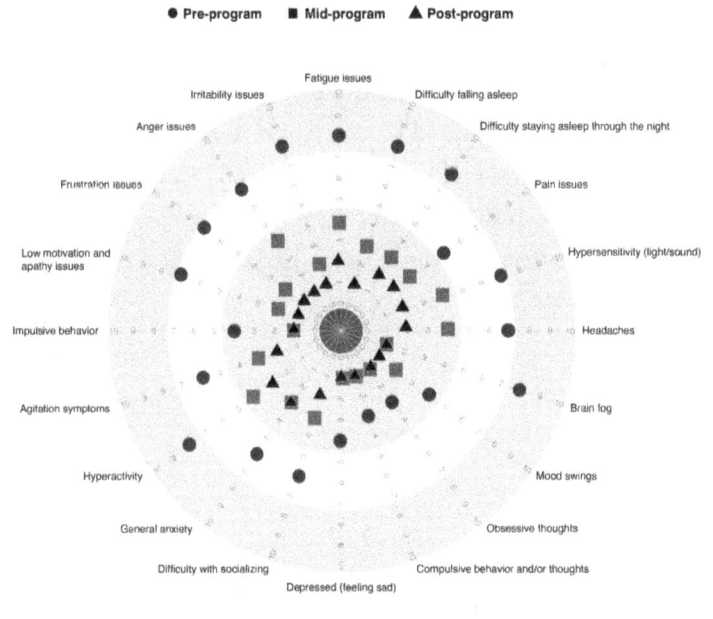

Total ● 124   Total ■ 35   Total ▲ 31

One goal at NeuroGrow was to help people achieve a positive mindset about their brains. In many cases, my patients were not doing what was necessary to fully recover from a head injury or manage something like ADHD or migraines. They felt they were suffering from cognitive decline caused by a horrible brain disease or permanent injury. Simply knowing how well their brains were working in areas they weren't appreciating and understanding the magical power of neuroplasticity to help them grow their brains set them on a new path to feeling better but also becoming more intelligent and cognitively sharper than they were before.

My program is designed to highlight strengths as well as detect deficits. The checklists on types of intelligence you went through at the beginning of this book were created for the same purpose—to show you that *you* are more intelligent than you think, and that intelligence comes in many forms and manifests in many different ways. But it is also my job, as a neurologist, to do a thorough investigation into my patients' brain health and cognitive performance, and we're going to do that with you, as well.

I always took some time to explain to my patients that following the five pillars of brain health in my program will help them improve blood flow in their brains, reduce inflammation, improve rinsing mechanisms, and grow new synapses and neurons. Learning about these facts energized them to follow and complete our program with enthusiasm.

In my experience, patients hardly ever decline in function once they have improved and understand how easy it is to feel and perform better in their daily lives. I will do all I can to ensure you keep boosting your brain performance and becoming smarter for years to come.

Let's begin by assessing your brain and getting you started on a new and life-changing journey!

12

ASSESS YOUR BRAIN FUNCTION

I hope you've had many "aha!" moments as you've read this book. I've found that change doesn't become easy until a patient has an "aha!" moment. Let's use your excitement and awe about the level of neuroplasticity in your brain and the knowledge of how easy it is to mold a newer, stronger brain to propel you through the twelve weeks of this program.

This multipronged intervention is appropriate for addressing the multifactorial soup of problems associated with day-to-day brain fog, aging in the brain, and the risk for Alzheimer's disease. It is also appropriate for increasing intelligence and optimizing brain function in anyone, at any age. Every person who starts my program has unique goals in mind. Is your goal to reduce your brain fog, improve your ADHD symptoms, reverse early signs of cognitive decline with aging, or get smarter to improve your job performance? Do you want to build a healthier brain, boost your intelligence, or do both? Start thinking about that now.

My Brain Fitness Program addresses your goals by focusing on the five pillars of brain health: fitness, sleep, nutrition, mindset, and brain training. Each of these pillars grows your brain, improves vascular health, mitigates inflammation, reduces amyloid accumulation, and has health benefits all over the body and in all the organs. Whatever your goals, this program can help you achieve them.

You may not need to work on all five pillars, or not all at once. In this chapter, I'll help you determine which of your daily habits or medical issues may impact your brain performance and what you need to work on to become sharper. You will also learn what medical issues you must discuss with your health care provider and what you must prioritize as you complete my program.

Since I cannot see you and ask you these questions in person, I am providing the exact questionnaires my patients completed at baseline, halfway through the program, and at the end. As such, you can make an inventory of the specific symptoms that bother you the most now and see them improve within weeks. This program is a powerful tool to make you sharper, happier, and stronger in a matter of weeks, and I am super excited to guide you on how you can get the most out of it.

Create Your Brain Portfolio

A Brain Portfolio is a collection of information about yourself and your plans and goals for achieving an invincible brain. I had each patient in my clinic keep a Brain Portfolio, and I'd like you to start one too.

Your Brain Portfolio will contain your goals, reasons for doing this program, test results and assessments, and tracked progress as you move through the program and beyond. You can create your Brain Portfolio (see template at the end of this chapter) in a notebook, on a computer, or online on my app (check my website: drfotuhi.com or use this QR code). Use it as both a tracker and a journal where you can record your wins and your frustrations. In this chapter, I'll review all the eight sections you can include in your Brain Portfolio and what to record there.

Brain Portfolio Section #1: Your "Why"

I would like you to contemplate the big-picture issues for your mind and brain. Let your thoughts on these questions kick off your Brain Portfolio:

Why *specifically* do you want to have a better-functioning brain in the future? What is your purpose in life?

As discussed in the third chapter, having a sense of purpose is critically important for living a long, rewarding, and cognitively sharp life. Please review that chapter and write down two to three things you feel passionate about, and how you think your sharper brain will help you achieve your long-term goals and dreams.

What short-term goals would you like to achieve in the next twelve weeks? What results are you going for?

In my experience, some people have primary concerns about their memory, while others worry about attention, being slow, or having disorganized thinking. Would you like to be able to memorize a list of one hundred words, finally learn a language you always wished you knew, get better at your golf game, sleep better, stress less, or become funnier (which is one of my short-term goals!)? Remember, you can improve any part of your brain and get better at anything you wish. Anything.

What percentage of your usual self are you these days, with regards to your brain functions and how you feel overall, compared to ten years ago? Are you at 90 percent or 25 percent of your usual self?

I always found it interesting how some people believed they had declined to 50 percent of their usual self during the previous ten years, only to get better and feel 100 percent of their usual self after they completed my program in twelve weeks. This happened for almost all our patients, who learned to believe (as I and my brain coaches did) in their potential to achieve anything they used to do in their past—and more. Usually, not much brain decline happens in ten years during midlife, so it is reasonable to reach that level of brain performance, and then exceed it.

Who is your role model?

Are there people in your family, work environment, or the public whom you admire? Perhaps you wish you could be more like your uncle, who is seventy years old and still exercises in a gym six days a week, or your sister who has managed to have a perfect balance of work and personal life, or your coworker who is always organized, or your close friend who seems to have a perfect memory for names. Be inspired to become more like any of the people you admire by imitating how they have achieved their goals. If they can do it, you can too.

Answering these questions will motivate you when your new habits feel hard. Let these answers help you keep your eye on the prize and be your guiding light.

Brain Portfolio Section #2: The Forty Questions

The next step is assessing where you are right now with regards to your mindset, habits, and medical issues by answering the same forty questions I asked all my patients who started my Brain Fitness Program. Write your answers in section two of your Brain Portfolio (or on the template on page 195). Just answering these questions will bring to your attention things you may not have thought about, or help you realize there are things you have been tolerating that you could do something about.

Answer honestly, based on what you have been doing and how you have been feeling for the most part or on average over the past few months. I have put these questions in specific categories of issues and conditions that affect you from head to toe. Consider putting a check mark next to each of the questions that apply to you.

Issues related to brain and mental health:
Do you consider yourself a pessimist?

If you aren't naturally optimistic, don't worry. Optimism is a skill you can learn, and that is worthwhile. Optimism is associated with lower rates of cognitive decline in a dose-dependent manner, meaning the most optimistic people tend to be the least likely to decline cognitively, according to a study of 4,624 people.[1] A study published in *JAMA* in 2023 showed that older individuals with MCI who held positive beliefs about aging were 30 percent more likely to regain normal cognitive function than those with negative age beliefs.[2] In a study of men with a mean age of 70.5, those who were more pessimistic had a much higher risk of MCI or dementia.[3]

Do you have insomnia?

You may be unable to think straight because you don't get enough sleep. If you want a high-functioning brain, you must take poor sleep seriously and prioritize fixing it. Insomnia shrinks your brain over time, and sleep problems correlate with Alzheimer's.[4]

Do you sleep too much?

Excessive sleeping could be due to several medical conditions, including sleep apnea, anemia, depression, vitamin deficiency, or thyroid abnormalities, all of which are treatable. If you sleep until 10:00 a.m. and still want to nap in the afternoon, please discuss these symptoms with your physician. The general recommendation for adults is to sleep between seven and nine hours per night, most nights.[5] One study found that individuals reporting sleep durations of nine hours or more had a 46 percent increased risk of developing dementia compared to those sleeping seven hours.[6]

Do you get migraine headaches?
When you have a severe headache, you can't think straight. Migraines are more than just headaches. You may also contend with hypersensitivity to light, sound, smell, or overstimulation in busy environments. I have migraines, and can't do complex thinking in large crowds, around loud noises, or if I have a messy desk. Migraine brains can become easily overwhelmed with too much information. People who get migraines even find it hard to talk to someone wearing clothes with a "loud" pattern, like a brightly striped shirt. They suffer from such nonheadache symptoms most days, even when they don't seem to have a migraine attack.

Only migraineurs know how much they have to modify their lives to suffer less. Their school and job performance and relationships may be compromised because their headaches and nonheadache symptoms can make them irritable and prevent them from paying attention to details, solving problems, and remembering things well. My twelve-week program can help you reduce the frequency of your migraine symptoms significantly, but if you have severe migraines that interfere with your ability to function well at work, home, or school, you need to see an experienced physician.

Have you had concussions?
For decades, research has linked head injuries with brain atrophy and Alzheimer's disease.[7] A study of college students showed that those who played football and had several concussions had a smaller hippocampus than those who played football but had not had a concussion, and both groups had a smaller hippocampus than those college students who had never played football.[8] The hippocampus of a young professional football player who has experienced hundreds of hard tackles or concussions could be the size of a person in their eighties. Retired football players are five

times more likely to die from Alzheimer's disease compared to the general population.[9] Of course, you don't have to play football to risk head injury. Any accident—bike, motorcycle, car, or something else—can put you at risk. Protect your head!

Do you often feel depressed?

There is a correlation between depression and hippocampal volume: The longer the depression lasts, the more the brain shrinks.[10] So, it makes sense that depression is a risk factor for Alzheimer's disease, vascular dementia, and all-cause dementia.[11] Depression, like heart disease or any other medical condition, is treatable. Unfortunately, an estimated 30 to 50 percent of people with depression do not seek medical help.[12]

Do you feel stressed regularly?

Chronic elevated levels of the stress hormone cortisol are toxic to the hippocampus, and higher cortisol levels are associated with a smaller hippocampus.[13] Several studies have linked chronic stress to increased risk of MCI and dementia.[14] Stress is often (not always) self-induced—it is a product of how you react to circumstances beyond your control. You could say you generate it with your own thoughts. Fortunately, this is something you can change.

Do you often feel anxious?

Anxiety, like chronic stress, increases cortisol levels, which shrink the hippocampus.[15] Chronic anxiety increases the risk of developing Alzheimer's disease within ten years by threefold, even after adjusting for other issues like depression.[16] A 2020 study showed a habit of negative thinking correlates with more amyloid, tau, and cognitive decline.[17] Like depression, anxiety is a treatable condition.

Do you dread challenging your brain?

Your brain is like a muscle. The more you use it, the stronger it gets. Those who are curious and like to seek out new information and learn new things every day tend to have better cognitive function.[18] In fact, higher education and lifelong learning can mitigate the genetic risk for Alzheimer's disease.[19] Many studies have shown that regularly engaging in cognitively stimulating activities grows the brain and improves cognitive function, even in those with MCI.[20]

Do you have ADHD?

People who have ADHD tend to be highly creative. They may ignore details in some situations but can think outside the box. I view ADHD as a different way of processing information, rather than a deficit. Many people with ADHD tend not to be bound by other people's expectations. A lot of executives have ADHD. They benefit from being risk-takers and seeing things differently than most. ADHD does come at a price, however. It can make school or work difficult, and people with ADHD may come to believe they are not as smart as others who do well in conventional learning and working environments. If you aren't sure whether or not you have ADHD, talk to your doctor about getting tested. If it interferes with your life and success, many therapies beyond the interventions in my program can help to boost your focus and concentration (along with my program, which has certainly helped many people with ADHD).

Do you feel lonely much of the time?

If you don't mingle with people, you have fewer opportunities to stimulate your brain. We don't fully understand why socialization is so essential for brain health and performance, but we know that dopamine levels are higher when individuals interact with each other than when interacting with a computer.[21] Positive social interactions are associated with better physical and mental health, faster healing, and higher quality of life.[22] In contrast, social isolation correlates with worse physical and psychological health, slower healing, lower quality of life, and a higher risk of dementia.[23]

Do you have a fixed mindset?

Unlike people with a fixed mindset, those with a growth mindset who are open to learning new things and becoming smarter are more likely to grow their brains and improve their cognitive skills with age.

Although much growth mindset research exists on children and young adults, a 2022 study examined the motivational influence of growth mindset training in older adults and found significant benefits for their cognitive functions.[24]

Do you work too much?

If you spend ten to fifteen hours working most days and come home so exhausted that all you can do is eat and fall onto a couch to watch TV, you may be on the wrong trajectory for brain aging. Achieving an invincible brain requires time and effort. You need to find room in your schedule to manage your chronic stress and engage in brain-friendly activities like exercising, cooking nutritious food, and socializing. There are always ways to delegate, be more efficient, and schedule priorities. You can make your brain health a top priority, and consider it as important as or even more important than your work!

Issues related to cardiovascular health:
Do you have heart problems?

People with untreated atrial fibrillation, heart disease, or heart failure are more likely to experience strokes, have reduced blood flow to the brain, and eventually experience shrinkage in their brains. As we discussed in chapter 8, there are many links between cardiovascular disease and Alzheimer's disease.[25] Heart disease is largely preventable, treatable, and reversible in most cases—remember that what is good for the heart is good for the brain and vice versa.

Have you had high blood pressure for a long time?

Untreated hypertension hardens the arteries, reducing the pulsation in the small brain arteries and impairing the effectiveness of the glymphatic system at clearing out toxic waste byproducts from your brain. Hardening of the arteries in the brain also increases the risk of stroke and Alzheimer's disease. Fortunately, this is reversible. Research from Johns Hopkins has indicated that people who are taking commonly prescribed blood pressure medications are half as likely to develop Alzheimer's as those who aren't.[26]

If you have high blood pressure, discuss this with your doctor and make sure you are receiving optimal treatment.

Do you have high LDL and/or low HDL cholesterol levels?

Several studies have linked high LDL cholesterol to dementia risk.[27] Statins, though they may cause mild side effects (such as muscle pain) in some people, can significantly lower cholesterol and may even reduce the risk of Alzheimer's disease,[28] likely because of their anti-inflammatory effect. Conversely, high HDL ("good") cholesterol levels are associated with better cognitive performance in individuals aged sixty and above.[29]

Do you have untreated diabetes?

Untreated diabetes is one of the worst culprits for causing heart attacks, stroke, brain shrinkage with aging, and a higher risk of Alzheimer's disease.[30] Some researchers call Alzheimer's disease type 3 diabetes.[31] Stay on top of your blood sugar numbers—ask your doctor to test your A1C every year at your annual physical. Persistent high sugar levels for years can damage your nerves, kidneys, and eyes.

Have you been diagnosed with metabolic syndrome?

People who have at least three of the following five conditions—hypertension, low HDL cholesterol level, abdominal obesity, insulin resistance, and high triglyceride level—meet the diagnostic criteria for metabolic syndrome. They are more likely to develop diabetes and suffer a wide range of cardiovascular problems and strokes. These individuals are also eleven times more likely to develop Alzheimer's disease compared to those without the syndrome.[32] You can ask your doctor to check you for this condition and treat you accordingly.

Do you have a sedentary lifestyle?

Are you fit? As you will see in chapter 13, regular exercise and optimal fitness are the most important ways to boost your brain functions and reduce your risk of cognitive decline with aging. For example, walking ten thousand steps a day is associated with a 50 percent lower risk for developing Alzheimer's disease.[33]

Do you eat junk food regularly?

Do you prefer sugar, salt, fried food, lots of bread and pasta, and sugary treats to lots of veggies, plenty of fiber, seafood, and cooking primarily with olive oil? A heart-healthy diet has a profound impact on reducing levels of plaques and tangles in the brain, lowering your risk of strokes and heart attacks, and soothing the inflammation that destroys the brain. Older people who eat a Mediterranean diet have brains that are eighteen years younger as measured by plaques and tangles.[34]

Issues related to your lungs, kidneys, and liver:
Do you smoke or vape anything?

I'm sure I don't have to tell you that smoking is toxic and damages the brain. Research has consistently linked smoking with increased Alzheimer's disease risk.[35] Vaping is a newer phenomenon, and many people who vape have done so to quit smoking. Vaping is probably preferable to smoking, but the research is still new on this, and there are some preliminary studies suggesting a link between vaping and cognitive decline.[36] Vaping is also just another way to get or stay addicted to nicotine.

Do you have untreated COPD?

One of the consequences of smoking for many years is damage to the airways and lung tissue, leading to chronic obstructive pulmonary disease (COPD). COPD can also happen for other reasons, like chronic exposure to polluted air. Reduced lung reserves send less oxygen to the brain, making exercising more difficult. Both can lead to brain shrinkage. Impaired lung function in patients with COPD is associated with a higher risk of dementia.[37]

Do you snore at night?

If you are overweight, snore many times every hour during sleep, and feel groggy during the day, you may be suffering from obstructive sleep apnea. Undiagnosed or untreated in about 80 percent of the cases,[38] sleep apnea is a significant brain shrinker: The more severe it is, the smaller the hippocampus.[39] Sleep apnea may also increase the risk of cognitive decline or Alzheimer's disease by more than twofold.[40] Sleep apnea is treatable, so if you snore or your bedmate says you stop breathing at night, talk to your doctor about it.

Do you live in a city with severe air pollution?

Research indicates that exposure to air pollution, especially fine particulate matter ($PM_{2.5}$), is associated with brain atrophy and an increased risk of Alzheimer's. A study published in *JAMA Internal Medicine* found that higher levels of $PM_{2.5}$ correlate with more dementia cases developing over time.[41] You may not be able to move to another city, but you can take steps to avoid air pollution whenever possible.

Do you have kidney disease?

Kidney disease is on the rise and, if untreated, can cause toxicity issues that can eventually impact cognitive function and brain size.[42]

Do you drink alcohol every day?

Heavy alcohol consumption (more than one or two drinks a day) is associated with increased risk of liver disease and cancer, but also with Alzheimer's disease.[43] While some studies suggest you should stay away from drinking any amount of alcohol, according to a recent extensive study in England, having two to three drinks *a week* can have some benefit for preserving brain functions with aging, though anything more than one drink a day can cause brain atrophy over time.[44]

Do you have liver disease?

Liver disease, due to alcohol, poor diet, sedentary lifestyle, or any other factor, has been associated with loss of brain volume as well as cognitive decline.[45] Having a damaged liver is associated with a higher risk of Alzheimer's disease and more significant brain atrophy.[46]

Issues related to your mouth, weight, GI tract, and digestion:
Do you have gum disease?

Oral bacteria that enter the bloodstream can infect the brain. Several extensive studies have linked gum disease with dementia or Alzheimer's disease. One study showed that patients with chronic periodontitis and gingivitis are 2.5 times more likely to develop dementia,[47] and another showed that those with chronic periodontitis were more likely to have Alzheimer's disease ten years later.[48]

Is your BMI greater than 30?

You can search "BMI calculator" online to find out. A healthy BMI is between 18.5 and 24.9. Overweight is defined as 25 to 29.9, although there is some controversy about whether this is unhealthy without other medical problems. Obesity is defined as 30 or greater, and severe obesity is defined as 40 or greater. Fact: Obesity shrinks your brain.[49] Although BMI is not always an accurate measure of obesity, many studies that assess the adverse health effects of being overweight use it. For example, one study showed that the higher the BMI, the smaller the brain.[50]

Do you have a big belly?

To determine this, you need to figure out your waist-to-hip ratio (WHR). Measure your waist at your belly button while standing straight and exhaling. Measure your hips at their widest point. Divide your waist measurement by your hip measurement. A WHR of more than 0.85 for women and 0.9 for men indicates abdominal obesity. A WHR higher than 1.0 indicates a much higher chance of health issues.[51] A high WHR correlates with heart disease risk[52] and Alzheimer's risk[53] in many studies.

Do you have frequent bloating, constipation, or diarrhea?

Having digestion problems could be due to known medical conditions such as Crohn's or ulcerative colitis. Other contributors to digestive issues are obesity, stress, and an imbalance of good and bad microbes in your GI tract due to consuming processed food. Another problem is "leaky gut" (intestinal permeability). When inflammation compromises your gut lining, food waste byproducts (i.e., stool content) can leak into your bloodstream and travel to your brain, where they can cause more inflammation and erode the linings of arteries. Leaky gut can lead to leaky brain.[54]

Issues related to your hormones:
Do you have a thyroid condition?

Both hypothyroidism and hyperthyroidism can affect cognitive function and brain volume.[55] Hypothyroidism is common, especially in women, and is due to the thyroid gland not producing enough thyroid hormones to control metabolism properly, leading to fatigue, obesity, cold intolerance, and other problems. Hyperthyroidism can cause nervousness, fatigue, and heart issues. Both can shrink the brain over time.[56] If you often feel tired for no apparent reason, you may have a thyroid issue or a problem with your other hormones. A doctor can assess and treat your hormonal issues.

Are you in menopause, or do you have low testosterone?

During menopause, hormonal fluctuations can profoundly affect a woman's sleep, weight management, and energy levels. These factors often cause significant memory loss as well as other cognitive and emotional symptoms, most of which subside when menopause ends. There are many remedies to deal with any residual symptoms. Older men who have low testosterone also experience a drop in their energy level, stamina, and cognitive capacity. Both conditions can be treated successfully with hormone replacement or natural remedies, under the care of an experienced clinician.

Do you have any vitamin deficiencies?

Low levels of vitamin B_{12} and vitamin D can contribute to memory loss, fatigue, slow thinking, difficulty problem-solving, depression, and a low zest for life. I check the serum levels of these two essential vitamins in all my patients and treat them effectively with supplements or medications.

Do you have anemia?

Iron is a key factor for the production and function of red blood cells and their ability to transport oxygen in the blood. Low iron levels can cause anemia, leading to fatigue, sluggish thinking, poor memory, difficulty maintaining attention for a long time, and cognitive deficits in young or middle-aged people. It has no substantial relation to brain atrophy or risk of Alzheimer's disease.[57]

Do you have low levels of omega-3 fatty acids?
Omega-3 fatty acids, especially DHA and EPA, are critical brain vitamins. DHA is a major component of neuronal membranes, representing up to 90 percent of all the polyunsaturated fatty acids and 20 percent of all the lipids in the brain.[58] I recommend omega-3 supplements to all my patients and take them myself daily (1,000 mg/day). Ask your doctor to test your levels.

Other issues:
Do you suffer from chronic pain?
Persistent back, knee, or shoulder pain for months or years can wear out a person and make them less sharp than usual. The medications for pain, such as gabapentin or opiates, can also contribute to memory loss and grogginess. Most often in middle-aged patients with uncontrolled pain, poor memory is not due to MCI or Alzheimer's disease but to a lack of sufficient sleep, frustration, depression, and the side effects of multiple sedating medications they take.

Do you take too many medications?
What are they, and what are they for? (List them.) Some medications, such as those for ulcers (proton pump inhibitors such as omeprazole), sleep/anxiety (benzodiazepines such as Valium), and allergies (antihistamines such as Benadryl), are linked to brain fog. When taken regularly for many years or decades, they create a higher risk for Alzheimer's disease.[59]

There are a few medications that may lead to a lower risk.[60] These include nonsteroidal anti-inflammatory medications (often used to treat arthritis), medications for diabetes (metformin and GLP-1 agonists such as Ozempic), antidepressants (such as Lexapro or Prozac), phosphodiesterase inhibitors (such as Viagra), and medications for the treatment of high blood pressure (such as calcium channel blockers). Some studies have suggested that statins are associated with memory loss, but others have shown they are associated with a lower risk of Alzheimer's disease, perhaps due to their anti-inflammatory effects.

Talk to your doctor about all the medications you take and whether you need to continue to take them. Ideally, taking fewer medications would be better, as they all have some side effects in some patients, but do not discontinue any medications without your doctor's approval.

Can you hear well?

We get so much mental stimulation from sound. Losing that input can significantly impact how well we interact with the world. Hearing loss can cause loneliness, isolation, and depression, which can all contribute to cognitive decline. You may feel embarrassed when you must keep asking what people are saying, discouraging you from socializing. Hearing loss can accelerate cognitive decline, leading to a higher risk of Alzheimer's disease.[61] One study showed that hearing aids reduced the rate of cognitive decline in older adults by almost 50 percent over three years.[62]

How is your vision?

Many people develop cataracts, glaucoma, or retinal atrophy as they age. When you cannot see very well, you get less brain stimulation. You may stay home more because you can no longer drive. You may be unable to read or use the computer, reducing learning and social interaction. One study of more than 3,800 people showed that seniors with vision problems were more likely to develop Alzheimer's.[63]

The above questions address about 90 percent of the issues that can impact a person's brain in the short and long term. However, there are other issues such as Lyme disease, mold exposure, chronic fatigue syndrome, post-Covid neurological symptoms, use of drugs like cannabis and cocaine, and a series of medical conditions such as fibromyalgia, cancer, and primary neurological disorders that I usually consider in patients who come to see me with concerns about their memory loss, poor focus, or general brain fog. A complete discussion of these issues and conditions is beyond the scope of this book. If you feel you may be suffering from any of them, please discuss them with your doctor.

There is one final question I ask all my patients and focus on discussing with them:

Are you happy?

Whether you are happy is the most important question of all. It may also be the most complex question. Deciding if you are happy is like determining how much money you need. You may realize things could be better, but you are happy where you are anyway. If you are doing all the right things for the biology of your brain, *and* you are happy, then great! But if you could do more right now to reduce your risk of cognitive decline in your eighties and nineties, you will be banking happiness for your future.

And if you are doing obvious things to increase your risk right now, like smoking, not treating your sleep apnea, eating lots of sugar every day, drinking too much alcohol, or never exercising, well . . . this is when I put aside my checklist and look the patient straight in the eye. I say, "It's not a matter of whether you will have a stroke or a heart attack in the future. It's a matter of when. It could be years down the line. It could be tomorrow."

You may be a wonderful person with a nice house, a good job, and a loving family, but how happy will you be if you develop a stroke or dementia and then can't walk or talk, or someone must change your diaper? These are miserable situations that don't happen out of the blue. They happen to people with risk factors. There are a small number of cases that are likely genetic, or of unknown origin, maybe 5 percent for dementia and 20 percent for strokes. Yet, stroke is the number one cause of disability in the United States and the number two cause of death in the world—and a major risk factor for Alzheimer's disease. In most cases, these issues can be prevented.

How's that for motivation?

Going through the above list has probably already given you some great ideas about things you would like to change about your health habits, medical conditions, social connections, and more. Please review this list again and jot down in your Brain Portfolio (the one you created for yourself, or on the template at the end of this chapter) the five things you feel are the most urgent to work on first. Over the next twelve weeks, I want you to be determined and serious about addressing these five issues by following my program and collaborating with your doctor. Fixing these issues may change your life forever. Now that you know the strong link between the five issues you picked and your brain vitality and performance, you will never go back to your old habits—instead, you'll follow lifestyle habits that can make you feel better, grow your brain, and reduce your risk for Alzheimer's disease.

Brain Portfolio Section #3: Blood Tests

Next, to fully understand the potential factors that can impact your brain function, I suggest obtaining the following battery of tests I ordered for my patients. You can request these from your doctor if you haven't had them recently. Keep track of all your test results with dates in your Brain Portfolio, and talk to your doctor about the next steps if anything is out of range or looks concerning. Repeat the tests yearly to track your progress. If something is going in the wrong direction, ask your doctor how you can intervene. *One of the secrets to the success of my program is my insistence that my patients address and treat all their medical issues.*

Below I have listed the basic tests I recommend, along with the range of preferred results (although every lab is different, so in the case of conflicting information, go with the results of the lab that did your test and listen to your doctor's advice). Please remember that the recommended level may vary for people with different medical conditions. For example, a person with a history of heart attacks needs to keep their LDL cholesterol at less than 55 to 70 mg/dL, much lower than people without any history of prior coronary artery disease. Also, please note that the normal range is not the same as the optimal results I list here, which are most conducive for an invincible brain. For example, the normal level of B_{12} in most laboratories is between 200 and 1000 pg/mL, but the optimal range is to have a B_{12} >500 pg/mL.

Total blood cholesterol: should be less than 200 mg/dL
LDL cholesterol: should be less than 100 mg/dL
HDL cholesterol: should be more than 60 mg/dL
Triglycerides (a component of the lipid panel): should be below 150 mg/dL
ApoB (predicts risk of heart attacks): should be less than 90 mg/dL
Lp(a) (another vascular risk factor): should be less than 30 mg/dL
Fasting blood glucose: should be between 70 mg/dL and 99 mg/dL
Fasting insulin (measure of insulin resistance): should be below 8 µIU/mL

Hemoglobin A1c (measure of blood sugar over 3 months): should be less than 5.7%

Ferritin (a measure of iron storage levels): should be 50 to 150 ng/mL

Omega-3 index: should be above 6% (ideal range is 8 to 12%)

Vitamin D: should be between 40–50 ng/ml

Vitamin B$_{12}$: should be over 500 pg/mL

Homocysteine (also a measure of B$_6$/B$_9$/B$_{12}$ deficiency): should be less than 8 μmol/L

Thyroid function: This is a panel of various measures that the lab should flag if any are abnormal.

C-reactive protein (a nonspecific measure of inflammation): should be less than 0.9 mg/L

Reproductive hormone levels (if you are in perimenopause, menopause, or have menstrual irregularities): Results depend on your age and stage

Testosterone: should be around 300–1000 ng/dL in men, and 15–70 ng/dL in women

Optional:
Alzheimer's blood biomarker tests

Consider these tests for someone who has cognitive deficits and is interested in understanding approximate levels of inflammation and neurodegeneration in their brain (while appreciating these tests are new and that they have not yet been fully standardized), to be done under the care of a physician only. It is important to note that these tests are only for people with cognitive deficits, and not those who are just worried about their memory or risk for Alzheimer's disease.

Amyloid-beta 42/40 ratio: should be >0.170:1, but may vary depending on different labs

p-tau-217/Abeta42 plasma ratio: should be < 0.007-0.008, but may vary depending on different labs, and some results may fall in the intermediate "gray zone"

p-tau-217: should be <0.34 ng/L, but may vary depending on different labs

Neurofilament light chain (NfL): varies by age and different labs—for a person in their 20s, <8.4 ng/L, and for a person in their 80s, <51.2 ng/L
Glial fibrillary acidic protein (GFAP): should be <80 ng/L, but may vary depending on different labs

Brain Portfolio Section #4: Fitness and ANS Tests

Fitness and stress management are two of the most important factors for optimal brain health and performance. But what are the tests to most accurately evaluate how fit you are and how well your body is handling your stress?

The best measure of fitness is VO_2 max measurement. As you will learn in more detail in chapter 13, this is the total amount of oxygen you can consume when you exercise at your peak. VO_2 max reflects how well your lungs, heart, muscles, and cardiovascular system work.

A cardiopulmonary exercise, or VO_2 max, test can be obtained in athletic or medical facilities. Smartwatches may also provide you with an approximate VO_2 max. You can also go for a timed run or walk to obtain your VO_2 max using calculations explained in chapter 13.

What about stress? I will go into detail about the autonomic nervous system (ANS), fight-or-flight, rest-and-digest, and how all of that relates to your heart rate variability (HRV) in chapter 16. For now, know that HRV reflects how calm or stressed you are. A higher HRV is better than a lower one because it shows that your heart is more adaptable and flexible, recovering more quickly from stress. Get some baseline HRV measurements at the same time each day for a few days in a row, so you can see how this will improve when you practice mindset and stress management interventions during the program.

Technology now makes it easy to measure HRV, which fluctuates throughout the day depending on your stress and activity level. Most smartwatches or other fitness trackers can give you your HRV measurements. While not perfectly accurate, they do provide fairly good estimates that you can use to monitor your progress with your stress management strategies. You can also ask your primary care physician or cardiologist for this test. Record your results in your Brain Portfolio section four, and get ready to make a plan for improving your fitness and your stress level.

Brain Portfolio Section #5: Miscellaneous Tests

Here are a few other tests to consider if you have issues in any of these areas, such as a suspicion that your hearing isn't as good as it could be, bleeding gums, snoring, or because your doctor recommends them. Ask your doctor about these. Record your results in your Brain Portfolio section five at the end of this chapter.

- Hearing test
- Vision test
- Dental check for gum disease
- Sleep study to check for insomnia and/or sleep apnea
- Cardiac stress test and/or a coronary calcium score (in patients who have multiple vascular risk factors for heart attacks and strokes)
- Brain MRI, if there are concerns about prior strokes or other primary neurological issues
- Skin biopsy Syn-One, if there is a concern for Parkinson's disease or Lewy body dementia
- A brain PET scan, if blood biomarkers for Alzheimer's are inconclusive and if you are being evaluated for receiving anti-amyloid medications
- Blood tests for heavy metals, Lyme disease, mold toxins, or other toxins and infections, if there is a concern for exposure to them or if cognitive symptoms are associated with overall fatigue, malaise, dizziness, rash, enlarged lymph nodes, or abnormal findings on medical history and examination

This list is not comprehensive. If you have symptoms suggestive of iron-deficiency anemia, fibromyalgia, cancer, or dozens of other medical conditions, your doctor will order the appropriate detailed tests for you. The critical point is that almost every illness or disease that impacts your body organs below your neck can affect your brain. *All your medical issues must be controlled and monitored if you want to have a supersharp memory and focus*, both now and in the future. Make sure your doctor has obtained a comprehensive set of blood tests and reviews the results with you in detail. Keep track of everything in your Brain Portfolio.

BRAIN FITNESS CALCULATOR RESULTS

	Your score
Energy level throughout the day (low: very tired to high: very energetic)	1 2 3 4 5
Fitness (low: totally out of shape to high: in great shape)	1 2 3 4 5
Peaceful state of mind (low: stressed out and nervous to high: calm and in control)	1 2 3 4 5
Organized (low: chaos at home and work to high: well-organized most of the time)	1 2 3 4 5
Positive attitude (low: life is tough; everything will fail to high: life is beautiful; everything will work out just fine)	1 2 3 4 5
Satisfactory sleep (low: trouble falling sleep or up all night to high: sleep well, about 8 hours a night)	1 2 3 4 5
Memory for names (low: can't remember anybody's name to high: remember everybody's name)	1 2 3 4 5
Taking Omega-3 Fatty Acid supplements (low: never or one day a week to high: 5 or more days a week)	1 2 3 4 5
Social engagement (low: prefer to stay alone by myself to high: busy with lots of social activities every week)	1 2 3 4 5
Sense of curiosity (low: not too much into figuring things out to high: love to discover new things and solve puzzles)	1 2 3 4 5
Love your daily routine (low: dread my day-to-day routine to high: enjoy and love my daily routine)	1 2 3 4 5
Heart healthy diet choices (low: fast food, donuts, French-fries to high: lots of fruits and vegetables, zero junk food)	1 2 3 4 5
Mindful of portion size (low: eat large portions and second servings to high: prefer small and reasonable portions)	1 2 3 4 5
Extracurricular activities / hobbies (low: do not enjoy participating in activities to high: enjoy trying new hobbies, participating in community activities, volunteering, or helping others in my community)	1 2 3 4 5
Usual mood (low: down and depressed to high: happy and cheerful)	1 2 3 4 5
Add up your score:	

Brain Portfolio Section #6: The Brain Fitness Calculator

Based on my knowledge of all the common factors affecting a person's brain functions, I developed a five-minute screening tool called the Brain Fitness Calculator (on the previous page) that anyone can take and score. This calculator focuses on what I believe to be the most essential brain care elements, to demonstrate to you how well you are taking care of your brain now, so you can assess what to work on during the twelve-week program. The score from this assessment can incentivize you to become proactive in building a stronger brain and appreciate how simple tweaks in your daily activities can reshape your brain for decades to come.

For each item, 1 is "low," and 5 is "high." Record your total score in your Brain Portfolio section six.

How to interpret your Brain Fitness score:

Green zone: 60–75

Good job, keep it up! It appears that you have already addressed many of the factors that can affect your brain. Now, you can improve your great results and go for an A+.

Yellow zone: 45–59

Your brain needs some work. You will benefit greatly from completing my Brain Fitness Program and should see great results quickly.

Red zone: 15–44

You are reporting noticeable problems, which could be due to depression, poor health habits, lack of sleep, uncontrolled medical conditions, or chronic stress. I recommend you start working on your lifestyle habits as soon as possible and complete every step of my Brain Fitness Program diligently. Also, please make an appointment with your doctor for a general workup and complete assessment. The problem is likely simple and treatable. You do not want to walk around with a series of treatable conditions that are shrinking your brain. Please do not ignore your low scores here, and make it a priority to discuss them with your doctor soon, especially for questions in which you gave yourself a score of one or two.

You will calculate your brain fitness score again after six weeks of doing the Brain Fitness Program and then again at the end of the twelve weeks. Record each score in your Brain Portfolio.

Brain Portfolio Section #7: Neurocognitive and Neurobehavioral Spidograms

Remember the spidograms from chapter 11? Now it's your turn. The following two assessments (on pages 192 and 193) aim to help you identify what specific brain-related issues you may suffer and how severe they are. Fill out these spidograms depicting neurocognitive and neurobehavioral symptoms on a scale of 1 to 10, with 1 being "no problem" and 10 being "a major issue that impacts my life." The outer circle represents severe symptoms. The middle circle represents moderate symptoms. The inner circle is minimal. Your results depict where you stand now with regard to your neurocognitive and neurobehavioral symptoms.

To determine the weight of your cognitive symptom load, you must add the numbers you circled for each of the fifteen items in the neurocognitive spidogram. Calculate your total load of neurocognitive symptoms by adding the scores you gave yourself for individual questions. Here, higher numbers are worse. So, red zone is for scores of 120 or higher, yellow zone is for scores of 75 to 119, and green zone is for scores below 74.

To determine the weight of your emotional/behavioral symptom load, add the scores for each of the twenty items in the neurobehavioral spidogram. Here red zone is for scores of 160 or higher, yellow zone is for scores of 100 to 159, and green zone is for any scores below 99.

You can monitor your improvement after six weeks and again after twelve weeks. Write this total number below the spidogram, and in your Brain Portfolio. The appendix shows additional spidograms to fill out for six weeks, twelve weeks, and beyond. These forms are also available on my website: drfotuhi.com.

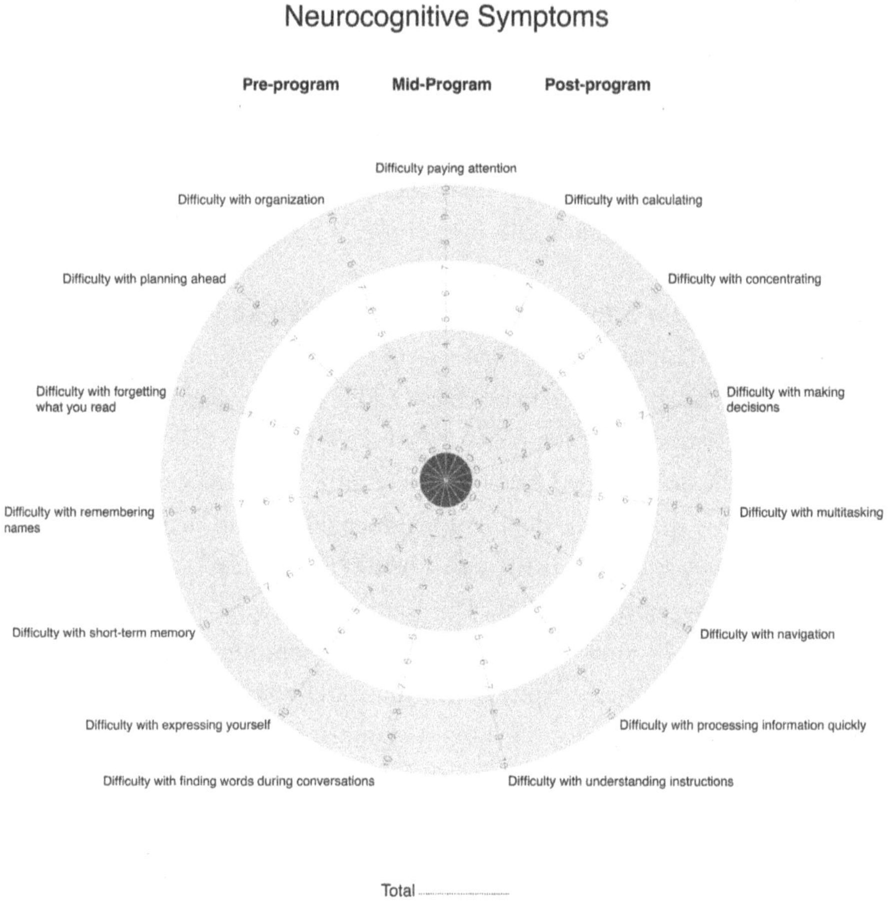

Neurocognitive Symptoms

Pre-program   Mid-Program   Post-program

(Radial chart with the following labels, going around: Difficulty paying attention, Difficulty with calculating, Difficulty with concentrating, Difficulty with making decisions, Difficulty with multitasking, Difficulty with navigation, Difficulty with processing information quickly, Difficulty with understanding instructions, Difficulty with finding words during conversations, Difficulty with expressing yourself, Difficulty with short-term memory, Difficulty with remembering names, Difficulty with forgetting what you read, Difficulty with planning ahead, Difficulty with organization)

Total _____

Brain Portfolio Section #8: Cognitive Testing

No single cognitive test can reflect all your talents, skills, and different forms of intelligence, nor can any test quantify your full brain potential. (Please remember that!) However, we can get a snapshot of how your brain functions in certain cognitive areas, including attention, memory, processing speed, and executive functions. A wide variety of paper-and-pencil and computer-based evaluations can tell you where you stand regarding these common cognitive domains compared to others in your age group.

An advantage of these tests is that they allow you to obtain an objective baseline evaluation and then monitor your progress periodically to see how your brain performance improves within these cognitive domains. It matters less where you are compared to others than it matters how you progress compared to your past scores.

Assess Your Brain Function

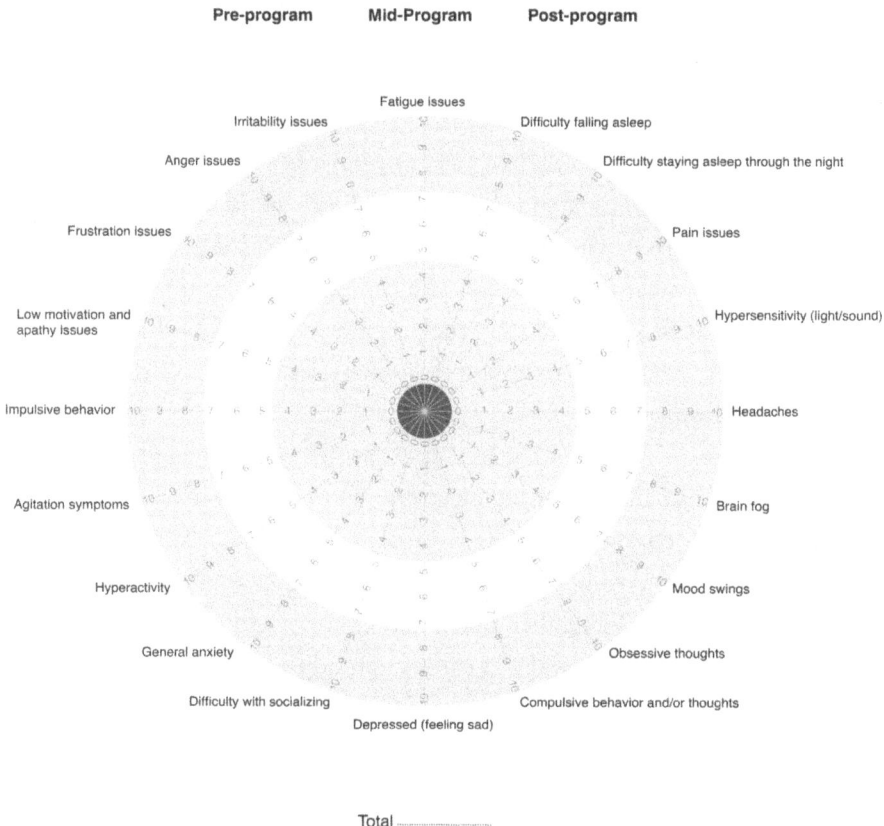

One way to do these tests is via a platform called Lumosity, a brain game app/program. After playing a handful of these games a couple of times, you can see how your scores compare to those of others your age. You can get a free thirty-day membership, and then continue using this platform to keep playing brain games and improving your scores if you enjoy it.

You can also ask your physician to order formal neurocognitive tests (also called a neuropsychological evaluation). These thorough exams, often administered by psychologists or psychometricians, may take six to sixteen hours to complete (done over multiple days) and provide an in-depth and comprehensive assessment of your brain functions. They can be repeated over time to see how your brain is improving (or if it has declined).

You can also consider doing an online version of these tests independently. Here are some companies you can consider for your at-home (confidential) cognitive evaluation: www.braincheck.com, www.creyos.com (previously www.cambridgebrainsciences.com), www.altoida.com, and www.totalbrain.com.

Ideally, you need to complete your assessments and record the results for all the eight sections of your Brain Portfolio checklist on the next page (or using your own method or the app) and then start the program. However, if you are eager to get started, you can complete the questionnaires in sections six and seven and start the program right now—while you are working with your doctor to obtain the other relevant parts of your Brain Portfolio assessments.

Choose two to three of the five brain health pillars, which I will review with you in the upcoming chapters. You can always switch to another track or focus on something else once you have made some progress or decide that something else is more important. Let yourself be flexible and keep working. Remember that small changes add up to significant results. Put in the effort, and you can feel proud that you are building an invincible brain.

Imagine as vividly as you can the version of yourself who is sharper, smarter, more confident, and happier, and then put in the work to get there within twelve weeks. This is such an exciting journey, and I am thrilled to give you specific instructions in the next five chapters on how to achieve your goals.

Brain Portfolio Template

		Findings
Section #1	Purpose:	* * *
	Short-term goals:	* * *
	% of baseline:	
	Your role models	* * *
Section #2	Based on answers to your 40 questions, list the five most important issues to be addressed.	* * * *
Section #3	Blood tests: List abnormal results	* * *
Sections #4	VO2 max results HRV results	* *

Brain Portfolio Template		
		Findings
Section #5	Results from additional tests (if done)	* * *
Section #6	Brain Fitness Calculator score	
Section #7	Scores for your neurocognitive & neurobehavioral questionnaires	* *
Section #8	Results of cognitive evaluation	* * * * *

13

FAST-TRACK YOUR FITNESS

If you could do only one thing, change only one lifestyle element, or adopt only one habit, your best bet for growing your brain and becoming invincible against cognitive decline would be to have a regular habit of daily (or mostly daily) physical activity.

Exercise is the fastest, easiest, most efficient, and most effective lifestyle intervention that has been consistently shown, including in my research and clinical experience, to stimulate growth in the cortex and hippocampus and make a noticeable difference in brain health, brain reserve, and resistance to cognitive decline. It is simply the best thing you can do for your brain and entire body. Whether you love it or hate it, there is no denying that exercise helps your brain grow bigger, function better, and even keep you happier, as it is a potent mood elevator.

If your assessment suggests that you have medical issues such as hypertension or diabetes that could be improved by exercise, and especially if you know you do not get regular exercise and do not work on all the essential aspects of fitness (aerobic capacity, endurance, strength, flexibility, and balance), this is the place to begin your fast-track experience. At NeuroGrow, our top priority after addressing major medical conditions was encouraging patients to boost their physical fitness.

What Good Is Exercise?

Exercise impacts you in numerous ways, such as strengthening, increasing energy, and boosting your self-esteem. You can see the change in your muscles and body shape. You can feel the difference when you go on a walk or climb a flight of stairs. However, there is much more happening when you exercise beyond the obvious. What exercise does biochemically is truly remarkable, so let's take a quick look at what happens inside your brain when you exercise.

Your Mighty Mitochondria

Exercise has a profound impact at the cellular level. Do you remember learning about the contents of a cell in middle school biology class? Every cell is encased in a membrane, has a nucleus at its center, and contains other cellular components, such as lysosomes, Golgi bodies, ribosomes, and mitochondria. The formation of new mitochondria in every cell in your body and brain is one of the most interesting aspects of exercise.

Mitochondria are often referred to as the powerhouses of the cell because they generate chemical energy in the form of adenosine triphosphate (ATP), which powers the cell's systems. You have mitochondria in cells throughout your body, which are highly responsive to your body's activities. Your muscles have a particularly high concentration of mitochondria. Because they produce energy, mitochondria are constantly "aware" of your energy needs. If you sit all day and never exert yourself too much, your mitochondria sense that you don't need very much energy, so they make less ATP. If you are active, using your muscles, the mitochondria in your muscle cells will replicate and increase their ATP production to meet your needs. The same applies to mitochondria in the cells of your heart, lungs, skin, and, of course, your brain.

Neurons have much in common with all your other cells, but are unique in that they have dendrites and an axon. The electric signals that travel down the axons, known as action potentials, require significant energy. Beyond providing fuel for the trillions of action potentials that occur in your brain every second, mitochondria also power all other metabolic activities within the neurons, such as processing the information received via dendrites, maintaining the flow of proteins and chemicals inside the cell, and managing the waste byproducts of these processes. The more mitochondria you have in your neurons, the more energy your brain has to perform its functions, and the more resilient your brain will become. Exercise is a powerful tool to generate fresh new mitochondria in brain cells (and throughout your body).[1]

Nitric Oxide Infusion

Another effect exercise has on the cell is the production of nitric oxide by the endothelial cells lining the blood vessels in your body and brain. Nitric oxide is a molecule that helps dilate blood vessels, allowing more blood, with its oxygen and nutrients, to pass through. This action has many benefits: It reduces blood pressure, plaque formation, and inflammation within blood vessels, and it lowers the risk of heart attacks and strokes while promoting angiogenesis, or the growth of new blood vessels.

Nitric oxide production depends on mitochondria. Mitochondria inside endothelial cells, which cover the inside lining of all the blood vessels in the body, generate the ATP required to produce nitric oxide. Since more exercise leads to increased mitochondria, this translates to higher nitric oxide production, resulting in healthier and more flexible blood vessels and wider channels for delivering oxygen and nutrients to the whole body and the brain.

BDNF Blast

Another excellent benefit of exercise is that it can trigger the release of brain-derived neurotrophic factor (BDNF). BDNF is a potent brain booster that helps grow more neurons and synapses, enhances neuroplasticity, and generally boosts overall brain health. More BDNF generally facilitates better cognitive functions such as improved memory, easier learning, and enhanced executive function. It also protects against Alzheimer's disease.[2] BDNF is something you want in your brain—the more, the better!

The way exercise produces BDNF is complex, but to simplify: Better blood flow and more mitochondria enhance nitric oxide production, which creates ideal conditions for making more BDNF. Exercise triggers this entire process better than any other activity.

The Big (Brain) Picture

Let's review: Exercise increases the demands on mitochondria, which results in more mitochondria producing more ATP in response. This enhances the production of nitric oxide and the dilation of blood vessels, allowing more blood, oxygen, and nutrients to pass through. Meanwhile, more BDNF is released, more blood vessels are formed (angiogenesis), more neurons are generated (neurogenesis), and more synapses and fiber bundles are created. Inflammation decreases, brain size increases, and on top of all that, exercise reduces amyloid[3] and tau levels.[4]

Exercise also makes you feel great. Your brain produces neurotransmitters that make you happy and energetic, thanks to the increased release of serotonin, dopamine, endorphins, and norepinephrine. In the moment, cortisol and adrenaline levels increase with exercise, but over time, these stress hormones decrease and remain lower as you exercise regularly. You will feel more motivated, have increased willpower, enjoy better concentration and focus, and experience greater pleasure and reduced pain. This ultimately leads to improved cognitive function, reduced signs of aging, and increased overall well-being and happiness.

If a magic drug could do all that, it would be the most expensive drug on earth! And yet, exercise is free. Isn't that wonderful?

On a practical level, regular exercise offers numerous benefits for the body. You will be physically stronger, so you can carry heavy things more easily, walk farther, climb more stairs, get up effortlessly from chairs or out of cars, get up quickly from the ground if you fall, and be less likely to fall because better fitness not only makes you stronger but improves core muscles and your balance.

Your bones will be stronger and less likely to break. You'll be more flexible, making you less likely to injure your joints. Exercise improves oxygen delivery to your lungs, heart, kidneys, skin, and endocrine system, all of which help every cell in your body function more effectively and feel younger and fresher. It enhances your metabolism and reduces your risk of diabetes. Increasing the strength of the muscles surrounding your joints can help relieve chronic joint pain. Exercise will sharpen your mind, enabling you to make better decisions, stay motivated, and increase your confidence while fostering a growth mindset. Exercise is the fountain of youth.

Just writing this makes me want to go for a bike ride!

How Fit Are You?

You may think you're fit, but how do you know for sure? Fitness is quantifiable, and understanding your current fitness level can provide a baseline to track your progress as you exercise more regularly. The best way to determine this is by measuring and monitoring your VO_2 max over time.

VO_2 max is a measure of your cardiovascular fitness and endurance and it is based on amount of oxygen you have available to you at maximum effort. This is how athletes determine their cardiovascular fitness and aerobic endurance. Technically, VO_2 max refers to the milliliters of oxygen consumed in one minute per kilogram of body weight. The more milliliters of oxygen you consume in a minute, the more fit you are and the better your lungs, muscles, blood vessels, and heart are at providing you with the oxygen you need to exert maximum effort.

To determine your VO_2 max, check your smartwatch or another fitness tracker. Many fitness trackers estimate your VO_2 max based on your heart rate and speed during exercise. They may have already estimated it or have a program you can use to test it.

For a truly accurate measure, you can visit a medical or athletic facility and run or walk on a treadmill or pedal on a stationary bike while wearing a mask that measures oxygen intake and carbon dioxide output. You can ask your doctor if you can do this in a medical facility, such as a sports medicine clinic, which will likely have the necessary equipment. You can also look for and consult with an exercise physiologist at local gyms in your area. Or, if you want to go low-tech, you can do the Cooper Running Test or the Rockport Walk Test. The Rockport Walk Test is a simple way to estimate your VO_2-max without special equipment. You walk one mile as fast as you can, record your time, and take your heart rate at the finish. Using your age, weight, time, and heart rate, you can calculate your VO_2-max, making this an easy option for tracking your stamina and fitness. I've put these calculations on my website and app at drfotuhi.com.

What Do Your Results Mean?

Although opinions differ somewhat on what constitutes a fit VO_2 max, in general, you can go by this chart or ask your doctor or trainer:

VO_2 Max Ranges for Men and Women (Ages 40–70+)

Age Group	Men (mL/kg/min)	Women (mL/kg/min)
40–49	Good: 42–46 | Average: 34–41	Good: 34–38 | Average: 26–33
50–59	Good: 38–42 | Average: 30–37	Good: 31–35 | Average: 24–30
60–69	Good: 34–38 | Average: 26–33	Good: 28–32 | Average: 20–27
70+	Good: 30–35 | Average: 22–29	Good: 25–29 | Average: 18–24

I suggest measuring your VO_2 max periodically, such as before you start exercising, at six weeks after you have begun working on your exercise goals, and then at twelve weeks. You will likely be amazed at how much your fitness improves when you consistently become more active and maintain that activity level.

A little motivation can go a long way. We have a family friend who is a psychiatrist in her sixties, and she, like so many other people, recently asked me what she could do for her brain to reduce her risk for developing Alzheimer's disease. I told her, "I can't go through everything—you'll have to read my book!—but if I can tell you just one thing, it is to increase your VO_2 max."

My friend looked at her smartwatch and discovered her VO_2 max was 28. I told her mine was 40 and that a watch only gives you an approximate number, but she could raise it by exercising.

My friend is a bit competitive. A group of us was dancing at a party a few weeks later, and my friend began to dance with even more energy. She told me, "I'm going to get my VO_2 max to 35 or 40!" Suddenly, she had a goal, and that made her happy. She was so inspired! She was enjoying herself before, but I could tell she was enjoying herself even more on the dance floor, knowing she was doing something to delay the onset of cognitive problems associated with aging.

Of course, one evening of vigorous dancing is not enough to significantly raise your VO_2 max, and you cannot transition from a sedentary person to someone engaging in high-intensity exercise in just one week without risking injury or burnout. You need to have a solid foundation that you can build upon gradually, starting with your current fitness level.

You might start by building up your step count. If you walk only a couple thousand steps daily, work up to 5,000, and eventually to 10,000. Don't jump right to 10,000 steps if you hardly ever walk. Let 10,000 steps be your goal, but increase it in increments as you become more accustomed to walking and gradually improve your fitness. A recent study showed that walking approximately 10,000 steps a day is associated with a 50 percent reduction in the risk of cognitive decline and Alzheimer's disease.[5] Get more active in general. Play Ping-Pong or pickleball. Go for a swim or a bike ride. Try some calisthenics or take an exercise class. If you think you might enjoy going to a gym, give it a try. Many will offer you a few complimentary personal training sessions. Try incorporating strength training on days when you don't do aerobic exercise. As you build your fitness confidence and abilities, as well as your strength, endurance, and cardiovascular capacity, your VO_2 max will increase.

If you are new to exercise, stay at a level that allows you to carry on a conversation, but be slightly out of breath. This is a great place to build fitness and gradually increase your aerobic capacity, which will increase your VO_2 max. You will be less likely to get injured and recover more quickly than you would from jumping into an intense exercise program.

That's not to say that intense exercise isn't a good idea from time to time. The more fit you become, the more you can include short periods of intensive exercise to further increase your VO_2 max. Do it when you feel ready, and don't sustain it longer than feels relatively comfortable—strenuous but not painful. You should not push yourself too hard to the point that you feel sick or can't catch your breath. It's more important to keep exercise enjoyable and safe.

You can also combine VO_2 max–increasing exercise with other activities that improve memory, learning, executive function, and more. Go on hikes with friends and engage in interesting conversations while enjoying nature. Listen to podcasts while walking or riding a stationary bike. Take golf, tennis, or Zumba lessons and practice your new moves with deep attention. Your VO_2 max will increase before you know it, and along with your muscles, your cortex and hippocampus will also grow larger.

Getting Fitter: The Guidelines

These are my cardinal rules for becoming a regular exerciser.

1. **Set a goal.** Aim to get 5,000 or more steps most days. Walking (for those who are able) is free and requires no special equipment, so it's easy to achieve this goal. In addition to getting as many steps as you can in one day, I also recommend getting a minimum of three hours of intentional exercise, such as running, swimming, or any other sports you enjoy, per week. You can play tennis for ninety minutes on a weekend and then get two forty-five-minute aerobic classes two days a week. Or you may go for a three-hour hike with your friends on a weekend. Set your goal and work up to it.

2. **Have fun.** When you first start exercising regularly, the most crucial concern is to do something you like. The best exercise in the world won't help you if you don't do it. Enjoying yourself is the secret to fitness success. Walking is a good place to start, but many options exist to mix up your routine. Perhaps you enjoy sports and want to learn tennis, pickleball, or take a dance class. If you don't like the gym, don't go to the gym. If you love the gym, start going more often. Maybe you prefer biking or swimming. Create a list of the activities you enjoy. The more items on the list, the more varied your exercise can be, which is excellent for someone who likes novelty. Or maybe you enjoy doing the same thing every day. That's fine too, but be sure to include some cardio, resistance, flexibility, and balance training.

3. **Cover your fitness bases.** Fitness doesn't just mean doing cardio daily, working a few weight machines at the gym, or doing only yoga. Those are all great ways to get and stay fit, but ideally, you should engage in some form of aerobic exercise to benefit your heart and lungs, some form of strength training to build your muscles, and some form of stretching and balance to keep you limber and on your feet. If you only do cardio, start incorporating weights into your routine a few times a week and add flexibility exercises, such as Pilates. If you only practice yoga, consider adding cardio and strengthening poses that require lifting your body weight. If you only do weightlifting, add some gentle

stretching afterward, and also include an aerobic activity to raise your heart rate.
4. **Start where you are.** Consider your current fitness level when creating your plan. If you are not exercising, don't jump into hour-long gym sessions; you will likely burn out or injure yourself. Keep it pleasant. Walk for five to seven minutes today, then take a break. Respect your body. If you exercise occasionally, continue your routine, but do it three times a week instead of once, or five times a week instead of three. If you already exercise daily but want to push yourself a little harder or longer, consider increasing your time by five or ten minutes, adding more resistance and weight, or incorporating a complementary activity.
5. **Be persistent and consistent.** Even when you don't feel like it, follow your plan and do it on a regular schedule as much as possible. This is how you build a habit. Once you become accustomed to exercising regularly, you won't feel good without it. Exercise on most days, rest when you are genuinely exhausted, get enough sleep, eat a balanced diet to support your efforts, and get back out there. When it feels challenging, remind yourself of the benefits of exercise on your brain. Reread the beginning of this chapter. And just. Keep. Going.

Make Your Plan

I've compiled a list of various fitness activities for you to choose from. Review this list and check all the items that appeal to you, are suitable for your fitness level and abilities, and that you are willing to try. No pressure—you can check something and never do it, but I want you to have options over the next twelve weeks. (Of course, you can add anything you like to do that isn't on this list.)

Once you have your list, select one to three tasks to accomplish every day. Make your daily choices based on your energy level, ability, and overall well-being. Some days, you will likely want to do more, and some days less, but always do something.

Fitness Activities to Choose From
- Walking
- Jogging
- Running
- Combined walking, jogging, and running along your route
- Any of the above on a treadmill
- Training for a 5K
- Long-distance running
- Training for a half-marathon or marathon
- Biking
- Stationary biking
- Swimming in a pool
- Water aerobics classes
- Swimming in open water
- Kayaking
- Paddleboarding
- Training for an Olympic triathlon or just a short sprint triathlon
- Weightlifting with weight machines or free weights (at home or the gym)
- Exercising with resistance bands at home
- Weight machines at a gym
- Free weights at a gym
- Weightlifting class (like BODYPUMP)
- Circuit training at a gym
- Calisthenics (e.g., sit-ups, push-ups, jumping jacks, jumping rope, burpees)
- Aerobics class
- Circus classes (such as aerial silks, trapeze, and pole fitness)
- Roller-skating/Rollerblading
- Jumping on a trampoline
- Ice-skating
- Tennis
- Pickleball
- Racquetball

- Golf (walk, no cart)
- Hitting balls at a batting cage
- Team sports (such as basketball, volleyball, soccer, baseball, and softball)
- Yoga (at home or in a class)
- Pilates (at home or in a class)
- Barre (at home or in a class)
- Dance classes (ballet, jazz, ballroom, Latin, Zumba, etc.)
- Martial arts class
- High-intensity interval training
- Swimming (long sessions)
- Biking (high intensity or long distances)
- Competitive sports (e.g., soccer, volleyball)
- Hiking
- Rock climbing
- Skiing or snowboarding
- Cross-country skiing
- Snowshoeing
- Yard work, like mowing, raking, or gardening
- Cleaning, like scrubbing, mopping, sweeping, and vacuuming
- Playing with kids or dogs (e.g., playground, tag, fetch)
- If you are injured, physical therapy exercises or simple chair exercise

Rate your progress regarding your fitness improvements either here or on the app. Give yourself a score of zero to 10, based on how well you exercise every day. Give yourself a zero if you don't do much activity on that day, and 10 if you feel very satisfied with your level of exercise. Determine your weekly score the same way, also from 0 to 10, based on how well you met your exercise goals for that week. Make sure to measure your VO_2 max at baseline, after six weeks, and after 12 weeks.

Your Exercise Tracker

Rate your progress each day and each week on a scale of 0 to 10

	MON	TUES	WED	THURS	FRI	SAT	SUN	WEEKLY SCORE
VO₂ MAX AT START:								
WEEK 1								
WEEK 2								
WEEK 3								
WEEK 4								
WEEK 5								
WEEK 6								
VO₂ MAX AFTER WEEK 6:								
WEEK 7								
WEEK 8								
WEEK 9								
WEEK 10								
WEEK 11								
WEEK 12								
VO₂ MAX AFTER WEEK 12:								

14

FAST-TRACK YOUR SLEEP

Sleep may seem like the most passive thing you do in twenty-four hours, but sleep is not passive at all. It's quite an active state. A lot goes on as you lie there, barely moving. Sleep is a biological necessity. During sleep, your body restores its energy, repairing muscles, clearing the brain of waste, repairing injuries and organ damage, consolidating memories, and processing experiences. It's like the cleaning crew coming into the building overnight to clean and repair everything. Over time, regular high-quality sleep reduces your risk of many health problems, including strokes and Alzheimer's disease.

Getting enough but not too much sleep and achieving good-quality sleep are the next most important things, after exercise, that you can do to prevent brain shrinkage, stay smarter, and maintain a good mood, a positive attitude, and a growth mindset. Even if you think you get enough sleep most of the time, you may be surprised at how much better you can feel if you regularly focus on maximizing the quality and quantity of your body's all-important nightly period of rejuvenation. During deep sleep, your brain repairs and refreshes everything that has broken down or worn out.

Sleeping well helps you stick to your resolve in many other areas, such as completing your work, focusing, concentrating, and making healthy food and exercise choices. Without enough sleep, all these things feel much more challenging. Do yourself a favor and allow yourself to operate at your highest level by getting seven to eight hours of satisfactory sleep!

If your assessment suggests that you have sleep issues, whether insomnia or sleep apnea, or you know you're not devoting enough time to sleep, this is the place to start your fast-track experience.

Stages of Sleep, Dreams, and Glymphatic Operations

The different stages of sleep are based on various brain wave patterns we all experience during sleep. There are four sleep stages: N1, N2, N3, and REM. During approximately the first hour of sleep, your brain waves gradually slow down, transitioning from N1, the light sleep stage, to N2, and then to N3, the deep sleep stage. During deep sleep, your body fully relaxes, breathing slows, and it becomes difficult to awaken. After about an hour, your brain quickly returns to N2, then to N1, and finally to REM sleep, which is the stage of sleep when you are dreaming and are closer to being awake. Your body muscles shut down during this stage—usually, you cannot move—but your brain remains quite active.

Under your closed eyelids, during REM sleep, your eyes dart back and forth quickly, hence the term REM, which stands for rapid eye movement. After five to twenty minutes of REM sleep, this seesaw pattern repeats itself. Your brain gradually dips deep into N2 and N3 deep sleep again, and after about an hour, it returns to REM sleep. You will experience four to five of these ninety-minute cycles throughout the night. During the first half of the night, you spend more time in the deep stages of sleep; during the second half, you spend more time in the REM stage, which explains why most people tend to dream more in the early-morning hours.

Because deep sleep tends to happen at the beginning of the night, staying up too late can sometimes keep you from getting enough deep sleep. You may switch too quickly into REM sleep, preventing your glymphatic system from having enough time to do its rinsing job. Going to bed a little earlier can make a big difference in getting enough deep sleep.

I've already told you about the glymphatic system—how it flushes your brain with cerebrospinal fluid (CSF) to clear out the byproducts of your brain's metabolism and remove accumulated amyloid as well as any foreign material that has leaked through the blood-brain barrier. As you remember from chapter 8, one of the primary ways to avoid Alzheimer's disease is to prevent the accumulation of amyloid. Sufficient deep sleep is crucial for maximizing amyloid clearance from the brain and minimizing the risk of brain atrophy and Alzheimer's disease.[1]

The glymphatic system is always working, but for some reason we do not fully understand, this process is most active during deep sleep (it also increases during exercise). During sleep, neurons and astrocytes contract, creating more space for CSF to flow in and out of brain tissue, likely facilitating the glymphatic cleaning and housekeeping process. Untreated insomnia, sleep apnea, or other factors that interfere with deep sleep (such as staying up too late working or watching television) can all shorten the rinsing time in your brain. Going to bed earlier can give your brain more time in deep sleep.

Without enough sleep, your body organs will begin to break down too. When muscles and other organs don't have enough repair time, they age more rapidly and function less efficiently. Meanwhile, you get irritable, grumpy, and tired. You may lose the willpower to maintain healthy lifestyle habits like making good food choices and exercising regularly, leading to a higher risk of obesity and other chronic diseases. I would even go so far as to say that optimal health becomes impossible without regular, uninterrupted sleep of seven to eight hours per night.

The Problem with Insomnia

Our drive to sleep, or sleep pressure, is influenced by the amount of sleep we got the night before and our level of tiredness during the day. The more physically and mentally challenged we are throughout the day, the more this sleep pressure increases. Typically, sleep pressure should be low in the morning when you are well-rested and high in the evening after an active day, so you feel ready to sleep. If you don't get good-quality sleep throughout the night because you stay up late too often, worry about things at night, work late, or toss and turn, this normal process can get out of sync. You may feel high sleep pressure in the morning and then feel so strung out that you have trouble relaxing enough to fall asleep at night.

Circadian rhythm, the natural sleep rhythm in humans (and animals), regulates sleep. In response to darkness, the pineal gland, a tiny, pea-shaped structure located deep within the brain, releases melatonin, which helps you fall asleep and stay asleep throughout the night. Exposing yourself to bright lighting or screens in the evening can confuse this natural process, delaying the release of melatonin and causing problems falling asleep.

Other factors that can disrupt your natural circadian rhythm include flying across time zones, which causes circadian rhythm disruption, and working the night shift. Working the night shift regularly may impact your brain health long-term. One study of nineteen nurses who worked the night shift and twenty nurses who worked the day shift showed that night-shift workers had more brain atrophy and were more likely to have depression.[2] Even switching to and away from daylight saving time can disrupt circadian rhythm for a few days.

The combination of regular poor-quality sleep and frequent disruption of circadian rhythm, as well as some medical conditions, can lead to chronic insomnia. The longer you suffer from insomnia, the more amyloid you accumulate in your brain and the more likely it is for you to suffer a heart attack or a stroke.

Do You Have Chronic Insomnia?

The criteria for a diagnosis of insomnia include the following symptoms:

- Having difficulty falling or staying asleep more than three times weekly for more than three months
- Early awakening
- Feeling tired during the day
- Having problems with mood and memory
- Feeling hyperactive and stressed

If you occasionally feel this way, that's normal, and the interventions in this chapter will likely help you. If, however, you think you might have chronic insomnia, talk to your doctor about testing and treatment. A standard questionnaire doctors use to assess insomnia is the Pittsburgh Insomnia Rating Scale, which can be found online.

Your doctor may order a sleep study, known as polysomnography, which records the frequency and duration of different sleep stages and measures your breathing, oxygen levels, muscle movements, snoring, eye movements, and heart rate changes. While sleep studies were once conducted in hospitals or sleep centers, they can now often be done at home using simple equipment. Your doctor can guide you on interpreting these results and providing you with a treatment plan. Additionally, consider the interventions listed at the end of this chapter.

Insomnia is a big problem for many people. It is the most common sleep disorder in the United States, affecting about 30 percent of the general population some of the time and 10 to 15 percent of the population chronically.[3]

There are many causes for chronic insomnia. These include overwhelming stress, physical pain, an irregular sleep schedule, mental health disorders like depression or anxiety, and medical conditions such as asthma, COPD, high blood pressure, heart failure, menopause, arthritis, fibromyalgia, reflux disorder, or cancer. Medications that have a sedating effect, like antihistamines or pain medications, can cause daytime fatigue, and sleeping during the day can then make it more difficult to sleep at night. Many sleep medications help you sleep when you need them, but they disrupt your sleep when you go off them (this is called rebound insomnia).[4] These medications include benzodiazepines and "Z-drugs," a class of non-benzodiazepine sleep medications including zolpidem (Ambien), zopiclone, and zaleplon.

Older people tend to have more insomnia than young people, at a rate of about 30 to 48 percent of people over sixty.[5] Older people may have pain conditions, depression, sleep apnea, or take medications that make it hard to fall or stay asleep. Other neurological issues can also cause insomnia, such as restless legs syndrome, peripheral neuropathy, sleepwalking, and less common disorders like sleep paralysis and REM behavior disorder (which can happen in people with Parkinson's disease).

Insomnia can also be caused by something as simple as eating too much or too close to bedtime (and/or the reflux and heartburn associated with it), having too much caffeine late in the day, drinking too much alcohol, or smoking too much. You may also be in the habit of staying up too late, scrolling on your phone, or binge-watching your favorite show. Oftentimes, there are multiple factors involved.

Chronic insomnia can trigger other health conditions like chronic stress and anxiety when your inability to fall asleep becomes its own source of stress. If you have chronic worry about work, school, money, or life circumstances such as being a caregiver to a child with autism or a spouse with cancer, you can have a physical response. Your body may release too much adrenaline and cortisol, making it feel impossible to relax, let alone fall asleep. Generalized anxiety disorder, depression, and repetitive negative thoughts can also interfere with sleep.

MRI studies of people with chronic insomnia show gray matter atrophy and reduced vitality and functions of fiber bundles in the brain. A study of 147 adults, with an average age of fifty-three, who underwent baseline and additional MRIs three to four years later, found that poor sleep quality was associated with reduced brain volume, particularly in adults over sixty.[6] The longer you experience insomnia, the smaller your hippocampus becomes. A bout of insomnia here and there, or even one that lasts a year or two, may not affect the size of your hippocampus, but research has shown that prolonged poor sleep, such as over twenty years, progressively shrinks the hippocampus.[7]

By elevating levels of inflammation in the brain, increasing the amount of amyloid plaques and tau tangles, and lowering levels of BDNF, chronic insomnia is associated with more than a twofold increased risk of developing Alzheimer's disease.[8] The consequences in everyday life include feeling tired or unwell, slower response times (which can increase the risk of accidents), poor memory, irritability, increased arguments with family members or co-workers, feelings of depression, withdrawal from social contact, and difficulty concentrating. Over the long term, that can lead to chronic anxiety and depression, chronic memory loss, depressed immune function, muscle pain and weakness, low sex drive, and a higher risk of hypertension, obesity, diabetes, heart attacks, and strokes. Eventually, it can even lead to a shorter lifespan!

Insomnia is certainly not something to accept as normal. Take action if your goal is to build brain reserve and prevent brain shrinkage. Here are some strategies you can consider.

Strategies for Treating Insomnia

Fortunately, many sleep issues are relatively easy to resolve, even if it may not feel that way to you right now. There are many effective interventions for sleep issues. Let's examine what they are and why they are so important:

Have a positive attitude toward resolving your sleep issues. In my experience, many people believe poor sleep, like stress and anxiety, is just a common problem that affects everyone and for which there is no permanent solution. This is the wrong mindset to approach insomnia. You need a positive attitude and to believe your sleep will improve in the next twelve weeks. The interventions listed here are effective for most people but require persistence. Picture how much better you will feel if you regularly get seven to eight hours of sleep most nights. Keep in mind that by doing so, you are also reducing your risk for many severe conditions, including heart attacks, strokes, and Alzheimer's disease.

Address medical issues robbing you of quality sleep. Talk to your doctor about chronic pain, fibromyalgia, lupus, menopause, or other hormone irregularities, heart failure, diabetes, gastric reflux, frequent urination at night, asthma, or other medical problems that are interfering with your ability to sleep well through the night. Successful treatment of these medical conditions will improve your sleep.

Consider healthy snacks before bed. Some foods can gently support better sleep by providing nutrients that promote relaxation and the production of melatonin, the body's natural sleep hormone. For example, yogurt is rich in calcium and tryptophan, which help the brain create melatonin and serotonin. Other great sleep-friendly options include cherries, which naturally contain melatonin, and kiwis, which are packed with antioxidants and serotonin. Bananas offer magnesium and vitamin B_6, both helpful for calming the nervous system, while almonds provide healthy fats and magnesium. Thanks to their complex carbohydrates and melatonin content, even a small bowl of oats can be beneficial. Pairing these foods with a warm cup of chamomile tea can make for a soothing bedtime routine.

Dig into psychological causes of your insomnia and address them. If too much stress, anxiety, or depression is keeping you awake at night, consider cognitive behavioral therapy for insomnia (CBT-I) before resorting to sleep medications. A therapist will help you review your thoughts, behaviors, and emotions associated with sleep and provide strategies such as limiting time in bed to improve sleep efficiency, using the bed only for sleep, addressing negative thoughts about sleep, and practicing relaxation techniques. CBT-I is typically delivered over several weeks and is considered the most effective long-term treatment for insomnia, often more effective than sleeping pills. Research shows that CBT-I can grow your brain, a solid indicator of its profound benefits for your brain.[9] I consider sleep medications a last resort due to the side effects and potential rebound insomnia.

Improve your sleep hygiene. Sleep hygiene refers to the regular practices that help you sleep better, such as taking a nightly hot shower, avoiding caffeine in the afternoon, keeping your bedroom as dark and quiet as possible, avoiding large or spicy meals in the evening, reading a book before bed, and practicing meditation or deep breathing exercises. These commonsense interventions, which I have listed at the end of this chapter, work very well. The problem is that people often don't do them religiously for at least two weeks, so they fail to see the full benefits. Join the ranks of successful sleepers by committing to good sleep hygiene.

Insomnia Intervention: Increase Your Sleep Pressure

For my patients who had chronic insomnia—maybe they get only four hours of sleep on most nights—I helped them use sleep pressure to their advantage. Once I established that they had no active medical issues causing their insomnia and had already tried the standard sleep hygiene recommendations, I would work with them to build up their sleep pressure. (Warning: This can be temporarily challenging during the day due to daytime sleepiness, so it may be beneficial to try this when you have some time off work or don't have responsibilities such as driving or caring for young children.)

I recommend you work with a therapist who has expertise in cognitive behavioral therapy for insomnia and do the following: Let's say you usually wake up at 8:00 a.m. Keep yourself awake until 4:00 a.m. on the first night, no matter what. Don't go to bed. Read, write, type, work, watch TV, whatever. Just don't go to bed until 4:00 a.m. Then, go to sleep and set your alarm for 8:00 a.m. (You can adjust these times to your standard wake-up time. The goal is to get just four hours of sleep. If you don't have a regular wake-up time, set one.)

Do this for three nights, sleeping only from 4:00 a.m. to 8:00 a.m. Do not take a nap during the day. You will notice yourself feeling increasingly tired over the three days—you are building up sleep pressure. You may feel like you are dying to go to sleep. Stay strong! You are doing this for yourself to help recalibrate your body and solve your insomnia. The more sleep pressure you build up, the easier it is to sleep regularly.

On the fourth day, add half an hour to your sleep. Go to bed at 3:30 and wake up at 8:00. The next night, add another half an hour, sleeping from 3:00 to 8:00. The next night, add another half hour, sleeping from 2:30 to 8:00. Keep going, adding just thirty minutes each night until you have gotten to your goal, such as sleeping for seven or eight hours.

If this feels too extreme, you can start with five hours a night and work up from there. This strategy proved highly effective for many of my patients.

The Problem with Sleep Apnea

Obstructive sleep apnea (OSA) is another common problem that interferes with sleep, sometimes severely. OSA is the most common sleep disorder globally, affecting 936 million adults between the ages of thirty and sixty-nine.[10] In the United States, 33.9 percent of men and 17.4 percent of women have OSA, but rates are also high in China, with 24.2 percent of both men and women afflicted. Rates in Germany, Japan, and Poland range from 20 to 40 percent.

OSA refers to a condition in which the airway is blocked during sleep as the soft tissues in the back of the throat collapse partially or completely, causing breathing to stop for up to 40 to 50 seconds. The person may wake up gasping for air but go back to sleep without realizing they experienced an episode unless their partner says something about snoring or gasping at night. In severe cases, this can happen 30 to 70 times an hour! Just imagine how horrible it would be for a person to wake up 200 to 300 times in one night, each time gasping for air because their oxygen levels have dropped dangerously low. No wonder patients with severe OSA feel tired and groggy during the day!

OSA is more common in men and increases with weight gain (it affects 45 percent of people with obesity) because excess fat tissue around the airways makes it easier for them to get compressed. It's also worse in smokers, who retain fluid in their upper airways, and in people who drink alcohol because of the relaxing effect on throat muscles. It's worse in people who sleep on their backs because the position allows the throat muscles to collapse more easily.

Symptoms of OSA, many of which are similar to having insomnia, include feeling tired during the day, irritability, mood swings, difficulty paying attention and concentrating, sexual dysfunction, and morning headaches due to low oxygen levels during the night. These can be severe. Sleep apnea increases cortisol levels, promotes excessive blood coagulation, and reduces blood flow to the brain. In a study of twenty patients with OSA and twenty-one without it, brain MRIs of the patients with OSA showed marked atrophy in many areas of the brain.[11]

OSA also targets the vulnerable hippocampus. Researchers examined sleep studies and brain MRI data from volunteers who had previously participated in an aging study but showed no cognitive symptoms. They found that individuals with mild or no respiratory distress due to OSA had normal hippocampal volume. In contrast, those with the most severe OSA and subsequent respiratory distress (experiencing oxygen levels below 89 percent for prolonged periods during the night) exhibited marked hippocampal atrophy.[12]

Even children can be affected, especially if they are obese. One study compared brain MRIs of sixteen children with OSA to two hundred healthy children, finding that kids with OSA had marked brain atrophy in many areas related to cognitive function and mood.[13]

When untreated over time, people with OSA have a much higher risk of strokes, heart attacks, congestive heart failure, irregular heartbeat (arrhythmia), depression, anxiety, obesity, diabetes, brain atrophy, progressive cognitive decline with age, and Alzheimer's disease.[14] Individuals with Alzheimer's disease are five times more likely to have OSA compared to age-matched controls, with approximately 50 percent of Alzheimer's patients experiencing OSA.[15] Among patients with a stroke, 70 percent have had OSA.[16]

Sleep apnea is not something to ignore in anyone of any age because it can have serious short-term and long-term effects. However, when treated successfully many consequences of OSA, including brain atrophy, can be successfully reversed.[17] Patients who receive treatment often report having more energy and feeling sharper.

OSA is a horrible disease that, unfortunately, many people do not take seriously. Fortunately, treating OSA can save your brain by reducing your risk for strokes and Alzheimer's disease.

Strategies for Treating Sleep Apnea

The first thing to do after receiving a confirmed diagnosis of OSA via a sleep study is to address causes and risk factors. Weight loss often helps people who are obese or overweight—in many cases, weight loss alone resolves mild cases of OSA. Other effective strategies include reducing or eliminating alcohol, avoiding back sleeping, and addressing respiratory issues like asthma, COPD, and allergies. In moderate to severe cases, CPAP therapy could save your life. CPAP (Continuous Positive Airway Pressure) is a treatment for sleep apnea that gently blows air through a mask to keep your airway open while you sleep. This prevents pauses in breathing, improves oxygen levels, and helps you feel more rested in the morning. CPAP machines are smaller, more comfortable, and more portable than they once were, and the oxygen they provide is critical for the brain.

Other options include oral appliances that can maintain your jaw forward, preventing your tongue from falling back and blocking your airways. You can get these from a dentist or an ENT doctor. There are also surgical options that remove the excess amount of soft tissue in the back of your throat. About twenty years ago, my wife had pointed out to me that I snored and my sleep study confirmed that I indeed had mild OSA. Knowing how important this issue is, I decided to undergo uvulopalatopharyngoplasty (UPPP), a surgical procedure that resected my uvula, soft palate, and tonsils (which were quite large). This procedure worked well for me and I never snored again.

There is now a less invasive procedure called hypoglossal nerve stimulation. It stimulates the cranial nerve that moves the tongue forward with each breath, creating more space for air to flow in the back of your throat. Consult with your doctor to discuss your options.

Make Your Plan

I've compiled a list of sleep hygiene interventions that can help you sleep better, longer, and more deeply, allowing you to achieve sufficient deep sleep and glymphatic system activity to clean your brain thoroughly. It's incredible how much better people feel when they regularly get adequate sleep—a sleep hygiene routine is worth every effort.

Review this list and check all the items you can do and are willing to try. Once you have your list, select one to three tasks to accomplish every night. If you still have trouble sleeping, try a few other things. If you're a good sleeper, try to get even better sleep. If you have the technology (or are willing to purchase it), use a sleep tracker to monitor your current sleep patterns and observe how your sleep improves as you gradually enhance your sleep hygiene.

SLEEP HYGIENE PRACTICES TO CHOOSE FROM

- Go to bed at the same time every night.
- Wake up at the same time every morning.
- If you can't sleep, don't toss and turn. Get up and do something calming, like reading. Let your sleep pressure build up.
- Sleep in total darkness, using a sleep mask to cover your eyes or blackout curtains.
- Sleep in total quiet, or use earplugs if you can't control the noise in your environment.
- Replace your mattress with a comfortable, supportive one that feels good and doesn't cause pain.
- Wash your sheets and pillowcases weekly.
- Keep your bedroom spotlessly clean. Please do not use it as a storage space.
- Decorate your bedroom in a way that makes you love being in there. It should feel relaxing and refreshing to be in your bedroom. Use it only for sleep, reading, and sex. Let it be your sanctuary.
- Remove any electronics from the bedroom, such as televisions and computers.
- Take a hot shower or bath before bed. Warm water stimulates blood flow to the extremities, which can help cool you off and improve your sleep quality.[18] Some people prefer a cold shower, but more research favors hot showers.
- Practice deep breathing for five minutes within the hour before bed. Try breathing in for a count of six, holding your breath for a count of three, and then exhaling for a count of six. Deep breathing helps increase melatonin production for a natural sleep aid produced in your brain.[19]
- Practice meditating before bed. A meta-analysis of eighteen studies involving more than 1,500 patients demonstrated that meditation can significantly enhance sleep quality.[20] Start with five minutes and work up to twenty minutes. There are apps with good sleep meditations you can follow or listen to.

- Do some relaxing yoga poses. Yoga can improve sleep quality, reduce anxiety and depression, and help with chronic insomnia.[21]
- Avoid loud noises, bright lights, and stimulating conversations (especially arguments) a few hours before bed.
- Try aromatherapy. Use a diffuser in your bedroom to gently diffuse essential oils known for their sleep-improving properties, such as lavender, chamomile, cedarwood, or sandalwood.
- Take a magnesium supplement before bed.[22]
- Try a melatonin supplement.[23] Some people say they have rebound insomnia when they stop taking melatonin, but in a 2023 review of the current studies on this subject, researchers determined there are no significant negative effects from taking or stopping melatonin.[24]
- Sip on relaxing herbal teas (no caffeine) before bed, such as chamomile.
- Play white noise or nature sounds, such as waves, wind, or birds, to help you sleep.
- Listen to a quiet, soothing story or relaxing music. Some apps have sleep tracks for this purpose.
- Read an actual book in bed rather than looking at your phone.
- Avoid looking at screens for at least one hour before going to bed.
- Do not eat anything other than small snacks to improve your sleep within three hours of bedtime.
- Stop all caffeine intake by noon.
- Don't drink alcohol.

Your Sleep Tracker

Rate your progress here or on the app. Score yourself from zero (very poorly) to 10 (wonderful), based on how well you have slept every night. Every week, give yourself a score from zero to 10 based on your overall sleep quality and quantity for that week and how well you met your goals. You can also keep track of how many hours you slept, to see if you improve over the twelve weeks.

	MON	TUES	WED	THURS	FRI	SAT	SUN	WEEKLY SCORE
Average hours of sleep per night at baseline:								
WEEK 1								
WEEK 2								
WEEK 3								
WEEK 4								
WEEK 5								
WEEK 6								
Average hours of sleep per night after six weeks:								
WEEK 7								
WEEK 8								
WEEK 9								
WEEK 10								
WEEK 11								
WEEK 12								
Average hours of sleep per night after twelve weeks:								

15

FAST-TRACK YOUR NUTRITION

For some reason, when it comes to preventing Alzheimer's and boosting your memory, people always ask about food first. Not exercise, not sleep. While I still believe exercise is the most significant influence on the brain, and sleep is necessary for brain health and energy to make lifestyle changes, there is no doubt that how you eat significantly affects your brain. Nutrition also impacts all parts of your body that directly influence your brain, such as your blood sugar levels, inflammation, the amount of BDNF you can generate, body fat percentage, and the composition of your gut microbiome.

But people don't often think of food in that functional context. They view food as a source of pleasure, a means to come together with friends, comfort, and a daily ritual. Food is all those things. It's such a big part of our lives, so it's no surprise we focus on it. Food has been a vital component of our survival for millions of years. We had to eat it, no matter how it tasted. Today, many of us are lucky enough to have enough food and the privilege of focusing on flavor and enjoyment. We can learn about nutrition and eating for good health. Yet even though we know that food affects our health and how we feel, these are not often the primary concerns when we are hungry for dinner.

But you can choose food that is pleasurable, comforting, *and* functional. For our purposes, food is medicine for the brain. It can be used like a medicine to help resolve or reduce metabolic issues, gastrointestinal problems, oxidative stress, and inflammation. It can be a pivotal support for brain health and function. However, food can also cause or contribute to metabolic issues, obesity, oxidative stress, inflammation, and brain shrinkage. Understanding which foods help and hurt is essential, and it's even more motivating if you know why.

If your Brain Portfolio assessments indicate that you have dietary issues related to nutritional deficiencies, inflammation, and/or metabolic health, this is a good area to focus on.

The Brain-Gut Connection

There is a special connection between the brain and the gut. The gut-brain axis is the direct line between the central nervous system and the digestive tract. Why are these two so especially connected? The gut has its own nervous system, known as the enteric nervous system. Yes, there are neurons in your digestive tract that operate independently of your brain, although they are constantly communicating with each other. This two-way communication happens through a major nerve highway called the vagus nerve. It originates in a few nuclei in the brain stem and extends through the heart, lungs, and digestive tract, ultimately reaching the colon.

Problems in the brain, how you feel, and your stress level can affect how well your digestive system functions and which types of microbes survive and thrive in your gastrointestinal tract. Digestive symptoms can affect the brain too, and cause nonspecific symptoms such as brain fog, fatigue, and mood swings. The inflammation that travels from the gut to the brain can alter the level of neurotransmitters, which can significantly impact your health and the vitality of your brain. Eating junk food consistently for decades can lead to brain atrophy and Alzheimer's disease.[1]

Who Are You Feeding?

You've probably heard of the gut microbiome. This collection of bacteria, fungi, viruses, and other microbes lives symbiotically with you inside your digestive tract. Technically, they are called the microbiota.

Many of these microbes are beneficial, and we rely on them to maintain good health. We feed them fiber, and they reciprocate by helping us with digestion and nutrient synthesis. The good bacteria can even improve your mood.[2] Yes, feeding fiber to the good bacteria in your gut can help your digestion and make you feel happier. A meta-analysis of eighteen studies on dietary fiber consumption and its relationship to depression showed that a high dietary fiber intake appeared protective against depression in a dose-response fashion, meaning that the higher the fiber intake, the less depression.[3] A high-fiber diet may not fully resolve depressive symptoms, but it can help to reduce their severity.

Your gut microbes ferment dietary fibers to produce beneficial compounds like short-chain fatty acids such as acetate, propionate, and butyrate. These wonderful small molecules help to keep the digestive tract environment healthy, make energy metabolism more efficient, strengthen the gut lining, and support healthy brain function by promoting more neurogenesis, reducing inflammation, strengthening the blood-brain barrier, and improving memory.[4] They support healthy insulin secretion and reduce the risk of diabetes by suppressing appetite.[5]

But every hero needs a villain. Our gut also houses unfriendly or pathogenic microbes. These guys feed on sugars and saturated fats, and in return, they cause inflammation and weaken the gut lining. Over time, gut contents can seep through this lining and reach the bloodstream. This is called "leaky gut." As I've mentioned before, the toxins that enter the bloodstream due to leaky gut can reach the blood vessels in the brain, causing leaky brain. As you know by now, leaky brain is associated with neuroinflammation, higher levels of amyloid, and a higher risk of developing Alzheimer's disease.[6]

Should You Take Probiotics?

Probiotics are live bacteria that you can take either via food or through supplements. You've likely seen advertisements for probiotics supplements, and a doctor may have even recommended that you take them. The jury is still out on how much probiotics help. Some studies show mild benefits, but most agree that the microbes in probiotics don't stick around for long, nor do they permanently colonize the gut.[7] They pass through but may have some positive effects as a result.

I believe the best way to obtain probiotics is through fermented foods.[8] I eat some yogurt every single day and have done so for decades. It has become a part of my routine. This preference of mine is so well known among my family and friends that whenever my wife and I go to friends' or family's houses for dinner, a small bowl of yogurt inevitably appears alongside my meal. I recommend yogurt without added sugar for the best effect.

There are other ways to get your probiotics through food: Kombucha, kefir, sauerkraut, kimchi, lacto-fermented pickled vegetables, miso, and tempeh are just some of the fermented foods readily available. If you want to take probiotics, it is unlikely that they will have any harmful effects, although some people may experience gastrointestinal issues if they take high doses.

In addition to natural probiotics, include prebiotics in your diet—these are types of fiber that nourish the beneficial bacteria already in your gut. Unlike probiotics, which introduce new microbes, prebiotics help nurture and support the growth of the beneficial bacteria you already have. They're found naturally in foods like garlic, onions, leeks, asparagus, bananas, oats, and chicory root. Think of them as fertilizer for your internal garden—they help your microbiome flourish, improve gut barrier function, and may even enhance brain health by supporting a healthy gut-brain axis.

So, consider this: Do you want to nourish the friendly microbes that help you digest your food, utilize its nutrients, build your immune system, and keep you feeling energetic and happy? Or do you want to feed the microbes that will cause inflammation, digestive problems, leaky gut, leaky brain, mental health issues, and a distressed immune system? Remember this the next time you make a food choice, and you may find yourself choosing differently.

I hope I've convinced you of the importance of feeding your good bacteria and providing your brain with all the necessary nutrition. So what does that look like? Most of us could improve our diets, so where you start depends on your current diet. My nutritional prescription includes three key components: what to avoid, what to include, and which supplements to take for optimal brain health.

What Not to Eat: Sugar, Refined Grains, and Ultra-Processed Food

Before you worry about supplements or a nutrient-dense diet, stop the inflammatory fire inside your body caused by consuming junk food. If you can drive up and get it through a window, or if comes in a package and it was made in a factory, it's junk food. Those foods might taste good to you now, but they increase inflammation, cause leaky gut, and contribute to metabolic diseases. Considering the potential damage they can cause, are they worth the momentary pleasure? Only you can decide.

If you can't resist salty, fried food, cut back on that first. If you have a diet soda habit, consider reducing the amount you drink. Even though diet soda has no calories, there is compelling evidence that artificial sweeteners alter the microbiome in ways that contribute to metabolic problems, such as obesity, increased visceral and subcutaneous fat, and fat infiltration into muscle tissue.[9]

If you have a sweet tooth, are unsure where to start with dietary change, or are prepared to make *only one dietary change*, start by eliminating added refined sugar. Cane sugar, beet sugar, and high-fructose corn syrup, sweetened soda, sugary coffee and tea drinks, candy, cookies, and pastries, plus processed foods with a high amount of added refined sugar, are all inflammatory. Sugar is just terrible for your brain. It can lead to severe metabolic problems like obesity and diabetes, and it damages your eyes, nerves, heart, kidneys, and brain. It drives blood sugar too high and causes inflammation and other problems that can lead to a shrinking brain and lower cognitive function.[10]

Sugar is hard to quit. Refined sugar, such as white sugar and high-fructose corn syrup, is significantly sweeter than anything in nature. Take a bite of a banana and compare it to a spoonful of white sugar, and you'll see what I mean. This is why fruit isn't addictive, but sugary treats like candy and cookies trigger a dopamine response in the brain very similar to what we see in someone who uses tobacco, alcohol, or cocaine.[11] Sugar may cause addiction-like cravings by overstimulating the brain's reward system, which, over time, can reduce its sensitivity to dopamine. As with drugs, this means that over time, you may need more sugar to get the same pleasurable feeling.[12] The more you consume sugar, the more you need it. These hyper-sweet tastes also desensitize your taste buds, making naturally sweet foods like fruit and natural sugars seem less satisfying and appealing. If you ask me, it's not worth the rush.

Your body can produce glucose, which your brain needs to operate, from complex carbohydrates found in fruits and whole grains. It doesn't need refined sugar to produce glucose. Glucose in the bloodstream signals the pancreas to release insulin, which unlocks a cell channel to allow glucose to enter. However, consuming sugar-sweetened foods with a high glycemic index (meaning they raise your blood sugar quickly) triggers the rapid release of a large amount of insulin, which removes too much sugar from your bloodstream, causing low blood sugar. The body thinks you are hungry again, even if you just ate a big meal. And so the cycle continues. Welcome to the blood sugar roller coaster.

Sugar can also affect your mood, stress levels, and emotions. A comprehensive review of more than three hundred studies[13] looking at the interaction of sugar consumption, anxiety, and emotions found "overwhelming evidence" to support the hypothesis that sugar consumption results in physical brain changes, altered emotional processing, and modified behavior in both rodents and humans.

Obesity and Your Brain

Many things contribute to obesity, which is a metabolic condition. Genetics, lack of exercise, chemicals in the food system, processed food, cultural pressure, stress, anxiety—obesity is its own soup of problems, but one of the primary ways to manage and reverse it is with diet, so without blame or shame—nobody tries to get a metabolic disorder—I want to talk about it briefly here.

The truth is that whether or not diabetes or a high-sugar diet is involved, obesity itself causes damage to your brain. The higher the BMI, the smaller the hippocampus, with or without diabetes.[14] Also, the higher the HbA1c (a measure of blood sugar over time, often used to diagnose diabetes and often associated with obesity), the more brain shrinkage. One study of 473 men and women between the ages of 20 and 87 showed that in those over 40, being overweight or obese was associated with a brain that looks up to 10 years older than a lean person's brain of the same age.[15] Another study of 10,001 adults with an average age of 53 found higher body fat levels were consistently associated with less volume all over the brain: especially in the hippocampus, temporal lobe, and front lobe.[16]

People with obesity, with or without diabetes, have much higher rates of sleep apnea,[17] lower blood flow to the brain,[18] less BDNF,[19] more atherosclerosis, elevated cortisol levels that are toxic to neurons, and more oxidative stress and inflammation in the brain. In 2013, I wrote an extensive review article, along with my student Brooke Lubinski (now a physician and instructor at Harvard Medical School), about the horrible effects of obesity on the brain.[20] The results of our review of the literature showed that obesity is linked to a 2.4 percent decrease in brain volume, especially in the hippocampus, cingulate gyrus, and frontal lobes; that a BMI of 30 or higher is associated with a decline in executive function over ten years; that a higher BMI correlates with reduced fiber bundle length, contributing to brain atrophy, especially in the temporal lobe; and that central obesity, indicated by a higher waist-to-hip ratio, is significantly associated with brain atrophy, including smaller hippocampal volume and a rise in white matter abnormalities.

The dopamine pathways in the brains of people with obesity are more active in response to sugar consumption. Their reward pathways light up much more in PET scans.[21] As an overweight person gradually becomes obese, food becomes a lot more rewarding to them and as such, they become addicted to eating. The orbitofrontal dopamine pathways take over food decisions, and the logical-leaning lateral prefrontal cortex is silenced. In this process, people who cross the line to obesity have a much harder time fighting back to manage their weight due in part to the negative neuroplasticity that has occurred in their brains—much like any other form of addiction modifies the brain. For all these reasons—to preserve your brain size and function—it is worth working hard and using all your resources to reverse obesity as much as possible at any age.

What can you do? Just as with Alzheimer's, the pharmaceutical industry continues to search for answers, with some degree of success. For all their issues and side effects, drugs like Ozempic and Mounjaro (GLP-1 agonists) appear to have many benefits for lowering blood sugar, reducing appetite, and significantly reducing inflammation. These drugs have also shown promising results for the prevention of Alzheimer's disease. As such, I favor these drugs for people who suffer from obesity and have had limited success with diet and exercise for managing their weight. Fat accumulation in the body, including inside the liver and muscles, has significant detrimental effects on the brain. The sooner they are managed and cleared, the better—ideally with a focus on natural weight-loss strategies and the use of drugs such as GLP-1 agonists as needed.

What to Eat: The Mediterranean Diet

I hope you've decided to quit sugar and junk food. If you've stopped eating the bad stuff, it's time for the next level: replacing junk with something good and preferably also delicious. Enter the Mediterranean diet.

The Mediterranean diet has been widely studied, and its primary components have been broken down and studied separately. Those who eat primarily a Mediterranean diet have slower cognitive decline and a lower risk that their MCI will progress to Alzheimer's disease, as well as a reduced risk of Alzheimer's disease itself.[22] Dr. Puja Agarwal and her colleagues in Chicago monitored the diet and cognitive functions of adults in their eighties and nineties for many years. After they passed away, researchers examined their brains for signs of Alzheimer's disease and found that those who had consumed a Mediterranean diet regularly had fewer plaques and tangles.[23] Dr. Agarwal, an assistant professor of internal medicine at the Rush University Medical Center in Chicago, made this statement in an interview with CNN: "Researchers found people who scored highest for adhering to the Mediterranean diet had average plaque and tangle amounts in their brains similar to being 18 years younger than people who scored lowest."[24] Countless studies show its benefits to the brain, mental health, and the heart, liver, kidneys, skin, and other organs.

There is no one specific Mediterranean diet, so how do you put this into practice? The Mediterranean diet is generally known for being high in vegetables and fruits, seafood, whole grains, olive oil, and a small glass of wine or other alcoholic beverage daily, along with an active lifestyle, strong social support, and ample time outdoors. It is also generally low in refined sugar and meat and does not include processed food. Additionally, portion sizes are typically smaller in the Mediterranean region, and a glass of wine is typically smaller than what we are used to in the United States.

It may feel overwhelming to take on all these changes at once, so let's break it down into a list of things to emphasize. These components of the Mediterranean diet all have research support and should be easy to incorporate into your meals, especially when you understand their brain benefits. I look at the ingredients of the Mediterranean diet in three main categories, though some food items fall under more than one category:

1. Foods that reduce inflammation

These classic Mediterranean dietary choices protect against brain atrophy, depression, cognitive decline, and Alzheimer's disease due to their polyphenols and other antioxidants, such as omega-3 fatty acids, that reduce oxidative stress and inflammation.

Fatty fish (such as salmon, mackerel, sardines, anchovies, and tuna): Seafood is a crucial component of the Mediterranean diet, but fatty fish in particular are rich in omega-3 fatty acids (EPA and DHA), which help lower inflammatory markers in the brain. An older study from 2003, which followed 815 people between the ages of sixty-five and ninety-four for nearly four years, found that those who consumed fish at least once a week had a 60 percent lower risk of Alzheimer's disease compared to those who rarely or never ate fish.[25] In 2009, my extensive review of the scientific literature in collaboration with my colleagues Dr. Payam Mohassel and Dr. Kristine Yaffe also showed that individuals with higher blood levels of omega-3 acids are less likely to develop Alzheimer's disease.[26]

Many studies have since confirmed this finding, including a 2020 study that showed fish intake may alter brain structure and enhance cognitive ability in healthy individuals.[27] A 2024 study examined the relationship between fish consumption, cognitive impairment, and dementia. It found that benefits start at about one ounce a day but increase with higher consumption.[28] There are concerns about mercury, which is why I recommend choosing low-mercury fish. The Natural Resources Defense Council publishes a list of fish with varying mercury content levels, categorized as having the least, moderate, high, or highest mercury content, in a format that can be easily cut out and kept in your wallet: www.nrdc.org/sites/default/files/walletcard.pdf.

Olive oil (extra-virgin): Olive oil is the primary fat used throughout the Mediterranean region, where olives grow naturally. One study reported that, in more than 92,000 adults followed for more than twenty-eight years, those who consumed over 7 grams of olive oil per day (approximately 1½ teaspoons) had a 28 percent lower risk of dementia-related death compared with those who rarely or never consumed olive oil.[29] A review of eleven studies on olive oil and brain health showed that consuming olive oil was associated with enhanced cognitive functioning and reduced cognitive decline.[30] Olive oil can also help with pain relief. Extra-virgin olive oil contains oleocanthal, a natural anti-inflammatory compound similar to ibuprofen.

Turmeric (curcumin): Curcumin, a compound in the turmeric root (a common spice), is a potent anti-inflammatory compound that crosses the blood-brain barrier and helps reduce neuroinflammation. It has antioxidant, cardioprotective, neuroprotective, anticancer, antirheumatic, hepatoprotective, and antimicrobial properties.[31] In the brain, it reduces oxidative stress,[32] activates BDNF,[33] inhibits the activation of microglia and astrocytes, suppresses inflammatory signaling, increases dopamine levels, promotes neuron survival,[34] and more. Turmeric is one of the most potent spices for protecting the brain, but you can get an even more concentrated dose of curcumin with supplements.

Berries (such as blueberries, strawberries, blackberries, and raspberries): Berries are high in flavonoids and anthocyanins, which reduce oxidative stress and inflammation, including inflammation in the digestive tract and brain. Berries are also low in sugar compared to some fruits. One study showed that they reduce inflammation caused by obesity.[35]

Leafy greens (such as spinach, kale, Swiss chard, collard greens, arugula): They are rich in antioxidants, fiber, and polyphenols that help protect neurons from damage. A 2023 study of the Mediterranean diet found an association with lower amyloid load in the brain. Among all measures, those with the highest intake of leafy green vegetables had the lowest levels of plaques and tangles.[36]

Nuts and seeds (such as walnuts, almonds, chia seeds, flaxseeds, and pumpkin seeds): High in polyphenols, vitamin E, fiber, and B vitamins, nuts and seeds combat oxidative stress and reduce inflammation while also specifically benefiting cognitive function.[37] Research indicates that individuals who consume more nuts are less likely to develop cardiovascular disease. Among nuts, the walnut appears to be most closely linked to cognitive health.[38]

2. Foods that increase BDNF

If you want more of this fertilizer for the brain, which is so powerful in the process of neurogenesis, neuroplasticity, and memory, eat more of these BDNF-stimulating Mediterranean foods:

Fatty fish (such as salmon, sardines, and mackerel): The DHA in fatty fish specifically promotes BDNF release, supporting the production of neurons and increased synaptic connections.[39]

Eggs: Egg yolks are rich in choline, a nutrient essential for producing acetylcholine, a neurotransmitter that plays a crucial role in memory and synaptic function. Research has shown that the choline from egg yolks can improve verbal memory in older adults and could play a role in preventing Alzheimer's disease.[40] Animal studies have shown that choline increases BDNF levels in the hippocampus.[41] High levels of vitamin B_{12} in eggs also have immense brain benefits beyond BDNF. Low B_{12} is associated with almost every neurological condition, including Alzheimer's disease.[42]

Dark chocolate (70+ percent cocoa): Cocoa contains flavonoids that boost BDNF and improve brain connectivity. Research has shown that consuming cocoa flavonols increases BDNF production and improves cognitive performance.[43]

Berries: Blueberries—my favorite fruit—are high in BDNF-boosting polyphenols. Research has shown that after consuming blueberries, adults exhibit higher BDNF levels and improved memory when recalling word lists.[44]

Legumes (such as lentils, chickpeas, black beans, and peas): Legumes contain zinc and magnesium, which enhance BDNF activity. Legumes are also an excellent source of fiber, vitamins, and protein. They serve as a primary protein source for vegetarians and are also an essential component of the Mediterranean diet, where meat consumption has traditionally been limited. Legumes are associated with improved cognitive performance in older adults.[45] They are also nutritious and filling foods that can aid in reducing body fat. A 2023 study of more than fifteen thousand U.S. adults found that those who regularly consumed legumes gained significantly less weight over the ten-year study period, had lower BMIs, and had leaner waists. One study showed that consuming more legumes and nuts was associated with higher levels of BDNF.[46]

Green tea: Although not traditionally part of the Mediterranean diet, I would like to add that green tea is rich in L-theanine and EGCG, which increase BDNF and protect against cognitive decline.[47]

3. Foods that improve blood flow to the brain

The brain needs a steady blood flow to function optimally. As you now know, poor circulation in the brain contributes to cognitive impairment, stroke risk, and brain atrophy. These traditional Mediterranean foods naturally enhance vascular health:

Beets and beet juice: Beets are rich in nitrates, stimulating nitric oxide production and dilating blood vessels. Native to Mediterranean countries, beets improve brain blood circulation. In one study, older adults who consumed beetroot juice exhibited improved circulation in brain areas associated with cognitive functions such as thinking and decision-making.[48] Studies have shown that diets high in nitrates can increase blood flow to the brain.[49]

Leafy greens (such as spinach, kale, arugula, and Swiss chard): Like beets, dark leafy greens are rich in nitrates, which improve blood flow to the brain.[50] They also contain folate and magnesium, which support healthy brain blood flow.

Citrus fruits (such as oranges, lemons, tangerines, and grapefruits): Citrus fruits contain flavonoids that improve circulation and reduce the risk of stroke. They are rich in vitamin C, which neutralizes free radicals, such as reactive oxygen species, and reduces oxidative stress. Citrus also contains many other bioactive compounds, such as flavanones, which have demonstrated neuroprotective effects. They are anti-inflammatory, are antioxidant, and strengthen the integrity of the blood-brain barrier.[51] Studies have shown a link between citrus juice and blood flow to the brain; however, consuming the whole fruit is even more beneficial due to the fiber and numerous other nutrients found in the pulp.

Walnuts: Walnuts, in particular, contain L-arginine, a compound that enhances nitric oxide production, which promotes the dilation of blood vessels in the heart[52] and brain.[53]

Olive oil: This healthy fat helps reduce arterial stiffness, which improves vascular health with aging, supporting long-term brain health. A recent study has demonstrated that extra-virgin olive oil enhances the blood-brain barrier function in individuals with MCI.[54]

Pomegranates: This delicious fruit, filled with juicy seeds, increases nitric oxide levels, improving oxygen flow to brain cells. Studies show that it can help increase blood flow, enhancing endurance during exercise.[55]

Dark chocolate (70+ percent cocoa): The flavonoids in dark chocolate increase nitric oxide production, thereby enhancing blood circulation in the brain and body. In a study of individuals with high blood pressure, consuming thirty grams of dark chocolate for fifteen days increased nitric oxide serum levels and decreased blood pressure.[56]

The Best Supplements for Your Brain

The third and last level of your nutrition fast track is supplementation, but you may be surprised to learn that I do not recommend multivitamins. These random assemblages of various vitamins and minerals contain nutrients that you may not need in doses that are often too small or too large for what most people require. I've seen patients who take many different supplements that either don't boost their low nutrient levels or drive them too high. I believe that food is generally the best source of nutrients.

For brain health, vitamin B_{12}, vitamin D, and iron are vital; however, I do not recommend taking these supplements unless you know your levels are low. Tests for these three nutrients are easy to obtain from your primary care physician, and they are inexpensive. If you are a little low in any of these, I recommend taking an over-the-counter supplement and rechecking every six months. If you are severely deficient in vitamin B_{12} (which can occur in individuals who avoid animal products or for other reasons), I recommend sublingual vitamin B_{12} or B_{12} injections, as this nutrient is crucial for maintaining healthy brain function.

The only exceptions in my mind when it comes to supplements are the following, which can be challenging to get from food alone in amounts that can be useful to your brain and which have the most research support for making a difference in brain health:

- **Omega-3 fatty acids.** These contain both EPA and DHA, which are only slightly different and can convert into each other. They both have excellent benefits. EPA is particularly beneficial for the heart and eyes, and DHA offers numerous advantages for the brain. You can take this in the form of fish or krill oil (look for mercury-free versions). Alternatively, you can opt for algae oil if you are a vegetarian. Fish are rich in omega-3 fatty acids because they eat algae, so you may as well go straight to the source. While research has raised doubts about the body's ability to convert nut and seed oils, including flaxseed oil, into DHA, algae oil increases EPA and DHA levels in the blood, similar to fish oil.[57]

  Look for an omega-3 supplement that contains at least 1,000 milligrams of EPA and DHA (not just any "fish oil" supplements).

  You can also have a blood test to measure your omega-3 index (should be above 6 percent) and take higher doses of these supplements, if needed.

If you want to do more, there are three other supplements I like for brain health:

- **Quercetin** (500 mg, twice daily) is beneficial for enhancing mitochondrial function. Best taken with fat-containing food for improved absorption. Look for formulations with bromelain or vitamin C to enhance bioavailability.

- **Resveratrol** is rich in antioxidants and helps reduce oxidative stress. 100 to 250 mg per day (standard for general brain and heart health). Higher doses (up to 500 mg/day) have been used in some Alzheimer's and metabolic studies. Absorption is low, so micronized, trans-resveratrol, or liposomal forms are preferred. Take with meals (some sources suggest fat-containing meals may enhance absorption).

- **Curcumin** is a potent anti-inflammatory. Look for formulas that include piperine, the active ingredient in black pepper extract, for improved absorption. Curcumin absorption and bioavailability increase by 2,000 percent when combined with 20 mg of piperine. You can also add turmeric and black pepper to your cooking. Turmeric is the primary source of curcumin, but a curcumin supplement is more concentrated. (The turmeric root contains only 2 to 8 percent curcumin by weight.) A typical dose of curcumin extract is 500 to 1,000 mg daily. Look for standardized forms with 95 percent curcuminoids. Must be combined with piperine (black pepper extract) or used in enhanced formulations, such as curcumin phytosome (Meriva) or liposomal curcumin (Theracurmin).

Make Your Plan

Here is a list of nutritional interventions that can help improve your diet to support and enhance your brain function. I've divided this list into three levels. It's up to you to decide which approach to take and whether to focus on elimination, addition, supplementation, or a combination of all three. Or, try some of these and then pick something different if you don't like them. Remember that changing only a few things at a time is more likely to lead to a sustainable habit.

Review this list and check all the items you think you can do and would be willing to try. I want you to have options over the next twelve weeks.

Nutrition Practices to Choose From

Elimination:
- No candy.
- No sweet baked goods, such as cookies, muffins, scones, cake, or pie.
- Replace sugar with honey or real maple syrup.
- Go the whole day without any added sugar.
- Skip all refined grains (white bread, white bagels, most baked goods, white rice, white pasta) today.
- Skip the drive-through or delivery and cook a meal at home.
- Go the whole day without any fried food. No French fries!
- Avoid eating anything from a package.
- Cut your portion sizes by 25 percent.
- No alcohol today.
- No cured meat (such as bacon, sausage, ham, or deli meat).
- No added salt today.

Addition:
- Have a big salad filled with leafy greens.
- Add berries to your yogurt or oatmeal.
- Make homemade kale chips.
- Try steamed collard greens or kale as a side dish.
- Eat an orange, tangerine, or grapefruit.
- Squeeze fresh lemon or lime into your water.
- Keep a small handful of nuts and/or seeds on hand for a quick snack.
- Put walnuts on your oatmeal.
- Have some bean soup. Try lentils, white beans, or black beans.
- Try scrambled tofu for breakfast. (Add some turmeric for color and anti-inflammation action.)
- Have a serving of salmon. Extra points for drizzling it with olive oil and squeezing citrus juice over it.

- Add salmon to your salad.
- Cook with turmeric or add a dash to your smoothie.
- Try mackerel or sardines.
- Add olive oil to your salad.
- Cook with olive oil.
- Dip your bread in olive oil or drizzle it on your toast instead of using butter.

Supplementation:
- Take a daily omega-3 fatty acid supplement containing at least 1000 mg of combined EPA and DHA.
- Take a quercetin supplement.
- Take a resveratrol supplement.
- Take a curcumin supplement with piperine for better absorption.
- Get blood tests for vitamins B_{12} and D, and iron. Supplement only if necessary for low levels.

Rate your progress here or on the app. Score yourself from zero to 10 based on how well you ate daily. Determine your weekly score, also from zero to 10, based on how well you met your weekly goals.

Your Nutrition Tracker

	MON	TUES	WED	THURS	FRI	SAT	SUN	WEEKLY SCORE
WEEK 1								
WEEK 2								
WEEK 3								
WEEK 4								
WEEK 5								
WEEK 6								

WEEK 7								
WEEK 8								
WEEK 9								
WEEK 10								
WEEK 11								
WEEK 12								

16

FAST-TRACK YOUR MINDSET

I considered calling this chapter "Fast-Track to Stress Management," but I felt something was missing from that title. The more I thought about it, the more I realized what I mean when I talk about this pillar of brain health—which involves managing stress, addressing anxiety, and taking care of your brain psychologically—is mindset.

Stress, anxiety, and worry are things we do to ourselves. They happen in our brains, not outside of us. Changing mindset can help lift these negative thought states. There is an old saying that goes something like this: *Depression is worrying about the past, anxiety is worrying about the future, and stress is worrying about the now.* There is up to 50 percent overlap of symptoms in these conditions.[1] These feelings can be uncomfortable, but knowing you can alter them through mindset may give you hope that you can escape chronic stress, anxiety, and worry.

There is a cognitive behavioral therapy (CBT) model that explains how behavior is formed. Thoughts lead to emotions, emotions lead to behaviors, and behaviors lead to more thoughts—and the cycle continues.

You can enter that circle at any point and get stuck. For example, you might think, "I'm completely overwhelmed at work because my coworkers don't do their share," or "I can't deal with this relationship anymore!" These are thoughts that can cause you to feel frustrated and stressed. Your behaviors toward your coworkers or spouse may change, whether you realize it or not. You may become quieter or sadder as you become consumed by your repetitive negative thoughts, or RNTs. People around you may begin to feel uncomfortable and act in ways that reinforce your negative thoughts, leading to more RNTs, until you are caught in a downward spiral.

You are not at the mercy of this cycle. You can change your thoughts to change your emotions. Depending on your emotional intelligence, you may also be able to change your emotions to change your behaviors. Your changed behaviors could inspire others to change their behaviors, improving your relationships. This is the essence of mindset.

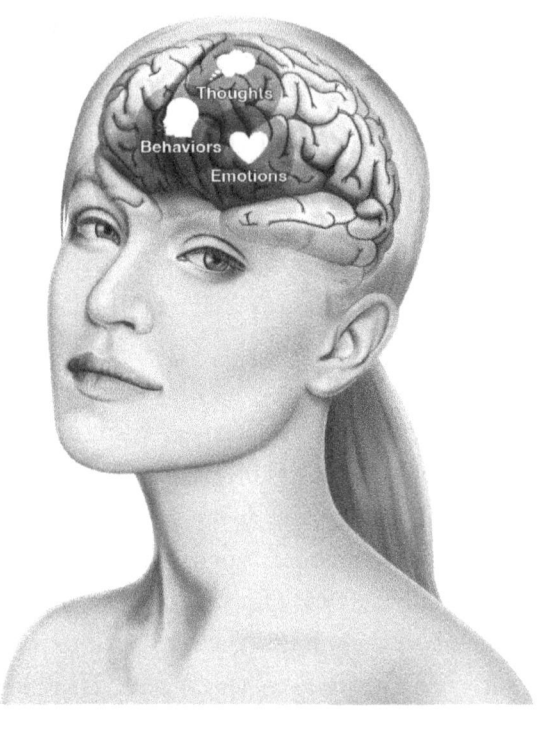

For example, let's say you become a little more forgiving toward your coworkers or spouse. Instead of complaining to them, you do something to surprise them and make them happy. They, in turn, may return the favor by acting kinder toward you, which confirms your positive thoughts about them and yourself. Now, you have repetitive positive thoughts (RPTs).

By simply changing your mindset, you and those around you can become happier, and you will experience less stress and anxiety in ways that impact your thoughts, emotions, and behaviors, ultimately determining the quality of your day. As long as you know you can change your perspective, you will see a way out of the downward spiral into your RNTs, which often lead to poor health, dysfunction, and cognitive decline.

Warning

Before we proceed, I would like to make an important distinction. The stress, anxiety, or low mood that people experience due to life events, workload, deadlines, financial problems, relationship conflicts, or other day-to-day situations that arise and pass is the kind of stress that responds to a mindset-based approach. This is different from having a diagnosis of general anxiety disorder, major depressive disorder, or bipolar disorder. People with these disorders suffer from their symptoms every day, even when they are not under external pressure, even when they are on vacation or spending time with loved ones, or doing nothing out of the ordinary. Their lives are seriously affected by their mental health condition. You can't just tell them to "Think positive!" or "Snap out of it!" or say, "Don't be depressed, you have a great life!"

Clinical depression and anxiety disorders are not about how good or bad someone's life is. They are biochemical in origin and can be genetic (due to variation in receptors for neurotransmitters in the brain), stem from childhood trauma, or be related to serious medical conditions such as thyroid problems, fibromyalgia, heart disease, insomnia, or chronic pain. Not only do they drastically lower a person's quality of life, but they can—if untreated—eventually injure the brain. For example, many studies of depressed adults of all ages have shown smaller hippocampal volume, smaller amygdala size, a thinner cortex, more white matter abnormalities, lower scores on memory and learning tests, and significant cognitive symptoms.[2] The longer the depression lasts, the smaller the hippocampus.[3]

These mental health issues require medical care, which could include cognitive behavioral therapy, participation in support groups, and/or medications. It is imperative to treat these conditions under the care of an experienced physician! Please seek help; these interventions can get you out of the crisis.

The Anatomy of Stress

Beyond your brain, which is your central nervous system, your body has an entire network of nerve endings that cover all your internal organs, from your heart and lungs to your stomach and bladder muscles. You don't have conscious awareness of this system of nerve networks, which is called your autonomic nervous system (ANS). The sympathetic branch of your ANS stimulates your body for action by increasing your heart rate, breathing, and blood perfusion to your muscles. This is fight-or-flight mode. The parasympathetic branch puts you in a rest-and-digest mode.

When you are stressed, your fight-or-flight sympathetic system is in overdrive, and your body is revved up. When you are relaxed, your parasympathetic system dominates, and your body is calm. When you are in a parasympathetic mode, there is a slight variability in the time between your heartbeats when you breathe in and out, which is good. Measuring your heart rate variability (HRV—I'll tell you how later in this chapter) can indicate if your body is stressed out or calm and relaxed. Ideally, you would like to spend most of your time in your parasympathetic mode, and gear up to sympathetic mode only when needed.

Of course, the whole process begins in the brain. Feelings of stress emerge from activity in the brain's emotional network, which includes the orbitofrontal cortex, prefrontal cortex, amygdala, hippocampus, basal ganglia, and hypothalamus. Based on your memories and experiences, you may perceive an event or comment as dangerous, concerning, or insulting. These thoughts and emotions directly trigger your hypothalamus to release adrenaline and cortisol, activating your fight-or-flight response through the sympathetic nervous system.

This is a survival response. Early humans had to have this ability to escape predators. We use it now too. Imagine you are about to cross the street, and suddenly a bus is zooming through the crosswalk. That internal emergency response system gives you quick reflexes to jump out of the way or pull someone else out. It is the source of those superhero-like feats we sometimes hear about, such as someone jumping into an icy river to rescue a drowning person, scaring off a grizzly bear, or the proverbial mother who lifts a car off a child.

When the body works normally, these stress hormones recede once the threat has passed. Your emotional network then orders your hypothalamus to stop producing adrenaline and cortisol. The parasympathetic nervous system takes over, triggering the rest-and-digest response. Heart rate, blood pressure, blood sugar, blood flow, pupils, and airways all return to baseline.

Chronic stress is a condition in which you stay in fight-or-flight mode even when there is no real threat to your survival. Work pressure, family problems, financial troubles, or any other issue that worries you can feel like a life-threatening emergency that doesn't go away. This constant stress causes you to stay in sympathetic nervous system mode for too long. Excessive, prolonged cortisol exposure is toxic to the hippocampus and accelerates aging. Human and animal studies have demonstrated that chronic stress can impair memory, neuroplasticity, neuronal firing, and even the structure of neurons, thereby suppressing neurogenesis and reducing the size of the hippocampus.[4]

Higher cortisol levels are associated with a smaller hippocampus in a dose-dependent manner.[5] A study of seventy adults in Japan with an average age of seventy-two, followed over seven years, found that those with the highest cortisol levels at the beginning of the study experienced the most significant atrophy in their hippocampus by the end.[6] Another study from Canada showed that older adults with a history of anxiety had higher levels of cortisol, a smaller hippocampus, and worse scores in memory tests.[7]

Even my kids (who have attended some of my talks) know that cortisol is toxic to the hippocampus. When my daughter Maya was in second grade, and I reminded her that she needed to work on her book report, she said, "Stop it, Dad. You're stressing me out, and that's bad for my hippocampus!" (I still made sure she did her homework, but she had a point.)

How to Think About Stress

Mindset can't solve every problem, but it can help you get into a state of mind that makes problem-solving easier. Remember in chapter 5, where we discussed how you can make decisions based on emotion or logic (depending on which part of the brain is in charge, the emotional or executive function network)? Which is your default? And what if you could use your executive function more often to help temper your emotional decisions or add more emotion into your perfectionist logical approach? Can you increase your emotional intelligence—the ability to recognize, understand, and manage your emotions, particularly in challenging situations—by becoming more aware of them rather than letting them dictate your behavior?

You can view your life as something that you make happen, or you can view it as something that happens to you. Although optimism and a sense of control over one's life may come more easily to some people than others and may have a genetic component, they are also skills that can be learned. You can become one notch better at cultivating a productive and positive mindset, just as you can cultivate a growth mindset even if you don't naturally think that way.

This can be challenging to do on your own. If you are stressed chronically, I highly recommend working with a CBT therapist. (Another type of therapy, called dialectical behavioral therapy, or DBT, has grown out of CBT and is especially good for working with trauma and posttraumatic stress disorder.) However, if your stress isn't too severe, there are some apps you can use to learn how to calm your mind, such as Woebot, Moodfit, Sanvello, Calm, and Bloom. You can also try some CBT techniques to help tweak your mindset:

Change your thoughts: This is called restructuring or reframing. What negative thoughts are you having? Name them. Say them out loud. Think about whether they are true. Thoughts aren't always a true manifestation of reality. It is humbling to remember that our thoughts, even our strongest beliefs, result from chemical processes in various networks within our brain, based on our limited perception of the world. These thoughts are malleable and can change over time.

If someone said something to you that upset you, you might think that this person is mean to you, hurt your feelings, or doesn't like you, or that you need to get back at them. But what if, instead, you had the thought: *That person's problem isn't my problem,* or *That person's opinion of me isn't any of my business,* or *That person must be going through a hard time to say something like that to someone*? Separating what the person said from your feelings can significantly affect your reaction and stress level. You may choose to ignore it or not escalate the situation, as doing so would have made it worse. You may even feel some compassion for someone who insulted you. What a difference mindset can make!

Change your feelings: This may feel challenging, but it is possible to change a feeling by altering the thought that triggered it. Pay attention to how you feel at this moment. Allow yourself to feel your emotions rather than suppressing them. Try to pinpoint the feeling in your body. Is it in your chest? Your stomach? Your head? When you've located it, focus on it and give it a name, such as "fear," "worry," or "overwhelm." Think about what is causing it. Can you trace it back to a thought you can restructure and reframe? Try this and see if you sense any easing of the physical feeling. Even if you don't know why you're feeling it, zeroing in on it can help you feel less overwhelmed and reactive. If nothing else, sometimes simply letting yourself fully feel the feeling lessens its intensity.

Here is something to remember next time someone says or does something that upsets you or makes you angry: When you are in this state of mind, your cortisol levels have spiked and are damaging the neurons in your hippocampus. Your blood adrenaline levels are also high, driving up your entire sympathetic nervous system, which over time harms your heart, kidneys, skin, brain, and every other organ in your body.

The longer you stay angry, and the longer your blood levels of cortisol and adrenaline remain high, the more harm you are doing to yourself! To keep your hippocampus and body young and strong, please find a way to view what happened from a different angle or forgive what happened. As you calm down, your parasympathetic nervous system will prevail, and your brain and body will be protected from further injury. One of the best books I have read is *Don't Sweat the Small Stuff . . . and It's All Small Stuff* by Richard Carlson. It shows how seemingly big problems are often minor issues in the grand scheme. As the teenagers I know often say, "It's not that deep."

Change your behaviors: Think about what you are doing that you would like to do differently. Are you stress-eating? Blowing off exercise? Snapping at loved ones or isolating yourself? Identify the feeling that causes you to exhibit or avoid these behaviors. What is the thought behind that feeling? Do you feel more motivated if you can restructure or reframe the thought and ease the emotion? Or, if this doesn't work just yet, focus on developing a new habit that makes you feel calm and peaceful, or reconnect with supportive friends or family. Do this weekly and notice how your feelings and thoughts change. Sometimes, changing your behavior can work its way backward through the cycle—good behavior can change a lousy feeling into a good feeling, which can transform a bad thought into a good idea.

It may not feel like you have control over your stress state, but for the most part, you do. Is that looming deadline overwhelming you, or is it an opportunity to finally get the thing done? Can you negotiate an extension, or are you so stressed that you can't discuss it? What's the worst that could happen? What's the best that could happen? What are some of the things in your life that you appreciate having? What are you thankful for? Are you taking all the good things in life for granted and focusing on the things that are not going well? Mindfully explore and discover what's happening. You may surprise yourself.

People with chronic stress often neglect their own needs as they operate in crisis mode, taking care of problems and other people. Another thing you can do to promote a more positive mindset is to get into the habit of stopping to take some long, deep breaths whenever you feel mounting stress. Ask yourself what you need. More focus? More downtime? More human connection? Every day, take at least ten minutes—anyone can spare ten minutes—to consider what you need, and you can begin to unravel the stress cycle and make different choices that help you feel better . . . and prevent brain atrophy.

Good Stress vs. Bad Stress

Stress can feel unpleasant, but it can also be beneficial and exciting. When I give lectures and presentations, even though I have done them thousands of times in the past thirty-plus years, I still get a little nervous, and I like it. I find it helpful to worry about whether I will explain things clearly, whether there is a new article or news related to my presentation that I haven't read, or any other concerns on my mind. This stress motivates me to research the literature and news on topics related to my lecture, practice my presentation multiple times, and be a little on edge when I take the podium or stage.

Short periods of stress followed by recovery can strengthen your resilience and reserves, just as lifting weights followed by recovery strengthens your muscles. Good stress, which has physiological and psychological benefits, is sometimes called eustress.[8] Eustress occurs in response to challenges that feel important to you and that you feel confident tackling. As you strive to meet a challenge, eustress activates your brain's reward system in the prefrontal cortex, increasing focus, alertness, and performance, thereby enhancing motivation and confidence.

Unlike chronic or extreme stress that damages the brain over time, eustress can increase resilience and reserve. Eustress is typically short-lived and is often followed by a period of recovery. The mild transient elevation in cortisol from eustress will not harm the hippocampus or the heart. One study in monkeys showed that exposure to moderate early-life stress leads to greater regulation of activity in the prefrontal cortex and more resilience later in life.[9]

To manage stress effectively, use it when needed without letting it become chronic. I find that people stress less when they manage their time and lives. I find that much of people's stress, especially in the United States, has to do with being too busy doing too many things. For example, parents working full-time must juggle their kids' activities with work projects and home chores. They often feel rushed and behind. Exercising, eating well, meditating, or simply taking some personal time becomes the last priority.

At NeuroGrow, we encouraged patients to prioritize organization to free up more time. I use an old-fashioned agenda booklet to jot down my plans for the next few months. I keep a list of projects I'm working on at the moment, as well as reflections on how things are progressing and my life in general (essentially, journaling). Every week, I have a list of specific tasks to attend to, and every morning, I create a list of high-priority tasks that I need to address for that day. This keeps me from worrying about the projects that I have allocated for another day or another week. I also try to be realistic and not make my to-do list too long. If one of my low-priority items doesn't get done that day, I plan to do it the next day. This system allows me to feel in control of my schedule and not feel overwhelmed.

You can't eliminate stress. Crises can sometimes occur, and when they do, everything else may need to be put on hold temporarily. Sometimes, the water heater breaks, a family member gets sick, or financial trouble appears out of nowhere. It is natural to feel overwhelmed when something new and unexpected happens. But even during these crises, you can stay calm and find ways to minimize extreme stress.

For example, I just traveled to Lisbon for a week when my brother was critically ill with cerebral malaria in the ICU. I was in the middle of writing this book and handling my many other responsibilities, but I had to pause, take this trip, and be there for my brother and his family. While I was there, in between being next to him in the ICU several hours a day, talking to his doctors, and soothing the stress of his wife and children, I spent a lot of time in the hospital's library, continuing to take care of my work matters. (Fortunately, he recovered and returned to being fit and healthy again two months later.) I already told you about my recent bike accident and broken kneecap. During that time, I decided to work on boosting my memory by doing a lot of brain exercises and postponing my work responsibilities. Both of these events were quite challenging, but because I manage my everyday stress effectively, I was able to navigate both events calmly and take the time to reflect on what I learned from these experiences.

Too often, my patients who feel stressed and overwhelmed ask, "Why me?" They forget that everyone's life has some degree of challenges, which could be financial, emotional, or health related. Having a mindset that allows us to appreciate the good things in our lives and experience gratitude for what we do have is helpful. There are many ways you can get into a zone of feeling free of stress, many of which I practice myself every day:

Do things that bring you joy. Scheduling activities that bring you joy can help mitigate the impact of stressful events in your life. For example, watching your kids play soccer, cooking dinner by yourself or with your spouse, or listening to your favorite music while driving can increase dopamine levels in your orbitofrontal cortex, giving you a relaxed feeling of well-being.

Calm yourself. Listen to relaxing music or engage in an activity that puts you in the zone, where time seems to fly by, and you feel completely immersed. I enjoy listening to calm music late at night while working on projects, such as writing this book. I plan something like this in my schedule every day.

Find your people. Socializing is a powerful way to reduce stress. Spending time with supportive friends and family members boosts comfort and well-being. Have deep conversations, learn from others, laugh together, or vent about your problems. Social exchanges of this nature create a stress buffer, stimulate the release of the bonding hormone oxytocin, and counteract the release of cortisol. Research shows that socializing improves mood as well as cognitive function and may significantly reduce symptoms of depression and anxiety.[10] Socializing also increases neurogenesis in the hippocampus.[11] It turns out that spending time with your favorite people is fun and also beneficial for your brain.

Meditate or pray. You don't have to be a meditation expert to meditate, and you don't have to be particularly religious to pray. Spending calm, focused time on spiritual reflection reduces stress and increases a sense of emotional well-being while lowering physiological measures of stress. Research has shown that a range of spiritual practices, including prayer, are linked to lower inflammation and improved immune function.[12]

Volunteer. Volunteering or helping others can take your mind off your problems and has significant stress-reducing effects. The pleasure you experience when you help others most likely originates from the release of dopamine and oxytocin in your brain. Helping others enhances emotional resilience, fosters a sense of purpose, and promotes greater empathy for others. One study found that individuals who volunteer regularly have lower cortisol and inflammation levels, while another showed lower rates of depression and greater life satisfaction among seniors who volunteer.[13]

Exercise vigorously. A gentle walk through the woods is relaxing, but a vigorous exercise session may be an even more powerful way to reduce feelings of stress. Physical exertion releases endorphins, which improve mood and increase BDNF, which enhances neurogenesis. Vigorous aerobic exercise reduces cortisol levels in the long term and fosters greater physical and emotional resilience. Several studies have shown that high-intensity exercise significantly lowers feelings of stress and anxiety[14] and increases hippocampal volume, especially in older adults.[15] Vigorous exercise does triple duty: improving physical fitness, reducing stress, and building resilience and growth in your brain.

Try yoga. Maybe you love it or think you're too inflexible to try it, but yoga is a potent stress reliever. The combination of physical movement, controlled breathing, and mindful awareness results in less stress, better body awareness, a calmer nervous system, and a feeling of restoration. Research has shown that people who practice yoga regularly have lower cortisol levels, better emotional regulation, and feel more resilient against stress.[16] Yoga can also significantly reduce feelings of depression and anxiety while increasing stress recovery and cognitive performance, according to a study that compared yoga to walking.[17] There are many types of yoga, from easy stretching to challenging high-intensity moves. You might enjoy it more than you think.

Measuring and Managing Stress

In my clinic, one of the ways we helped our patients gauge their stress levels and work on improving their sense of calm and peace was through the measurement and training of heart rate variability. This is an indirect measurement of the state of your autonomic nervous system. HRV is a measure of the tiny differences in time between heartbeats. While your heart may beat at a steady rate—say, sixty beats per minute—it doesn't beat exactly once per second. Instead, the time between beats might be 0.98 seconds, then 1.02 seconds, then 0.95 seconds, and so on.

This natural variation is beneficial—it means your heart is adaptable and can adjust to subtle changes during your breathing cycles (your heart rate increases slightly when you breathe in and slows somewhat when you breathe out). A reflection of optimal and balanced functions of your sympathetic and parasympathetic nerves, a higher HRV generally indicates that your body is better at handling stress and bouncing back from challenges. In comparison, a lower HRV can be a sign of stress, fatigue, or even poor health.

Measuring HRV is easier than ever, thanks to modern technology. Many smartwatches, fitness trackers, and chest-strap heart monitors can automatically track your HRV. Check whether your watch, ring, or other tracking device has this feature. Your HRV can vary significantly based on your baseline stress level, as well as your fitness, diet, and sleep, and even from moment to moment throughout the day and night. For consistency, measure your HRV at the same time every day. An average healthy HRV is typically 40 to 60 milliseconds, but rather than shooting for a particular number, find your average HRV after monitoring daily for two weeks and then work to raise it above what it is now by 10 points in six weeks. If yours is 30, try to increase it to 40. If it's 10, try to increase it to 20. If it's 60, try to increase it to 70. When you've reached your HRV goal, set a new one.

One of the best ways to increase the beat-to-beat variability of your heart is through slow breathing. This simple intervention reduces the sympathetic tone in your body and promotes a calmer, more relaxed state in your brain. Slow breathing appears to set a rhythm in the vagus nerve, the primary pathway for information transmission from your heart and lungs to your brain, which establishes a calmer tone for the rest of your brain.[18] It's easy to do.

Find a quiet place, sit down, close your eyes, and take deep breaths for 5 to 10 minutes. In our office, we often used the 6–3–6 technique: breathe in for a count of 6, hold your breath for a count of 3, then breathe out for a count of 6. There is also evidence that breathing through your nose rather than your mouth releases more nitric oxide into your blood. This opens your blood vessels, further improving HRV. Even pausing for two minutes to breathe deeply during a stressful situation can help reduce your stress and calm you down.

If you are tracking your HRV, you receive feedback on your HRV to determine what works. You will notice a significant increase when you practice slow, deep breathing daily. Practice this regularly, and your body learns how to do it automatically, improving your overall HRV, even when you aren't practicing deep breathing.

Some people find it challenging to maintain their slow breathing pattern for five to ten minutes. Fortunately, many biofeedback devices can help you achieve better results by displaying images on a screen that reflect how well you are breathing and how much your HRV is improving.

We used an HRV biofeedback program from the HeartMath company in our office. To use this program, you place a pulse sensor on your fingertip or earlobe to measure your pulse and HRV. On your phone screen, you view a balloon in an open field before a blue sky and follow a suggested breathing pattern designed to produce the most significant improvements in your HRV. As you follow the screen prompt for your slow breathing (follow a sinusoidal wave in the corner), you see the balloon rise in the sky. The better you follow the breathing prompt, the higher your balloon rises (reflecting a higher HRV).

There are many options for the feedback, ranging from a black-and-white drawing that turns into a color illustration to flowers blooming. This app is relatively expensive but effective. These days, you can find many similar gadgets on the internet, or use one of the apps that facilitate your HRV biofeedback training. These include HRV4Biofeedback, Elite HRV, Welltory, Breathwrk, Resonate, and Apple Health.

Some clinical trials show that HRV biofeedback can have lasting benefits for patients with anxiety or depression. In one study, a group of patients with depression did HRV biofeedback training for fifteen minutes three times a week. After four weeks, the HRV group reported feeling better and the placebo group did not; one month after the study was completed, the HRV group still had lower depression rates than the placebo group.[19] Another study assessed HRV biofeedback's effect on mental health symptoms in general and found that just five sessions reduced stress and other mental health symptoms in people working on the front line during the Covid-19 pandemic.[20]

HRV biofeedback can help grow parts of your brain's emotional network. In one randomized clinical trial, participants engaged in daily HRV biofeedback sessions through slow-paced breathing for five weeks. The findings revealed that older adults in the training group exhibited increased volume in specific hippocampal regions.[21] In another study, participants who engaged in daily HRV biofeedback for five weeks exhibited increased volume in the left orbitofrontal cortex, an area associated with emotion regulation and decision-making.[22]

Several factors beyond slow breathing can improve HRV. One of the most effective is meditation. Many studies show that meditation over time increases HRV,[23] lowers stress, improves anxiety, and reduces the risk of many chronic diseases.[24] Other ways to boost HRV include regular exercise, optimal sleep, yoga, a healthy diet, and omega-3 fatty acids, but among all these options, slow and deep breathing appears to be the most effective.

It is essential to recognize that biofeedback will not be effective if the basics of a healthy lifestyle are not in place. If you have a poor diet, you never exercise, and you have untreated sleep apnea, then don't expect biofeedback to make you into a whole new person. This is why I placed those fast-track chapters first. However, many individuals who combine HRV biofeedback with other interventions are amazed by how much better and happier they feel.

Make Your Plan

I've made a list of mindset interventions and stress management techniques here that can help you maintain a more positive frame of mind, break out of the stress cycle, and manage situational anxiety and depression. These are habits to stick with because we all know we can't eliminate stress. There will always be stressful situations; sometimes you need that stress response to get you through an emergency. However, the secret to preserving your brain health and protecting it from chronic stress is learning to get yourself out of a stress state when you no longer need it.

Once you have your list, select one to three tasks to accomplish every day. If you have a lot of stress, begin with just a few things that feel doable. If you don't feel too stressed, focus on increasing your HRV with deep breathing exercises. Keep tracking it and monitor your progress, which will be motivating!

Mindset and Stress Management Practices to Choose From

- ☐ Practice mindfulness meditation. Notice your thoughts, feelings, and behaviors and how they are interconnected. Mindfulness practices are associated with lower stress[25] and better executive function.[26] A simple way to start is to count your breaths. See how far you can get before your mind wanders. This exercise is beneficial for reducing stress and engaging your prefrontal cortex (which is why people's executive functions also improve).

- ☐ Find one repetitive negative thought (RNT) and restructure or reframe it. See if this makes a difference in how you feel. Research supports reframing as an effective method for improving responses to stress.[27]

- ☐ Identify one recurring uncomfortable feeling and see if you can trace it to a thought that you can restructure or reframe.

- ☐ Find one behavior you want to stop doing or one you want to start doing. See if you can identify the feeling or thought holding you back. Can you change your thoughts to change your feelings, making stopping or starting the behavior easier?

- ☐ Take ten minutes each day to relax, feel calm, and focus on what you need to do for yourself that day.

- ☐ Exercise on most days. By raising endorphin levels in the brain, exercise helps to calm anxiety and boost mood. It will also increase your HRV and help to improve your emotional resilience to stress.[28]

- ☐ Try deep breathing exercises. Try a slow inhale through the nose for six counts, hold for three counts, and a slow exhale through the nose or mouth for six counts. Try to do this for one minute daily, then gradually increase to five or ten minutes.

- ☐ Use a meditation app you like and follow along, take a class, or read about different techniques and try them. Numerous studies support the benefits of regular meditation for improving mindset and mood and promoting calmness. Bonus: Regular meditation leads to a larger hippocampus.[29]

- ☐ Increase your intake of omega-3 fatty acids by consuming fish or algae oil supplements, as well as two to three servings of fatty fish per week. These fats can have brain effects that reduce the reactivity of the sympathetic nervous system and cardiac stress effects.[30]

- ☐ Get enough sleep. Sleep deprivation can contribute to an unstable mood and lower your HRV. Get seven to eight hours of high-quality sleep each night, and you will likely notice an improvement in your mood and mindset.

- ☐ Consider complementary medicine treatments, such as acupuncture, therapeutic massage, yoga, or tai chi.

- ☐ Consider calming supplements like magnesium,[31] ashwagandha,[32] L-theanine,[33] and a B-vitamin complex.[34]

Track your progress here or on the app. Every day, score yourself from zero to 10 based on your stress management and mindset. Give yourself zero if you felt stressed out and overwhelmed most of the day and 10 if you felt calm most of the day and maintained a positive mindset. Determine your weekly score based on how well you reach your goal for that week, also from zero to 10.

Your Mindset and Stress Tracker

	MON	TUES	WED	THURS	FRI	SAT	SUN	WEEKLY SCORE
Your HRV at baseline:								
WEEK 1								
WEEK 2								
WEEK 3								
WEEK 4								
WEEK 5								
WEEK 6								
Your HRV after six weeks:								
WEEK 7								
WEEK 8								
WEEK 9								
WEEK 10								
WEEK 11								
WEEK 12								
Your HRV after twelve weeks:								

17

FAST-TRACK YOUR BRAIN TRAINING

Having an invincible brain isn't just about preventing Alzheimer's disease in the future; it is about becoming sharper now. Everyone would agree that having a sharp mind is better than feeling slow, experiencing brain fog, and struggling to grasp concepts or articulate their thoughts and feelings. It's good to be sharp. You accomplish more, achieve better job performance, engage in more interesting conversations, listen more effectively, and grasp concepts more quickly. When you feel smarter, you gain more confidence in yourself and will soon notice an improvement in your quality of life.

Everybody can get smarter. You know that now. With effort, everyone can get at least one notch sharper, faster, more productive, and more detail oriented. When you work to train your brain, you may not turn into an Einstein-level genius, but you will increase your current cognitive capacity in noticeable and measurable ways. It's like training your muscles to get stronger. Exercise the "muscle" that is your brain, and it will get stronger. "Use it or lose it" applies to your brain just as much as to your muscles.

Challenging your brain yields results, whether you do it through hands-on brain games or computer-based programs and apps. Daily brain training with apps such as Lumosity, Brain HQ, Elevate, Name Shark, and Peak, for twelve weeks, will result in significant improvements in the cognitive domains you focus on. Explore the various apps and determine which ones look the most interesting to you, considering your budget, as some are free. For a complete list and brief descriptions of the brain games used in NeuroGrow's Brain Fitness Program—verbal memory, reaction time, attention, processing speed, working memory, or executive function—please visit my website at drfotuhi.com.

What about recent reports that brain training games do not lower the risk of Alzheimer's disease? While the research is mixed, such reports, in my opinion, are misleading. Doing a daily brain game and nothing else will, of course, not make much of a dent in the mix of problems that is Alzheimer's disease. However, I guarantee that brain training combined with the other four pillars of brain health will have a significant and noticeable impact on your cognitive abilities and will have a protective effect against cognitive decline in the future. The areas you work on will improve. If you work on improving your memory, it will become better. If you work on focusing, your focus will improve. If you train your brain regularly in multiple areas, you will get smarter—several studies have demonstrated how brain training can increase your IQ![1] Let brain training be one piece of the puzzle as you seek to get smarter and stay sharper with age.

Brain Cross-Training

If you want to be fit, would you only work on your biceps and triceps? Of course not. You would do cardio to benefit your heart and lungs, strength training to target your upper body, lower body, and core, and stretching to improve flexibility. However, if you genuinely want to build up your leg or shoulder strength, you will focus more on those areas than the others.

Your brain is the same. When you begin your brain-training exercises, you can focus on improving specific brain functions, such as attention, memory, executive function, or processing speed. You can easily enhance some of these cognitive abilities by 10 to 15 percent in three months. I suggest planning to work on two or three cognitive domains during your twelve weeks in this program. You won't fully challenge your cognitive capacity if you engage in only one type of brain training. The daily crossword doesn't reap benefits if that's the only brain training you've done for years. It becomes easy, or even if it still feels challenging, it only works certain parts of your brain.

Instead, cross-train your brain. Begin by powering up your prefrontal cortex, the central hub of your brain's attention network. Your ability to maintain focus for an extended period is a common denominator in many other brain activities. It's a very efficient way to begin upgrading your brain.

Then, power up your hippocampus, the most integral hub for your brain's learning and memory network. For my patients at NeuroGrow, we prioritized improving attention and memory, since these are two cognitive domains that tend to decline with aging. Working on them provides a meaningful difference in people's lives.

Once you are satisfied with your level of attention and memory, continue to challenge your brain with new hobbies, experiences, brain games, and other cognitive challenges, as everything you do will engage multiple parts of your brain. As I mentioned in our first chapter, learning a new language, juggling, practicing balancing yourself, taking golf lessons or piano lessons, and any other activity you practice repeatedly will increase the size of various parts of your cortex and hippocampus. Remember, practice makes cortex!

Regular brain training is like a daily tune-up, keeping your prefrontal cortex, hippocampus, and other key brain areas in tip-top shape. As you find ways to challenge your brain every day, you create more synapses, build new connections in your brain, enhance the efficiency of neuronal networks, increase the number of blood vessels in your brain, and boost levels of BDNF, a critical factor in the process of neurogenesis in your hippocampus.

Brain training isn't a chore. Think of it as an enjoyable upgrade as you progress toward building an invincible brain. You don't need more than five or ten minutes a day on most days, but do something to challenge your brain *daily* to increase your brain reserve. Check the end of this chapter for brain-training ideas.

You can expect to see a noticeable change in your brain performance in a matter of weeks. Just as regular and challenging physical exercise for twelve weeks leads to perceptible changes in your strength and body shape, brain exercises for twelve weeks will result in tangible cognitive improvements in your daily life. People around you will also notice that you have become sharper. This was one of the most common types of feedback we received from patients who completed our Brain Fitness Program.

Physical Exercise + Brain Training = Better Mental Stamina

Recent research has uncovered the surprising synergistic benefits of combining cognitive tasks with exercise. A recent study of thirty-one professional soccer players found that those who combined complex mental tasks with their physical training sessions showed improvement in both areas—focus and concentration increased, and they experienced reduced mental fatigue and enhanced soccer skills.[2] Another study compared groups of sedentary women between the ages of 65 and 78; one group performed a challenging cognitive task for 20 minutes before exercising for 45 minutes, and the other group exercised for 45 minutes only. The women who trained their brains and bodies increased their cognitive function by 7.8 percent and their physical endurance by 29.9 percent. The group that only exercised increased their cognitive function by just 4.5 percent and their physical endurance by just 22.4 percent.[3]

One study reviewed multiple clinical trials to determine whether combining physical exercise with cognitive training benefits older adults experiencing subjective cognitive decline—an early stage of decline preceding MCI.[4] Analyzing data from eleven trials with 1,713 participants, researchers found that engaging in physical and mental activities, such as memory training and movement-based exercises, significantly improved cognitive function in older adults.

Another study tested whether combining physical exercise with brain training would be more helpful even for people who suffer from MCI.[5] Over twelve weeks, ninety-five older adults were divided into two groups: One performed only cognitive exercises, while the other engaged in physical and cognitive activities. The results showed that those who combined movement with brain challenges demonstrated better balance, strength, flexibility, walking ability, memory, problem-solving skills, and verbal fluency compared to those who only underwent brain training.

Racquet sports, by themselves, are a form of brain training. A recent review highlights how playing badminton can significantly enhance multiple cognitive functions.[6] Unlike repetitive exercises like running, badminton requires rapid decision-making, hand-eye coordination, and strategic thinking, which engage multiple brain areas. The study found that regular badminton play improves executive function, processing speed, working memory, attention, and visuospatial skills, even with as little as ten to twenty minutes of high-intensity play per week. I am sure playing tennis or pickleball would have similar brain benefits. Physical exercise, particularly activities that combine movement and mental engagement, is a powerful tool for maintaining and improving your cognitive vitality.

Why not try this yourself? Do puzzles or brain games while on a stationary bike. Take a dance class. Listen to language-learning apps or audiobooks while walking or running. Consider finding creative solutions to complex problems while swimming or lifting weights. Or find your own way to combine mentally and physically challenging training.

Learning How to Focus

Focus is a skill that can be easily trained and improved. When you want to engage in deep work or serious thought that requires absolute concentration, you can train yourself. Let's say you want to focus on solving a complex problem, studying for exams, preparing a presentation for work, or writing a paper. The first thing to do is to make sure you are not interrupted.

Distraction is a prevalent feature of modern life. Our attention is frequently fragmented. You may finally be getting into your flow of deep thought, and then your phone dings to alert you to a message or an email. Of course, you have to see who it is and what it's about, so you go to your phone, check it, maybe answer it, maybe look up something or contact someone to get the answer, maybe see something online that looks interesting, and before you know it, an hour has gone by. What happened to your focus?

Once you've returned to your project after making a phone call, you'll need to regain your concentration level before being interrupted. It may take ten to fifteen minutes to return to your deep-focus zone. And then it happens again—ding, ding, ding, all through the workday and evening. Someone knocks on your office door to ask you a question. A family member calls to check in or to share something with you. The dog scratches at the door to go outside. These dings bring us back to the surface level. How will you learn to concentrate and sustain attention if this continues? You won't.

Sometimes, it takes me half an hour from sitting in front of my computer to getting fully immersed in my work, such as writing this chapter. I check the news, review my emails, and respond to some. I then decide what I will do and create an outline of tasks. During that time, I'm preparing to do deep work. I let my family know I will be focusing for a specific period. I put on some nature sounds so I'm not distracted by noises and slowly sink into that deep-focus zone. Getting there is a great feeling, but it takes some work.

When you want to get into a deep-focus zone, you must minimize or eliminate the distractions first. Forget multitasking. Research indicates that multitasking is less productive than focusing on a single activity, as it requires time to switch focus repeatedly.[7] Pick one thing to focus on. Turn off the alerts and the ringer on your phone. Better yet, turn your phone off while you are working. Not everyone can do this because they may need to be available in an emergency. If you have children or are a caregiver, turn the sound and ringer off. Stop alerts on your computer. If you don't need the internet, turn that off too, so you aren't tempted to start scrolling or checking social media.

It's also worth considering when you will be best able to focus. Are you more alert and focused in the mornings or at night? I like to work at night when my family is asleep and the house is quiet. I'm able to concentrate intensely without interruption. Other people prefer to work early in the morning before the family wakes up. For others, peak concentration occurs in the middle of the day, so they must be even more vigilant about eliminating distractions. Some self-employed people rent a quiet space to work. Some people who work in busy offices put Do Not Disturb signs on their doors and alerts on their phones during focus time.

Begin with twenty to thirty minutes focused on something you want to accomplish without any external distractions. Set a timer for the start and end of your focus session. As this becomes easier, work up to more extended periods of focus. I can now focus deeply for about five hours, with ten-minute breaks every hour (to do push-ups, go for a short walk, or get a healthy snack).

This level of undistracted focus time, lasting a few hours, requires training. If you were training for a marathon, would you ever be ready if, every time you started to go for a run, someone called you to return home to deal with something? You would never get to the point where you could run twenty-six miles.

Don't let trivial matters interfere with your goal to build a supersharp brain! Set aside specific times, get deep into your thoughts, and enjoy the magnificent results of sustained concentration! Being in the deep-focus zone is enjoyable, much like when you get into a zone while running and experience that runner's high. Additionally, since sustained attention is the foundation for all forms of learning, having better focus will open many doors for other parts of your brain to expand and flourish.

Boredom to Stimulate Creativity

Sometimes, the best thing to do for your brain is to do nothing. Creativity often emerges when you are not working. If you want to be more creative in your work or life, try daydreaming or exercising without distractions, such as audiobooks, podcasts, or music. Let your mind wander and let your brain wonder about things. You will be surprised at what creative ideas and solutions to problems emerge at the forefront of your consciousness.

Try this by taking a quiet, solitary walk. Many people say they get most inspired and come up with their best ideas when they are in natural areas. I often get my creative "aha!" moments and inspirations for solving problems during my long bike rides on trails through wooded areas. This system has worked well for me, as I get fit and enjoy the outdoors while coming up with new ideas, including many for this book. I also get creative ideas when I'm swimming. Ideas just come to me, and they will come to you too if you make the space for them.

Exercising without distractions may feel boring, but it's the first step. Our brains get creative in response to boredom. Research supports this, showing that engaging in mundane tasks can increase creativity. Daydreaming also promotes creativity. Let yourself get bored, dream without external stimulation, such as media devices, and see what you find on the other side of boredom. You might come up with your best idea yet!

Make Your Plan

I've created a list of brain-training exercises to help you work your brain like a muscle daily. Review this list and check all the items you would like to try. Once you have your list, select one to three tasks to accomplish every day. Begin with a few things that feel doable, such as memorizing four to five new names daily. You can then set new challenges for yourself. Using apps like Lumosity, you can track your progress in specific cognitive functions.

Brain-Training Practices to Choose From

ATTENTION AND FOCUS
- ☐ Practice focused concentration by working on one task for twenty minutes or more without distractions, gradually increasing your focus to two to three hours.
- ☐ Train your brain with something challenging for at least five minutes a day, such as brain games on an app like Lumosity.

- Limit digital distractions by spending time away from screens each day.
- Listen actively to TED Talks, speeches, podcasts, or audiobooks without distractions. See how long you can maintain focus.
- Practice mindful observation by selecting an object, such as a tree or a building, and studying it for two minutes. Then, close your eyes and recall as many details as possible.
- Engage in deep conversations by actively listening and recalling key details.

MEMORY AND LEARNING
- Practice active recall by summarizing key conversation points in your mind and testing yourself later.
- Memorize helpful information such as credit card numbers, grocery lists, license plate numbers, or frequently used phone numbers with the techniques you learned in our memory chapter.
- Memorize recipes and test yourself on ingredients and steps for making the dishes you love.
- Learn from others by asking questions and absorbing knowledge from professionals in different fields.
- Expand your vocabulary by learning and using five to ten new words daily.
- Read challenging material such as classic literature or complex science books.
- Learn how to play a musical instrument and practice daily.
- Start learning a new language with a language app for a few minutes daily.

EXECUTIVE FUNCTION AND PROBLEM-SOLVING
- Play strategy games like chess, Risk, or sudoku to challenge your problem-solving skills.
- Debate yourself by picking a topic you believe in and arguing against your viewpoint.
- Solve word puzzles, like the crossword, Wordle, Connections, or Spelling Bee.

- Solve real-world puzzles by navigating without GPS, estimating distances, or calculating tips without a calculator.
- Describe a complex idea in simple terms to someone without expertise in that field, ensuring they have a complete understanding.
- Try reverse puzzle solving by designing a crossword or sudoku instead of solving one.
- Play what-if scenarios by imagining alternative historical events or business strategies.

PROCESSING SPEED

- Time yourself while playing thinking games, such as Wordle, crossword puzzles, and reaction-based video games. Can you decrease your time?
- Memorize visual details quickly by looking at a scene for ten seconds, closing your eyes, and recalling everything you saw.
- Increase your reading speed while ensuring you still understand the key concepts.

Rate your progress here or on the app. Score yourself from zero to 10 based on whether you challenged your brain daily. Give yourself zero if you did not challenge your brain at all and 10 if you did specific brain-training exercises or focused to learn something new that day. Determine your weekly score based on how well you met your weekly goals, again with a score from zero to 10.

Your Brain-Training Tracker

	MON	TUES	WED	THURS	FRI	SAT	SUN	WEEKLY SCORE
WEEK 1								
WEEK 2								
WEEK 3								
WEEK 4								
WEEK 5								
WEEK 6								
WEEK 7								
WEEK 8								
WEEK 9								
WEEK 10								
WEEK 11								
WEEK 12								

18

YOUR INVINCIBLE FUTURE

Even less than one hundred years ago, cardiologists thought we were each allotted a certain number of heartbeats in a lifetime, and if we used too many of them with exercise, we would wear out our hearts and die sooner. Especially for those who had experienced heart issues, rest was the prescription. Doctors feared that strenuous activity would overstrain the heart and lead to sudden death, which they had seen in the case of a marathon runner. Vigorous exercise was suspect, or recommended only for the healthiest young men.[1]

One of the first studies to begin shifting this belief was published in 1953.[2] This study looked at the cardiac function of bus drivers and bus conductors. The study found that the conductors, who were on their feet and moving around all day, going up and down the steps to direct and assist people on and off the buses, had a significantly lower incidence of coronary heart disease than the drivers, who spent most of their workday seated. In 1979, results from a famous large-scale study called the Framingham Study showed that death due to cardiovascular and ischemic heart disease was more likely in sedentary men than in active men, but that the effect was not significant in women.[3]

Dr. Paul Dudley White, the personal physician for President Dwight Eisenhower, who took care of him after his heart attack in 1955, was among a few cardiologists who went against the mainstream and insisted that exercise was good for the heart.[4] Dr. Ralph Paffenbarger's study of seventeen thousand Harvard alums in the 1970s and 1980s, which showed that men who exercised more were less likely to develop heart disease, contributed to a paradigm shift toward the benefits of vigorous physical activity.[5] However, it took considerable time for mainstream medicine to agree. Now, in the first half of the twenty-first century, it is well known that exercise is beneficial for the heart, for both men and women, and even for most individuals with heart disease. Few would question it. In retrospect, it's obvious. Why didn't they see it?

I think we are in those early stages concerning brain health. Mainstream medicine still generally insists that if you are going to get Alzheimer's disease, there isn't much you can do about it. Amyloid accumulation cannot be reversed (without the latest expensive medications), intelligence is static, and you cannot grow your brain. A handful of us doctors and researchers go against the mainstream and insist that cognitive decline can be reversed, amyloid load can be reduced without medication, one can become more brilliant tomorrow than they are today, and the brain can be measurably enlarged. I firmly believe that in twenty years, nobody will question the power of lifestyle changes on brain health, brain growth, and cognitive longevity.

What's more, in my clinic, we saw more than 80 percent of our patients, whether they had cognitive decline with aging, concussion, or ADHD, improve their symptoms and cognitive scores within twelve weeks. No drug can boast that level of improvement. *Not* improving on our program was unusual. I'm not alone in demonstrating this effect. I published this ten years ago, but since then, I have found references to more than fifty additional studies and programs demonstrating brain improvements.[6]

In recent years, several studies have shown that even patients who already have developed MCI or early-stage Alzheimer's can benefit from lifestyle interventions. Dr. Dean Ornish and his colleagues in California showed not only that their patients improved their memories, but also that they experienced a reduction in amyloid accumulation in their brains.[7] As we reviewed in chapter 9, four other randomized controlled trials showed patients with MCI improved their cognitive scores with a set of lifestyle interventions. And all of them showed superior results compared to the clinical trials for the new Alzheimer's medications that solely target removing amyloid in the brain—as I presented at the recent international Alzheimer's conference in Toronto.

So far, my research is the only published study to show cognitive improvement and growth specifically in the hippocampus in patients with MCI in three months; however, this was so evident in my clinic that it is only a matter of time before others demonstrate it. There are now more than twenty new lifestyle-intervention programs in various stages of development. Some are just beginning their research, and others are nearly complete. There is much more to be learned about lifestyle and the brain, but we are on our way to discovery.

In early 2025, when I attended the NIH Alzheimer's conference here in Washington, DC, many more people were doing these lifestyle interventions and collecting more data on a variety of measures like VO_2 max, HRV, heart rate, weight, visceral fat, and MRI data—all the things I've told you about in this book. I believe that in the next two to three decades many more programs like mine will be available, and this trend will only increase.

It was once challenging to publish studies on multimodal interventions. I had difficulty publishing my paper on my twelve-week program when I initially submitted it for publication in 2016. The reviewers kept commenting that I was doing too many things for too many different people in my program. They wanted me to test one group on a diet, one on exercise, one on brain training, and so on. But I was persistent. I argued that to live, you need water, food, oxygen, and sleep. You can't just say, "Okay, group one gets oxygen only. Group two gets food only." The point is that we now know that late-life cognitive decline is a soup of problems, and the best way to address a soup with many ingredients is to do a program with many interventions.

My follow-up paper, published in 2023, establishes that it's not just older people who have multiple reasons why they struggle to think clearly. There are concussion patients who have migraine symptoms, attention issues, sleep problems, and anxiety issues—they have their own soup of problems. So do ADHD patients. Sometimes, patients who have ADHD are diagnosed with anxiety, insomnia, depression, or other conditions that have overlapping symptoms with ADHD.

Neuroplasticity principles apply universally, regardless of the specific brain issue. Whether you have experienced a flood, fire, or termite damage, the principles of renovating a house remain the same. You clean it, go through the junk, and eliminate what's ruined. You rebuild the broken parts, apply a fresh coat of paint, and relandscape.

Brain repair and rehabilitation principles are the same—the formation of new synapses, improvement or formation of new fiber bundles, enhancement of the glymphatic system, elevation of BDNF levels, creation of new blood vessels, and the birth or maturation of new neurons. Regarding brain rehabilitation, there are not fifty different things to do for fifty different conditions. A few simple principles are universally helpful for all brains. What's good for one brain is good for every brain. It's not so complicated after all.

Your brain becomes stronger when your cortex and hippocampus are denser, are thicker, and have volume. Our goal is to generate more vascularization, more neurons, and more synapses, with a more substantial blood-brain barrier that doesn't leak. When inflammation resolves and amyloid disperses, when mitochondria multiply and generate more and more ATP in response to the brain's energy needs, when the glymphatic system has broad, clear channels for waste removal, brain issues resolve across the board. Brain fog clears. Memory, attention, and executive function improve.

Results emerge by addressing those five pillars of brain health: increasing your fitness with exercise; increasing glymphatic function with longer and better-quality sleep; increasing nutrient density and addressing weight, blood sugar, and lipid issues with diet; raising HRV by improving mindset and managing stress; and directly exercising the brain with brain training in lots of different ways every single day.

I eagerly await the day mainstream medicine acknowledges the power of the five pillars of brain health to make the brain more resilient against cognitive decline and Alzheimer's disease. But you don't have to wait for that. Just by reading this book, you've already begun building your invincible brain.

Maintain Your Brain Portfolio

I hope you've already created your Brain Portfolio, as I encouraged you to do in chapter 12. Your Brain Portfolio can help you see that your overall symptom load decreases significantly when you follow my program. After twelve weeks, perhaps you will discover you've improved by just 10 to 20 percent in five areas, so you don't notice it, but a 10 to 20 percent improvement in five areas significantly reduces your overall symptom load. When you begin to feel better, it can be easy to forget how bad you felt before you started this program, but your Brain Portfolio can show you how far you've come. Keep going, and you'll see positive changes accumulate until feeling sharp, strong, and bright is your everyday reality. Soon, people around you will notice and comment on your new, brighter side.

I asked you this in chapter 12, as you were preparing to create your Brain Portfolio, but let's consider the question again: "Compared to how you felt ten years ago, how much do you feel like yourself—what percent of your usual self are you today?" This was one of my favorite and most valuable questions I asked my patients. It was surprisingly helpful, as it put things in perspective regarding how they began and how much they had progressed. Some patients would say they felt like 80 percent of their usual selves, or 50 percent. Some would say they felt only 10 percent of their usual selves, or they would say, "Dr. Fotuhi, I feel like zero percent of my usual self. I don't even know where that person went." Then they would work hard, and in three months, I would ask them again: "What percent of your usual self do you feel now?" With my patients, this number almost invariably rose with every visit. By the end, some were even so enthusiastic that they felt like 200 percent of their usual selves!

I encourage you to monitor this for yourself in this way. What percentage of yourself do you feel you are before starting the program? At the halfway point? At the end of the twelve weeks? Then, six months after that, a year, and so on? Mark that percentage in your Brain Portfolio. You are working to get back to who you once were. The part of you full of hopes, dreams, and plans is still alive. You are excavating your true self so you can make your comeback.

Ultimately, what matters is how much better you feel about yourself. It's not so much the scores. The scores are informative, but the bottom line is: Are you feeling more like yourself every day? Are you starting to feel better than you've ever felt before? I can't wait for you to answer yes to those questions.

What's Next?

When people undertake a program, a diet, an exercise challenge, or a similar initiative, they often wonder what happens when it's over. Do you do it again? Do you return to your old ways because you are now "fixed"? Is there a maintenance phase?

What I found interesting about my program was that even at our visits three, six, and twelve months after they finished the program, my patients' test scores were almost always slightly better than when they initially completed the program. The reason is because they stayed committed to it. The changes you experience while doing the Brain Fitness Program are the motivation to make your lifestyle interventions permanent habits.

This is not a "do-it-and-forget-it" program because if you want an invincible brain, you need to do the things that build an invincible brain, not just occasionally but as a regular part of your brain-optimizing life. Even a year or more after the program was completed, my patients continued to tell me how much they loved the program and felt like a new person, or like they had reclaimed the person they used to be. You don't want to return once you get to that level. Why would you trade your newfound clarity and sharpness for the old brain fog, confusion, and decline?

It takes twenty-one days to form a habit, but that's twenty-one days of consistently practicing. It takes some time to get to the point where you do it regularly, which is why my program lasts twelve weeks instead of three. The habit clock doesn't start from the day you start trying. It starts from the day you become consistent. For some, that can be a few days. For others, it's a month or longer. We have families, we have jobs, we have busy lives. However, people make time for what is important to them. If retaining and growing your brain is essential to you, you will make healthy brain habits part of your life and never look back.

It doesn't have to be complicated. It doesn't have to take hours. You don't have to drive to the gym, get dressed, exercise, drive home, shower, and lose three hours of your day. Even a walk out your front door, some jumping jacks and sit-ups, a weekend game of tennis, or a few yoga sessions will put you on the right track. You don't have to make it a production. All you have to do is establish small habits that can grow at your own pace.

You can even incorporate memory training into your leisure time. Play cards, board games, or word games with your family or friends. Challenge each other to puzzle games. Share brain-training scores once you've learned how fun and rewarding it is to memorize things, which can also become part of your leisure time. You've already seen how easy it is to exercise your memory. If you dedicate just a few minutes daily to memorizing names, within a month, you will be one of those people with a good memory for names. You will no longer say you have a terrible memory. You can regain your memory and improve it with just a few minutes a day.

How about working on cognitive stamina? You know what stamina is. If you can go up only one flight of stairs at first, doing it every day will eventually enable you to climb two flights of stairs, and then, if you continue, ten flights of stairs. If you can walk only one mile today, with regular walking and running, you can eventually run a mile, then two miles, and eventually ten miles, or you can run those one or two miles faster and faster.

Just as you can improve your physical stamina, you can improve your cognitive stamina. There is no question. You'll get better at whatever you practice. Nobody questions whether doing biceps curls daily will strengthen your arms or whether taking piano lessons and practicing every day will improve your piano playing. If you want to become a cognitive athlete, go for it! Train for it. I predict that memory prowess will become a more popular sport in the years to come as people discover how easy it is to excel. I practice it regularly and enjoy it. I don't expect I'll ever get as good as Memory Champion Nelson Dellis, who, I recently discovered, has memorized the pi number up to ten thousand digits! Now, that is above and beyond. However, simply memorizing things every day will lead to significant improvement.

You can improve your ability to focus for extended periods by training your brain through meditation or entering the zone, or flow state, where you perform your task efficiently, with interest, and uninterrupted concentration. You can get more creative, coming up with ideas you never would have thought of in a brain fog. You can have more rewarding relationships as you get better at socializing and improve your emotional and social intelligence.

So many rewards await you at the end of this program and beyond! You could never discover them all in twelve weeks. What an exciting road you have ahead! One of the most tremendous benefits you will soon discover is more happiness.

Happiness Intelligence

In chapter 2 and a few other sections throughout this book, I briefly mention that happiness intelligence may be the most important intelligence. Why have it all if you aren't happy? Health can certainly enhance happiness, and a sharp and optimized brain will be less subject to conditions that can interfere with happiness, such as anxiety, depression, brain fog, and cognitive decline. The program in this book is an excellent happiness insurance policy.

This is my favorite formula:

Happiness = Reality − Expectations

I have noticed over the years how much expectations can interfere with the pure joy of appreciating your life. For instance, I remember buying my first car as a graduate student. I had never owned a car. I fled Iran at age twenty (during the Iran-Iraq War) and came to Canada with no money in my pockets. For years, buying a car was not even on my radar. Only after much hard work and becoming a graduate student at Johns Hopkins with a full scholarship (a long story for another time) could I scrape together $500 to buy a used Honda. This occurred around 1988 or 1989. I was in my late twenties.

This Honda was nothing special. It was an old car with a hundred thousand miles on it, but to me, it was the most thrilling experience to drive that old Honda around. I was on cloud nine. I could not believe I owned my own car. I remember my friend and I cruising down the highway, and I was thrilled. That old Honda brought me so much happiness!

This is so true of everything in life. Imagine someone who has never flown on an airplane before, getting a window seat in basic economy and taking off for the first time, looking down as the earth falls away. What a thrill! Contrast that to the person in first class complaining because the onboard Wi-Fi doesn't work, or they are told to put their laptop away. The person in basic economy, elated to be on an airplane, has no expectations. They are happy. The complainer in first class is full of expectations, and when they are thwarted, they become unhappy.

The same applies to relationships, which are crucial for happiness. It's incredible how you can get along with someone or not based on your expectations. People are often surprised when I say the secret to a happy marriage is lowering your expectations.

Interestingly, people often place higher expectations on their spouses than on their friends or other family members. "If only they would do this one thing I want them to do!" "If only they would stop doing that thing I hate!" "Why does he spend so much money?" "Why does she spend so much time with her friends?" Instead of expecting, look to yourself. Instead of trying to make your partner make you happy, what can you do to make that person happy? People are happier when those around them are happy. It makes people happy to make other people happy. This may be why volunteering leads to happiness,[8] and social support underpins happiness.[9] In my opinion, lowering your expectations for your partner, children, and parents in favor of accepting them for who they are while encouraging them to become their best selves, supporting their efforts, and trying to make them happy is the shortest path to happiness.

Expectations can foil many other kinds of relationships. Have you ever found yourself irritated or angry because someone doesn't just do something they should do, or can't seem to solve their obvious problem, or because someone cut you off in traffic or said something to you that you didn't like, or has a different opinion than you about politics or religion? If you assume the best—perhaps that person is going through a difficult time, has an emergency, possesses a different kind of intelligence than you, or was brought up differently—then you may find yourself much happier and less easily derailed by what other people do and say. Another saying I like is: "Other people's opinion of you is none of your business." And here is another one my uncle likes to say: "If you don't have a solution for a problem, then it's not your problem."

What can you let go of today to feel happier?

There is considerable stress and difficulty in the world today. Many people are unhappy, many for reasons of tragedy, trauma, anxiety, or depression. If we all step back and see each other as fellow humans trying to navigate life as best we can, we may all find more happiness.

Why say all this in a book about the brain? Because frustration and chronic stress kill your synapses, damage the blood vessels in your brain, increase your risk of heart attacks and strokes, accelerate your aging process, shrink your brain, and contribute to your risk of developing Alzheimer's disease.[10] Happiness is good for your brain. Life satisfaction can keep your mind healthy by building more reserve in your brain and other organs. As your brain gradually becomes invincible against anxiety, depression, brain fog, and cognitive decline, and as you continue to get brighter and sharper, and as you work to be the best person you can be while letting go of your expectations for anyone other than yourself, I predict your happiness will grow exponentially.

I'll end this book with a joke. So, this guy is driving down the highway in a brown minivan and has the radio on. Suddenly, a voice interrupts the music. It's a breaking news alert. The voice says, "Attention, attention, someone in a brown minivan is driving the wrong way on the highway, so beware!" The guy looks around, then says, "Hmmm, that's strange. They're wrong. There isn't just one person going the wrong way on this highway. Everybody is going the wrong way!"

Sometimes, the problem isn't "everybody else." Sometimes, it's just you, which is great because you are the only one you can do something about. Maybe you aren't going in the right direction. Perhaps you need a new perspective. You can pull over and turn your car around, metaphorically speaking. Reevaluate your situation.

What kind of person do you want to be? You can make that happen by thinking about what you want out of your life. What makes you happy, and why aren't you doing that? What makes you unhappy, and why do you continue to do that?

Establishing why you are here and what you live for can make a surprising change in your life. Pursuing your goals with hope and optimism translates into positive brain chemistry. What would happen if you consciously tried to do what makes you happy more often? You can make a transition, set a goal, and do it. Your brain will then experience pockets of joy and frequent bursts of dopamine.

There is no reason to waste another minute feeling sad, irritable, angry, and unhappy. It's time to get to work. Start simple. Set manageable goals and hold yourself accountable. You owe it to yourself to make your brain as strong as possible, and your mind will follow. All you have to do to get started is pick one thing:

- Raise your VO_2 max.
- Go on a walk.
- Help someone.
- Make more BDNF.
- Sleep longer and better.
- Eat more nutrients.
- Eat less sugar.
- Raise your HRV.
- Calm yourself.
- Breathe deeper.
- Go outside.
- Be alone less.
- Learn something.
- Practice something.
- Play games.
- Challenge yourself.
- Practice memory tricks.
- Look on the bright side.
- Believe you can do it.
- Find your purpose.
- Find your joy.
- Be grateful for what you have.
- Expect less.
- Live more.
- Make people happy.
- Let yourself be happy.

Keep going, keep trying, and do your best for your brain. Once you've mastered the basics of creating an invincible brain and happiness intelligence, you will be on the direct path to a bright future and a long, happy life. That's where I'm headed, and I hope to see you there!

Sincerely,

Dr Majid Fotuhi

APPENDIX

Brain Fitness Calculators and Spidograms for Ongoing Tracking

You can make copies of these to track your progress at six weeks, twelve weeks, six months, one year, and beyond. It's always good to keep an eye on your scores for these assessments, so you can keep going in the right direction.

BRAIN FITNESS CALCULATOR RESULTS

	Your score
Energy level throughout the day (low: very tired to high: very energetic)	1 2 3 4 5
Fitness (low: totally out of shape to high: in great shape)	1 2 3 4 5
Peaceful state of mind (low: stressed out and nervous to high: calm and in control)	1 2 3 4 5
Organized (low: chaos at home and work to high: well-organized most of the time)	1 2 3 4 5
Positive attitude (low: life is tough; everything will fail to high: life is beautiful; everything will work out just fine)	1 2 3 4 5
Satisfactory sleep (low: trouble falling sleep or up all night to high: sleep well, about 8 hours a night)	1 2 3 4 5
Memory for names (low: can't remember anybody's name to high: remember everybody's name)	1 2 3 4 5
Taking Omega-3 Fatty Acid supplements (low: never or one day a week to high: 5 or more days a week)	1 2 3 4 5
Social engagement (low: prefer to stay alone by myself to high: busy with lots of social activities every week)	1 2 3 4 5
Sense of curiosity (low: not too much into figuring things out to high: love to discover new things and solve puzzles)	1 2 3 4 5
Love your daily routine (low: dread my day-to-day routine to high: enjoy and love my daily routine)	1 2 3 4 5
Heart healthy diet choices (low: fast food, donuts, French-fries to high: lots of fruits and vegetables, zero junk food)	1 2 3 4 5
Mindful of portion size (low: eat large portions and second servings to high: prefer small and reasonable portions)	1 2 3 4 5
Extracurricular activities / hobbies (low: do not enjoy participating in activities to high: enjoy trying new hobbies, participating in community activities, volunteering, or helping others in my community)	1 2 3 4 5
Usual mood (low: down and depressed to high: happy and cheerful)	1 2 3 4 5
Add up your score:	

Appendix 287

Neurocognitive Symptoms

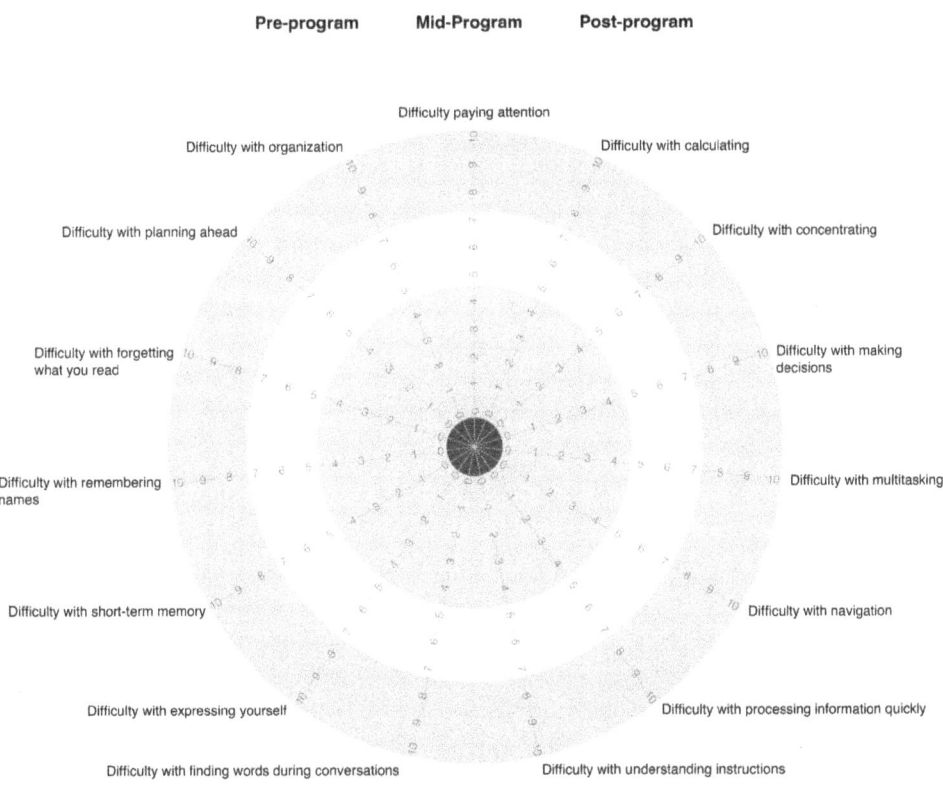

Total _____

Appendix

Total _____

ACKNOWLEDGMENTS

Writing this book has been a labor of love, and I am deeply grateful to the many people who helped bring it to life.

First and foremost, I want to thank Eve Adamson, my brilliant co-writer. She always showed immense curiosity and care for the complexity of the science behind this book. She patiently took the time to understand the nuances of Alzheimer's disease, neuroplasticity, and the compelling evidence supporting lifestyle interventions for successful aging. I often joked with her that she has now become more of an expert in this field than many of my physician colleagues. She was never in a hurry—always willing to explore another layer, revise a chapter one more time, and push for clarity so that readers could experience that "aha!" moment that is so vital for lasting change in their lifestyle habits. Eve was enthusiastic, detail oriented, and a joy to work with. I will miss our collaboration deeply and am already brainstorming a new book idea just so that I can work with her again.

I am also grateful to my literary agent, Alex Glass. Alex has an extraordinary gift for understanding both the heart of a project and the realities of the publishing world. He guided this book from conception to publication with wisdom, strategy, and patience. Thanks to his tireless advocacy, we secured international publishing contracts, reaching audiences I never imagined I could reach. He was always available, always kind, and always believed in the mission of this book.

My sincere thanks go to my editor at HarperCollins, Sarah Pelz, who loved the idea of this book from the moment we had our first conversation via a Zoom call. She was able to appreciate the immediacy of this topic, my contributions to this field, and the large impact this book can have on the lives of millions of people around the world. Her keen editorial instincts, thoughtful feedback, and passion for the subject matter helped shape this book into what it is. She brought structure, flow, and a deep understanding of what readers need in order to stay engaged with complex ideas.

I was fortunate to work with one of the best medical illustrators in this field, Tatiana Gandlin. A gifted artist, she was meticulous in making sure she created the most accurate versions of scientific figures, graphs, and drawings I shared with her. She turned my rough sketches into beautiful illustrations, and was always ready and enthusiastic to make more tweaks and adjustments, as needed. I also thank her for incorporating my wife Bita's image in some of our illustrations.

To the thousands of patients who trusted me with their care: Thank you. Being invited into your lives was one of the greatest privileges of my career. Your stories, your questions, and your compliments brought me joy every single day.

To my students at Johns Hopkins, George Washington University, and Harvard Medical School: Thank you for challenging me with your questions and inspiring me with your enthusiasm. Teaching you pushed me to keep learning and growing.

To my many research collaborators and colleagues over the past thirty-plus years: Thank you for your brilliance and your commitment to discovery. I am especially grateful to my PhD mentor, Dr. Solomon Snyder, whose guidance at Johns Hopkins shaped the scientist I became. And to Dr. David Zee, my fellowship supervisor and a true star in the world of neurology, thank you for your mentorship and your example. You have always been my role model on how to treat patients with utmost respect, patience, and genuine care to attend to all their issues. Watching how your patients admired you inspired me to replicate your way of practicing medicine.

To my parents and siblings, thank you for your love, encouragement, and belief in me throughout the years. Your support has been a steady foundation in my life, and I am grateful for the ways—both big and small—you've shaped who I am.

I want to particularly thank my father for planting in me a passion for the brain and for believing in the power of the mind to shape our destiny. From the time I was in elementary school, he inspired me to set ambitious goals and pursue them with determination. His voice—cheering me on, reminding me that nothing was out of reach—has never left me. This book exists because he helped me believe that it could. He passed away last year, and since then, I have been remembering him every single day.

To my brother Leo, thank you for being more than a sibling—for being a fellow traveler with me in understanding the world of thoughts, emotions, and behavior. Our long conversations about growth mindset, neuroscience, and the deeper questions of life have deeply enriched my thinking. Some of those conversations made their way into this book.

To my daughters, Nora and Maya, I am endlessly proud of you. You have both written your own books, and I admire your drive, your intelligence, your maturity, and your open hearts. You are my inspiration. Everything I do—this book included—is ultimately for you.

And finally, to my wife, Bita—the heart of our family and the soul of my life. You are my partner in everything that matters. Thank you for giving me the time, space, and encouragement to write this book, and for standing by me through every challenge and triumph in our lives together. You helped with every aspect of this project—from the earliest brainstorming sessions to the choice of figures, to shaping the narrative and flow of each chapter. Your brilliance and insight are woven into these pages.

But even beyond your contributions to the book, I am most grateful for the life we've built together. I love your beautiful smiles, your quick wit, and your warm sense of humor. I treasure our evening walks, our ballroom dances, and the quiet joy of just being beside you. Your cooking nourishes our family in every sense of the word. You are strong, humble, and devoted, always putting us first—yet somehow still finding time to take care of your health, your mind, and your career goals with grace and discipline. You are a true role model for successful aging. I am certain you will always remain energetic, athletic, and bubbly—even when you are one hundred years old.

I am so proud of you, Bita. I love you more than words can ever fully express. This book would not exist without you—and neither would the happiest parts of my life.

NOTES

Introduction
1. Gill Livingston, Jonathan Huntley, Kathy Y. Liu, et al. "Dementia Prevention, Intervention, and Care: 2024 Report of the *Lancet* Standing Commission." *The Lancet* 404, no. 10452 (2024): 572–628. Accessed April 9, 2025. https://doi.org/10.1016/S0140-6736(24)01296-0.
2. M. Fotuhi, B. Lubinski, N. Hausterman, et al. "A Personalized 12-Week 'Brain Fitness Program' for Improving Cognitive Function and Increasing the Volume of Hippocampus in Elderly with Mild Cognitive Impairment." *The Journal of Prevention of Alzheimer's Disease* 3, no. 3 (2016): 133–137. https://doi.org/http://dx.doi.org/10.14283/jpad.2016.92.
3. M. Fotuhi, A. Y. Ebadi, P. Dwivedy, et al. "Retrospective Analysis of a Comprehensive Concussion Recovery Program." *Journal of Rehabilitation* 86, no. 1 (2020): 20–31 https://neurogrow.com/wp-content/uploads/2020/07/Fotuhi-JOR-published-2020-1.pdf.
4. Majid Fotuhi, Noah D. Khorrami, and Cyrus A. Raji. "Benefits of a 12-Week Non-Drug 'Brain Fitness Program' for Patients with Attention-Deficit/Hyperactive Disorder, Post-Concussion Syndrome, or Memory Loss." *Journal of Alzheimer's Disease Reports* 7, no. 1 (2023): 675–697. https://doi.org/10.3233/ADR-220091.

Chapter 1: The Unlimited Potential of the Invincible Brain
1. Associated Press. "Iranian Woman Born Without Arms Teaches Others to Live with Disability." Fox News. May 1, 2015. https://www.foxnews.com/world/iranian-woman-born-without-arms-teaches-others-to-live-with-disability.
2. M. M. Merzenich, J. H. Kaas, J. T. Wall, M. Sur, R. J. Nelson, and D. J. Felleman. "Progression of Change Following Median Nerve Section in the Cortical Representation of the Hand in Areas 3b and 1 in Adult Owl and Squirrel Monkeys." *Neuroscience* 10, no. 3 (1983): 639–665. https://doi.org/10.1016/0306-4522(83)90208-7.
3. Emma G. Duerden and Danièle Laverdure-Dupont. "Practice Makes Cortex." *Journal of Neuroscience* 28, no. 35 (2008): 8655–8657. https://doi.org/10.1523/JNEUROSCI.2650-08.2008.
4. Maguire, Eleanor A., David G. Gadian, Ingrid S. Johnsrude, et al. "Navigation-related Structural Change in the Hippocampi of Taxi Drivers." *Proceedings of the National Academy of Sciences* 97, no. 8 (2000): 4398-4403. https://doi.org/10.1073/pnas.070039597.
5. J. Mårtensson, J. Eriksson, N. C. Bodammer, et al. "Growth of Language-Related Brain Areas After Foreign Language Learning." *NeuroImage* 63, no. 1 (2012): 240–244. https://doi.org/10.1016/j.neuroimage.2012.06.043. PMID: 22750568.
6. Bogdan Draganski, Christian Gaser, Volker Busch, Gerhard Schuierer, Ulrich Bogdahn, and Arne May. "Changes in Grey Matter Induced by Training." *Nature* 427 (2004): 311–312. https://doi.org/10.1038/427311a.
7. Bogdan Draganski, Christian Gaser, Gerd Kempermann, et al. "Temporal and Spatial Dynamics of Brain Structure Changes During Extensive Learning." *Journal of Neuroscience* 26, no. 23 (2006): 6314–6317. https://doi.org/10.1523/JNEUROSCI.4628-05.2006.

8. Midori Kodama, Takashi Ono, Fumio Yamashita, et al. "Structural Gray Matter Changes in the Hippocampus and the Primary Motor Cortex on An-Hour-to-One-Day Scale Can Predict Arm-Reaching Performance Improvement." *Frontiers in Human Neuroscience* 12 (2018): 209. https://doi.org/10.3389/fnhum.2018.00209.
9. Janina Boyke, Joenna Driemeyer, Christian Gaser, Christian Büchel, and Arne May. "Training-Induced Brain Structure Changes in the Elderly." *Journal of Neuroscience* 28, no. 28 (2008): 7031–7035. https://doi.org/10.1523/JNEUROSCI.0742-08.2008.
10. Taubert, Marco; Bogdan Draganski; Alfred Anwander; et al. "Dynamic Properties of Human Brain Structure: Learning-Related Changes in Cortical Areas and Associated Fibre Connections." *Journal of Neuroscience* 30, no. 35 (2010): 11670-11677. https://doi.org/10.1523/JNEUROSCI.2567-10.2010.
11. Sagi, Yuki, Kotaro Tavor, Takuya Hofstetter, et al. "Learning in the Fast Lane: New Insights into Neuroplasticity." *Frontiers in Human Neuroscience* 12 (2018): 209. https://doi.org/10.3389/fnhum.2018.00209.
12. Tom Popomaronis. "Billionaire Jeff Bezos: To Live a Happy Life with No Regrets by Age 80, Ask Yourself These 12 Questions." CNBC Make it. April 7, 2019. https://www.cnbc.com/2019/04/05/amazon-billionaire-ceo-jeff-bezos-ask-yourself-these-12-questions-to-live-a-long-happy-life.html.
13. Johnny L. Matson and Lindsey W. Williams. "The Making of a Field: The Development of Comorbid Psychopathology Research for Persons with Intellectual Disabilities and Autism." *Research in Developmental Disabilities* 35, no. 1 (2014): 234–238. https://doi.org/10.1016/j.ridd.2013.09.043.
14. G. H. Roid and M. Pomplun. "The Stanford-Binet Intelligence Scales, Fifth Edition." In D. P. Flanagan and P. L. Harrison, eds., *Contemporary Intellectual Assessment: Theories, Tests, and Issues*, 3rd ed. (The Guilford Press, 2012): 249–268. https://psycnet.apa.org/record/2012-09043-010.
15. Sarah Cassidy, Bryan Roche, Dylan Colbert, Ian Stewart, and Ian M. Grey. "A Relational Frame Skills Training Intervention to Increase General Intelligence and Scholastic Aptitude." *Learning and Individual Differences* 47 (2016): 222–235. https://doi.org/10.1016/j.lindif.2016.03.001.

Chapter 2: You Are Smarter Than You Think You Are
1. "What Are Mirror Neurons?" News-Medical.net. February 27, 2019. https://www.news-medical.net/health/What-are-Mirror-Neurons.aspx.
2. S. Lyubomirsky, R. Dickerhoof, J. K. Boehm, and K. M. Sheldon. "Becoming Happier Takes Both a Will and a Proper Way: An Experimental Longitudinal Intervention to Boost Well-Being." *Emotion* 11, no. 2 (2011): 391–402. https://doi.org/10.1037/a0022575.

Chapter 3: The Invincible Brain Mindset
1. Majid Fotuhi and Sara Mehr. "The Science Behind the Powerful Benefits of Having a Purpose." *Practical Neurology* (2015): 32–33. https://practicalneurology.com/diseases-diagnoses/alzheimer-disease-dementias/the-science-behind-the-powerful-benefits-of-having-a-purpose/30530/.
2. Login S. George and Crystal L. Park. "Are Meaning and Purpose Distinct? An Examination of Correlates and Predictors." *The Journal of Positive Psychology* 8, no. 5 (2013): 365–375. https://doi.org/10.1080/17439760.2013.805801.
3. Ajay Kumar Nair, Nagesh Adluru, Anna J. Finley, et al. "Purpose in Life as a Resilience Factor for Brain Health: Diffusion MRI Findings from the Midlife in the U.S. Study." *Frontiers of Psychology* 15 (2024): 1355998. https://doi.org/10.3389/fpsyt.2024.1355998.

4. Georgia Bell, Timothy Singham, Robert Saunders, Amber John, and Joshua Stott. "Positive Psychological Constructs and Association with Reduced Risk of Mild Cognitive Impairment and Dementia in Older Adults: A Systematic Review and Meta-Analysis." *Ageing Research Reviews* 77 (2022): 101594. https://doi.org/10.1016/j.arr.2022.101594.
5. Patricia A. Boyle, Aron S. Buchman, Robert S. Wilson, Lei Yu, Julie A. Schneider, and David A. Bennett. "Effect of Purpose in Life on the Relation Between Alzheimer Disease Pathologic Changes on Cognitive Function in Advanced Age." *Archives of General Psychiatry* 69, no. 5 (2012): 499–504. https://doi.org/10.1001/archgenpsychiatry.2011.1487.
6. Angelina R. Sutin, Martina Luchetti, and Antonio Terracciano. "Sense of Purpose in Life and Healthier Cognitive Aging." *Trends in Cognitive Sciences* 25, no. 11 (2021): 917–919. https://doi.org/10.1016%2Fj.tics.2021.08.009.
7. Lei Yu, Patricia A. Boyle, Robert S. Wilson, Steven R. Levine, Julie A. Schneider, and David A. Bennett. "Purpose in Life and Cerebral Infarcts in Community-Dwelling Older People." *Stroke* 46, no. 4 (2015): 1071–1076. https://doi.org/10.1161/STROKEAHA.114.008010.
8. Cohen, Randy; Chirag Bavishi; Alan Rozanski. "Purpose in Life and Its Relationship to All-Cause Mortality and Cardiovascular Events." *Psychosomatic Medicine* 78, no. 2 (2016): 122–133. https://doi.org/10.1097/PSY.0000000000000274.
9. Eric S. Kim, Koichiro Shiba, Julia K. Boehm, and Laura D. Kubzansky. "Sense of Purpose in Life and Five Health Behaviors in Older Adults." *Preventive Medicine* 139 (2020): 106172. https://doi.org/10.1016/j.ypmed.2020.106172.
10. Marlijn E. Besten, Marie-José van Tol, Jacolien van Rij, and Marieke K. van Vugt. "The Impact of Mood-Induction on Maladaptive Thinking in the Vulnerability for Depression." *Journal of Behavior Therapy and Experimental Psychiatry* 81 (2023): 101888. https://doi.org/10.1016/j.jbtep.2023.101888.
11. Patrick L. Hill, Nancy L. Sin, Nicholas A. Turiano, Anthony L. Burrow, and David M. Almeida. "Sense of Purpose Moderates the Associations Between Daily Stressors and Daily Well-Being." *Annals of Behavioral Medicine* 52, no. 8 (2020): 724–729. https://doi.org/10.1093/abm/kax039.
12. P. L. Hill, G. Olaru, and M. Allemand. "Do Associations Between Sense of Purpose, Social Support, and Loneliness Differ Across the Adult Lifespan?" *Psychology and Aging* 38, no. 4 (2023): 345–355. https://doi.org/10.1037/pag0000733.
13. John Franklin Donaldson. "Letters to the Editor." *Menopause: The Journal of the North American Menopause Society* 19, no. 2 (2012): 245. https://doi.org/10.1097/gme.0b013e3182455545.
14. Aliya Alimujiang, Ashley Wiensch, Jonathan Boss, et al. "Association Between Life Purpose and Mortality Among US Adults Older Than 50 Years." *JAMA Network Open* 2, no. 5 (2019): e194270. https://doi.org/10.1001/jamanetworkopen.2019.4270.
15. Roy F. Baumeister, Ellen Bratslavsky, Catrin Finkenauer, and Kathleen D. Vohs. "Bad Is Stronger Than Good." *Review of General Psychology* 5, no. 4 (2001): 323–370. https://doi.org/10.1037/1089-2680.5.4.323.
16. Lang Chen, Hyesang Chang, Jeremy Rudoler, et al. "Cognitive Training Enhances Growth Mindset in Children Through Plasticity of Cortico-Striatal Circuits." *npj Science of Learning* 7 (2022): 30. https://doi.org/10.1038/s41539-022-00146-7.
17. Emma G. Duerden and Danièle Laverdure-Dupont. "Practice Makes Cortex." *Journal of Neuroscience* 28, no. 35 (2008): 8655–8657. https://doi.org/10.1523/jneurosci.2650-08.2008.
18. Robert Goldman and Stephen Papson. *Nike Culture: The Sign of the Swoosh* (Sage Publications, 1999), 49.
19. Michael Jordan and Mark Vancil. *I Can't Accept Not Trying: Michael Jordan on the Pursuit of Excellence* (HarperSanFrancisco, 1994), 129.

Chapter 5: Memory, Plasticity, and Habit Change
1. Nikola Vukovic, Brian Hansen, Torben Ellegaard Lund, Sune Jespersen, and Yury Shtyrov. "Rapid Microstructural Plasticity in the Cortical Semantic Network Following a Short Language Learning Session." *PLoS Biology* 19, no. 6 (2019): e3001290. https://doi.org/10.1371/journal.pbio.3001290.

Chapter 6: How to Improve Your Memory
1. Frank J. Walters, Lori B. Chibnik, Reem Waziry, et al. "Twenty-Seven-Year Time Trends in Dementia Incidence in Europe and the United States: The Alzheimer Cohorts Consortium." *Neurology* 95, no. 5 (2020): e519–e531. https://doi.org/10.1212/WNL.0000000000010022.
2. Gabriel A. Radvansky, Sabine A. Krawietz, and Andrea K. Tamplin. "Walking Through Doorways Causes Forgetting: Further Explorations." *Quarterly Journal of Experimental Psychology* 64, no. 8 (2011): 1632–1645. https://doi.org/10.1080/17470218.2011.571267.

Chapter 7: Epigenetics Overrides Genetics for Alzheimer's Disease and Beyond
1. Brian H. Chen, Riccardo E. Marioni, Elena Colicino, et al. "DNA Methylation-Based Measures of Biological Age: Meta-Analysis Predicting Time to Death." *Aging* 8, no. 9 (2016): 1844–1865. https://doi.org/10.18632/aging.101020.
2. Elad Lax. "DNA Methylation as a Therapeutic and Diagnostic Target in Major Depressive Disorder." *Frontiers in Behavioral Neuroscience* 16 (2022): 759052. https://doi.org/10.3389/fnbeh.2022.759052.
3. Charlotte A. M. Cecil, Esther Walton, and Essi Viding. "DNA Methylation, Substance Use and Addiction: A Systematic Review of Recent Animal and Human Research from a Developmental Perspective." *Current Addiction Reports* 2 (2015): 331–346. https://doi.org/10.1007/s40429-015-0072-9.
4. Kristine Williams, Germán D. Carrasquilla, Lars Roed Ingerslev, et al. "Epigenetic Rewiring of Skeletal Muscle Enhancers After Exercise Training Supports a Role in Whole-Body Function and Human Health." *Molecular Metabolism* 53 (2021): 101290. https://doi.org/10.1016/j.molmet.2021.101290.
5. Paula Etayo-Urtasun, Mikel L. Sáez de Asteasu, and Mikel Izquierdo. "Effects of Exercise on DNA Methylation: A Systematic Review of Randomized Controlled Trials." *Sports Medicine* 54 (2024): 2059–2069. https://doi.org/10.1007/s40279-024-02033-0.
6. Yongjeon Cheong, Shota Nishitani, Jinyoung Yu, et al. "The Effects of Epigenetic Age and Its Acceleration on Surface Area, Cortical Thickness, and Volume in Young Adults." *Cerebral Cortex* 32, no. 24 (2022): 5654–5663. https://doi.org/10.1093/cercor/bhac043.
7. Amy L. Proskovec, Michael T. Rezich, Jennifer O'Neill, et al. "Association of Epigenetic Metrics of Biological Age with Cortical Thickness." *JAMA Network Open* 3, no. 9 (2020): e2015428. https://doi.org/10.1001/jamanetworkopen.2020.15428.
8. Denise Head, Julie M. Bugg, Alison M. Goate, et al. "Exercise Engagement as a Moderator of the Effects of APOE Genotype on Amyloid Deposition." *Archives of Neurology* 69, no. 5 (2012): 636–643. https://doi.org/10.1001/archneurol.2011.845.
9. Ibid.
10. R. Pedrero-Chamizo, K. Zhuang, A. Juarez, M. Janabi, W. J. Jagust, and S. M. Landau. "Alzheimer's Disease Prevention: Apolipoprotein e4 Moderates the Effect of Physical Activity on Brain BetaAmyloid Deposition in Healthy Older Adults." *Journal of Science and Medicine in Sport* 27, no. 6 (2024): 402–407. https://doi.org/10.1016/j.jsams.2024.03.012. PMID: 38664148.
11. Sevilay Tokgöz and Jurgen A. H. R. Claassen. "Exercise as Potential Therapeutic Target to Modulate Alzheimer's Disease Pathology in APOE ε4 Carriers: A Systematic

Review." *Cardiology and Therapy* 10 (2021): 67–88. https://doi.org/10.1007/s40119-020-00209-z.
12. M. Kivipelto, T. Ngandu, T. Laatikainen, B. Winblad, H. Soininen, and J. Tuomilehto. "Risk Score for the Prediction of Dementia Risk in 20 Years Among Middle Aged People: A Longitudinal, Population-Based Study." *The Lancet Neurology* 5, no. 9 (2006): 735–741. https://doi.org/10.1016/s1474-4422(06)70537-3. PMID: 16914401.
13. Majid Fotuhi, Vladimir Hachinski, and Peter J. Whitehouse. "Changing Perspectives Regarding Late-Life Dementia." *Nature Reviews Neurology* 5, no. 12 (2009): 649–658. https://doi.org/10.1038/nrneurol.2009.175.

Chapter 8: Alzheimer's Disease Is Not What We Thought

1. F. J. Wolters, L. B. Chibnik, R. Waziry, et al. "Twenty-Seven-Year Time Trends in Dementia Incidence in Europe and the United States: The Alzheimer Cohorts Consortium." *Neurology* 95, no. 5 (2020): e519–e531. https://doi.org/10.1212/wnl.0000000000010022. PMID: 32611641; PMCID: PMC7455342.
2. Ibid.
3. C. DeCarli, P. Maillard, M. P. Pase, et al. "Trends in Intracranial and Cerebral Volumes of Framingham Heart Study Participants Born 1930 to 1970." *JAMA Neurology* 81, no. 5 (2024): 471–480. https://doi.org/10.1001/jamaneurol.2024.0469.
4. J. A. Pillai, J. Bena, L. Bekris, et al. "Metabolic Syndrome Biomarkers Relate to Rate of Cognitive Decline in MCI and Dementia Stages of Alzheimer's Disease." *Alzheimer's Research and Therapy* 15 (2023): 54. https://doi.org/10.1186/s13195-023-01203-y.
5. K. M. Langa, E. B. Larson, E. M. Crimmins, et al. "A Comparison of the Prevalence of Dementia in the United States in 2000 and 2012." *JAMA Internal Medicine* 177, no. 1 (2017): 51–58. https://doi.org/10.1001/jamainternmed.2016.6807.

    F. D. Testai, P. B. Gorelick, P.-Y. Chuang, et al. "Cardiac Contributions to Brain Health: A Scientific Statement From the American Heart Association." *Stroke* 55, no. 12 (2024): e425–e438. https://doi.org/10.1161/STR.0000000000000476. Erratum in: *Stroke* 56, no. 1 (2025): e39. https://doi.org/10.1161/STR.0000000000000483. PMID: 39387123.
6. It is quoted in this paper: Janna Dinneweth and Sylvie Gadeyne. "Unravelling the Evolution of Neurodegenerative Disease Mortality: Insights from 50 Years of Belgian Data." *Espace populations sociétés* (2023/3–2024/1). It attributes this assertion to the obscure reference "Jameson, 1811, pp. 129–130." https://doi.org/10.4000/12tpx.

    It's also mentioned here: N. C. Berchtold and C. W. Cotman. "Evolution In the Conceptualization of Dementia and Alzheimer's Disease: Greco-Roman Period to the 1960s." *Neurobiology of Aging* 19, no. 3 (1998): 173–189. https://doi.org/10.1016/S0197-4580(98)00052-9.
7. All this history comes from section two in Dinneweth and Gadeyne's "Unravelling the Evolution," which includes references regarding Hippocrates (Papavramidou, 2018) and Cicero (Boller & Forbes, 1998).
8. Tanner Jensen. "Origins of Alzheimer's: The Life and Research of Dr. Alois Alzheimer." Being Patient. August 29, 2019. https://www.beingpatient.com/alois-alzheimer-life-and-research/.

    Majid Fotuhi, Vladimir Hachinski, and Peter J. Whitehouse. "Changing Perspectives Regarding Late-Life Dementia." *Nature Reviews Neurology* 5, no. 12 (2009): 649–658. https://doi.org/10.1038/nrneurol.2009.175.
9. R. N. Kalaria and T. Erkinjuntti. "Small Vessel Disease and Subcortical Vascular Dementia." *Journal of Clinical Neurology* 2, no. 1 (2006): 1–11. https://doi.org/10.3988/jcn.2006.2.1.1.
10. J. A. Hardy and G. A. Higgins. "Alzheimer's Disease: The Amyloid Cascade Hypothesis." *Science* 256, no. 5054 (1992): 184–185. https://doi.org/10.1126/science.1566067.

11. N. Cherbuin, K. Sargent-Cox, M. Fraser, P. Sachdev, and K. J. Anstey. "Being Overweight Is Associated with Hippocampal Atrophy: The PATH Through Life Study." *International Journal of Obesity* 39, no. 10 (2015): 1509–1514. https://doi.org/10.1038/ijo.2015.106.
12. Erick Gómez-Apo, Alejandra Mondragón-Maya, Martina Ferrari-Díaz, and Juan Silva-Pereyra. "Structural Brain Changes Associated with Overweight and Obesity." *Journal of Obesity* 2021, no. 1 (2021): 6613385. https://doi.org/10.1155/2021/6613385.
13. E. J. Kim, B. Pellman, and J. J. Kim. "Stress Effects on the Hippocampus: A Critical Review." *Learning & Memory* 22, no. 9 (2015): 411–416. http://doi.org/10.1101/lm.037291.114. PMID: 26286651; PMCID: PMC4561403.
14. J. F. Strain, K. B. Womack, N. Didehbani, et al. "Imaging Correlates of Memory and Concussion History in Retired National Football League Athletes." *JAMA Neurology* 72, no. 7 (2015): 773–780. http://doi.org/10.1001/jamaneurol.2015.0206.
15. E. D. Bigler, D. D. Blatter, C. V. Anderson, et al. "Hippocampal Volume in Normal Aging and Traumatic Brain Injury." *American Journal of Neuroradiology* 18, no. 1 (1997): 11–23. https://www.ajnr.org/content/18/1/11.
16. D. F. Cechetto, V. Hachinski, and S. N. Whitehead. "Vascular Risk Factors and Alzheimer's Disease." *Expert Review of Neurotherapeutics* 8, no. 5 (2008): 743–750. https://doi.org/10.1586/14737175.8.5.743. PMID: 18457531.
17. Majid Fotuhi, Vladimir Hachinski, and Peter J. Whitehouse. "Changing Perspectives Regarding Late-Life Dementia." *Nature Reviews Neurology* 5, no. 12 (2009): 649–658. https://doi.org/10.1038/nrneurol.2009.175.
18. Miia Kivipelto, Tiia Ngandu, Tiina Laatikainen, Bengt Winblad, Hilkka Soininen, and Jaakko Tuomilehto. "Risk Score for the Prediction of Dementia Risk in 20 Years Among Middle Aged People: A Longitudinal, Population-Based Study." *The Lancet Neurology* 5, no. 9 (2006): 735–741. https://doi.org/10.1016/S1474-4422(06)70537-3.
19. M. Kivipelto, F. Mangialasche, H. M. Snyder, et al. "World-Wide FINGERS Network: A Global Approach to Risk Reduction and Prevention of Dementia." *Alzheimer's & Dementia* 16, no. 7 (2020): 1078–1094. https://doi.org/10.1002/alz.12123. PMID: 32627328; PMCID: PMC9527644.
20. T. Ngandu, J. Lehtisalo, A. Solomon, et al. "A 2 Year Multidomain Intervention of Diet, Exercise, Cognitive Training, and Vascular Risk Monitoring Versus Control to Prevent Cognitive Decline in At-Risk Elderly People (FINGER): A Randomised Controlled Trial." *The Lancet* 385, no. 9984 (2015): 2255–2263. https://doi.org/10.1016/S0140-6736(15)60461-5. PMID: 25771249.
21. M. Fotuhi, D. Do, and C. Jack. "Modifiable Factors That Alter the Size of the Hippocampus with Ageing." *Nature Reviews Neurolology* 8 (2012): 189–202. https://doi.org/10.1038/nrneurol.2012.27.
22. M. Fotuhi, B. Lubinski, N. Hausterman, et al. "A Personalized 12-Week 'Brain Fitness Program' for Improving Cognitive Function and Increasing the Volume of Hippocampus in Elderly with Mild Cognitive Impairment." *The Journal of Prevention of Alzheimer's Disease* 3, no. 3 (2016): 133–137. https://doi.org/10.14283/jpad.2016.92. PMID: 29205251.
23. D. A. Snowdon, L. H. Greiner, J. A. Mortimer, K. P. Riley, P. A. Greiner, and W. R. Markesbery. "Brain Infarction and the Clinical Expression of Alzheimer Disease. The Nun Study." *JAMA* 277, no. 10 (1997): 813–817. https://doi.org/10.1001/jama.277.10.813. PMID: 9052711.
24. A. Kapasi, C. DeCarli, and J. A. Schneider. "Impact of Multiple Pathologies on the Threshold for Clinically Overt Dementia." *Acta Neuropathologica* 134, no. 2 (2017): 171–186. https://doi.org/10.1007/s00401-017-1717-7.
25. Salvatore Spina, Renaud La Joie, Cathrine Petersen, et al. "Comorbid Neuropathological Diagnoses in Early Versus Late-Onset Alzheimer's Disease." *Brain* 144, no. 7 (2021): 2186–2198. https://doi.org/10.1093/brain/awab099.

26. E. Vataja, G. Ratti, A. Safa, et al. "Exploring the Intersection of Atherosclerosis and Alzheimer's Disease: The Role of Inflammation and Complement Activation." *Inflammation Research* 74 (2025): 102. https://doi.org/10.1007/s00011-025-02069-6.
27. J. N. Davis II and J. C. Chisholm. "Alois Alzheimer and the Amyloid Debate." *Nature* 400, no. 6747 (1999): 810. https://doi.org/10.1038/23571.
28. G. Livingston, J. Huntley, K. Y. Liu, et al. "Dementia Prevention, Intervention, and Care: 2024 Report of the *Lancet* Standing Commission." *The Lancet* 404, no. 10452 (2024): 572–628. https://doi.org/10.1016/S0140-6736(24)01296-0. PMID: 39096926.

Chapter 9: A Revolution in the Testing and Treatment of Alzheimer's Disease

1. J. Jia, Y. Ning, M. Chen, et al. "Biomarker Changes During 20 Years Preceding Alzheimer's Disease." *New England Journal of Medicine* 390, no. 8 (2024): 712–722. https://doi.org/10.1056/NEJMoa2310168. PMID: 38381674.
2. Lawren VandeVrede and Suzanne E. Schindler. "Clinical Use of Biomarkers in the Era of Alzheimer's Disease Treatments." *Alzheimer's & Dementia* 21, no. 1 (2024): e14201. https://doi.org/10.1002/alz.14201.
3. I. C. M. Verheggen, J. J. A. de Jong, M. P. J. van Boxtel, et al. "Imaging the Role of Blood-Brain Barrier Disruption in Normal Cognitive Ageing." *GeroScience* 42, no. 6 (2020): 1751–1764. https://doi.org/10.1007/s11357-020-00282-1.
4. C. H. van Dyck, C. J. Swanson, P. Aisen, et al. "Lecanemab in Early Alzheimer's Disease." *New England Journal of Medicine* 388, no. 1 (2023): 9–21. https://doi.org/10.1056/NEJMoa2212948. PMID: 36449413.
5. J. R. Sims, J. A. Zimmer, C. D. Evans, et al. "Donanemab in Early Symptomatic Alzheimer Disease: The TRAILBLAZER-ALZ 2 Randomized Clinical Trial." *JAMA* 330, no. 6 (2023): 512–527. https://doi.org/10.1001/jama.2023.13239.
6. Rudolph J. Castellani, Elisheva D. Shanes, Matthew McCord, et al. "Neuropathology of Anti-Amyloid-β Immunotherapy: A Case Report." *Journal of Alzheimer's Disease* 93, no. 2 (2023): 803–813. https://doi.org/10.3233/JAD-221305.
7. J. C. Arbanas, C. L. Damberg, M. Leng, et al. "Estimated Annual Spending on Lecanemab and Its Ancillary Costs in the US Medicare Program." *JAMA Internal Medicine* 183, no. 8 (2023): 885–889. https://doi.org/10.1001/jamainternmed.2023.1749.
8. J. W. Han, H. Lee, J. W. Hong, et al. "Multimodal Cognitive Enhancement Therapy for Patients with Mild Cognitive Impairment and Mild Dementia: A Multi-Center, Randomized, Controlled, Double-Blind, Crossover Trial." *Journal of Alzheimer's Disease* 55, no. 2 (2017): 787–796. https://doi.org/10.3233/JAD-160619. PMID: 27802233.
9. Hyuntae Park, Jong H. Park, Hae R. Na, et al. "Combined Intervention of Physical Activity, Aerobic Exercise, and Cognitive Exercise Intervention to Prevent Cognitive Decline for Patients with Mild Cognitive Impairment: A Randomized Controlled Clinical Study." *Journal of Clinical Medicine* 8, no. 7 (2019): 940. https://doi.org/10.3390/jcm8070940.
10. Train the Brain Consortium, "Randomized Trial on the Effects of a Combined Physical/Cognitive Training in Aged MCI Subjects: The Train the Brain Study." *Scientific Reports* 7, no. 1 (2017): 1–15. https://doi.org/10.1038/srep39471.
11. M. Montero-Odasso, G. Zou, M. Speechley, et al. "Effects of Exercise Alone or Combined with Cognitive Training and Vitamin D Supplementation to Improve Cognition in Adults with Mild Cognitive Impairment: A Randomized Clinical Trial." *JAMA Network Open* 6, no. 7 (2023): e2324465. https://doi.org/10.1001/jamanetworkopen.2023.24465. PMID: 37471089; PMCID: PMC10359965.
12. D. Ornish, C. Madison, M. Kivipelto, et al. "Effects of Intensive Lifestyle Changes on the Progression of Mild Cognitive Impairment or Early Dementia Due to Alzheimer's

Disease: A Randomized, Controlled Clinical Trial." *Alzheimer's Research & Therapy* 16 (2024): 122. https://doi.org/10.1186/s13195-024-01482-z.

Chapter 10: The Gracefully Aging Invincible Brain

1. Michael Woodward, David A. Bennett, Tatjana Rundek, George Perry, and Tomasz Rudka. "The Relationship Between Hippocampal Changes in Healthy Aging and Alzheimer's Disease: A Systematic Literature Review." *Frontiers in Aging Neuroscience* 16 (2024): 1390574. https://doi.org/10.3389/fnagi.2024.1390574.
2. Hiroyuki Shimada, Takehiko Doi, Sangyoon Lee, and Hyuma Makizako. "Reversible Predictors of Reversion from Mild Cognitive Impairment to Normal Cognition: A 4-Year Longitudinal Study." *Alzheimer's Research & Therapy* 11 (2019): 24. https://doi.org/10.1186/s13195-019-0480-5.
3. B. R. Levy and M. D. Slade. "Role of Positive Age Beliefs in Recovery from Mild Cognitive Impairment Among Older Persons." *JAMA Network Open* 6, no. 4 (2023): e237707. https://doi.org/10.1001/jamanetworkopen.2023.7707.
4. M. Canevelli, G. Grande, E. Lacorte, et al. "Spontaneous Reversion of Mild Cognitive Impairment to Normal Cognition: A Systematic Review of Literature and Meta-Analysis." *Journal of the American Medical Directors Association* 17, no. 10 (2016): 943–948. https://doi.org/10.1016/j.jamda.2016.06.020. PMID: 27502450.
5. Harshad Devarbhavi, Sumeet K. Asrani, Juan Pablo Arab, Yvonne Ayerki Nartey, Elisa Pose, and Patrick S. Kamath. "Global Burden of Liver Disease: 2023 Update." *Journal of Hepatology* 79, no. 2 (2023): 516–537. https://doi.org/10.1016/j.jhep.2023.03.017.
6. A. Rovira, J. Alonso, and J. Córdoba. "MR Imaging Findings in Hepatic Encephalopathy." *American Journal of Neuroradiology* 29, no. 9 (2008): 1612–1621. https://doi.org/10.3174/ajnr.A1139.
7. Kwangsik Nho, Alexandra Kueider-Paisley, Shahzad Ahmad, et al. "Association of Altered Liver Enzymes with Alzheimer Disease Diagnosis, Cognition, Neuroimaging Measures, and Cerebrospinal Fluid Biomarkers." *JAMA Network Open* 2, no. 7 (2019): e197978. https://doi.org/10.1001/jamanetworkopen.2019.7978.
8. Prashanthi Vemuri, Cynthia Davey, Kirsten L. Johansen, et al. "Chronic Kidney Disease Associated with Worsening White Matter Disease and Ventricular Enlargement." *Journal of Alzheimer's Disease* 83, no. 4 (2021): 1729–1740. https://doi.org/10.3233/JAD-210604.
9. Johannes B. Scheppach, Aozhou Wu, Rebecca F. Gottesman, et al. "Association of Kidney Function Measures with Signs of Neurodegeneration and Small Vessel Disease on Brain Magnetic Resonance Imaging: The Atherosclerosis Risk in Communities (ARIC) Study." *American Journal of Kidney Diseases* 81, no. 3 (2023): 261–269. https://doi.org/10.1053/j.ajkd.2022.07.013.
10. Chun-Yun Zhang, Fang-Fang He, Hua Su, Chun Zhang, and Xian-Fang Meng. "Association Between Chronic Kidney Disease and Alzheimer's Disease: An Update." *Metabolic Brain Disease* 35 (2020): 883–894. https://doi.org/10.1007/s11011-020-00561-y.

    Kenji Maki, Tomoyuki Ohara, Jun Hata, et al. "CKD, Brain Atrophy, and White Matter Lesion Volume: The Japan Prospective Studies Collaboration for Aging and Dementia." *Kidney Medicine* 5, no. 3 (2022): e100593. https://pubmed.ncbi.nlm.nih.gov/36874508/.
11. Min Zhang, Shunze Hu, and Xuying Sun. "Alzheimer's Disease and Impaired Bone Microarchitecture, Regeneration and Potential Genetic Links." *Life* 13, no. 2 (2023): 373. https://doi.org/10.3390/life13020373.
12. Chun-Hao Tsai, Chieh-Sen Chuang, Chih-Hung Hung, et al. "Fracture as an Independent Risk Factor of Dementia: A Nationwide Population-Based Cohort Study." *Medicine* 93, no. 26 (2014): e188. https://doi.org/10.1097/MD.0000000000000188.

13. Ji Hee Yu, Regina E. Y. Kim, Jin-Man Jung, et al. "Sarcopenia Is Associated with Decreased Gray Matter Volume in the Parietal Lobe: A Longitudinal Cohort Study." *BMC Geriatrics* 21 (2021): 622. https://doi.org/10.1186/s12877-021-02581-4.
14. Chen, Nan; Jianying Li; Chengjie Cai; et al. "Regional Gray Matter Density Associated with Fast-Paced Walk Performance among Older Adults: A Voxel-Based Morphometry Study." *Journal of Gerontology. Series A, Biological Sciences and Medical Sciences* 75, no. 8 (2020): 1530–1536. https://doi.org/10.1093/Gerona/glaa091
15. Rongtao Jiang, Margaret L. Westwater, Stephanie Noble, et al. "Associations Between Grip Strength, Brain Structure, and Mental Health in > 40,000 Participants from the UK Biobank." *BMC Medicine* 20 (2022): 286. https://doi.org/10.1186/s12916-022-02490-2.
16. Minmin Yin, Haibao Wang, Xianwei Hu, Xiaoshu Li, Guanghe Fei, and Yongqiang Yu. "Patterns of Brain Structural Alteration in COPD with Different Levels of Pulmonary Function Impairment and Its Association with Cognitive Deficits." *BMC Pulmonary Medicine* 19 (2019): 203. https://doi.org/10.1186/s12890-019-0955-y.
17. Anna Frey, Roxane Sell, György A. Homola, et al. "Cognitive Deficits and Related Brain Lesions in Patients with Chronic Heart Failure." *Journal of the American College of Cardiology: Heart Failure* 6, no. 7 (2018): 583–592. https://doi.org/10.1016/j.jchf.2018.03.010.
18. M. Chen, Z. Wang, H. Xu, P. Teng, W. Li, and L. Ma. "Association Between Modifiable Lifestyle Factors and Telomere Length: A Univariable and Multivariable Mendelian Randomization Study." *Journal of Translational Medicine* 22 (2024): 160. https://doi.org/10.1186/s12967-024-04956-8.
19. Estelle Balan, Anabelle Decottignies, and Louise Deldicque. "Physical Activity and Nutrition: Two Promising Strategies for Telomere Maintenance?" *Nutrients* 10, no. 12 (2018): 1942. https://doi.org/10.3390/nu10121942.
20. Eli Puterman, Jordan Weiss, Jue Lin, et al. "Aerobic Exercise Lengthens Telomeres and Reduces Stress in Family Caregivers: A Randomized Controlled Trial—Curt Richter Award Paper 2018." *Psychoneuroendocrinology* 98 (2018): 245–252. https://doi.org/10.1016/j.psyneuen.2018.08.002.
21. L. M. C. Puhlmann, S. L. Valk, V. Engert, et al. "Association of Short-Term Change in Leukocyte Telomere Length with Cortical Thickness and Outcomes of Mental Training Among Healthy Adults: A Randomized Clinical Trial." *JAMA Network Open* 2, no. 9 (2019): e199687. https://doi.org/10.1001/jamanetworkopen.2019.9687.
22. Dean Ornish, Jue Lin, June M. Chan, et al. "Effect of Comprehensive Lifestyle Changes on Telomerase Activity and Telomere Length in Men with Biopsy-Proven Low-Risk Prostate Cancer: 5-Year Follow-Up of a Descriptive Pilot Study." *The Lancet Oncology* 14, no. 11 (2013): 1112–1120. https://doi.org/10.1016/S1470-2045(13)70366-8.
23. Anya Topiwala, Thomas E. Nichols, Logan Z. J. Williams, et al. "Telomere Length and Brain Imaging Phenotypes in UK Biobank." *PLoS One* 18, no. 3 (2023): e0282363. https://doi.org/10.1371/journal.pone.0282363.

Chapter 11: The Brain Fitness Program
1. M. Fotuhi, B. Lubinski, N. Hausterman, et al. "A Personalized 12-Week 'Brain Fitness Program' for Improving Cognitive Function and Increasing the Volume of Hippocampus in Elderly with Mild Cognitive Impairment." *The Journal of Prevention of Alzheimer's Disease* 3, no. 3 (2016): 133–137. http://doi.org/10.14283/jpad.2016.92. PMID: 29205251.
2. Majid Fotuhi, Pritty Dwivedy, Lauren H. Yeom, et al. "Retrospective Analysis of a Comprehensive Concussion Recover Program." *Semantic Scholar* (2020). https://www.semanticscholar.org/paper/Retrospective-Analysis-of-a-Comprehensive-Recovery-Fotuhi-Dwivedy/685524c4f6faa7c0532adf1a61933ceee71d20b2.

3. M. Fotuhi, N. D. Khorrami, and C. A. Raji. "Benefits of a 12-Week Non-Drug 'Brain Fitness Program' for Patients with Attention-Deficit/Hyperactive Disorder, Post-Concussion Syndrome, or Memory Loss." *Journal of Alzheimer's Disease Reports* 7, no. 1 (2023): 675–697. https://doi.org/10.3233/ADR-220091.

Chapter 12: Assess Your Brain Function

1. Katerina Gawronski, Eric S. Kim, Kenneth M. Langa, and Laura D. Kubzansky. "Dispositional Optimism and Incidence of Cognitive Impairment in Older Adults." *Psychosomatic Medicine* 78, no. 7 (2016): 819–828. https://doi.org/10.1097/PSY.0000000000000345.
2. B. R. Levy and M. D. Slade. "Role of Positive Age Beliefs in Recovery from Mild Cognitive Impairment Among Older Persons." *JAMA Network Open* 6, no. 4 (2023): e237707. https://doi.org/10.1001/jamanetworkopen.2023.7707.
3. B. C. Sachs, S. A. Gaussoin, G. A. Brenes, et al. "The Relationship Between Optimism, MCI, and Dementia Among Postmenopausal Women." *Aging & Mental Health* 27, no. 6 (2023): 1208–1216. https://doi.org/10.1080/13607863.2022.2084710. PMID: 35694859; PMCID: PMC9741664.
4. A. Gaur, A. Kaliappan, Y. Balan, V. Sakthivadivel, K. Medala, and M. Umesh. "Sleep and Alzheimer: The Link." *Maedica* 17, no. 1 (2022): 177–185. https://doi.org/10.26574/maedica.2022.17.1.177. PMID: 35733758; PMCID: PMC9168575.
5. National Heart, Lung, and Blood Institute. "How Sleep Works: How Much Sleep Is Enough?" https://www.nhlbi.nih.gov/health/sleep/how-much-sleep.
6. I. Bulycheva, Y. Watanabe, K. Kitamura, et al. "Self-Reported Sleep Duration and Bedtime Are Associated with Dementia Risk in Community-Dwelling People Aged 40–74 Years: The Murakami Cohort Study." *Journal of Alzheimer's Disease* 99, no. 2 (2024): 535–547. https://doi.org/10.3233/JAD-231104. PMID: 38669530.
7. D. X. Rasmusson, J. Brandt, D. B. Martin, and M. F. Folstein. "Head Injury as a Risk Factor in Alzheimer's Disease." *Brain Injury* 9, no. 3 (1995): 213–219. https://doi.org/10.3109/02699059509008194.

    J. Ramos-Cejudo, T. Wisniewski, C. Marmar, et al. "Traumatic Brain Injury and Alzheimer's Disease: The Cerebrovascular Link." *eBioMedicine* 28 (2018): 21–30. https://doi.org/10.1016/j.ebiom.2018.01.021. PMID: 29396300; PMCID: PMC5835563.

    E. A. Rogers, T. Beauclair, J. Martinez, et al. "The Contribution of Initial Concussive Forces and Resulting Acrolein Surge to β-Amyloid Accumulation and Functional Alterations in Neuronal Networks Using a TBI-on-a-Chip Model." *Lab on a Chip* 23, no. 15 (2023): 3388–3404. https://doi.org/10.1039/d3lc00248a. PMID: 37337817.
8. T. B. Meier, L. Y. España, A. J. Kirk, et al. "Association of Previous Concussion with Hippocampal Volume and Symptoms in Collegiate-Aged Athletes." *Journal of Neurotrauma* 38, no. 10 (2021): 1358–1367. https://doi.org/10.1089/neu.2020.7143. PMID: 33397203; PMCID: PMC8082726.
9. Drake Foundation. "Football and Dementia: Former Players over Five Times More Likely to Die of Alzheimer's, Says Landmark Study." October 21, 2019. https://www.drakefoundation.org/football-and-dementia-former-players-over-five-times-more-likely-to-die-of-alzheimers-says-landmark-study/.
10. Mark Nolan, Elena Roman, Anurag Nasa, et al. "Hippocampal and Amygdalar Volume Changes in Major Depressive Disorder: A Targeted Review and Focus on Stress." *Chronic Stress* 4 (2020): 2470547020944553. https://doi.org/10.1177/2470547020944553.
11. O. Sáiz-Vázquez, P. Gracia-García, S. Ubillos-Landa, et al. "Depression as a Risk Factor for Alzheimer's Disease: A Systematic Review of Longitudinal Meta-Analyses." *Journal of Clinical Medicine* 10, no. 9 (2021): 1809. https://doi.org/10.3390/jcm10091809.

12. Eisho Yoshikawa, Toshiatsu Taniguchi, Nanako Nakamura-Taira, Shin Ishiguro, and Hiromichi Matsumura. "Factors Associated with Unwillingness to Seek Professional Help for Depression: A Web-Based Survey." *BMC Research Notes* 10 (2017): 673. https://doi.org/10.1186/s13104-017-3010-1.
13. S. White, R. Mauer, C. Lange, et al. "The Effect of Plasma Cortisol on Hippocampal Atrophy and Clinical Progression in Mild Cognitive Impairment." *Alzheimer's & Dementia: Diagnosis, Assessment & Disease Monitoring* 15, no. 3 (2023): e12463. https://doi.org/10.1002/dad2.12463. PMID: 37583892; PMCID: PMC10423926.
14. J. Wallensten, G. Ljunggren, A. Nager, et al. "Stress, Depression, and Risk of Dementia—A Cohort Study in the Total Population Between 18 and 65 Years Old in Region Stockholm." *Alzheimer's Research and Therapy* 15 (2023): 161. https://doi.org/10.1186/s13195-023-01308-4.
15. Raffael Kalisch, Mirjam Schubert, Wolfgang Jacob, et al. "Anxiety and Hippocampus Volume in the Rat." *Neuropsychopharmacology* 31, no. 5 (2006): 925–932. https://doi.org/10.1038/sj.npp.1300910.
16. Patricia Gracia-García, Juan Bueno-Notivol, Darren M. Lipnicki, Concepción de la Cámara, Antonio Lobo, and Javier Santabárbara. "Clinically Significant Anxiety as a Risk Factor for Alzheimer's Disease: Results from a 10-Year Follow-Up Community Study." *International Journal of Methods in Psychiatric Research* 32, no. 3 (2023): e1934. https://doi.org/10.1002/mpr.1934.
17. N. L. Marchant, L. R. Lovland, R. Jones, et al. "Repetitive Negative Thinking Is Associated with Amyloid, Tau, and Cognitive Decline." *Alzheimer's & Dementia* 16, no. 7 (2020): 1054–1064. https://doi.org/10.1002/alz.12116. PMID: 32508019.
18. Allison N. Grossberg, Brianne M. Bettcher, Kim A. Gorgens, and Aurélie Ledreux. "Curiosity-Based Interventions Increase Everyday Functioning Score but Not Serum BDNF Levels in a Cohort of Healthy Older Adults." *Frontiers in Aging* 2 (2021): 700838. https://doi.org/10.3389/fragi.2021.700838.
19. Xuping Li, Yushi Zhang, Chengcheng Zhang, Ying Zheng, Ruilin Liu, and Shuiyuan Xiao. "Education Counteracts the Genetic Risk of Alzheimer's Disease Without an Interaction Effect." *Frontiers in Public Health* 11 (2023): 1178017. https://doi.org/10.3389/fpubh.2023.1178017.
20. Manuela Adcock, Mélanie Fankhauser, Jennifer Post, et al. "Effects of an In-Home Multicomponent Exergame Training on Physical Functions, Cognition, and Brain Volume of Older Adults: A Randomized Controlled Trial." *Frontiers in Medicine* 6 (2019): 321. https://doi.org/10.3389/fmed.2019.00321.

    S. A. Schultz, J. Larson, J. Oh, et al. "Participation in Cognitively-Stimulating Activities Is Associated with Brain Structure and Cognitive Function in Preclinical Alzheimer's Disease." *Brain Imaging and Behavior* 9 (2015): 729–736. https://doi.org/10.1007/s11682-014-9329-5.

    Jody S. Nicholson, Elizabeth M. Hudak, Christine B. Phillips, et al. "The Preventing Alzheimer's with Cognitive Training (PACT) Randomized Clinical Trial." *Contemporary Clinical Trials* 123 (2022): 106978. https://doi.org/10.1016/j.cct.2022.106978.
21. Seth R. Batten, Dan Bang, Brian H. Kopell, et al. "Dopamine and Serotonin in Human Substantia Nigra Track Social Context and Value Signals During Economic Exchange." *Nature Human Behaviour* 8, no. 4 (2024): 718–728. https://doi.org/10.1038/s41562-024-01831-w.
22. J. Holt-Lunstad. "Why Social Relationships Are Important for Physical Health: A Systems Approach to Understanding and Modifying Risk and Protection." *Annual Review of Psychology* 69 (2018): 437–458. https://doi.org/10.1146/annurev-psych-122216-011902. PMID: 29035688.

23. Jisca S. Kuiper, Marij Zuidersma, Richard C. Oude Voshaar, et al. "Social Relationships and Risk of Dementia: A Systematic Review and Meta-Analysis of Longitudinal Cohort Studies." *Ageing Research Reviews* 22 (2015): 39–57. https://doi.org/10.1016/j.arr.2015.04.006.

    J. T. Cacioppo and S. Cacioppo. "Older Adults Reporting Social Isolation or Loneliness Show Poorer Cognitive Function 4 Years Later." *Evidence-Based Nursing* 17, no. 2 (2014): 59–60. https://doi.org/10.1136/eb-2013-101379.

24. Pamela Sheffler, Esra Kürüm, Angelica M. Sheen, et al. "Growth Mindset Predicts Cognitive Gains in an Older Adult Multi-Skill Learning Intervention." *The International Journal of Aging and Human Development* 96, no. 4 (2022): 501–526. https://doi.org/10.1177/00914150221106095.

25. J. Leszek, E. V. Mikhaylenko, D. M. Belousov, et al. "The Links Between Cardiovascular Diseases and Alzheimer's Disease." *Current Neuropharmacology* 19, no. 2 (2021): 152–169. https://doi.org/10.2174/1570159X18666200729093724. PMID: 32727331; PMCID: PMC8033981.

26. "Blood Pressure and Alzheimer's Risk: What's the Connection?" Johns Hopkins Medicine: Health (newsletter). https://www.hopkinsmedicine.org/health/conditions-and-diseases/alzheimers-disease/blood-pressure-and-alzheimers-risk-whats-the-connection.

27. E. L. Ferguson, S. C. Zimmerman, C. Jiang, et al. "Low- and High-Density Lipoprotein Cholesterol and Dementia Risk over 17 Years of Follow-Up Among Members of a Large Health Care Plan." *Neurology* 101, no. 21 (2023): e2172–e2184. https://doi.org/10.1212/WNL.0000000000207876. PMID: 37793911; PMCID: PMC10663022.

28. N. E. Shepardson, G. M. Shankar, and D. J. Selkoe. "Cholesterol Level and Statin Use in Alzheimer Disease: I. Review of Epidemiological and Preclinical Studies." *Archives of Neurology* 68, no. 10 (2011): 1239–1244. https://doi.org/10.1001/archneurol.2011.203.

29. Georgina E. Crichton, Merrill F. Elias, Adam Davey, Kevin J. Sullivan, and Michael A. Robbins. "Higher HDL Cholesterol Is Associated with Better Cognitive Function: The Maine-Syracuse Study." *Journal of the International Neuropsychological Society* 20, no. 10 (2014): 961–970. https://doi.org/10.1017/S1355617714000885.

30. "Your Brain and Diabetes." CDC Diabetes (newsletter). July 16, 2024. https://www.cdc.gov/diabetes/diabetes-complications/effects-of-diabetes-brain.html.

31. Suzanne M. de la Monte and Jack R Wands. "Alzheimer's Disease Is Type 3 Diabetes—Evidence Reviewed." *Journal of Diabetes Science and Technology* 2, no. 6 (2008): 1101–1113. https://doi.org/10.1177/193229680800200619.

32. Y. J. Kim, S. M. Kim, D. H. Jeong, S.-K. Lee, M.-E. Ahn, and O.-H. Ryu. "Associations Between Metabolic Syndrome and Type of Dementia: Analysis Based on the National Health Insurance Service Database of Gangwon Province in South Korea." *Diabetology & Metabolic Syndrome* 13 (2021): 4. https://doi.org/10.1186/s13098-020-00620-5.

33. B. del Pozo Cruz, M. Ahmadi, S. L. Naismith, and E. Stamatakis. "Association of Daily Step Count and Intensity with Incident Dementia in 78,430 Adults Living in the UK." *JAMA Neurology* 79, no. 10 (2022): 1059–1063. https://doi.org/10.1001/jamaneurol.2022.2672.

34. Puja Agarwal, Sue E. Leurgans, Sonal Agrawal, et al. "Association of Mediterranean-DASH Intervention for Neurodegenerative Delay and Mediterranean Diets with Alzheimer Disease Pathology." *Neurology* 100, no. 22 (2023): e2259–e2268. https://doi.org/10.1212/WNL.0000000000207176. PMID: 36889921; PMCID: PMC10259273.

35. Timothy C. Durazzo, Niklas Mattsson, and Michael W. Weiner. "Smoking and Increased Alzheimer's Disease Risk: A Review of Potential Mechanisms." *Alzheimer's & Dementia* 10, no. 3 Suppl. (2014): S122–S145. https://doi.org/10.1016/j.jalz.2014.04.009.

36. E. S. Prasedya, Y. Ambana, N. W. R. Martyasari, et al. "Short-Term E-Cigarette Toxicity Effects on Brain Cognitive Memory Functions and Inflammatory Responses In

Mice." *Toxicological Research* 36 (2020): 267–273. https://doi.org/10.1007/s43188-019-00031-3.

Nathan A. Heldt, Nancy Reichenbach, Hannah M. McGary, and Yuri Persidsky. "Effects of Electronic Nicotine Delivery Systems and Cigarettes on Systemic Circulation and Blood-Brain Barrier: Implications for Cognitive Decline." *The American Journal of Pathology* 191, no. 2 (2021): 243–255. https://doi.org/10.1016/j.ajpath.2020.11.007.

37. P. L. Lutsey, N. Chen, M. C. Mirabelli, et al. "Impaired Lung Function, Lung Disease, and Risk of Incident Dementia." *American Journal of Respiratory and Critical Care Medicine* 199, no. 11 (2019): 1385–1396. http://doi.org/10.1164/rccm.201807-1220OC. PMID: 30433810; PMCID: PMC6543713.

38. T. Young, L. Evans, L. Finn, and M. Palta. "Estimation of the Clinically Diagnosed Proportion of Sleep Apnea Syndrome in Middle-Aged Men and Women." *Sleep* 20, no. 9 (1997): 705–706. http://doi.org/10.1093/sleep/20.9.705. PMID: 9406321.

39. C. André, E. Kuhn, S. Rehel, et al. "Association of Sleep-Disordered Breathing and Medial Temporal Lobe Atrophy in Cognitively Unimpaired Amyloid-Positive Older Adults." *Neurology* 101, no. 4 (2023): e370–e385. https://doi.org/10.1212/WNL.0000000000207421. PMID: 37258299; PMCID: PMC10435067.

40. F. Emamian, H. Khazaie, M. Tahmasian, et al. "The Association Between Obstructive Sleep Apnea and Alzheimer's Disease: A Meta-Analysis Perspective." *Frontiers in Aging Neuroscience* 8 (2016): 78. https://doi.org/10.3389/fnagi.2016.00078. PMID: 27148046; PMCID: PMC4828426.

41. B. Zhang, J. Weuve, K. M. Langa, et al. "Comparison of Particulate Air Pollution from Different Emission Sources and Incident Dementia in the US." *JAMA Internal Medicine* 183, no. 10 (2023): 1080–1089. https://doi.org/10.1001/jamainternmed.2023.3300. PMID: 37578757; PMCID: PMC10425875.

42. Yuhan Jiang, Bingbing Gao, Mingshuai Li, et al. "Relations of Hippocampal Subfields Atrophy Patterns with Memory and Biochemical Changes in End Stage Renal Disease." *Scientific Reports* 13 (2023): 2982. https://doi.org/10.1038/s41598-023-29083-0.

43. Laurel R. Seemiller, Julio Flores-Cuadra, Keith R. Griffith, Grace C. Smith, and Nicole A. Crowley. "Alcohol and Stress Exposure Across the Lifespan Are Key Risk Factors for Alzheimer's Disease and Cognitive Decline." *Neurobiology of Stress* 29 (2024): 100605. https://doi.org/10.1016/j.ynstr.2024.100605.

44. Remi Daviet, Gökhan Aydogan, Kanchana Jagannathan, et al. "Associations Between Alcohol Consumption and Gray and White Matter Volumes in the UK Biobank." *Nature Communications* 13 (2022): 1175. Accessed April 21, 2025. https://doi.org/10.1038/s41467-022-28735-5.

45. Zhongsheng Peng, Michael R. Duggan, Heather E. Dark, et al. "Association of Liver Disease with Brain Volume Loss, Cognitive Decline, and Plasma Neurodegenerative Disease Biomarkers." *Neurobiology of Aging* 120 (2022): 34–42. https://doi.org/10.1016/j.neurobiolaging.2022.08.004.

46. Y. Shang, L. Widman, and H. Hagström. "Nonalcoholic Fatty Liver Disease and Risk of Dementia: A Population-Based Cohort Study." *Neurology* 99, no. 6 (2022): e574–e582. https://doi.org/10.1212/WNL.0000000000200853. PMID: 35831178; PMCID: PMC9442617.

47. N.-S. Tzeng, C.-H. Chung, C.-B. Yeh, et al. "Are Chronic Periodontitis and Gingivitis Associated with Dementia? A Nationwide, Retrospective, Matched-Cohort Study in Taiwan." *Neuroepidemiology* 47, no. 2 (2016): 82–93. https://doi.org/10.1159/000449166. PMID: 27618156.

48. C.-K. Chen, Y.-T. Wu, and Y.-C. Chang. "Association Between Chronic Periodontitis and the Risk of Alzheimer's Disease: A Retrospective, Population-Based, Matched-Cohort Study." *Alzheimer's Research & Therapy* 9 (2017): 56. https://doi.org/10.1186/s13195-017-0282-6.

49. Qi Zhou, Wanlin Zhu, Xueli Cai, et al. "Obesity and Brain Volumes: Mediation by Cardiometabolic and Inflammatory Measures." *Stroke and Vascular Neurology* 10, no. 2 (2024): e003045. https://doi.org/10.1136/svn-2023-003045.
50. M. A. Ward, C. M. Carlsson, M. A. Trivedi, M. A. Sager, and S. C. Johnson. "The Effect of Body Mass Index on Global Brain Volume in Middle-Aged Adults: A Cross Sectional Study." *BMC Neurology* 5 (2005): 23. https://doi.org/10.1186/1471-2377-5-23.
    R. K. West, A. Livny, R. Ravona-Springer, et al. "Higher BMI Is Associated with Smaller Regional Brain Volume in Older Adults with Type 2 Diabetes." *Diabetologia* 63 (2020): 2446–2451. https://doi.org/10.1007/s00125-020-05264-8.
51. Lana Burgess. "Why Is the Hip-Waist Ratio Important?" MedicalNewsToday. March 28, 2025. https://www.medicalnewstoday.com/articles/319439.
52. C. Zhang, K. M. Rexrode, R. M. van Dam, T. Y. Li, and F. B. Hu. "Abdominal Obesity and the Risk of All-Cause, Cardiovascular, and Cancer Mortality: Sixteen Years of Follow-Up in US Women." *Circulation* 117, no. 13 (2008): 1658–1667. https://doi.org/10.1161/CIRCULATIONAHA.107.739714. PMID: 18362231.
53. Deborah R. Gustafson and José A. Luchsinger. "High Adiposity: Risk Factor for Dementia and Alzheimer's Disease?" *Alzheimer's Research & Therapy* 5 (2013): 57. https://doi.org/10.1186/alzrt221.
54. Margo B. Heston, Kendra L. Hanslik, Katie R. Zarbock, et al. "Gut Inflammation Associated with Age and Alzheimer's Disease Pathology: A Human Cohort Study." *Scientific Reports* 13 (2023): 18924. https://doi.org/10.1038/s41598-023-45929-z.
55. Tom Chambers, Richard Anney, Peter N. Taylor, et al. "Effects of Thyroid Status on Regional Brain Volumes: A Diagnostic and Genetic Imaging Study in UK Biobank." *The Journal of Clinical Endocrinology & Metabolism* 106, no. 3 (2021): 688–696. https://doi.org/10.1210/clinem/dgaa903.
56. F. J. de Jong, T. den Heijer, T. J. Visser, et al. "Thyroid Hormones, Dementia, and Atrophy of the Medial Temporal Lobe." *The Journal of Clinical Endocrinology & Metabolism* 91, no. 7 (2006): 2569–2573. https://doi.org/10.1210/jc.2006-0449. PMID: 16636121.
57. Woon-Man Kung, Sheng-Po Yuan, Muh-Shi Lin, et al. "Anemia and the Risk of Cognitive Impairment: An Updated Systematic Review and Meta-Analysis." *Brain Sciences* 11, no. 6 (2021): 777. https://doi.org/10.3390/brainsci11060777.
58. Michael J. Weiser, Christopher M. Butt, and M. Hasan Mohajeri. "Docosahexaenoic Acid and Cognition Throughout the Lifespan." *Nutrients* 8, no. 2 (2016): 99. https://doi.org/10.3390/nu8020099.
59. Niti Sharma, Seong Soo A. An, and Sang Yun Kim. "Medication Exposure and Risk of Dementia and Alzheimer's Disease." *International Journal of Molecular Sciences* 25, no. 23 (2024): 12850. https://doi.org/10.3390/ijms252312850.
60. B. R. Underwood, I. Lourida, J. Gong, et al. "Data-Driven Discovery of Associations Between Prescribed Drugs and Dementia Risk: A Systematic Review." *Alzheimer's & Dementia: Translational Research & Clinical Interventions* 11, no. 1 (2025): e70037. https://doi.org/10.1002/trc2.70037. PMID: 39839078; PMCID: PMC11747987.
61. Hadeel Y. Tarawneh, Dona M. P. Jayakody, Hamid R. Sohrabi, Ralph N. Martins, and Wilhelmina H. A. M. Mulders. "Understanding the Relationship Between Age-Related Hearing Loss and Alzheimer's Disease: A Narrative Review." *Journal of Alzheimer's Disease Reports* 6, no. 1 (2022): 539–556. https://doi.org/10.3233/ADR-220035.
62. F. R. Lin, J. R. Pike, M. S. Albert, et al. "Hearing Intervention Versus Health Education Control to Reduce Cognitive Decline in Older Adults with Hearing Loss in the USA (ACHIEVE): A Multicentre, Randomised Controlled Trial." *The Lancet* 402, no. 10404 (2023): 786–797. https://doi.org/10.1016/S0140-6736(23)01406-X. PMID: 37478886; PMCID: PMC10529382.

63. O. J. Killeen, Y. Zhou, and J. R. Ehrlich. "Objectively Measured Visual Impairment and Dementia Prevalence in Older Adults in the US." *JAMA Ophthalmology* 141, no. 8 (2023): 786–790. https://doi.org/10.1001/jamaophthalmol.2023.2854. PMID: 37440238; PMCID: PMC10346499.

Chapter 13: Fast-Track Your Fitness
1. J. L. Steiner, E. A. Murphy, J. L. McClellan, M. D. Carmichael, and J. M. Davis. "Exercise Training Increases Mitochondrial Biogenesis in the Brain." *Journal of Applied Physiology* 111, no. 4 (2011): 1066–1071. http://doi.org/10.1152/japplphysiol.00343.2011.
2. S.-S. Jiao, L.-L. Shen, C. Zhu, et al. "Brain-Derived Neurotrophic Factor Protects Against Tau-Related Neurodegeneration of Alzheimer's Disease." *Translational Psychiatry* 6, no. 10 (2016): e907. https://doi.org/10.1038/tp.2016.186.
3. Riya Thomas, Scott D. Zimmerman, Kayla M. Yuede, et al. "Exercise Training Results in Lower Amyloid Plaque Load and Greater Cognitive Function in an Intensity Dependent Manner in the Tg2576 Mouse Model of Alzheimer's Disease." *Brain Sciences* 10, no. 2 (2020): 88. https://doi.org/10.3390/brainsci10020088.
4. S. A. Kim, D. Shin, H. Ham, et al. "Physical Activity, Alzheimer Plasma Biomarkers, and Cognition." *JAMA Network Open* 8, no. 3 (2025): e250096. https://doi.org/10.1001/jamanetworkopen.2025.0096.
5. B. del Pozo Cruz, M. Ahmadi, S. L. Naismith, and E. Stamatakis. "Association of Daily Step Count and Intensity with Incident Dementia in 78,430 Adults Living in the UK." *JAMA Neurology* 79, no. 10 (2022):1059–1063. https://doi.org/10.1001/jamaneurol.2022.2672.

Chapter 14: Fast-Track Your Sleep
1. Jana Harenbrock, Heinz Holling, Graham Reid, and Ivan Koychev. "A Meta-Analysis of the Relationship Between Sleep and β-Amyloid Biomarkers in Alzheimer's Disease." *Biomarkers in Neuropsychiatry* 9 (2023): 100068. https://doi.org/10.1016/j.bionps.2023.100068.
2. Chang-hyun Park, Mirim Bang, Kook Jin Ahn, Woo Jung Kim, and Na-Young Shin. "Sleep Disturbance–Related Depressive Symptom and Brain Volume Reduction in Shift-Working Nurses." *Scientific Reports* 10 (2020): 9100. https://doi.org/10.1038/s41598-020-66066-x.
3. Susan McNamara, Benjamin C. Spurling, and Pradeep C. Bollu. "Chronic Insomnia." NIH National Library of Science web page, StatPearls [Internet]. Updated March 28, 2025. https://www.ncbi.nlm.nih.gov/books/NBK526136/.
4. Colin Tuft, Elie Matar, Zoe Menczel Schrire, Ronald R. Grunstein, Brendon J. Yee, and Camilla M. Hoyos. "Current Insights into the Risks of Using Melatonin as a Treatment for Sleep Disorders in Older Adults." *Clinical Interventions in Aging* 18 (2023): 49–59. https://doi.org/10.2147/CIA.S361519.
5. Alexa Fry. "Insomnia and Older Adults." Sleep Foundation. Updated July 10, 2025. https://www.sleepfoundation.org/insomnia/older-adults.
6. Claire E. Sexton, Andreas B. Storsve, Kristine B. Walhovd, Heidi Johansen-Berg, and Anders M. Fjell. "Poor Sleep Quality Is Associated with Increased Cortical Atrophy in Community-Dwelling Adults." *Neurology* 83, no. 11 (2014): 967–973. https://doi.org/10.1212/WNL.0000000000000774.
7. Hyun Jin Noh, Eun Yeon Joo, Sung Tae Kim, et al. "The Relationship Between Hippocampal Volume and Cognition in Patients with Chronic Primary Insomnia." *Journal of Clinical Neurology* 8, no. 2 (2012): 130–138. https://doi.org/10.3988/jcn.2012.8.2.130.
8. S. Sadeghmousavi, M. Eskian, F. Rahmani, and N. Rezaei. "The Effect of Insomnia on Development of Alzheimer's Disease." *Journal of Neuroinflammation* 17 (2020): 289. https://doi.org/10.1186/s12974-020-01960-9.

9. Christina S. McCrae, Jennifer M. Mundt, Ashley F. Curtis, et al. "Gray Matter Changes Following Cognitive Behavioral Therapy for Patients with Comorbid Fibromyalgia and Insomnia: A Pilot Study." *Journal of Clinical Sleep Medicine* 14, no. 9 (2018): 1595–1603. https://doi.org/10.5664/jcsm.7344.
10. Salim Surani and Pahnwat Taweesedt. "Obstructive Sleep Apnea: New Perspective." *Medicina* 59, no. 1 (2023): 75. https://doi.org/10.3390/medicina59010075.
11. Paul M. Macey, Luke A. Henderson, Katherine E. Macey, et al. "Brain Morphology Associated with Obstructive Sleep Apnea." *American Journal of Respiratory and Critical Care Medicine* 166, no. 10 (2002): 1382–1387. https://doi.org/10.1164/rccm.200201-050oc.
12. Chase E. Taylor, Kate E. Sprecher, Nicholas M. Vogt, et al. "O1-03-04: Hypoxia During Sleep Is Associated with Hippocampal Volume in Cognitively Unimpaired Adults." *Alzheimer's & Dementia* 14, no. 7S Part 4 (2018): P220–P221. https://doi.org/10.1016/j.jalz.2018.06.2345.
13. Mona F. Philby, Paul M. Macey, Richard A. Ma, Rajesh Kumar, David Gozal, and Leila Kheirandish-Gozal "Reduced Regional Grey Matter Volumes in Pediatric Obstructive Sleep Apnea." *Scientific Reports* 7 (2017): 44566. https://doi.org/10.1038/srep44566.
14. C. Lal, I. Ayappa, N. Ayas, et al. "The Link Between Obstructive Sleep Apnea and Neurocognitive Impairment: An Official American Thoracic Society Workshop Report." *Annals of the American Thoracic Society* 19, no. 8 (2022): 1245–1256. https://doi.org/10.1513/AnnalsATS.202205-380ST.
15. F. Emamian, H. Khazaie, M. Tahmasian, et al. "The Association Between Obstructive Sleep Apnea and Alzheimer's Disease: A Meta-Analysis Perspective." *Frontiers in Aging Neuroscience* 8 (2016): 78. https://doi.org/10.3389/fnagi.2016.00078.
16. Xiaodi Liu, David Chi-Leung Lam, King Pui Florence Chan, Hiu-Yeung Chana, Mary Sau-Man Ip, and Kui Kai Lau. "Prevalence and Determinants of Sleep Apnea in Patients with Stroke: A Meta-Analysis." *Journal of Stroke and Cerebrovascular Diseases* 30, no. 12 (2021): 106129. https://doi.org/10.1016/j.jstrokecerebrovasdis.2021.106129.
17. Hea Ree Park, Hye Ryun Kim, Joon-Kyung Seong, and Eun Yeon Joo. "Effects of Continuous Positive Airway Pressure on White Matter Microstructure in Patients with Obstructive Sleep Apnea." *Sleep Medicine Research* 14, no. 1 (2023): 31–36. https://doi.org/10.17241/smr.2022.01459.

    N. Canessa, V. Castronovo, S. F. Cappa, et al. "Obstructive Sleep Apnea: Brain Structural Changes and Neurocognitive Function Before and After Treatment." *American Journal of Respiratory and Critical Care Medicine* 183, no. 10 (2011): 1419–1426. https://doi.org/10.1164/rccm.201005-0693OC.
18. Yoshiaki Tai, Kenji Obayashi, Yuki Yamagami, et al. "Hot-Water Bathing Before Bedtime and Shorter Sleep Onset Latency Are Accompanied by a Higher Distal-Proximal Skin Temperature Gradient in Older Adults." *Journal of Clinical Sleep Medicine* 17, no. 6 (2021): 1257–1266. https://doi.org/10.5664/jcsm.9180.
19. Ravinder Jerath, Connor Beveridge, and Vernon A. Barnes. "Self-Regulation of Breathing as an Adjunctive Treatment of Insomnia." *Frontiers in Psychiatry* 9 (2019): 780. https://doi.org/10.3389/fpsyt.2018.00780.
20. Heather L. Rusch, Michael Rosario, Lisa M. Levison, et al. "The Effect of Mindfulness Meditation on Sleep Quality: A Systematic Review and Meta-Analysis of Randomized Controlled Trials." *Annals of the New York Academy of Sciences* 1445, no. 1 (2019): 5–16. https://doi.org/10.1111/nyas.13996.
21. Denis Turmel, Sarah Carlier, Anne Violette Bruyneel, and Marie Bruyneel. "Tailored Individual Yoga Practice Improves Sleep Quality, Fatigue, Anxiety, and Depression in Chronic Insomnia Disorder." *BMC Psychiatry* 22 (2022): 267. https://doi.org/10.1186/s12888-022-03936-w.
22. Michael J. Breus, Stephanie Hooper, Tarah Lynch, and Heather A. Hausenblas. "Effectiveness of Magnesium Supplementation on Sleep Quality and Mood for Adults

with Poor Sleep Quality: A Randomized Double-Blind Placebo-Controlled Crossover Pilot Trial." *Medical Research Archives* 12, no. 7 (2024). https://doi.org/10.18103/mra.v12i7.5410.
23. "Melatonin: What You Need to Know." National Center for Complementary and Integrative Health. https://www.nccih.nih.gov/health/melatonin-what-you-need-to-know.
24. Colin Tuft, Elie Matar, Zoe Menczel Schrire, Ronald R. Grunstein, Brendon J. Yee, and Camilla M. Hoyos. "Current Insights into the Risks of Using Melatonin as a Treatment for Sleep Disorders in Older Adults." *Clinical Interventions in Aging* 18 (2023): 49–59. https://doi.org/10.2147/CIA.S361519.

Chapter 15: Fast-Track Your Nutrition
1. Yimin Han, Boya Wang, Han Gao, et al. "Vagus Nerve and Underlying Impact on the Gut Microbiota-Brain Axis in Behavior and Neurodegenerative Diseases." *Journal of Inflammation Research* 15 (2022): 6213–6230. https://doi.org/10.2147/JIR.S384949.
2. Sydney E. Martin, Colleen S. Kraft, Thomas R. Ziegler, Erin C. Millson, Lavanya Rishishwar, and Greg S. Martin. "The Role of Diet on the Gut Microbiome, Mood and Happiness." Preprint. *MedRXiv*, March 21, 2023. https://doi.org/10.1101/2023.03.18.23287442.
3. Faezeh Saghafian, Maryam Hajishafiee, Parisa Rouhani, and Parvane Saneei. "Dietary Fiber Intake, Depression, and Anxiety: A Systematic Review and Meta-Analysis of Epidemiologic Studies." *Nutritional Neuroscience* 26, no. 2 (2023): 108–126. https://doi.org/10.1080/1028415x.2021.2020403.
4. Ygor Parladore Silva, Andressa Bernardi, and Rudimar Luiz Frozza. "The Role of Short-Chain Fatty Acids from Gut Microbiota in Gut-Brain Communication." *Frontiers in Endocrinology* 11 (2020): 25. https://doi.org/10.3389/fendo.2020.00025.
5. Wei Ling Lau and Nosratola D. Vaziri. "Gut Microbial Short-Chain Fatty Acids and the Risk of Diabetes." *Nature Reviews Nephrology* 15, no. 7 (2019): 389–390. https://doi.org/10.1038/s41581-019-0142-7.
6. Margo B. Heston, Kendra L. Hanslik, Katie R. Zarbock, et al. "Gut Inflammation Associated with Age and Alzheimer's Disease Pathology: A Human Cohort Study." *Scientific Reports* 13 (2023): 18924. https://doi.org/10.1038/s41598-023-45929-z.
7. Shengyi Han, Yanmeng Lu, Jiaojiao Xie, et al. "Probiotic Gastrointestinal Transit and Colonization After Oral Administration: A Long Journey." *Frontiers in Cellular and Infection Microbiology* 11 (2021): 609722. https://doi.org/10.3389/fcimb.2021.609722.
8. Natasha K. Leeuwendaal, Catherine Stanton, Paul W. O'Toole, and Tom P. Beresford. "Fermented Foods, Health and the Gut Microbiome." *Nutrients* 14, no. 7 (2022): 1527. https://doi.org/10.3390/nu14071527.
9. Brian T. Steffen, David R. Jacobs, So-Yun Yi, et al. "Long-Term Aspartame and Saccharin Intakes Are Related to Greater Volumes of Visceral, Intermuscular, and Subcutaneous Adipose Tissue: The CARDIA Study." *International Journal of Obesity* 47, no. 10 (2023): 939–947. https://doi.org/10.1038/s41366-023-01336-y.
10. Kerri M. Gillespie, Melanie J. White, Eva Kemps, Halim Moore, Alexander Dymond, and Selena E. Bartlett. "The Impact of Free and Added Sugars on Cognitive Function: A Systematic Review and Meta-Analysis." *Nutrients* 16, no. 1 (2023): 75. https://doi.org/10.3390/nu16010075.
11. Nicole M. Avena, Pedro Rada, and Bartley G. Hoebel. "Evidence for Sugar Addiction: Behavioral and Neurochemical Effects of Intermittent, Excessive Sugar Intake." *Neuroscience & Biobehavioral Reviews* 32, no. 1 (2008): 20–39. https://doi.org/10.1016/j.neubiorev.2007.04.019.
12. Michael Winterdahl, Ove Noer, Dariusz Orlowski, et al. "Sucrose Intake Lowers µ-Opioid and Dopamine D2/3 Receptor Availability in Porcine Brain." *Scientific Reports* 9 (2019): 16918. https://doi.org/10.1038/s41598-019-53430-9.

13. Angela Jacques, Nicholas Chaaya, Kate Beecher, Syed Aoun Ali, Arnauld Belmer, and Selena Bartlett. "The Impact of Sugar Consumption on Stress Driven, Emotional and Addictive Behaviors." *Neuroscience & Biobehavioral Reviews* 103 (2019): 178–199. https://doi.org/10.1016/j.neubiorev.2019.05.021.
14. Hannah Bruehl, Oliver T. Wolf, Victoria Sweat, Aziz Tirsi, Stephen Richardson, and Antonio Convit. "Modifiers of Cognitive Function and Brain Structure in Middle-Aged and Elderly Individuals with Type 2 Diabetes Mellitus." *Brain Research* 1280 (2009): 186–194. https://doi.org/10.1016/j.brainres.2009.05.032.
15. Lisa Ronan, Aaron F. Alexander-Bloch, Konrad Wagstyl, et al. "Obesity Associated with Increased Brain Age from Midlife." *Neurobiology of Aging* 47 (2016): 63–70. https://doi.org/10.1016/j.neurobiolaging.2016.07.010.
16. Cyrus A. Raji, Somayeh Meysami, Sam Hashemi, et al. "Visceral and Subcutaneous Abdominal Fat Predict Brain Volume Loss at Midlife in 10,001 Individuals." *Aging and Disease* 15, no. 4 (2024): 1831–1842. https://doi.org/10.14336/AD.2023.0820.
17. Gabriella Pugliese, Luigi Barrea, Daniela Laudisio, et al. "Sleep Apnea, Obesity, and Disturbed Glucose Homeostasis: Epidemiologic Evidence, Biologic Insights, and Therapeutic Strategies." *Current Obesity Reports* 9, no. 1 (2020): 30–38. https://doi.org/10.1007/s13679-020-00369-y.
18. Alex C. Birdsill, Cynthia M. Carlsson, Auriel A. Willette, et al. "Low Cerebral Blood Flow Is Associated with Lower Memory Function in Metabolic Syndrome." *Obesity* 21, no. 7 (2013): 1313–1320. https://doi.org/10.1002/oby.20170.
19. Bente K. Pedersen, Maria Pedersen, Karen S. Krabbe, Helle Bruunsgaard, Vance B. Matthews, and Mark A. Febbraio. "Role of Exercise-Induced Brain-Derived Neurotrophic Factor Production in the Regulation of Energy Homeostasis in Mammals." *Experimental Physiology* 94, no. 12 (2009): 1153–1160. https://doi.org/10.1113/expphysiol.2009.048561.
20. Majid Fotuhi and Brooke Lubinski. "The Effects of Obesity on Brain Structure and Size." *Practical Neurology* (2013): 20–34. https://practicalneurology.com/articles/2013-july-aug/the-effects-of-obesity-on-brain-structure-and-size/pdf.
21. Lauri Nummenmaa, Jussi Hirvonen, Jarna C. Hannukainen, et al. "Dorsal Striatum and Its Limbic Connectivity Mediate Abnormal Anticipatory Reward Processing in Obesity." *PloS One* 7, no. 2 (2012): e31089. https://doi.org/10.1371/journal.pone.0031089.
22. Catherine Féart, Cécilia Samieri, and Pascale Barberger-Gateau. "Mediterranean Diet and Cognitive Function in Older Adults." *Current Opinion in Clinical Nutrition and Metabolic Care* 13, no. 1 (2010): 14–18. https://doi.org/10.1097/MCO.0b013e3283331fe4.
23. Puja Agarwal, Sue E. Leurgans, Sonal Agrawal, et al. "Association of Mediterranean-DASH Intervention for Neurodegenerative Delay and Mediterranean Diets with Alzheimer Disease Pathology." *Neurology* 100, no. 22 (2023): e2259–e2268. https://doi.org/10.1212/WNL.0000000000207176.
24. American Academy of Neurology (2023). "MIND and Mediterranean Diets Associated with Fewer Alzheimer's Plaques and Tangles." https://www.aan.com/PressRoom/Home/PressRelease/5060.
25. Martha Clare Morris, Denis A. Evans, Julia L. Bienias, et al. "Consumption of Fish and N-3 Fatty Acids and Risk of Incident Alzheimer Disease." *Archives of Neurology* 60, no. 7 (2003): 940–946. https://doi.org/10.1001/archneur.60.7.940.
26. Majid Fotuhi, Payam Mohassel, and Kristine Yaffe. "Fish Consumption, Long-Chain Omega-3 Fatty Acids and Risk of Cognitive Decline or Alzheimer Disease: A Complex Association." *Nature Reviews Neurology* 5, no. 3 (2009): 140–152. https://doi.org/10.1038/ncpneuro1044.
27. Keisuke Kokubun, Kiyotaka Nemoto, and Yoshinori Yamakawa. "Fish Intake May

Affect Brain Structure and Improve Cognitive Ability in Healthy People." *Frontiers in Aging Neuroscience* 12 (2020): 76. https://doi.org/10.3389/fnagi.2020.00076.

28. Justyna Godos, Agnieszka Micek, Walter Currenti, et al. "Fish Consumption, Cognitive Impairment and Dementia: An Updated Dose-Response Meta-Analysis of Observational Studies." *Aging Clinical and Experimental Research* 36, (2024): 171. https://doi.org/10.1007/s40520-024-02823-6.

29. Anne-Julie Tessier, Marianna Cortese, Changzheng Yuan, et al. "Consumption of Olive Oil and Diet Quality and Risk of Dementia-Related Death." *JAMA Network Open* 7, no. 5 (2024): e2410021. https://doi.org/10.1001/jamanetworkopen.2024.10021.

30. Asra Fazlollahi, Kimia Motlagh Asghari, Cynthia Aslan, et al. "The Effects of Olive Oil Consumption on Cognitive Performance: A Systematic Review." *Frontiers in Nutrition* 10 (2023): 1218538. https://doi.org/10.3389/fnut.2023.1218538.

31. Javad Sharifi-Rad, Youssef El Rayess, Alain Abi Rizk, et al. "Turmeric and Its Major Compound Curcumin on Health: Bioactive Effects and Safety Profiles for Food, Pharmaceutical, Biotechnological and Medicinal Applications." *Frontiers in Pharmacology* 11 (2020): 01021. https://doi.org/10.3389/fphar.2020.01021.

32. Jingxian Wu, Qiong Li, Xiaoyan Wang, et al. "Neuroprotection by Curcumin in Ischemic Brain Injury Involves the Akt/Nrf2 Pathway." *PLoS One* 8, no. 3 (2013): e59843. https://doi.org/10.1371/journal.pone.0059843.

33. J. Yang, S. Song, J. Li, and T. Liang. "Neuroprotective Effect of Curcumin on Hippocampal Injury in 6-OHDA-Induced Parkinson's Disease Rat." *Pathology—Research and Practice* 210, no. 6 (2014): 357–362. https://doi.org/10.1016/j.prp.2014.02.005.

34. Pranay Srivastava, Yogesh K. Dhuriya, Vivek Kumar, et al. "PI3K/Akt/GSK3β Induced CREB Activation Ameliorates Arsenic Mediated Alterations in NMDA Receptors and Associated Signaling in Rat Hippocampus: Neuroprotective Role of Curcumin." *NeuroToxicology* 67 (2018): 190–205. https://doi.org/10.1016/j.neuro.2018.04.018.

35. Hannah L. Lail, Rafaela G. Feresin, Dominique Hicks, Blakely Stone, Emily Price, and Desiree Wanders. "Berries as a Treatment for Obesity-Induced Inflammation: Evidence from Preclinical Models." *Nutrients* 13, no. 2 (2021): 334. https://doi.org/10.3390/nu13020334.

36. Puja Agarwal, Sue E. Leurgans, Sonal Agrawal, et al. "Association of Mediterranean-DASH Intervention for Neurodegenerative Delay and Mediterranean Diets with Alzheimer Disease Pathology." *Neurology* 100, no. 22 (2023): e2259–e2268. https://doi.org/10.1212/WNL.0000000000207176.

37. Stephanie K. Nishi, Aleix Sala-Vila, Jordi Julvez, Joan Sabaté, and Emilio Ros. "Impact of Nut Consumption on Cognition Across the Lifespan." *Nutrients* 15, no. 4 (2023): 1000. https://doi.org/10.3390/nu15041000.

38. Abha Chauhan and Ved Chauhan. "Beneficial Effects of Walnuts on Cognition and Brain Health." *Nutrients* 12, no. 2 (2020): 550. https://doi.org/10.3390/nu12020550.

39. S. Ziaei, S. Mohammadi, M. Hasani, et al. "A Systematic Review and Meta-Analysis of the Omega-3 Fatty Acids Effects on Brain-Derived Neurotrophic Factor (BDNF)." *Nutritional Neuroscience* 27, no. 7 (2024): 715–725. https://doi.org/10.1080/1028415X.2023.2245996.

40. Soyogu Yamashita, Naoki Kawada, Wei Wang, et al. "Effects of Egg Yolk Choline Intake on Cognitive Functions and Plasma Choline Levels in Healthy Middle-Aged and Older Japanese: A Randomized Double-Blinded Placebo-Controlled Parallel-Group Study." *Lipids in Health and Disease* 22 (2023): 75. https://doi.org/10.1186/s12944-023-01844-w.

41. Bin Liu, Jing Tang, Jinxia Zhang, Shiying Li, Min Yuan, and Ruimin Wang. "Autophagy Activation Aggravates Neuronal Injury in the Hippocampus of Vascular Dementia Rats." *Neural Regeneration Research* 9, no. 13 (2014): 1288–1296. https://doi.org/10.4103/1673-5374.137576.

42. Etsuko Oshima, Seishi Terada, Shuhei Sato, et al. "Frontal Assessment Battery and Brain Perfusion Imaging in Alzheimer's Disease." *International Psychogeriatrics* 24, no. 6 (2012): 994–1001. https://doi.org/10.1017/S1041610211002481.
43. María A. Martin, Luis Goya, and Sonia de Pascual-Teresa. "Effect of Cocoa and Cocoa Products on Cognitive Performance in Young Adults." *Nutrients* 12, no. 12 (2020): 3691. https://doi.org/10.3390/nu12123691.
44. Phuong H. L. Tran and Thao T. D. Tran. "Blueberry Supplementation in Neuronal Health and Protective Technologies for Efficient Delivery of Blueberry Anthocyanins." *Biomolecules* 11, no. 1 (2021): 102. https://doi.org/10.3390/biom11010102.
45. X. Chen, Z. Liu, P. S. Sachdev, et al. "Association of Dietary Patterns with Cognitive Function and Cognitive Decline in Sydney Memory and Ageing Study: A Longitudinal Analysis." *Journal of the Academy of Nutrition and Dietetics* 122, no. 5 (2022): 949–960. e15. https://doi.org/10.1016/j.jand.2021.10.018.
46. Mohammad J. Assi, Donya Poursalehi, Shahnaz Amani Tirani, et al. "Legumes and Nuts Intake in Relation to Metabolic Health Status, Serum Brain Derived Neurotrophic Factor and Adropin Levels in Adults." *Scientific Reports* 13 (2023): 16455. https://doi.org/10.1038/s41598-023-43855-8.
47. U. Gundimeda, T. H. McNeill, T. K. Fan, et al. "Green Tea Catechins Potentiate the Neuritogenic Action of Brain-Derived Neurotrophic Factor: Role of 67-kDa Laminin Receptor and Hydrogen Peroxide." *Biochemical and Biophysical Research Communications* 445, no. 1 (2014): 218–224. https://doi.org/10.1016/j.bbrc.2014.01.166.
48. Tennille D. Presley, Ashley R. Morgan, Erika Bechtold, et al. "Acute Effect of a High Nitrate Diet on Brain Perfusion in Older Adults." *Nitric Oxide* 24, no. 1 (2011): 34–42. https://doi.org/10.1016/j.niox.2010.10.002.
49. Ibid.
50. Ibid.
51. Matthew G. Pontifex, Mohammad M. A. H. Malik, Emily Connell, Michael Müller, and David Vauzour. "Citrus Polyphenols in Brain Health and Disease: Current Perspectives." *Frontiers in Neuroscience* 15 (2021): 640648. https://doi.org/10.3389/fnins.2021.640648.
52. Emilio Ros. "Nuts and Novel Biomarkers of Cardiovascular Disease." *American Journal of Clinical Nutrition* 89, no. 5 (2009): 1649S–1656S. https://doi.org/10.3945/ajcn.2009.26736R.
53. Abha Chauhan and Ved Chauhan. "Beneficial Effects of Walnuts on Cognition and Brain Health." *Nutrients* 12, no. 2 (2020): 550. https://doi.org/10.3390/nu12020550.
54. Ibid.
55. Eric T. Trexler, Abbie E. Smith-Ryan, Malia N. Melvin, Erica J. Roelofs, and Hailee L. Wingfield. "Effects of Pomegranate Extract on Blood Flow and Running Time to Exhaustion." *Applied Physiology, Nutrition, and Metabolism* 39, no. 9 (2014): 1038–1042. https://doi.org/10.1139/apnm-2014-0137.
56. V. Sudarma, S. Sukmaniah, and P. Siregar. "Effect of Dark Chocolate on Nitric Oxide Serum Levels and Blood Pressure in Prehypertension Subjects." *Acta Medica Indonesiana* 43, no. 4 (2011): 224–228. PMID: 22156352.
57. K. Lane, E. Derbyshire, W. Li, and C. Brennan. "Bioavailability and Potential Uses of Vegetarian Sources of Omega-3 Fatty Acids: A Review of the Literature." *Critical Reviews in Food Science and Nutrition* 54, no. 5 (2014): 572–579. https://doi.org/10.1080/10408398.2011.596292.

Chapter 16: Fast-Track Your Mindset
1. S. Mineka, D. Watson, and L. A. Clark. "Comorbidity of Anxiety and Unipolar Mood Disorders." *Annual Review of Psychology* 49 (1998): 377–412. https://doi.org/10.1146/annurev.psych.49.1.377.

2. Y. I. Sheline, P. W. Wang, M. H. Gado, J. G. Csernansky, and M. W. Vannier. "Hippocampal Atrophy in Recurrent Major Depression." *Proceedings of the National Academy of Sciences USA* 93, no. 9 (1996): 3908–3913. https://doi.org/10.1073/pnas.93.9.3908.

   J. D. Bremner, M. Narayan, E. R. Anderson, et al. "Hippocampal Volume Reduced in Major Depression." *African Journal of Psychiatry* 12, no. 2 (2009): 168. https://www.walshmedicalmedia.com/open-access/hippocampal-volume-reduced-in-major-depression-jop-12-247.pdf.

   L. Schmaal, D. J. Veltman, T. G. M. van Erp, et al. "Subcortical Brain Alterations in Major Depressive Disorder: Findings from the ENIGMA Major Depressive Disorder Working Group." *Molecular Psychiatry* 21, no. 6 (2015): 806–812. https://doi.org/10.1038/mp.2015.69.

   Bradley S. Peterson, Virginia Warner, Ravi Bansal, et al. "Cortical Thinning in Persons at Increased Familial Risk for Major Depression." *Proceedings of the National Academy of Sciences USA* 106, no. 15 (2009): 6273–6278. https://doi.org/10.1073/pnas.0805311106.

   Julie Coloigner, Jean-Marie Batail, Olivier Commowick, et al. "White Matter Abnormalities in Depression: A Categorical and Phenotypic Diffusion MRI Study." *NeuroImage: Clinical* 22 (2019): 101710. https://doi.org/10.1016/j.nicl.2019.101710.

3. Y. I. Sheline, P. W. Wang, M. H. Gado, J. G. Csernansky, and M. W. Vannier. "Hippocampal Atrophy in Recurrent Major Depression." *Proceedings of the National Academy of Sciences USA* 93, no. 9 (1996): 3908–3913. https://doi.org/10.1073/pnas.93.9.3908.

4. Eun Joo Kim, Blake Pellman, and Jeansok J. Kim. "Stress Effects on the Hippocampus: A Critical Review." *Learning & Memory* 22 (2015): 411–416. https://doi.org/10.1101/lm.037291.114.

5. Sonia J. Lupien, Mony de Leon, Susan de Santi, et al. "Cortisol Levels During Human Aging Predict Hippocampal Atrophy and Memory Deficits." *Nature Neuroscience* 1, no. 1 (1998): 69–73. https://doi.org/10.1038/271.

6. Ryuzo Orihashi, Yoshiomi Imamura, Shigeto Yamada, Akira Monji, and Yoshito Mizoguchi. "Association Between Cortisol and Aging-Related Hippocampus Volume Changes in Community-Dwelling Older Adults: A 7-Year Follow-Up Study." *BMC Geriatrics* 22 (2022): 765. https://doi.org/10.1186/s12877-022-03455-z.

7. Sonia J. Lupien, Mony de Leon, Susan de Santi, et al. "Cortisol Levels During Human Aging Predict Hippocampal Atrophy and Memory Deficits." *Nature Neuroscience* 1, no. 1 (1998): 69–73. https://doi.org/10.1038/271.

8. Kirstin Aschbacher, Aoife O'Donovan, Owen M. Wolkowitz, Firdaus S. Dhabhar, Yali Su, and Elissa Epel. "Good Stress, Bad Stress and Oxidative Stress: Insights from Anticipatory Cortisol Reactivity." *Psychoneuroendocrinology* 38, no. 9 (2013): 1698–1708. https://doi.org/10.1016/j.psyneuen.2013.02.004.

9. David M. Lyons and Karen J. Parker. "Stress Inoculation-Induced Indications of Resilience in Monkeys." *Journal of Traumatic Stress* 20, no. 4 (2007): 423–433. https://doi.org/10.1002/jts.20265.

10. I. Kawachi and L. F. Berkman. "Social Ties and Mental Health." *Journal of Urban Health* 78, no. 3 (2001): 458–467. https://doi.org/10.1093/jurban/78.3.458.

11. D. Ibi, K. Takuma, H. Koike, et al. "Social Isolation Rearing-Induced Impairment of the Hippocampal Neurogenesis Is Associated with Deficits in Spatial Memory and Emotion-Related Behaviors in Juvenile Mice." *Journal of Neurochemistry* 105, no. 3 (2008): 921–932. https://doi.org/10.1111/j.1471-4159.2007.05207.x.

12. H. G. Koenig. "Religion, Spirituality, and Health: The Research and Clinical Implications." *ISRN Psychiatry* 2012 (2012): 278730. https://doi.org/10.5402/2012/278730.

13. N. D. Anderson, T. Damianakis, E. Kröger, et al. "The Benefits Associated with Volunteering Among Seniors: A Critical Review and Recommendations for Future Research." *Psychological Bulletin* 140, no. 6 (2014): 1505–1533. https://doi.org/10.1037/a0037610.
14. M. P. Herring, P. J. O'Connor, and R. K. Dishman. "The Effect of Exercise Training on Anxiety Symptoms Among Patients: A Systematic Review." *Archives of Internal Medicine* 170, no. 4 (2010): 321–331. https://doi.org/10.1001/archinternmed.2009.530.
15. K. I. Erickson, M. W. Voss, R. S. Prakash, et al. "Exercise Training Increases Size of Hippocampus and Improves Memory." *Proceedings of the National Academy of Sciences USA* 108, no. 7 (2011): 3017–3022. https://doi.org/10.1073/pnas.1015950108.
16. N. P. Gothe, J. M. Hayes, C. Temali, and J. S. Damoiseaux. "Differences in Brain Structure and Function Among Yoga Practitioners and Controls." *Frontiers in Integrative Neuroscience* 12 (2018): 26. https://doi.org/10.3389/fnint.2018.00026.
17. C. C. Streeter, T. H. Whitfield, L. Owen, et al. "Effects of Yoga Versus Walking on Mood, Anxiety, and Brain GABA Levels: A Randomized Controlled MRS Study." *Journal of Alternative and Complementary Medicine* 16, no. 11 (2010): 1145–1152. https://doi.org/10.1089/acm.2010.0007.
18. Andy Schumann, Feliberto de la Cruz, Stefanie Köhler, Lisa Brotte, and Karl-Jürgen Bär. "The Influence of Heart Rate Variability Biofeedback on Cardiac Regulation and Functional Brain Connectivity." *Frontiers in Neuroscience* 15 (2021): 691988. https://doi.org/10.3389/fnins.2021.691988.
19. Perciliany M. de Souza, Miriam de Cássia Souza, Luiza Araújo Diniz, et al. "Long-Term Benefits of Heart Rate Variability Biofeedback Training in Older Adults with Different Levels of Social Interaction: A Pilot Study." *Scientific Reports* 12 (2022): 18795. https://doi.org/10.1038/s41598-022-22303-z.
20. Thais Castro Ribeiro, Pau Sobregrau Sangrà, Esther García Pagès, et al. "Assessing Effectiveness of Heart Rate Variability Biofeedback to Mitigate Mental Health Symptoms: A Pilot Study." *Frontiers in Physiology* 14 (2023): 1147260. https://doi.org/10.3389/fphys.2023.1147260.
21. Hyun J. Yoo, Kaoru Nashiro, Shubir Dutt, et al. "Daily Biofeedback to Modulate Heart Rate Oscillations Affects Structural Volume in Hippocampal Subregions Targeted by the Locus Coeruleus in Older Adults but Not Younger Adults." *Neurobiology of Aging* 132 (2023): 85–99. https://doi.org/10.1016/j.neurobiolaging.2023.08.010.
22. Hyun J. Yoo, Kaoru Nashiro, Jungwon Min, et al. "Heart Rate Variability (HRV) Changes and Cortical Volume Changes in a Randomized Trial of Five Weeks of Daily HRV Biofeedback in Younger and Older Adults." *International Journal of Psychophysiology* 181 (2022): 50–63. https://doi.org/10.1016/j.ijpsycho.2022.08.006.
23. Aravind Natarajan. "Heart Rate Variability During Mindful Breathing Meditation." *Frontiers in Physiology* 13 (2023): 1017350. https://doi.org/10.3389/fphys.2022.1017350.
24. Bassam Khoury, Tania Lecomte, Guillaume Fortin, et al. "Mindfulness-Based Therapy: A Comprehensive Meta-Analysis." *Clinical Psychology Review* 33, no. 6 (2013): 763–771. https://doi.org/10.1016/j.cpr.2013.05.005.
25. Larissa Bartlett, Marie-Jeanne Buscot, Aidan Bindoff, Richard Chambers, and Craig Hassed. "Mindfulness Is Associated with Lower Stress and Higher Work Engagement in a Large Sample of MOOC Participants." *Frontiers in Psychology* 12 (2021): 724126. https://doi.org/10.3389/fpsyg.2021.724126.
26. Wan L. Yue, Kwun Kei Ng, Amelia Jialing Koh, et al. "Mindfulness-Based Therapy Improves Brain Functional Network Reconfiguration Efficiency." *Translational Psychiatry* 13 (2023): 345. https://doi.org/10.1038/s41398-023-02642-9.
27. Jenny J. Wen Liu, Maureen Reed, and Kristin Vickers. "Reframing the Individual Stress

Response: Balancing Our Knowledge of Stress to Improve Responsivity to Stressors." *Stress and Health* 35, no. 5 (2019): 607–616. https://doi.org/10.1002/smi.2893.
28. Emma Childs and Harriet De Wit. "Regular Exercise Is Associated with Emotional Resilience to Acute Stress in Healthy Adults." *Frontiers in Physiology* 5 (2014): 161. https://doi.org/10.3389/fphys.2014.00161.
29. Britta K. Hölzel, James Carmody, Mark Vangel, et al. "Mindfulness Practice Leads to Increases in Regional Brain Gray Matter Density." *Psychiatry Research: Neuroimaging* 191, no. 1 (2011): 36–43. https://doi.org/10.1016/j.pscychresns.2010.08.006.
30. Annelise A. Madison, Martha A. Belury, Rebecca Andridge, et al. "Omega-3 Supplementation and Stress Reactivity of Cellular Aging Biomarkers: An Ancillary Substudy of a Randomized, Controlled Trial in Midlife Adults." *Molecular Psychiatry* 26, no. 7 (2021): 3034–3042. https://doi.org/10.1038/s41380-021-01077-2.
31. Gisèle Pickering, André Mazur, Marion Trousselard, et al. "Magnesium Status and Stress: The Vicious Circle Concept Revisited." *Nutrients* 12, no. 12 (2020): 3672. https://doi.org/10.3390/nu12123672.
32. "Ashwagandha: Is It Helpful for Stress, Anxiety, or Sleep?" National Institutes of Health. December 5, 2024. https://ods.od.nih.gov/factsheets/Ashwagandha-HealthProfessional/.
33. Shinsuke Hidese, Shintaro Ogawa, Miho Ota, et al. "Effects of L-Theanine Administration on Stress-Related Symptoms and Cognitive Functions in Healthy Adults: A Randomized Controlled Trial." *Nutrients* 11, no. 10 (2019): 2362. https://doi.org/10.3390/nu11102362.
34. Sara-Jayne Long and David Benton. "Effects of Vitamin and Mineral Supplementation on Stress, Mild Psychiatric Symptoms, and Mood in Nonclinical Samples: A Meta-Analysis." *Psychosomatic Medicine* 75, no. 2 (2013): 144–153. https://doi.org/10.1097/psy.0b013e31827d5fbd.

Chapter 17: Fast-Track Your Brain Training
1. Sarah Cassidy, Bryan Roche, Dylan Colbert, Ian Stewart, and Ian M. Grey. "A Relational Frame Skills Training Intervention to Increase General Intelligence and Scholastic Aptitude." *Learning and Individual Differences* 47 (2016): 222–235. https://doi.org/10.1016/j.lindif.2016.03.001.
2. M. Slimani, N. L. Bragazzi, D. Tod, et al. "Do Cognitive Training Strategies Improve Motor and Positive Psychological Skills Development in Soccer Players? Insights from a Systematic Review." *Journal of Sports Sciences* 34, no. 24 (2016): 2338–2349. https://doi.org/10.1080/02640414.2016.1254809.
3. Jesús Díaz-García, Tomás García-Calvo, and Christopher Ring. "Brain Endurance Training Improves Sedentary Older Adults' Cognitive and Physical Performance When Fresh and Fatigued." *Psychology of Sport and Exercise* 76 (2025): 102757. https://doi.org/10.1016/j.psychsport.2024.102757.
4. Qianqian Sun, Shurui Xu, Shuai Guo, Yue You, Rui Xia, and Jiao Liu. "Effects of Combined Physical Activity and Cognitive Training on Cognitive Function in Older Adults with Subjective Cognitive Decline: A Systematic Review and Meta-Analysis of Randomized Controlled Trials." *Evidence-Based Complementary and Alternative Medicine* 2021 (2021): 882961. https://doi.org/10.1155/2021/8882961.
5. Y. Castellote-Caballero, M. del Carmen Carcelén Fraile, A. Aibar-Almazán, D. Fernando Afanador-Restrepo, and A. María González-Martín. "Effect of Combined Physical–Cognitive Training on the Functional and Cognitive Capacity of Older People with Mild Cognitive Impairment: A Randomized Controlled Trial." *BMC Medicine* 22 (2024): 281. https://doi.org/10.1186/s12916-024-03469-x.
6. Ayame Oishi and Takao Yamasaki. "Benefits of Badminton for Preventing Cognitive Decline and Dementia." *Encyclopedia* 4, no. 2 (2024): 984–996. https://doi.org/10.3390/encyclopedia4020063.

7. "Multitasking: Switching Costs." American Psychological Association. March 20, 2006. https://www.apa.org/topics/research/multitasking.

Chapter 18: Your Invincible Future
1. V. Heggie. "A Century of Cardiomythology: Exercise and the Heart c.1880–1980." *Social History of Medicine* 23, no. 2 (2010): 280–298. https://doi.org/10.1093/shm/hkp063.
2. J. N. Morris, J. A. Heady, P. A. B. Raffle, C. G. Roberts, and J. W. Parks. "Coronary Heart-Disease and Physical Activity of Work." *The Lancet* 262, no. 6796 (1953): 1111–1120. https://doi.org/10.1016/S0140-6736(53)91495-0.
3. W. B. Kannel and P. Sorlie. "Some Health Benefits of Physical Activity: The Framingham Study." *Archives of Internal Medicine* 139, no. 8 (1979): 857–861. https://doi.org/10.1001/archinte.1979.03630450011006.
4. Paul Oglesby. *Take Heart: The Life and Prescription for Living of Dr. Paul Dudley White* (Harvard University Press, Countway Library, 1986).
5. R. S. Paffenbarger Jr., R. Hyde, A. L. Wing, and C.-C. Hsieh. "Physical Activity, All-Cause Mortality, and Longevity of College Alumni." *New England Journal of Medicine* 314, no. 10 (1986): 605–613. https://doi.org/10.1056/NEJM198603063141003.
6. C. Zou, D. Amos-Richards, R. Jagannathan, and A. Kulshreshtha. "Effect of Home-Based Lifestyle Interventions on Cognition in Older Adults with Mild Cognitive Impairment: A Systematic Review." *BMC Geriatrics* 24 (2024): 200. https://doi.org/10.1186/s12877-024-04798-5.

    Claudie Hooper, Nicola Coley, Julien Delrieu, and Sophie Guyonnet. "Lifestyle Factors and Plasma Biomarkers of Alzheimer's Disease: A Narrative Review." *The Journal of Prevention of Alzheimer's Disease* 12, no. 6 (2025): 100130. https://doi.org/10.1016/j.tjpad.2025.100130.
7. D. Ornish, C. Madison, M. Kivipelto, et al. "Effects of Intensive Lifestyle Changes on the Progression of Mild Cognitive Impairment or Early Dementia Due to Alzheimer's Disease: A Randomized, Controlled Clinical Trial." *Alzheimer's Research & Therapy* 16 (2024): 122. https://doi.org/10.1186/s13195-024-01482-z.
8. F. Borgonovi. "Doing Well by Doing Good. The Relationship Between Formal Volunteering and Self-Reported Health and Happiness." *Social Science & Medicine* 66, no. 11 (2008): 2321–2334. https://doi.org/10.1016/j.socscimed.2008.01.011.
9. Z. Beygi, M. Solhi, S. F. Irandoost, and A. F. Hoseini. "The Relationship Between Social Support and Happiness in Older Adults Referred to Health Centers in Zarrin Shahr, Iran." *Heliyon* 9, no. 9 (2023): e19529. https://doi.org/10.1016/j.heliyon.2023.e19529.
10. Nicholas J. Justice. "The Relationship Between Stress and Alzheimer's Disease." *Neurobiology of Stress* 8 (2018): 127–133. https://doi.org/10.1016/j.ynstr.2018.04.002.

INDEX

abdominal (belly) fat, 180
acquisition and memory, 60–61, 82
addiction, 56, 69, 70, 91, 230, 231–32
ADHD (attention-deficit/hyperactivity disorder), xii, xiv, 3, 150, 175, 275
   Hannah's case, 163–64
   memory and, 86
   testing, 16
adrenaline, 54, 200, 214, 246, 249
Agarwal, Puja, 232–33
aging. *See also* gracefully aging invincible brain
   Alzheimer's disease and, *113*, 113–14, *114*, *115*, 132–36, *133*, *134*
   forgetting and memory, 68
   methylation and, 91–92
   organ reserve and, 136–41
"aha!" moments, 116, 169, 268
air pollution, 98, 179
air travel and sleep, 212
alcohol, 140, 179, 233
   Alzheimer's disease and, 114
   brain chaos and, 53
   happiness and, 184
   John's case, 131
   liver disease and, 137–38, 179
   memory and forgetting, 67, 70
   osteoporosis and, 139
   Renaissance and dementia, 103
   sleep problems and, 213, 218, 219, 223
allergies, 67, 182, 220
almonds, 215, 235
alpha-synuclein, 106, 108, 114
Alzheimer, Alois, xv–xvi, 103–4, 116
Alzheimer's Association International Conference, x, 127, 274
Alzheimer's disease, ix–xii, xv–xvi, 101–18
   Brain Fitness Program for. *See* Brain Fitness Program
   brain training and, 126, 262
   causes of, 101–2, 106–10, 115–16, 138, 139
   declining rates of, 102–3
   diagnosis of (testing), 119–22, 186–87
   Dynamic Polygon Hypothesis, *107*, 107–10
   early-onset, ix, 105, 108, 118, 120, 134, 274
   evolving understanding of, 103–5
   genes and genetics, ix–x, xvi, 89, 93–98, *94*
   late-onset, 89, 94, 105, 108, 109, 114, 125
   medications for, 123–25, *127*, 127–29, *128*, *129*
   multimodal lifestyle interventions for, 98–99, 115–18, 120, 125–29, *129*, 274, 275. *See also specific interventions*
   optimal rinsing and blood flow, 110–12, *111*, 117
   origin of term, 103–4
   overdiagnosis of, 107
   plaques and tangles, 32, 103–5, 107–10, 116
   sense of purpose and, 32
   successful aging and, *113*, 113–14, *114*, *115*, 132–36, *133*, *134*
   vascular risk factors, 115–17
Alzheimer's Disease Assessment Scale-Cognitive Subscale (ADAS-Cog), 123–28
Alzheimer's Disease Research Center, xi, 106–7
"Alzheimer's gene," 93–98, *94*
Ambien, 214

amygdala, 54–55, 62, *62*, 65
amyloid, xv–xvi, 93–95, 104–5, 108, 116, 123, 210, 274
Amyloid Cascade Hypothesis, 104, 108
ancient Greece, 80, 103
anemia, 181–82, 188
angiogenesis, 199–200
"animal whisperers," 22
anthocyanins, 234–35
anti-amyloid monoclonal antibodies, 123–25, 127–29, *129*
antioxidants, 216, 233, 234, 235, 237, 239
anxiety, 174, 243–45, 275, 282
  Alzheimer's disease and, 122
  brain reserve and, 136
  diet and, 230
  exercise for, 254, 258
  forgetting and memory, 67
  genetic predisposition, 26
  HRV biofeedback, 256–57
  medications, 67, 182
  sleep problems and, 214–17, 219
ApoE (apolipoprotein E), 93–98, *94, 95*
  testing, 123–24
apps, 152–53
  Brain Portfolio, 170, 194
  brain training and games, 193, 261, 268
  cognitive tests, 194
  exercise, 201
  heart rate variability, 256
  meditations, 259
  VO₂ max, 201
ARIA (amyloid-related imaging abnormalities), 124
Aristotle, 103
aromatherapy, 222
arthritis, 182, 214
ashwagandha, 259
asking of name, 77
assessing brain function. *See* Brain Portfolio
astrocytes, *50*, 50–51, 52–53, 55, 181

atherosclerosis, 231
ATP (adenisone triphosphate), 90–91, 198–200, 276
atrial fibrillation, 176
attention
  memory and, 64–65
  practicing focus, 265–67, 268–69
attitude, 78, 135, 215, 250
autonomic nervous system (ANS), 187–88, 245–46
axons, 31, 49–50

balance, 8, 11, 200, 204
Baltimore Longitudinal Study of Aging (BLSA), xi, 106–7
bananas, 215, 228
basal ganglia, 62, *62*, 63
baths (bathing), 221
BDNF (brain-derived neurotrophic factor), 53, 90–91, 139, 263
  exercise and, 199–200
  foods increasing, 235–36
beans and legumes, 236, 240
bedroom environment, 221
bedtime routine, 215, 221–22
beets (beet juice), 236
behavior, changing, 249–50
belly fat, 180
benzodiazepines, 182, 213
berries, 234–35, 236, 240
Bezos, Jeff, 12–13
Binet, Alfred, 13–14
biofeedback, 152, 158, 256–57
biological age, 91–92
biomarker tests, 119–22, 186–87
bloating, 180–81
blood-brain barrier, 112, 121–22, 140, 211, 276
blood pressure, high. *See* high blood pressure
blood tests, 119–22, 185–87
body mass index (BMI), 180, 231
body movement intelligence, 21
bone-brain connection, 139
bones, exercise for, 200
book-smart intelligence, 21
boredom and creativity, 267–68

Index 319

brain, ix–x
 assessing function. *See* Brain Portfolio
 chaos in the, 52–53
 functions of, 3–5, *4,* 45–56. *See also* cortex; hippocampus
 gut connection, 226–27
 invincible mindset. *See* mindset
 network of connections, 46–49, *48*
 organ reserve and successful aging, 136–41
 plasticity. *See* neuroplasticity
 sense of purpose and, 31–34
 testing. *See* cognitive tests
 thoughts and emotions, 54–55
 training your. *See* brain games; brain training
 unlimited potential of, 3–9
brain blood flow, xvi, 112, 117, 121–22, 168
 ApoE4 and, 95
 foods improving, 236–327
 heart disease and, 176
 Lisa's case, 158
 liver disease and, 138
 negative thoughts and, 54
 obesity and, 231
 sleep apnea and, 219
 vascular dementia, xvi, 105, 174
brain-derived neurotrophic factor. *See* BDNF
Brain Fitness Calculator, 150, 153, 154, *189,* 190–91, *286*
Brain Fitness Program, xii–xiii, xvii, 16, 117–18, 147–68
 Carlos's case, 164–66
 Carol's case, 147–49
 five pillars of, 150–53. *See also* brain training; diet; exercise; mindset; sleep
 Hannah's case, 163–64
 Lisa's case, 154–63
brain fog, xii, 53, 66, 138, 169, 182, 183
 brain training and, 261, 276, 278, 279
 diet and, 226
 happiness and, 280, 282

brain function assessment. *See* Brain Portfolio
brain games, 75, 152, 261, 269–70, 279
 apps, 193, 261
 Lisa's case, 164
brain mindset. *See* mindset
Brain Portfolio, xvii, 170–94
 maintaining, 276–77
 section #1: your "why," 170–71
 section #2: the forty questions, 172–85
 section #3: blood tests, 185–87
 section #4: fitness and ANS tests, 187–88
 section #5: miscellaneous tests, 188
 section #6: The Brain Fitness Calculator, *189,* 190–91
 section #7: neurocognitive and neurobehavioral spidograms, 191, *192*
 section #8: cognitive testing, 192–94
 template, *195–96*
brain reserve, 110, 136–37
brain size
 DNA hypermethylation, 98–99
 exercise and, 200
 increasing (growing), xiii, xvi, 4–9, 143
 kidney disease and, 179
 sleep problems and, 109, 215
 successful aging and, 113–14, 132, 143
brain training, xiii, 152, 261–71, 279. *See also* brain games
 Alzheimer's disease and, 126, 174–75
 cross-training, 262–63
 exercise and, 264–65
 focus, 265–67
 plan, 268–70
 practice makes cortex, 6–7, 9, *10,* 40–41, 55, 63–64, 82
 tracker, *271*
breathing. *See* deep breathing
Broca, Paul, 46
Broca's area, 46, 47, *48,* 48–52, *52*

caffeine, 140, 214, 217, 223
calcium channel blockers, 182
calming the brain, 222, 253
   supplements, 259
cancer, 71, 91, 101, 179, 183, 188, 214, 215
"can't do it" mentality, 67
cardiac stress test, 188
cardiovascular disease. *See* heart disease
cardiovascular health. *See* heart health
Carlson, Richard, 249
Carper, Jean, 96
car, remembering where parked, 79–80
cataracts, 183
central nervous system, 116, 226, 245
cerebellum, 62, *62*, 63
cerebral cortex. *See* cortex; prefrontal cortex
cerebrospinal fluid (CSF), 52, 86, 110–12, *111,* 120, 140, 210–11
chamomile tea, 215, 222
children
   ADHD, xiv
   growth mindsets, 38–39, 176
   intelligence and, 12, 13, 14
   sleep apnea and, 219
cholesterol, 112, 115, 116, 117, 121, 131, 140, 177
   Antonio's case, 115–16
   lipid panel, 121, 185–86
chronic insomnia, 212–17
chronic obstructive pulmonary disease (COPD), 139–40, 178, 213, 219
chronic pain, 182, 215, 245
Cicero, 103
circadian rhythms, 211–12
citrus fruits, 237
cocoa, 235
coffee. *See* caffeine
cognition, overview of, 6–7
cognitive behavioral therapy (CBT), 243, 248
cognitive behavioral therapy for insomnia (CBT-I), 216, 217
cognitive flexibility intelligence, 25

cognitive function, 13–14, 47–48
cognitive impairment (dementia). *See also* Alzheimer's disease; *and specific types*
   common types of, 105–6
cognitive tests, xii, 13–16, 192–94
   Brain Fitness Program, 149, *149*
   children and growth mindsets, 38–39
   value and limits of, 16–18
cognitive training. *See* brain training
concussions, 173–74
   postconcussion syndrome, xiii–xiv, 16–17, 150
consolidation of memories, 61
constipation, 180–81
cooking intelligence, 22
Cooper Running Test, 201
coronary calcium score, 188
cortex, 3–5, *4,* 46, 51. *See also* orbitofrontal cortex; prefrontal cortex
   Alzheimer's disease and, 108, 113, 116–17, 120, 133
   Carol's case, 148
   diet and, 231
   exercise and, 197, 203
   memory and, 57, 61, 63–64, 82
   practice makes (training), 6–7, 9, *10,* 40–41, 55, 63–64, 82, 89, 142, 143, 262–63, 276
   telomeres and, 142–43
cortisol
   exercise and, 200
   obesity and, 231
   sleep problems and, 214, 218
   stress and, 152, 174, 246–47, 249, 251, 253, 254
CPAPs (Continuous Positive Airway Pressure), 147, 219–20
creative intelligence, 23
creativity, 267–68
credit card numbers, 80–82
Crohn's disease, 180–81
crossword puzzles, 10, 262, 269, 270
cultural biases and IQ tests, 14
curcumin, 234, 239
curiosity, 174–75

dancing, 15, 21, 41, 63, 202
Danz, Hailey, 5
dark chocolate, 235, 237
daydreaming, 24, 267
daylight saving time, 213
deep breathing, 141, 216, 221, 250, 255–57, 258
deep-focus, 265–67
Dellis, Nelson, 8–9, 74–75, 279
dementia (cognitive impairment). *See also* Alzheimer's disease; *and specific types*
   common types of, 105–6
dendrites, 31, 49–50, *50,* 51
dental problems, 180
depression, 174, 243–45, 280
   Alzheimer's disease and, 110, 122
   brain reserve and, 136
   brain, thoughts and emotions, 54–55
   chronic pain and, 182
   diet for, 227, 233
   forgetting and memory, 67
   genetic predisposition, 26
   hearing loss and, 183
   lifestyle changes for, 252–54, 256
   MCI and, 135
   medications, 166, 182
   methylation and, 91
   Renaissance and dementia, 103
   sense of purpose and, 32, 33
   sleep problems and, 172–73, 213, 214, 215, 220
DHA (docosahexaenoic acid), 182, 238, 241
diabetes, 177
   Alzheimer's disease and, 106, 121
   ApoE2 and, 95
   brain chaos and, 53
   diet for, 227, 229, 231
   exercise for, 197, 200
   liver problems, 137–38, 219
   medications, 120, 182
   obesity and, 231
   sense of purpose, 32
   sleep problems and, 216, 220

diarrhea, 180–81
diet, 152, 225–42
   Alzheimer's disease and, 126–27
   brain reserve and, 136
   forgetting and memory, 67
   gut microbiome, 226–29
   liver problems, 137–38
   obesity. *See* obesity
   plan, 239–41
   sense of purpose, 32
   sleep and, 215
   for stress, 259
   supplements, 237–39, 241
   telomere length and, 142
   tracker, *241–42*
   what not to eat, 229–30, 240
   what to eat, 232–37, 240–41
dietary fiber, 226–27
digestive issues, 180–81
digestive tract, 226–27
digital distractions, 213, 223, 269
digital/machine intelligence, 25
distractions, 67, 265–67, 269
DNA hypermethylation, 91, 98–99
DNA methylation, 90–93, 142
donanemab, 123–25
Don't Sweat the Small Stuff (Carlson), 249
dopamine, xvi, 54, 65, 283
   diet and, 230, 231–32, 234
   exercise and, 200
   memory and habit changes, 69–72
   mental health and, 175, 252, 253
dreams (dreaming), 210–11. *See also* daydreaming
Dynamic Polygon Hypothesis, *107,* 107–10

early-onset Alzheimer's disease, ix, 105, 108, 118, 120, 134, 274
eating. *See* diet
Edison, Thomas, 36
eggs, 235
Einstein, Albert, 11
emotional intelligence, 16, 20, 243–44, 247
emotional memory, 59, 64–65, 71

emotions
  brain chemistry and, 54–55
  habits and, 71–72
empathic intelligence, 23–24
endorphins, 200, 253–54, 258
environment and epigenetics, 90–93
EPA (eicosapentaenoic acid), 182, 238, 241
epigenetic age, 91–92
epigenetics, xvi, 90–93, 98, 99
estrogen, 54, 67, 139
eustress, 251
evolution, 65
executive function, xvi, 47, 269–70
  Alzheimer's disease and, 110, 112, 126
  brain training, 261, 262, 269–70
  cognitive tests, 16, 17, 192
  exercise for, 199, 203, 265
  Lisa's case, 158
  obesity and, 231
  stress management, 258
exercise, 151–52, 197–208
  Alzheimer's disease and, 126–27
  ApoE and, 93–95
  benefits of, 197–200
  brain training and, 264–65, 268
  epigenetic age and, 92
  fitness tests, 187–88
  guidelines, 204
  for heart health, 273–74
  plan, 205–7
  sense of purpose, 32
  for stress, 253–54, 258
  telomere length and, 142
  tracker, *208*
  VO$_2$ max, 152, 201–3

fatty fish, 233–34, 235, 240, 259
fatty liver disease, 137–38
ferritin, 186
fiber bundles, 9, 49–50, 51, 55, 57–58, 112, 135, 136, 138, 200, 214, 231, 276
fiber, dietary, 226–27
fibromyalgia, 183, 188, 214, 216, 245

fight-or-flight response, 187, 246–47
FINGER (Finnish Geriatric Intervention Study to Prevent Cognitive Impairment and Disability), 108–9
fish and seafood, 233–34, 235, 240, 259
fitness. *See* exercise
fitness tests, 187–88
fixed mindset, 36–40, 175–76
flavonoids, 234, 235, 237
focus, 265–67, 268–69, 279
fogginess. *See* brain fog
food. *See* diet
food portion sizes, 233, 240
football concussions, 173–74
foreign-language intelligence, 21
forgetting, 66–68
forty questions, 172–85
fractures, 139
Framingham Heart Study, 102, 273
Frech, Ezra, 5
fried foods, 178, 229
frontotemporal dementia (FTD), 105–6, 122
future self and memory, 78–79

Gandhi, Mahatma Mohandas, 36
Gardner, Howard, 14
general anxiety disorder, 244–45
genes and genetics, ix–x, xvi, 12, 26, 89–93
  epigenetics vs., 90–93
genetic testing, 95–96, 123
George Washington University, xiv
Gladwell, Malcolm, 40
glaucoma, 183
GLP-1 agonists, 120, 232
glucose, 50, 185, 230
glymphatic drainage, 110–12, *111*, 148, 211–12
glymphatic system, 52, 140, 176, 210–11, 220, 276
goal-setting, 171, 204
gracefully aging invincible brain, 131–43

Index 323

Alzheimer's disease and, 132–36, *133*
John and Brian, 131
organ reserve and, 136–41
gray matter, 51
green tea, 236
grocery lists, memorizing, 83–86
growth mindsets, 36–40, 58, 248
  how to cultivate, 38–40
gum disease, 180
gut-brain axis, 226–27
gut microbiome, 226–29

habit formation, 32, 68–72, 278
Hachinski, Vladimir, 107–8
happiness, 184, 252
happiness intelligence, 25–26, 280–83
Hardy, John, 104
Harvard Medical School, ix, x, xi, xiv
headaches (migraines), xii, 173, 275
  Hannah's case, 164, 166
  Lisa's case, 154, 156, 160
  sleep apnea and, 219
  Sue's case, 17
hearing loss, 183
heart attacks, 282
  Alzheimer's disease and, 116–17
  diabetes and, 177
  diet and, 178
  LDL cholesterol and, 185
  nitric oxide infusion and, 199
  sense of purpose and, 32
  sleep problems and, 213, 215, 216, 220
  tests for, 188
heartbeat, 52, 86
heart-brain connection, 140
heartburn, 71, 213
heart disease, 140, 176, 245
  Alzheimer's disease and, 115–17, 124
  belly fat and, 180
  exercise for, 273–74
  sense of purpose and, 32, 33
heart health
  Brain Portfolio, 176–78
  diet for, 233, 237, 238

exercise for, 273–74, 282
sense of purpose for, 32–33
tests for, 188
HeartMath, 256
heart rate variability (HRV), 187–88, 246, 254–57
hemoglobin A1c, 186
herbal teas, 215, 222
Higgins, Gerald, 104
high blood pressure (hypertension), 176–78
  Alzheimer's disease and, 106, 121
  Antonio's case, 115–16
  ApoE2 and, 95
  brain chaos and, 53
  brain, thoughts and emotions, 54–55
  exercise for, 197, 199
  kidney function and, 138
  medications, 182
  sense of purpose and, 32, 33
  sleep problems and, 214
hippocampus, 3–5, *4*, 51
  Alzheimer's disease and, 104–5, 108, 109, 116–17, 120, 132, 133
  Carol's case, 148
  concussions and, 173
  diet and, 231, 235
  exercise and, 197, 203
  heart failure and, 140
  late-onset Alzheimer's disease, 108
  Lisa's case, 158
  London taxi drivers, 6–7
  memory and, 57, 61–65
  sleep problems and, 179, 214, 218–19
  stress and cortisol, 174, 246, 247, 249, 251
  telomeres and, 142–43
  training, 9, *10*, 89, 143, 149, 259, 263, 274–75, 276
homocysteine, 186
humor and memory, 78, 79
humor intelligence, 23
hypermethylation, 91, 98–99

hypertension. *See* high blood pressure
hyperthyroidism, 181
hypothalamus, 54
hypothyroidism, 181

imitation intelligence, 22–23
inflammation, 200
   brain and, 50, 51, 54, 136, 214
   brain chaos and, 53
   diet and, 67, 91, 228
   foods reducing, 233–35
   methylation and, 90, 98
insomnia. *See* sleep problems
inspirational/motivational
   intelligence, 25
intelligence, 10–13, 55
   culturally accepted markers of,
      10–12
   definition of, 12, 13, 15, 16
   Gardner's types of, 14
   thirty types of, 20–28
intrapersonal intelligence, 20
invincible brain mindset. *See* mindset
invincible future, 273–84
IQ tests, 10, 13–16
iron, 238
iron levels, 181–82
irritability, 150, 157, 163, 164, 173, 212, 215, 219, 283

Jack, Clifford, 109
Johns Hopkins University, ix, x, xi–xii, xiv, 68, 280
Jordan, Michael, 40–41
Journal of Prevention of Alzheimer's Disease, xii, 109, 149
joy, 252
junk food, 51, 95, 110, 137, 178, 226, 229, 232
"just one more time," 69

Karolinska Institute, 108
Kennedy, John F., 36
kidney-brain connection, 138
kidney disease, 138, 179
Kivipelto, Miia, 108–9
Kraepelin, Emil, 103–4

Lancet, The, x, 117
language network, 47
late-onset Alzheimer's disease, 89, 94, 105, 108, 109, 114, 125
laughter, 23, 253
leafy greens, 141, 235, 236, 240
leaky brain, 112, 113, 114, 121–22, 148, 181, 227, 228
leaky gut, 180–81, 227, 228, 229
lecanemab, 123–25
legumes, 236, 240
Lewy body dementia (LBD), xvi, 106, 108, 122, 188
lifestyle intelligence, 24
lifestyle interventions, ix–x, xiii, xv, 29, 51, 274–75. *See also* brain training; diet; exercise; mindset; sleep
   for Alzheimer's disease, 98–99, 108–10, 112, 115–18, 125–29, *129*
   ApoE and, 93–98, *94, 95*
   epigenetics and, 91–92
   hypermethylation, 91, 98–99
limbic network, 47, 65
limbic-predominant age-related TDP-43 encephalopathy (LATE), 106, 114, 122
lipid panel, 121, 185–86
liver-brain connection, 137–38
liver disease, 137–38, 179
logical/analytical intelligence, 20
London taxi drivers, 6–7
loneliness, 33, 175, 183
longevity
   sense of purpose for, 33
   telomeres and, 141–43
long-term memory, 62–63, 66
love and brain, 54
Lubinski, Brooke, 231
Lumosity, 193, 261, 268
lung-brain connection, 139–40
lung cancer, 71
lung disease, 139–40, 178
lungs, Brain Portfolio, 178–79

magnesium, 215, 222, 236, 259
math and growth mindset, 38–39

Mayo Clinic, 109
MCI. *See* mild cognitive impairment
medications, 182–83
   for Alzheimer's disease, 123–25
   forgetting as side effect, 67
   GLP-1 agonists, 120, 232
   for sleep, 213
meditation, 142, 221, 253, 258, 259
Mediterranean diet, 141, 159, 178, 232–37, 240–41
melatonin, 211–12, 215, 221, 222
memory, 8–9, 57–86
   anatomy of, 60–62
   emotional, 64–65
   forgetting, 66–68
   habit change, 68–72
   is now, 58–60
   menopause and, 66
   types of, 62–64
"memory bank," 60
Memory Champion, US, 8–9, 74–75, 80, 279
Memory Cure, The (Fotuhi), x, xi
memory intelligence, 21–22
memory palace, 80–82
memory retrieval, 61
memory training (tricks and exercises), 8–9, 73–86, 269, 279
   credit card numbers, 80–82
   names, 73, 76–78
   prefrontal cortex, 82
   twenty things, 82–86
   "Where did I park the car?", 79–80
   "Where did I put that . . . ?", 78–79
   "Why did I come into this room?", 79
menopause, 66, 181, 186, 214
mental fog. *See* brain fog
mental health. *See also* mindset; sleep problems; stress
   Brain Portfolio, 172–76
   diet for, 228, 232–33
mercury, in fish, 234, 238
metabolic syndrome, 177

methylation, 90–93
microglia, *50,* 50–55, 112, 138
migraines. *See* headaches
mild cognitive impairment (MCI), 134–35
   chronic stress and, 174
   diet for, 232, 237
   exercise for, 264
   multimodal lifestyle interventions for, xii, xiii, 102, 109, 115, 117, 120, 126–27, 135, 149, 175, 274–77
   positive attitude and, 135, 172
mindfulness. *See* meditation
mindset, 29–41, 152, 243–60. *See also* growth mindset
   anatomy of stress, 245–47
   finding purpose, 29–35
   good vs. bad stress, 250–54
   how to think about stress, 247–50
   plan, 257–59
   tracker, *260*
mirror neurons, 23
misplacing, 78–79
mitochondria, 198–200, 239, 276
Mohassel, Payam, 91, 233
mood (mood swings), 163–64, 253–54
   diet and, 226–27, 230
   sleep and, 210, 219, 220
Morris, John, 94
motivation, 184–85
motor cortex, 8, 46, 47, *48,* 48–49, 62
motor network, 47
Mount Sinai Hospital, 32
MRIs (magnetic resonance imaging), 6–7, 31, 38–39, 45–46, 51, 188
   Alzheimer's disease and, 109, 112, 120, 122, 124
   memory and, 57–58
   sleep problems and, 214
multitasking, 67, 266
muscle-brain connection, 139
musical instruments, 269
musical intelligence, 22
myelin, *50,* 50–51

names, 73, 76–78
  forgetting and memory, 3, 58, 62, 64, 67
  four-step process for remembering, 76–77
nature intelligence, 22
nature therapy, 267–68
navigational/spatial intelligence, 24
neurobehavioral spidograms, 191, *192*, 288
  Lisa's case, 156–57, *157, 159,* 159–60, *161, 162*
neurocognitive spidograms, 191, *192*, 287
  Lisa's case, 156, *156, 158,* 158–59, *160, 162*
neurogenesis, xvi
NeuroGrow Brain Fitness Center, xii–xiii, 150, 251, 263
neurons, 6, 49–50, *50,* 52–53, 55, 57–58, 91, 136
  mitochondria and, 198–200
neuroplasticity, xii, xvi, 5, 8, 17, 55, 58, 68–69, 91, 134, 275
Newton, Isaac, 36
nicotine, 69, 178
nitric oxide infusion, 199
nonbenzodiazepines ("Z-drugs"), 213
norepinephrine, 200
normal pressure hydrocephalus (NPH), 106, 122
notice and memorization, 76–77, 79–80
numerical intelligence, 21
Nun Study, 109–10
nutrition. *See* diet
nuts and seeds, 235, 237

obesity, 230–32
  Alzheimer's disease and, 104–5
  Antonio's case, 115–16
  brain chaos and, 53
  hypermethylation and, 98
  liver problems and, 137–38
  sense of purpose and, 32
  sleep apnea and, 219

obstructive sleep apnea. *See* sleep apnea
oligodendrocytes, *50,* 50–51, 52–53
olive oil, 234, 237
omega-3 fatty acids, 141, 154, 182, 186, 233, 238, 241, 257, 259
101 Ways to Avoid Alzheimer's & Dementia (Carper), 96
optimism, 25, 32, 33, 78, 135, 172, 215, 250
orbitofrontal cortex, 65, *70,* 70–71, 72, 232–32, 246, 252, 257
organizational/procedural intelligence, 24
organ reserve, 136–41
Ornish, Dean, 126–27, 274
osteoporosis, 139
Outliers: The Story of Success (Gladwell), 40
Öztürk, Sevilay, 5

Paffenbarger, Ralph, 273
Paralympics, 5
Parkinson's disease, ix, xvi, 106, 108, 188, 213
perivascular space, *50,* 110
persuasive intelligence, 21
pessimism, 172
PET (positron emission tomography) imaging, 120, 188
Plato, 103
pollution, 98, 179
polysomnographies, 188, 213
pomegranates, 237
portion sizes, 233, 240
positive attitude, 78, 135, 172, 215, 250
postconcussion syndrome, xiii–xiv, 16–17, 150
practice makes cortex, 6–7, 9, *10,* 40–41, 55, 63–64, 82
prayer, 23, 253
prebiotics, 228
prefrontal cortex, *48,* 48–49, 158, 251, 258
  memory and, 60, 62, *62,* 64–65, *70,* 70–71, 72, 82
  training, 82, 262–63

Princeton University, 12
probiotics, 227–28
procedural intelligence, 24
procedural memory, 63–64
purpose. *See* sense of purpose
puzzles, 10, 152, 262, 265, 269, 270, 279
Pythagoras, 103

quercetin, 239
quick learning intelligence, 25

refined grains, 229, 240
reframing, 248
religion, 23, 253
REM behavior disorder, 213
REM sleep, 210–11
repetitive negative thoughts (RNTs), 74, 243–44, 258
repetitive positive thoughts (RPTs), 74, 244
restructuring, 248
resveratrol, 239
retinal atrophy, 183
retrieval of memories, 61
reward system, 65, 68, 70–71
rock-paper-scissors, 82
Rockport Walk Test, 201
role models, 171
Ryff, Diane, 31, 34
Ryff Scale of Measurement, 31

salient attention network, 47
Saltaneh, Zohreh Etezad, 4–5
screen time, 213, 222, 223, 269
seafood, 233–34, 235, 240, 259
sedentary lifestyle, 67, 136, 177–78
  Antonio's case, 115–16
self-awareness, 45–46
self-esteem, 197–98
senile dementia of Alzheimer's Type (SDAT), 104
sense of purpose, 29–35, 71, 170
  brain benefits of, 31–34
  finding your, 35
sensory/intuitive intelligence, 22

serotonin, 54, 200, 215
sex (sex drive), 33, 54, 215, 219
shift workers and sleep, 212
short-term memory, 62
"silent strokes," 112, 113
Sinai Hospital of Baltimore, xi–xii, 107
sleep, 152, 209–23
  plan, 220–22
  sense of purpose and, 32
  stages of, 210–11
  for stress, 259
  tracker, 222, *223*
sleep apnea, 172–73, 217–20
  Alzheimer's disease and, 96, 109, 112, 179, 219
  Antonio's case, 115–16
  brain reserve and, 136
  brain, thoughts and emotions, 54–55
  Carol's case, 147
  forgetting and memory, 67
  happiness and, 184
  liver problems, 137–38
  medications, 213
  snoring, 178–79, 218
  symptoms, 218
  treatment, 219–20
sleep hygiene, 152, 216, 221–22
sleep pressure, 216–17
sleep problems (insomnia), 152, 178–79, 211–17
  Alzheimer's disease and, 96, 122
  ApoE2 and, 95
  brain chaos and, 53
  brain reserve and, 136
  Carlos's case, 166
  causes of, 213–14
  diagnosis of, 188, 212–13
  excessive sleep, 172–73
  medications, 213
  treating, 215–17
slow breathing. *See* deep breathing
smells and memories, 65, 68
smoking, 71, 136, 178. *See also* vaping
  Alzheimer's disease and, 114, 117, 121

brain reserve and, 137
happiness and, 184
hypermethylation and, 98
John's case, 131
osteoporosis and, 139
sense of purpose and, 32
sleep apnea and, 214–15, 219
snacks (snacking), 215, 222
snoring, 178–79, 218
Snowdon, David, 109–10
social intelligence, 20, 24
socialization, 28, 33, 75, 98, 110, 126, 142, 175, 253
spatial intelligence, 24
spiritual intelligence, 23
Stanford-Binet IQ test, 13–14
Stanford University, 13
step counts, 203
storage of memories, 61
street-smart intelligence, 21
stress, 174, 243–45
   Alzheimer's disease and, 105
   anatomy of, 245–47
   brain chaos and, 53
   brain, thoughts and emotions, 54
   forgetting and memory, 67
   good vs. bad, 250–54
   how to think about, 247–50
   hypermethylation and, 98
   measuring and managing, 254–57
   sense of purpose and, 32, 33
   sleep problems and, 214
   tracker, *260*
stress management, 254–59. *See also* mindset
   HRV tests, 187–88, 254–57
   plan, 257–59
stretching, 204–5, 254, 262
strokes, 32, 33, 46, 106–9, 112, 124, 219
Stutzman, Matt, 5
sugar, 229–30, 240
supplements, 237–39, 241, 259
Swedish Armed Forces, 7
sympathetic nervous system, 245–47, 249, 259
synapse, 49–50
synapses, 49, *50*, 51, 57–58, 91, 136
Syn-One, 188
syphilis, 103

tactile intelligence, 23
tau protein, 104, 105–6, 108, 109, 110, *111*, 120, 123
telomeres, 141–43
Terman, Lewis, 13
testosterone, 54, 67, 181, 186
Textbook of Psychiatry (Kraepelin), 103–4
theanine, 259
thyroid function, 186
thyroid problems, 181, 245
trauma, 5, 59, 166, 245, 248
triglycerides, 177, 185
turmeric, 234, 239
twenty things, memorizing, 76, 82–86

ulcerative colitis, 180–81
ulcers, 182
ultra-processed food, 229–30, 240
University of Pittsburgh, 15
University of Wisconsin, 31
"use it or lose it," 58, 261
uvulopalatopharyngoplasty (UPPP), 220

vagus nerve, 226, 255
vaping, 68–70, 178
vascular dementia, xvi, 105, 174
Viagra, 182
vision, 183
vision tests, 188
visualization intelligence, 24
visual network, 47
vitamin B_6, 186, 216
vitamin B_{12}, 186, 235
   deficiency, 50–51, 164, 238
vitamin C, 237, 239
vitamin D, 138, 139, 181, 186, 238
vitamin deficiencies, 181
vocabulary, 21, 57–58, 269
volunteering, 253

VO$_2$ max, 151–52, 187, 201–3
    ranges for men and women, *202*

waist-to-hip ratio (WHR), 180
walking, 177–78, 203, 204, 206, 267–68
walnuts, 237
Wechsler Intelligence Scale, 14
weight gain. *See also* obesity
  sleep apnea and, 219
weightlifting, 204–5, 206
Wernicke, Carl, 46
Wernicke's area, 46, 47, 48, *48,* 49–50
"Where did I park the car?", 79–80
"Where did I put that . . . ?", 78–79
White, Dudley, 273

Whitehouse, Peter, 107–8
white matter, 51
white noise, 222
whole-body health, 136–41
whole-body organ reserve, 137
"Why did I come into this room?", 79
working memory, 62, 64–65
work life, 176

Yaffe, Kristine, 233
Yale University, 135
yoga, 21, 126, 204, 222, 228, 254, 259, 278

zaleplon, 213
zolpidem (Ambien), 213
zopiclone, 213

ABOUT THE AUTHOR

Dr Majid Fotuhi is a pioneering neurologist, neuroscientist, and author with more than thirty years of experience in brain health, memory, neuroplasticity, and the prevention of Alzheimer's disease. His career spans cutting-edge research, clinical innovation, and public education.

Dr. Fotuhi earned his PhD in neuroscience from Johns Hopkins University in 1992, followed by his medical training at Harvard Medical School. He returned to Johns Hopkins to complete his residency in neurology. He later held faculty positions simultaneously at both Harvard Medical School and Johns Hopkins for many years. He currently serves as an adjunct professor at George Washington University and Johns Hopkins University.

Author of several books, Dr. Fotuhi is a gifted communicator who is known for making complex science accessible and inspiring readers to take charge of their cognitive health. His contributions to medical education earned him the prestigious teaching award from the American Academy of Neurology.

Dr. Fotuhi has published his research discoveries in peer-reviewed scientific journals, presented at major conferences including the American Academy of Neurology and the Alzheimer's Association International Conference; his research has been cited by thousands of scientists worldwide.

Founder and medical director of the NeuroGrow Brain Fitness Center, Dr. Fotuhi has developed a comprehensive twelve-week program that has helped thousands of patients with memory loss, brain fog, concussion, mild cognitive impairment, and early Alzheimer's disease.

Dr. Fotuhi has been featured in more than fifty national and international media outlets, including CNN, NBC News, the *Today* show, ABC News, *The New York Times*, *The Washington Post*, and *The Times* (London). His ability to communicate the power of neuroplasticity has reached millions of people around the world.

In both his clinical practice and public lectures, Dr. Fotuhi emphasizes that it is never too late to grow new brain cells, build brain reserve, and reclaim cognitive vitality. His five-pillar approach—focusing on fitness, sleep, nutrition, mindset, and cognitive training—offers a practical road map for lifelong brain health and the prevention of Alzheimer's disease.

Outside of his professional life, Dr. Fotuhi enjoys spending time with his wife and their two daughters. His hobbies include ballroom dancing, long-distance biking, cooking, skiing, and tennis.

RAISING READERS
Books Build Bright Futures

Dear Reader,

We'd love your attention for one more page to tell you about the crisis in children's reading, and what we can all do.

Studies have shown that reading for fun is the **single biggest predictor of a child's future life chances** – more than family circumstance, parents' educational background or income. It improves academic results, mental health, wealth, communication skills, ambition and happiness.[1]

The number of children reading for fun is in rapid decline. Young people have a lot of competition for their time. In 2024, 1 in 10 children and young people in the UK aged 5 to 18 did not own a single book at home.[2]

Hachette works extensively with schools, libraries and literacy charities, but here are some ways we can all raise more readers:

- Reading to children for just 10 minutes a day makes a difference
- Don't give up if children aren't regular readers – there will be books for them!
- Visit bookshops and libraries to get recommendations
- Encourage them to listen to audiobooks
- Support school libraries
- Give books as gifts

There's a lot more information about how to encourage children to read on our website: **www.RaisingReaders.co.uk**

Thank you for reading.

---

[1] OECD, '21st-Century Readers: Developing Literacy Skills in a Digital World', 2021, https://www.oecd.org/en/publications/21st-century-readers_a83d84cb-en.html

[2] National Literacy Trust, 'Book Ownership in 2024', November 2024, https://literacytrust.org.uk/research-services/research-reports/book-ownership-in-2024